The Judgment of the Provinces

Roman law is justly famous, but what was its relationship to governing an empire? In this book, Ari Z. Bryen argues that law, as the learned practice that we know today, emerged from the challenge of governing a diverse and fractious set of imperial subjects. Through analysis of these subjects' political and legal ideologies, Bryen reveals how law became the central topic of political contest in the Roman Empire. Law offered a means of testing legitimacy and evaluating government, as well as a language for asking fundamental political questions. But these political claims did not go unchallenged. Elites resisted them, and jurists, in collaboration with emperors, reimagined law as a system that excluded the voices of the governed. The result was to separate, for the first time, "law" from "society" more broadly, and to define law as a primarily literate and learned practice, rather than the stuff of everyday life.

Ari Z. Bryen is Associate Professor in the Department of History and the Department of Classical and Mediterranean Studies at Vanderbilt University. He is the author of *Violence in Roman Egypt: A Study in Legal Interpretation* (2013).

See the Studies in Legal History series website at
http://studiesinlegalhistory.org/

Studies in Legal History

Other books in the series:

James M. Campbell, *Reluctant Abolitionists: Britain and the End of the Colonial Death Penalty*
Sonia Tycko, *Captured Consent: Contract Labor in English Charity, Colonization, and War, 1600–1700*
Jenny Huangfu Day, *Transborder Fugitives, Extradition, and Political Crimes in Modern China*
Maurits den Hollander, *Court, Credit, and Capital: Amsterdam's Insolvency Legislation in the Dutch Golden Age*
Zachary Herz, *The God and the Bureaucrat: Roman Law, Imperial Sovereignty, and Other Stories*
Kevin Arlyck, *The Nation at Sea: The Federal Courts and American Sovereignty, 1789–1825*
Ivan Lee, *Extradition and Empire: Sovereignty and Subjecthood in Hong Kong*
James Q. Whitman, *From Masters of Slaves to Lords of Lands: The Transformation of Ownership in the Western World*

(Continued after the Index)

The Judgment of the Provinces

The Roman Empire and the Origins of Law and Society

ARI Z. BRYEN
Vanderbilt University

CAMBRIDGE
UNIVERSITY PRESS

CAMBRIDGE
UNIVERSITY PRESS

Shaftesbury Road, Cambridge CB2 8EA, United Kingdom

One Liberty Plaza, 20th Floor, New York, NY 10006, USA

477 Williamstown Road, Port Melbourne, VIC 3207, Australia

314–321, 3rd Floor, Plot 3, Splendor Forum, Jasola District Centre, New Delhi – 110025, India

103 Penang Road, #05–06/07, Visioncrest Commercial, Singapore 238467

Cambridge University Press is part of Cambridge University Press & Assessment, a department of the University of Cambridge.

We share the University's mission to contribute to society through the pursuit of education, learning and research at the highest international levels of excellence.

www.cambridge.org
Information on this title: www.cambridge.org/9781009730372

DOI: 10.1017/9781009730341

When citing this work, please include a reference to the DOI 10.1017/9781009730341

First published 2026

Cover image: MET/BOT / Alamy Stock Photo.

A catalogue record for this publication is available from the British Library

A Cataloging-in-Publication data record for this book is available from the Library of Congress

ISBN 978-1-009-73037-2 Hardback

To Kim

Contents

Figures

Acknowledgments

This book has taken a long time, and bears the marks of many friends, colleagues, and institutions. It began as a very different project, during a postdoctoral fellowship at New York University's Institute for the Study of the Ancient World, in 2008–2009. The time that I spent in New York allowed me to read broadly in law and social science. A conversation with Rob Tempio encouraged me to move from my stated project to paint on a broader canvas. The immediate result of this was an article, eventually published in 2012, that served as the framework for my broader thinking about how to tell the story of the changes of law in the Roman world over the course of the Roman period, broadly conceived. A subsequent fellowship from the American Council of Learned Societies (the heroic "New Faculty Fellows" program, designed to protect vulnerable PhDs in the wake of the 2008 economic crisis) allowed me to spend two years in the Departments of Rhetoric and Classics at the University of California, Berkeley. My time at Berkeley was formative for exposing me to new modes of thinking about rhetoric and language, about how speech might act in the world, and about how law and legality inflected and emerged from such speech acts. The Rhetoric department is also, in some key respects, a department devoted to investigating the meaning and consequences of a commitment to *logos*; my time there thus casts a long shadow over the manuscript as a whole. My special thanks at Berkeley are due to Marianne Constable, who saw the potential of the earlier versions of this book, and who encouraged me to read broadly in the "law and society" literature; and to Felipe Gutterriez, who was a constant source of intellectual engagement and challenge. Felipe's encouragement, broad reading, and generous conversation are greatly missed.

I began thinking more systematically about how to approach this book during my time at West Virginia University. There, a writing group consisting of Kate Staples, Brian Luskey, Tyler Boulware, Kimberly Welch, and Joshua Arthurs pushed me to clarify my thinking and urged me to apply for support to develop the project. They were also a constant source of joy, as well as periodic gut-busting laughter. A fellowship at the Institute for Advanced Study (School of Historical Studies) in 2014–2015, aided by another fellowship from the American Council of Learned Societies, was essential for the early-stage research. With the support of Angelos Chaniotis, I spent a year working through the papyrological sources for this project, as well as beginning to think about how to integrate the work of the jurists. During my time at the Institute, Sara McDougall, Jim Whitman, Ted Lendon, John Marincola, John Bodel, Patrick Sänger, and Stephen Harrison served as friends and interlocutors. I remain grateful to them. During the summers while at West Virginia University, the American Bar Foundation (ABF) was often my home-away-from home. I am grateful for the ABF's support, and for Robert Nelson and Laura Beth Nielsen in particular.

The next major tranche of writing was done as a fellow at the Stanford Humanities Center, with aid from a grant from the Loeb Classical Library Foundation. There, Brian DeLay and Gerry Cadava kept me company as we descended into Covid-times. Fellowships from Vanderbilt University offered me much needed summer support and the ability to spend time at the very fine libraries of Oxford University. My thanks are due to Georgy Kantor, Lisa Eberle, and Hannah Skoda for their hospitality and their help in setting up these visits. Two visits to the Kommission für Alte Geschichte und Epigraphik in Munich, and the generosity of my host there, Rudolf Haensch, enabled the completion of several chapters. Finally, the writing of the book was completed during a sabbatical from Vanderbilt, spent again in the beautiful surroundings of Oxford University.

I owe a special debt of gratitude to my colleagues at Vanderbilt. They constantly endeavored to support me, to protect me, and to make my life easier as I brought this project to completion. Special thanks are due to Joel Harrington and Emily Greble, and to the generosity of a group of colleagues who gathered to read and comment on a first complete draft of the manuscript: Tom McGinn, Leor Halevi, Katie Crawford, Niki Hemmer, and Dan Sharfstein. The workshop on the draft was fundamental for testing out ideas, and I owe especial thanks to a panel of outside readers who came to Vanderbilt to help: Clifford Ando, Barbara Welke, and Laura Nasrallah. Michael Peachin was not able to make it, but generously commented on the entire manuscript, nonetheless. Finally, my dean's office has been unfailingly supportive. Special thanks are due to Lauren Benton, John Geer, Cindy Kam, and Kamal Saggi.

As a dilettante when it comes to Jewish texts, I have benefited from the expertise of Natalie Dohrmann, Ishay Rosen Zvi, and especially for the remarkable generosity of Amit Gvaryahu, who entertained many queries with deep learning and remarkable patience.

Many others have also helped improve this book. Maud Gleason gave essential comments on what would eventually become Chapter 7. Ishay Rosen Zvi and Georgy Kantor read the entire manuscript and saved me from many errors. Clifford Ando has been a constant interlocutor and read both the finished manuscript and chapters in draft. In addition to the institutions mentioned above, audiences at the Katz Center for Advanced Judaic Studies, the University of Pennsylvania, the University of Chicago, Yale University, Oxford University, the University of Southern California, the University of Virginia, and the University of Michigan have offered feedback on other chapters.

My intellectual home over the past few years has been the American Society for Legal History. I am most pleased to have this book appear in its series, and the editorial work and patience of Tom McSweeney have improved the final product a great deal, especially with the urgent task of shortening what was an excessively long text. Special thanks are also due to Cecelia Cancellaro and to Michael Sharp of Cambridge University Press, as well as to Victoria Phillips, who helped me move the manuscript through production.

To thank friends and family is always a pleasure. Clifford Ando, Cam Grey, Jill Weinberg, Michelle McKinley, Jefferson Cowie, Mickey Casad, Lauren Benton, Joel and Beth Harrington, Sara McDougall, Jim Whitman, Noel Lenski, Rachel Mairs, Emily Greble,

Matt Worsnik, Chiara Sulprizio, Katie Crawford, Niki Hemmer, Barbara Welke, and Jon and Cortney Novak have all been sources of support during this process. My parents, Stephen and Shoshana Bryen, have encouraged me for a long time indeed, as have my sisters, Gabrielle, Sarah, and Mollie Bryen. Over the course of the last decade or more I have also been lucky to enjoy the good humor and hospitality of my extended family, including Wells and Leslie Person, Jim and Lee Person, Michael and Mary Welch, Matt Ludwig and Anna Welch, Barry and Jenny Ludwig, Hilary Ludwig, Sarah Mensinger, and Dan Bell.

The book is dedicated to my wife, Kimberly Welch, who has done more than anyone to encourage this process: to read drafts, to bat around ideas, to protect my time, and to laugh and complain about the fundamental absurdity of the amount of time that we spend doing the work of historical research. During the writing process, Lena Grace Bryen was added to our family; her endless curiosity, energy, and courage have both inspired me and kept my sense of humor on its toes.

Note on the Text

Ancient sources are abbreviated according to the conventions of the *Oxford Classical Dictionary* (4th ed., Oxford University Press, 2012); Papyri are abbreviated according to the *Checklist of Editions of Greek, Latin, Demotic, and Coptic Papyri, Ostraca, and Tablets* (https://papyri.info/docs/checklist). Translations of juristic sources from Justinian's *Digest* are adapted from the edition of Alan Watson (*The Digest of Justinian*, Philadelphia: University of Pennsylvania Press, rev. ed. 2011). Translations from the Loeb Classical Library are noted as LCL. Other sources for translation are recorded in the notes. In many cases I have adapted these as necessary. Throughout the book, I have endeavored only to cite bibliography directly useful to me. I have made no effort to be comprehensive.

Roman governors had different titles. Thus, for example, the governor of Egypt was known as the *prefect*, whereas the governor of Asia was a *proconsul*. For the purposes of this book, this matters little; they were all chief executives of their various provinces. Accordingly, I use the English word "governor" to describe all of them.

I

Introduction

In the towns and cities of the Roman world, over the first centuries AD, the law was alive. It was something that people thought with, something that they wrote about, copied, excerpted, edited, fought over, joked about, imitated, and parodied; something, in other words, that they invested with meaning and animated with narratives. By the end of the fourth century AD, it was no longer so: it was a specialized technology, held in books, and propounded by experts. A great separation had taken place: law became divorced from society; it became something to be applied to subjects, recalcitrant or not, and measured on the basis of its efficacy. *The Judgment of the Provinces* is about this transformation: when, why, and how it happened, and with what effects on provincial and metropolitan culture more generally, and political and rhetorical culture more specifically.

***

The main thread of this story runs through the eastern half of the Roman Empire: a vast and heterogeneous swathe of land running from Greece and Macedonia through Asia Minor, into Syria and the Levant, and down to Egypt and Cyrenaica (see Figure 1.1). Within this densely populated world, a frenzy of hermeneutic activity took place. Christians, Jews, and polytheists all told stories of the righteous individuals confronting imperial governors in court. They laughed at the lawyerly logic-chopping of the crafty slave Aesop. They recopied administrative documents into petitions and used

FIGURE 1.1 Map of the Eastern Roman Empire. Barbara Levick, *High Tide of Empire* (Cambridge: Cambridge University Press, 2023), p. 9.

them to make claims on representatives of the imperial state. Among these populations, the language of law makes its appearance in texts both humble and learned, urban and rural. And yet the texts themselves are only the ripples on a surface, attempts to fix in writing a move or gesture in a larger conversation about the nature, content, and legitimacy conditions of the world their writers inhabited – the world of empire. As such, law was the starting point for a distinctly provincial political theory.

These provincial interpreters were interested in law not as an abstract system, but as a practical manifestation of authority. They engaged the courtroom as fact and symbol, interpreting legal interactions through their local understandings of power, of legitimacy, and of the ideal relationship between legal rules, administrative practices, ethical demands, and rhetorical performance. In other words, within this imperial context, law was vastly more than mere *nomos* (a mode of declaring a statute or a binding rule). It was also *logos* (a mode of speaking and reasoning), *aisthēsis* (a mode of sensing and feeling), and *erōs* (a mode of longing and desiring).[1] It was a register of speaking about problems that was deeply normative, generative of thinking and feeling, and constitutive of communities.

How are we to explain this historical horizon? Why did law come to be among the most important discourses through which subordinated people sought to explain the nature of empire, of administration, and of community?[2] Who conceived it, in which ways, and to what effect? Why, more generally, are empires so productive of legal interpretation?[3] What effects did these discourses have on the imperial center? And why, eventually, did the center try mightily to make this culture go away? These are the questions that structure what follows.

***

Before attempting an answer – even a brief answer – to these questions, it might be useful to gesture at some ways that contemporary scholarship has framed the problem of law in the Roman world more generally, if only to give a sense of what this book is *not*. The goal of writing the legal history of the Roman Empire, and even of the Roman provinces, is hardly new. Some reason for this is simply the profusion of legal evidence, both from the metropole and from the provinces. Rome was, in an important sense, the great regulator: Roman elites settled disputes between communities, including

1 I take inspiration here from Kahana and Mayse 2017.

2 The only real competing discourse was the language of religion or cult; it is nonetheless interesting that in some provincial communities the two discourses intermingled. See further below, Chapters 7–8. On imperial cult, see Price 1984. There is an important late antique analogue to this story, namely, that over the fourth and fifth centuries AD the discourse of theology was similarly important for understanding one's place in the world and entangled with similar questions about the nature of authority and community. See, most importantly, Lim 1995, and the Epilogue.

3 On the legal politics of empires compare esp. Benton 2010; Benton and Ross 2013, and from the Spanish empire, Yannakakis 2008; Premo 2017.

communities over which they did not formally rule; they wrote constitutions for subject communities like municipalities; passed laws and decrees regulating the legal status of communities that were subject to them; exercised jurisdiction over their own citizens and others; and granted legal privileges to some and imposed disabilities upon others. We know of this legal activity not least because, in a great number of cases, communities that were the objects of such regulation took it upon themselves to carve the words of such declarations of law into stone, thus memorializing such legal discourse in permanent media.[4] In other cases, the records of such attempts at regulation come through the sheer luck of their having been written on papyri that have been preserved in dry climates. Periodically, too, the traces of such regulation were written down in texts aspiring to the status of "literature" and passed through the medieval manuscript tradition. Given the vagaries of this process, in which the great majority of evidence was surely lost, the preservation of substantial amounts of legal regulation surely speaks to its more general importance among the communities of the Roman world.[5]

Law was implicated in Rome's attempts to regulate, structure, and describe its empire from the earliest period of Roman expansion. Roman magistrates announced, in solemn idioms, what "the rules" were to be, to whom they were going to apply, and by whom they were going to be enforced. At times the Romans announced rules to other peoples because those peoples had requested that Rome settle a dispute that occurred among them or between themselves and their neighbors or requested that a privilege be granted or confirmed. But often this process of announcing rules to a population was done at

[4] For a provocative recent study of local pride in inscribed codes, see Eck 2020.

[5] The evidence is vast; representative samples can be found in Sherk 1969 (for republican period regulation of Greek communities); for imperial legislation by emperors preserved on stone and papyrus, see Oliver 1989 (with the supplement of Anastasiades and Souris 2000), Purpura 2009; legislation by emperors preserved in juristic texts is gathered by Gualandi 2012. Much valuable material can also be found in Riccobono et al. 1940, now in the process of being updated (on which see Purpura 2012). Crawford 1996 gathers all extant republican legislation, including legislation for subordinate communities, such as the municipal laws that might be said to have served as their constitutions; see more generally Abbott and Johnson 1926 (still useful though badly out of date); González and Crawford 1986. Purpura 1992 collects edicts of Roman governors of Egypt, a province exceptional for its documentation.

the barrel of a gun (or at swordpoint, if one likes), in the wake of conquest, when Roman magistrates simply dictated to other communities how they were to be structured. It ought to be added that a key part of these Roman regulatory schemes involved Roman magistrates declaring that communities ought to be independent and autonomous – that they use their own laws or some version thereof, rather than those of the Romans.[6]

Three impulses motivated these decisions. First, Rome often lacked the desire, and at times lacked the capacity, to involve Roman magistrates in the day-to-day affairs of subject cities. Second, as a matter of policy, Rome rewarded the most loyal of allied cities with the right to self-government. Third, Rome was reluctant to impose Roman legal frameworks on peoples and territories that were not juridically "Roman" but rather, in the terminology of Roman jurists, *peregrini* or "foreigners." According to the Roman jurists, the Roman *ius civile* applied to Roman citizens alone. This claim was truer in theory than in practice, but it performed the important ideological work of marking the uniqueness of Rome vis-à-vis its subjects. As a result, only a small proportion of the inhabitants of the eastern Mediterranean would have held Roman citizenship before AD 212, when the emperor Caracalla granted citizenship to all free inhabitants of the empire.[7] Nonetheless, even in these acts of refusing to provide substantive rules to many communities, Roman magistrates were essentially legislating for them constitutionally, and thus, in a sense, governing their empire through law. What is more, Rome attempted, through the language of law, to regulate its own

[6] Laws imposed upon conquered communities: Livy 45.29–30 (Aemilius Paulus dictating terms to Macedonians – technically a *senatus consultum*); Cic. II *Verr.* 2.32 (reporting details of "what they [sc., the Sicilians] call the *lex Rupilia*"); Plin. *Ep.* 10.112, 114. Mandating the use of local laws: *AE* 1986.304 (*Tabula Alcantarensis*), ll.8-11; *RDGE* 1 (*senatus consultum* guaranteeing freedom and autonomy for Delphi, 189 BC); *RS* 19.8-11 (*lex Antonia de Termessibus*, granting Termessus use of local laws, subject to the provision that the use of such laws did not conflict with other provisions of the Roman grant).

[7] *Ius civile* applied only to Roman citizens: Gai. *Inst.* 1.1, 1.55. On the interpenetration of Roman rules and procedures of civil law in legally alien communities: Ando 2011. On the ways Rome incorporated foreigners within the system of Roman private law, see Alonso 2020. On the extent of citizenship prior to AD 212, see now Lavan 2016; Lavan and Ando 2021.

magistrates when they acted abroad. Such men, it was well understood, might prove politically dangerous.[8]

This profusion of legal acts has not failed to excite scholars, not least because it would appear that, from such acts, a relatively straightforward story of Roman legal practice can be told across the first four centuries AD. Earlier, relatively doctrinal scholarship sought to think of this flurry of legislative action as providing an aperçu into Roman imperial structures along the lines of a more contemporary, rationalized constitution with various actors exercising well-defined powers and offices. The more recent tendency has been to see these various pronouncements within an arc of historical development.[9] This is surely correct and salutary, at least in part.

Within this arc of development there were tendencies towards both fragmentation and homogeneity, both acting in productive tension. The pragmatic demands of governance tended to produce fragmentation. Though Roman magistrates produced texts written in authoritative language that purported to regulate behavior from the Republic onwards, the texts themselves were often ad hoc responses to particular problems and challenges. The edicts of governors tend to address highly localized problems: a famine here, the abuses of detachments of soldiers there, and so forth. This is hardly surprising: the Mediterranean itself, and the eastern Mediterranean in particular, was geographically, linguistically, and politically fragmented. Egypt might require a particular rule, Bithynia another. The patchwork of political units across this landscape further complicated matters: some areas were filled by cities that enjoyed varying degrees of independence, whereas others were crisscrossed by imperial properties that presented different regulatory challenges. In some areas, the imperial government had placed colonies of Roman citizens who had particular status and privileges; in others, the territory was imagined to be completely unurbanized, and thereby subject to different types of rules. While at the ideological level Roman administrators and provincial subjects might have been committed to the proposition

8 E.g., *RS* 12 (*lex de praetoriis provinciis*), Cnidos copy, col. III, ll.1–15, col. IV, 31–19.

9 The modern literature is vast, and in what follows all citations should be taken *exempli gratia*.

that imperial law may have suffused these areas, in practice it did so unevenly, and in some places not at all. Law thus tended to mark regional and political difference, rather than bringing together diverse territories under a single constitutional regime.[10]

By the same token, however, there were patterns to such responses, and they become more pronounced during the first three centuries AD as the advent of emperors and a nascent imperial bureaucracy began to homogenize some aspects of the Roman imperial system. Some of this stability emerges from ruling ideology: Roman administrators often sought to project a sense of conservatism in their legislation, sometimes to the extent of simply copying whole paragraphs of earlier texts. Such was the case, for instance, in crafting constitutions for municipalities, the majority of which existed only in the Roman west. In other cases, stability and consistency emerged from the brute necessities of governing a vast territory: Roman administration depended largely on a governor, who divided the territory into a series of *conventus* centers – locations to which he would ride circuit, to hear cases within his jurisdiction and to check on matters that required his oversight. These visits were necessary as a matter of management, not least because they operated to oversee processes of taxation and material extraction. They also had important ideological and symbolic value, for jurisdiction was expressive of Roman sovereignty in a time of peace. It should be added that the *conventus* districts did not follow the contours of local cultural, geographic, or linguistic divisions. By dividing the province, the *conventus* districts tended to group dissimilar people together and in so doing attempted to collapse local modes of distinction. Finally, we might add that in all territories Roman rule was imagined to operate hierarchically: the

[10] Ad hoc responses to problems: the classic account of imperial reactivity is Millar 1992; see also the papers collected in Millar 2002, especially volumes 1 and 2; a useful general survey of imperial administration can be found in Lintott 1993. Geographic fragmentation: Horden and Purcell 2000. Governors addressing discrete problems: e.g., *AE* 1925.126 (governor addressing a famine in Pisidian Antioch, 93); *SEG* 26 1392 (governor addressing the abuse of free transport by soldiers and others, 14–21). The importance of regional studies, especially of well-documented provinces, has highlighted the ways in which legal cultures were particular to regions: Fournier 2010; Kantor 2013 (on Phrygia); Kantor 2015 (providing a more synoptic view); Czajkowski and Eckhardt 2020. On Roman colonies in the Greek world see now Brélaz 2017. See more generally the studies collected in Eck 1999. Ideological claims of law suffusing all subject territories: Aristid. *Or.* 26.30–33 (Behr).

governor was the chief authority over his province, and was in charge of subordinate officials; but he was also subject to the emperor, who could be appealed to under particular circumstances.[11]

Overall, this tension between homogeneity and particularity seems mostly to have been productive, rather than problematic. Though hard to quantify, it appears that large numbers of subjects settled their disputes in provincial courts. From Egypt, the province that affords us the most granular documentation, we see not only a flurry of petitions to both local and imperial officials, but also a flurry of correspondence between those who travelled great distances to have their cases heard, and those who stayed back, awaiting the results. Moreover, this movement across the landscape continued despite the personal status of the individual complainants, most of whom were not Roman citizens. Cities, in turn, competed to host the governor's assizes, a badge of their importance vis-à-vis their neighbors.

If in fact the penetration of legal institutions was spotty, the ideological importance of such institutions nonetheless coaxed them into the intimate disputes even of country towns and villages. It bears adding, of course, that we get only rare glimpses of those disputes that people chose *not* to settle in formal venues – because they thought them unacceptably alien, because the cost of litigation was too high, or simply because they did not speak or did not care to speak the official language of such a venue. Still, at the ideological level, this flurry of litigation was guaranteed by the emperor himself, who was imagined to be available to his subjects to rule even on matters approaching the terribly mundane, both in person and via written correspondence. But one sees the deep penetration of legal institutions in ways independent of litigation: one can see it in the migration of

[11] On the *leges municipales* see González and Crawford 1986; on the earlier process of Italian municipalization, Bispham 2007: esp. 205–46; see now the evidence of a *municipium* at Troesmis: Eck 2014. Colonies were more common in the eastern provinces: see recently the papers collected in Brélaz 2017, and MacMullen 2000 on the demographic transformation of the Roman landscape at the start of the Principate. On the question of centralization over the first centuries AD, see Burton 1998 (arguing against centralization, but in favor of rationalization). On assizes: Burton 1975; Ando 2010b: 31–40. On appeals, see Garnsey 1966. Others have seen a process of homogenization in the first centuries AD on the basis of the spread of Roman citizenship: most importantly Sherwin-White 1973 (but see now Lavan 2016; Lavan and Ando 2021). For an overview emphasizing homogeneity and similarity, Galsterer 2000.

legal forms for structuring official documents, in the development of archival practices, or in the development, against the background of Roman law, of forms of contractual and property rights that resulted in burgeoning trade. Legal forms also operated, in some communities, as indices of identity, which might urge us to consider this shared legal culture as an index of "Romanization." Even if such a term makes us anxious, the picture that is revealed is nonetheless that of an empire suffused with law and legal practice.[12]

***

The picture I have been painting thus far is of legal history in the institutional register. It operates from a central assumption, which might be termed legal positivism: that law is, primarily, a practice of the state – and in particular, a practice of the state in which binding commands are issued to guide the practice of either a subordinate official or a non-state end-user. Accordingly, in institutional legal history one begins by drawing a map of the universe of state pronouncements (be they pragmatic and local, or ambitious and universalizing), or even a map of state capacities to make such pronouncements, and then measuring the extent to which that map adequately describes practice "on the ground." How, that is, law enforcing institutions operate, or how institutions affect the behavior of non-state actors.

A few things might be said in favor of such an approach. To begin with, this method at times produces empirical findings of great significance: it matters, for instance, to know the extent to which local institutions continued, over the first three centuries AD, to produce legislation and to what extent, if any, the shape of those institutions changed.[13] Second, insofar as institutional history creates maps of

[12] Petitions: *P.Yale* 61 (205); *P.Euphr.* 1 (245); petitions from communities: Hauken 1998. On the business of assizes cf. Dio *Or.* 35.15-17, Bryen 2012a, and infra, Chapter 3. On the role of petitions in dispute resolution more generally, Kelly 2010. On the costs of courts, Haensch 2015. The emperor's handling of low-level provincial cases: *P.Col.* VI 123 (199–200), Severus' *apokrimata*; *SEG* 17 759 (216), Caracalla hearing the case of the Goharieni; more generally Millar 1992. Emperors delegating jurisdiction to manage caseloads: Peachin 1996. On the penetration of legal forms as indices of identity, see Mélèze Modrzejewski 1970, 1988; Cotton 1993; Czajkowski 2017; Czajkowski and Eckhardt 2018; Czajkowski and Eckhardt 2020; Furstenberg 2023. Property rights: Kehoe 2007; with respect to archives, Lerouxel 2015.

[13] E.g., Kantor 2016.

complex processes, maps of this sort are often useful. They simplify messy realities by abstracting salient details from a universe of empirical noisiness. It does indeed matter to have a sense of which organs were – or thought themselves – capable of constraining the behavior of others, even if they were, in actuality, limited in their ability to actualize such constraints.

Third, and on related grounds, it might make sense to begin with the authoritative pronouncements of the imperial Roman state (and those authorized to speak in its name). It possessed the power to enforce its commands with violence. It often did so in a way that was regarded, by other Romans in positions of power at least, as final. The importance of violence ought not to be underrated, and more will be said about it in the course of what follows. For now it will suffice to note that violence is often at the foundation of systems of incentives (and on some accounts law simply *is* a system of incentives).[14] More to the point, Roman administrators were perfectly content to deploy violence to enforce their dictates when they deemed it necessary.[15] The possibility that someone would suffer material loss (of money, of status, or of flesh and skin) does with regularity influence behavior. It is a good reason to give these sorts of state commands an important role in crafting our maps of provincial legal practice.

Its advantages to one side, it might also be said that the institutional account of Roman legal history rests on two assumptions, each of which will be interrogated in what follows. First, the institutional account assumes that law consists primarily in commands, and second, that the goal of such commands is ultimately enforcement. A third assumption, as well, has sneaked in, one characteristic of the "law and society" literature that began to gain currency in the second half of the twentieth century: that the goal of writing legal history is essentially that of measuring the gap between edict and

[14] Whitman 2012: 189–206.

[15] On the importance of violence to Roman administrators, see the important studies of Coleman 1990 and Gleason 1999 on spectacular violence; on the assumption that administrators ought to be able to punish even informally, cf. Cic. II *Verr.* 5.133; *Dig.* 1.16.9.3 = Ulp. 1 *Off. Proc.*, Frg. 2151 Lenel; evidence that they did so or threatened to do so is extensive: cf. *P.Oxy.* IV 706 (c.115 AD); *P.Oxy.* LXXIII 4960 (AD II); Acts 22:24–25; Jos. *BJ* 2.241–44, and infra. On the importance of violence in constructing the elite Roman habitus more generally, Peachin 2007.

enforcement, between "law on the books" and "law in action." The purpose, ultimately, is to assess the health and strength of the state.[16] It is here that what follows parts ways with the institutional account of Roman legal history.

***

We might raise several critiques of this model of writing legal history. The first is methodological. Attempts to measure state efficacy in incentivizing the application of its own rules only have salience as part of a comparative endeavor: that is, to understand the effectiveness of Roman state pronouncements only makes sense in comparison to the effectiveness of other states in enforcing their pronouncements. Yet in many institutional histories of the Roman world, this explicit comparison is simply omitted. The result of such inquiries is thus often unsatisfying.[17] No more satisfying are institutional histories that seek to sidestep this problem by claiming a more restricted purpose, namely, of simply showing how things "actually" worked (normally in comparison to an ideal, articulated or not).

But there is also a second, perhaps more consequential objection: on what grounds do we privilege the state as the source of law in the first place? In other words, to what degree ought our histories of law in the Roman world be founded on an account of legal positivism – that is, the claim that law is, and just is, what the state declares it to be? Or even upon a modified version of legal positivism, one adapted to the study of empires, that law ought to be understood as the command both of the imperial metropole and of subordinate units?[18] I would suggest that such an account is, at best, only partial.[19]

[16] See Sarat 1985. On fetishization of state capacity in antiquity, see (in a different context) the important discussions of Richardson 2012 and Richardson 2017.

[17] This seems to be especially the case with respect to works about policing: e.g., Fuhrmann 2011, and, for the Hellenistic period, Bauschatz 2013.

[18] On the importance of imperial forms of sovereignty, see Benton 2010; Benton and Ross 2013.

[19] I follow here in the footsteps of Hartog 1985, a piece that deserves to be read by more ancient historians. Similarly important are Cover 1992b; Constable 1994, 2014. Cover 1992a states the problem succinctly: "[Understanding law as a bridge between what is and what ought to be] is a plea to grant all collective behavior entailing systematic understandings of our commitments to future worlds equal claim to the word 'law'. The upshot of such a claim, of course, is to deny to the nation state any special status for the collective behavior of its officials or for their

Consider the following example. At the start of his second-century textbook, the *Institutes*, the Roman jurist Gaius attempted to delimit the field of study by anticipating a student's question, namely, where was one to go to learn the Roman civil law (*ius civile*)? To begin with, Gaius explains, there was not one single source of law (*ius*); Roman civil law consisted, rather, in multiple sources of authoritative discourse (*iura*):[20]

> The *iura* of the Roman people consist of statutes, plebiscites, opinions of the senate, orders of the emperors, the edicts of those who have the right to issue edicts, and the *responsa* of the jurists.

Gaius continues from here, defining the nature of each of these, and giving the background that a student would require: thus, a statute is said to be "what the *populus* decrees or orders," a plebiscite is what the plebeians decree or order, and so forth.

We need not detain ourselves over the well-known problems that this text poses, not least that there are rival attempts at defining the content of the *ius civile* by other authors, namely Cicero and Pomponius, crafted under different circumstances and pressed into doing different sorts of work. Nor do we need to worry about what seems to be a sleight of hand: that Gaius' account of the *ius civile* is substantially positivist and written, relying heavily on official orders coming from the state, while in point of fact much of *ius* was oral – so much so that what was written down by jurists hewed closely to this tradition, copying much of its oral style. Jurisprudence is another puzzle in Gaius' account. He gestures at it in his claim that the *ius civile* also includes the *responsa* of jurists – the replies of learned men – but

systematic understandings of some special set of 'governing' norms. The status of such 'official' behavior and 'official' norms is not denied the dignity of 'law.' But it must share the dignity with thousands of other social understandings. In each case the question of what is law and for whom is a question of fact about what certain communities believe and with what commitments to those beliefs. The organized behavior of other groups and the commitments of actors within them have as sound a claim to the word 'law' as does the behavior of state officials. The most important consequence of this radical relativization of law is that violence – a special problem in the analysis of any community's commitments to its future – must be viewed as problematic in much the same way whether it is being carried out by order of a federal district judge, a mafioso or a corporate vice-president."

20 Gai. *Inst.* 1.2.

for this to be accurate we would have to take "responsa" in a much broader sense than Gaius seems to intend.[21]

We should instead focus on the "frame" that structures this sort of definitional activity. Gaius is not stating a fact: that is, that Roman law *just is* these six things – for in fact it was more. He is rather engaging in an act of deixis: he is pointing a student, his imagined reader, to a body of materials, materials that have been elevated to the status of texts that deserve commentary and study.[22] And as with all such acts of deixis or pointing, defining one body of materials as deserving of study does two further pieces of work. First, it operates to create community: those who comment on *these* texts are discussing the *ius civile*. Second, and relatedly, by creating community in one place it operates to exclude other, rival understandings of the relationship between texts and communities: those who comment on *these* texts (and not *those* texts) are discussing the *ius civile*. He is, in effect, issuing an invitation: join me in discussing *these* texts, follow my lead in learning *how* to discuss them, and you will join me in a learned community – with all of its attendant privileges. This act of pointing cannot be separated from values, or from status. It is also political: these texts, the invitation suggests, constitute *us* as a political community. To join in their interpretation is to partake of our history and our values, and to share in, or at least become habituated to, our deepest assumptions about optimal social and political ordering.[23]

Gaius' account of the *ius civile* can be contrasted to another example of deixis. This one comes from a text known as the *Mekhilta*

[21] Other definitions: Cic. *Top.* 28; *Dig.* 1.2.2.12 = Pomp. *Ench.*, Frg. 178 Lenel. The later version of Justinian (*Inst.* 1.2) is radically different in its framing. On *ius* as a practice transcending mere statute, see Schiavone 2012; on the genres in which one could speak about *ius*, see Schulz 1946; on orality in juristic composition, see *Dig.* 1.2.2.5, 1.2.2.12, Honoré 2002: 37–75. On *responsa* more specifically, Bryen 2019b. Gaius' definition of *responsa prudentium* (1.7) makes certain that he thinks positivistically: *responsa prudentium sunt sententiae et opiniones eorum, quibus permissum est iura condere. quorum omnium si in unum sententiae concurrunt, id, quod ita sentiunt, legis vicem optinet; si vero dissentiunt, iudici licet quam velit sententiam sequi.* ("The *responsa* of jurists are the rulings and opinions of those *who have been given the authority* to establish the law; of these, if they are unified on a question, they obtain the force of statute; but if they differ, the judge is permitted to follow the opinion he chooses.")

[22] On the work of deixis in the context of Republican legislation, see Ando 2019.

[23] Cf. the Jewish approach: *infra*, page 237.

de-Arayot, a Rabbinic commentary on selections from the book of Leviticus that was later preserved in some editions of *Sifra*, another commentary on Leviticus which was edited or compiled from yet earlier materials in the Roman provinces sometime probably in the third or fourth century.[24] Like Gaius, the authors of this passage worried about the content of the law, and worried more particularly about the relationship of the law as written in the Torah to the authoritative pronouncements of the Roman state.[25] It is a text that worries, in other words, about the nature of community, and of order, in relation to law. It took up these questions in its discussion of Leviticus 18:3, "and in their statutes you shall not walk":[26]

"And in their statutes (*bi-huqutekhem*) you shall not walk": What did Scripture leave unsaid (that this need be stated)? Is it not already written (Deut. 18:10–11) "There shall not be found among you one who passes his son or daughter through fire ... and casts spells, etc."? What, then, is the intent of "and in their statutes you shall not walk"? In their customs (*nimosot*) – those things that are inscribed for them – such as theatres (*tiyatrot*), circuses (*qirqusot*), and arenas (*hasteryot*). R. Meir says: These are "the ways of the Amorites," which the sages enumerated. R. Yehudah b. Betheira says: that you not preen yourself, and not cultivate locks, and not wear the hair *qomi*. And lest you say: "They have statutes and we have no statutes" – It is, therefore, written (18:9) "My judgments shall you do and My statutes you shall heed to walk in them; I am the Lord your God." – But there is still "hope" for the evil instinct to reflect and say "But theirs are more beautiful than ours!" – It is, therefore, written (Deut. 4:6) "And you shall heed and you shall do. For this is your wisdom and your understanding."

To make sense of the biblical text, the authors of the *Sifra* seek to understand the nature of "statutes": what does it mean that one must not "walk" in them? A separate biblical prohibition had already covered religious acts: child sacrifice, augury, and the casting of spells. So as not to replicate this prohibition, the authors perform an act of

[24] Kahana 2006: 86–87.

[25] As a salutary reminder that Rabbinic Jews were themselves provincial subjects, and need to be included in discussions of provincial activity more broadly, see Lapin 2012; on Jewish legalism as an effect of empire, see Dohrmann 2013.

[26] *Sifra, Aharei Mot* 13, trans. sefaria.org with modifications based on the discussion of Dohrmann 2003. Dohrmann's discussion of *Mekhilta de Rabbi Ishmael* on Ex. 21:1 contains another example of a similar sort of deixis. On the passage discussed herein (and its compositional issues) see the discussion of Berkowitz 2011: 89–111.

redefinition: statutes are not just written prohibitions, but rather *customs* (*nimosot*, from the Greek *nomos*, both "custom" and "law") – things that suffuse daily life and serve to define communities. To avoid "walking" in "their statutes," one must avoid theatres, circuses, and arenas; one must similarly avoid certain types of personal grooming, such as avoiding wearing one's hair *qomi* (presumably from the Greek for long hair: *komē*). For Rabbi Meir, these things, taken together, can be captured through an act of deixis: *these*, he asserts, are the ways of the Amorites and are thus prohibited.

"Statute," on this reading, is more than the command of the state. It is what archaeologists might refer to as a cultural assemblage: it encompasses architecture and urban space, hairstyle and dress. The things that make them *them* are the things that *we* must avoid; since the text posits a *we* that is constituted by statutes (by Torah), so by deduction there must also be a *they*, similarly constituted.[27] It ought immediately to be added that the *we* posited by this text is a rhetorical construct with only a tenuous relationship to the realities of Roman Palestine.[28] But the author goes farther, and in so doing manages to capture something essential about the experience of pluralism in an empire: a sense of longing for the culture of the dominant, either by noting an absence in one's own culture ("They have statutes and we have no statutes"), or by judging alien practices to be aesthetically superior ("But theirs are more beautiful than ours!"). Law, on such a reading, is far from just positive law declarations: it is also the object of aesthetic contemplation, indeed even of erotic desire.[29] It is in this context that the reference to the "evil instinct," the *yetzer ha-raʿ*, makes sense: the desire for the laws of others here is imagined as a sort of base if not sexualized yearning, to be countered with authoritative, Biblical injunctions, to which the reader is directed through another act of deixis.

Both Gaius and the *Sifra* can be read as attempting, through their own idioms, to define the category of Roman law. For Gaius it is

[27] For law (in this case *nomothesia*) as a cultural assemblage, compare Tatian, *Orat.* 26 (focused on sexual practices).

[28] Useful surveys of this issue: Schwartz 2001a: 110–23; Cohen 2014: 213–22, and more generally Berthelot 2021. Cases judged by Rabbis, Lapin 2012: 98–125.

[29] Dohrmann 2003: 71. On *eros*, cf. the analysis of Richardson 2014: esp. 71, who asks a similar question from the perspective of the archaic state. On the nature of the longing posed by the *yetzer ha-raʿ*, see Rosen-Zvi 2011.

restricted and positive, whereas for the *Sifra* it is extensive and manifested in things as diverse as hairstyle and entertainment. It will not do, at this juncture, to suggest that the *Sifra* was simply incorrect or tendentious in claiming such an extensive territory for "their" laws. To begin with, Roman jurists and administrators themselves at times imagined that legal practices, and legal statuses in particular, were just parts of one's habitus, one's way of being in the world.[30] The institutions of the city – theaters, circuses, and arenas – were, among the Greek speaking populations of the empire at least, the signs of civilization, and they might easily be imagined as the physical instantiation of law, a reflection of privileged status, and a source of collective pride in one's political community. The *Sifra*, then, gives a fairly workable definition of how a substantial part of the population of the empire imagined the law of the empire: as a habitus, a package of traits that determined how one ought to live. What is more, such a definition would have made sense to a Roman, even to a Roman jurist, who would also have recognized that, even among communities of juridically "Roman" status, there would necessarily be variation in local customs, which would have to be accounted for in the absence of positive law.[31]

The point, then, is not that one definition is tendentious and the other is not. They both are. We might say that both Gaius and the *Sifra*, and many other texts besides, engaged in struggles to define the content and boundaries of law. To privilege one account a priori – normally, in modern literature, the account of Gaius – comes at the cost of missing this broader hermeneutic struggle. It also, if perhaps quietly, tends to give priority to the Roman imperial state, simply, so far as I can tell, because it claimed to be the final authority on what sorts of violence against subjects might be taken as authoritative.

[30] Cf. *FIRA* I 71, the grant of citizenship to the Anauni by Claudius, after they had been usurped it for generations. On Claudius and citizenship more generally, see Suet. *Claud.* 15.41, where citizenship is assumed to be expressed through one's clothing (cf. *Dig.* 47.10.15.15 = Ulp. 77 *Ed.*, Frg. 1352 Lenel). On dress and citizen status more generally, see Edmondson 2008; Suet. *Claud.* 16.2, where citizenship is assumed to be encoded in language; cf. Suet. *Gramm.* 22.2, on "giving citizenship" to Greek loanwords in Latin (and for similar examples, Kaster 1995: 226–27).

[31] On the problem of urban space see further Ando 2012b. Custom and its relation to statute: e.g., *Dig.* 21.2.6 = Gai. 10 *Ed. Prov.*, Frg. 242 Lenel; *Dig.* 1.3.32–1.3.40; *Dig.* 22.5.3.6 = Callist. 4 *Cog.*, Frg. 28 Lenel; cf. *Dig.* 48.22.7.5 = Ulp. 10 *Off. Proc.*, Frg. 2243 Lenel. See, with further references, Humfress 2011, who rightly emphasizes the fluidity of the category, and the complexity of its interface with Roman "law."

As such, it leads scholars to take institutions – courts, law-creating organs, personnel, even rules and statutes themselves – as *presumptively* authoritative and binding because they emanate from the power of states to actualize their claims, either through persuasion or violence. To be sure, the best institutional histories can show, often in great detail, that a given institution might work better or worse, persist or transform, and so on. But the ways that institutions operate as *claims* upon spaces is often elided.

But institutions never just *are*; they are the product of particular human desires to organize a space or a practice in a particular way. They are therefore also the product of normative claims – that justice is done here, at this time, and in this way not because that is simply how it is done, but because that is how it *ought* to be done. Institutions, one might say, complete the act of deixis in a particular way. They attempt to instantiate or reify a particular act that defines law as one thing but not the other. To be sure, this often works: people can operate through institutions because they find their claims persuasive or profitable, or because they have been induced – or terrified – into compliance. They can naturalize the existence of some institutions, to the point where competing ones might be perceived as unnatural or abnormal. They can even be convinced that an *is* and an *ought* are identical: that the way that "we" solve problem X is just the way problem X is solved.

But when we see such claims we ought to imagine that behind them sit – or at some point sat – processes of struggle, competing acts of deixis, and alternative modes of imagining that have been effaced or made illegitimate. In other words, for every Gaius, there was also a *Sifra*. If Roman historians have tended to privilege Gaius and not the *Sifra*, we ought to ask why. And we cannot assume that the answer is just, "state violence," or even the forms of authority that follow on the back of such violence. We need instead to interrogate the category, ask what it can and cannot do, to whom and under what circumstances, and with what sort of effects for governance more generally.[32]

***

32 I follow here in the footsteps of important work on the nature and effect of the Roman state and its role in transforming local understandings of justice and disputes: see, most importantly, Shaw 2009; Shaw 2011. See further the essays collected in Ando and Richardson 2017.

Legal history in the institutional register has a further shortcoming. In its acts of mapping, it does a very good job of reconstructing certain phenomena that admit of ready reconstruction: the existence of courts, the careers of officials, the edicts of emperors, and so forth. These things tend to be especially amenable to mapping precisely because they claimed official status and were thus amenable to memorialization. But it does a rather poorer job of explaining how law came to be a register for creating meaning in the first place. Yet throughout the Roman world, discussions of law – along with discussions and stories of trials, of judges, and of other "legal" phenomena – came to serve as loci of meaning, as generative of theories of governance and of empire more generally. That law came to serve as a mode of meaning-making and political theorizing, largely independent of legal institutions themselves, calls for explanation.

We might consider two examples. Both are what we could call legal storytelling or even mythmaking: foundation stories that use legal action to point towards other phenomena of government and governance, and in so doing serve to make sense of, and to make claims upon, the world of empire. Mythmaking of this sort was a common practice throughout the empire, and the stories range from brief vignettes to elaborate, multi-stage narratives, encompassing a wide range of genres.[33] I shall have more to say about such mythmaking in what follows, but for present purposes I want to single out two texts to give some sense of the ways law is generative of meaning in other spheres, and to probe the broader consequences of this form of meaning-making. The first text comes from the learned second-century florilegium of Aulus Gellius, who recounts a story about the emperor Hadrian, confronted in Rome with a difficult case:

> There was a distinguished woman of good morals, whose faithfulness was beyond question. In the eleventh month after the death of her husband she had given birth, and on account of the length of time since her husband's death she was accused as having conceived after the death of her husband, since the *decemviri* had written that children are born within ten months

[33] A few recent studies have done much to clarify the importance of such narratives: see Schwartz 2017 on the importance of trial narratives in the Greek novel; Harker 2008 on the *Acta Alexandrinorum*; and Tuori 2016 on imperial adjudication. On stories about legal origins, see in particular, Fögen 2002. See also Bryen 2014a for an attempt to articulate some methodological principles.

(of conception), not eleven. But the divine Hadrian, upon hearing the case, decreed (*decrevisse*) that it was possible for children to be born in the eleventh month as well; and we have read (*legimus*) his very decision (*decretum*) in this case. In this decision Hadrian says that he ruled (*statuere*) this way after having read the opinions (*sententiis*) of the ancient philosophers and physicians.[34]

One can read Gellius' story in two ways. One can read it through lawyerly, institutional eyes, as a "case": in this sense, we might say that it is a story in which a legal outlier (an unquestionably virtuous woman with an exceptionally long pregnancy) comes before an emperor, similarly renowned for his legal innovations and good character. Faced with an exception to the rule, the emperor chooses not to apply the law as written, originally, by the decemviri (the authors of the Twelve Tables, the original source of Roman statutory law). Rather than subordinate the demands of justice to a body of ancient writing, the emperor can show his innate sense of justice by extending the law.

Such a story is meant to be exemplary, to serve a pedagogical purpose. It insists that a good emperor will behave in a similar way; it also reminds readers that it is only emperors – rather than others – who have the temperament and moral capacity to exercise such a prerogative. Read along these lines, as an example of legal mythmaking, the story fits comfortably within a larger framework in which good emperors, through their ability to recognize virtue, contribute to the body of law itself.[35] On such a reading, this vignette works to explain the internal development of the legal system. This system develops through the intervention of virtuous men like Hadrian who seek to achieve substantive justice by transcending the confines of written tradition – but only when necessary. On such a reading, Gellius' story is the kind of legal myth that one would tell a law

[34] Aul. Gell. *NA* 3.16.12.

[35] See Tuori 2016: 214. Similar stories about transcending tradition were told in the Republican period of the praetors: cf. Aul. Gell. *NA* 20.1.13 (quoting from M. Antistius Labeo's commentary *On the Twelve Tables*). The explanation of Pomponius (*Dig.* 1.1.7.1 = *Ench.*, Frg. 178 Lenel) seeks to naturalize what must have been a remarkable power grab by explaining that the praetors added to the civil law only for the sake of "improving, supplementing, or correcting it for the sake of public interest" (*adiuvandi vel supplendi vel corrigendi iuris civilis gratia propter utilitatem publicam*). See, most importantly, Frier 1985.

student: it seeks to domesticate the actions of an emperor by providing an ethical framework that explains them. The emperor changed the law because he was a moral actor faced with empirical realities that demanded remedy. More importantly, it explains these interventions as a necessary and natural part of jurisdiction more generally.

But there is another way to approach this story. We might begin by noting that stories of miraculous fecundity seemed to attach themselves to the emperors, Hadrian in particular. Jurists repeatedly recounted these stories – an odd fact, since jurists were in general loathe to comment on such sorts of paradoxa. Multiple or unusual births, we might say (with apologies for the pun), served as a fertile locus for thinking through some particular aspect of imperial power. So far as the jurists' stories go, they all turn on the relationship between the natural and the unnatural and the extent to which law might be made to account for the latter.[36] This is, to a certain extent, what is going on in this case: the question is whether the emperor ought to change the law itself in order to account for the outermost possibilities of the human capacity for parturition.

But Gellius adds an important twist. The reason for changing the law was not because the emperor had an innate sense of justice or equity, but rather because he had done his reading. Because he went to consult the "ancient philosophers and physicians," he could effect a change in the fabric of law: accordingly, he ruled (*statuere*) that birth was indeed possible in the eleventh month. Note that, on Gellius' telling, Hadrian is no longer ruling on the particular case of the woman – that is, he is not announcing that, for legal purposes, a pregnancy in the eleventh month after the death of a husband will simply be counted as, or deemed to be, the product of a marital union. Rather, he rules "that it was possible for children to born in the eleventh month as well." Law, on this reading, does not expand or change simply from the personal good (or ill) will of the sovereign; it operates, ideally, in the light of "scientific" learning external to it, and defers to learned consensus.

Such a story is a myth of legal legitimacy. It uses a moment of judgment to comment on the conditions of law's legitimacy vis-à-vis

[36] I gather and analyze the relevant sources in Bryen 2016b: 22–28. Cf. Thomas 2011 on nature.

other, competing modes of learning. Gellius told it in the context of a larger discursive system in which similar stories were told and retold, to competing purposes. Within such a system, stories of law are never purely descriptive. They are always interested, ideological, and eventually political. Like the acts of deixis to which I referred earlier, they isolate particular moments that they deem to be exemplary acts of lawmaking, and then narrate these moments to teach a broader lesson about the foundations of legal and political authority more generally.

For much of the population of the Roman world, I shall argue, these sorts of myths or stories were the most important ways to frame these larger issues. Lacking a contemporary social scientific vocabulary to talk in the abstract about institutions, institutional performance, and legitimacy, the inhabitants of the Roman Empire deployed the narrative, the exemplum, and the myth as tools to make sense of their political, legal, and institutional worlds. It should quickly be added that this is no shortcoming on their part: among the most powerful ideas of history have been parables, fables, or aphorisms. Narratives, as every historian knows, focus the attention on salient matters and make them vivid; storytelling (and the additional interpretive endeavors – the *commentaries* – that stories invite) is a powerful tool for explaining the world in which one lives and for imagining the world in which one might.[37]

I should like to take a very broad view of such mythmaking in what follows. These myths could be communicated in texts, and indeed this is the way that contemporary scholars encounter them. But they did not have to be. Often such stories were performed in public spaces, displayed as tableaus for inquisitive audiences, for the purpose of teaching lessons. Sometimes, as scholars like Maud Gleason and Kathleen Coleman have made clear in the case of capital punishment, these tableaus were meant to inspire a sense of horror and dread – a fear of the consequences of not respecting legal authority – as well as the satisfaction of knowing that it was ultimately someone deserving who was being so violently disposed of.[38]

But myths can be performed in many ways besides, and throughout the world of the Roman provinces, they often were. My second example of the ways law comes to serve as an important symbolic

[37] Cover 1992b. [38] Coleman 1990; Gleason 1999. Cf. Shaw 1996.

resource comes from a text, Philo's *Against Flaccus*, purporting to describe a public ritual in the city of Alexandria in the early first century AD. The background to the story is the worsening relations between the population of Jews resident in the city of Alexandria, and the Alexandrian citizens themselves. A catalyst for the riots that soon followed was the visit to Alexandria of Herod Agrippa (Julius Agrippa), the tetrarch in charge of northeast Galilee. Though the deep causes of the tension between the Jews and the Alexandrians were complicated, in this case, the arrival of a Jewish monarch in Alexandria was particularly problematic because it raised the specter of a realignment of the relations between the two communities. The Alexandrians had been treated badly in the course of the Roman conquest of Egypt, some sixty years before, while the Jews had been given privileges. In the intervening years, a *modus vivendi* was worked out, where the two had agreed to tolerate each other, but probably only at arm's length. Agrippa's arrival threatened to upset the balance.[39]

According to Philo, Alexandrian motives were far simpler: the Alexandrians were incensed "that a Jew had become a king," and began to mock Agrippa publicly. Part of this came in the form of mimes and jests but eventually it took the form of a public performance, an inversion of Jewish sovereignty:[40]

Now there was a lunatic named Karabas, whose madness was not of the wild and savage kind, against which neither the madmen themselves nor those in their vicinity can protect themselves, but of the more relaxed and gentler variant. He spent both day and night naked on the streets, not discouraged by heat or cold, a plaything of the children and the youngsters who were idling about. Together they drove this poor man into the gymnasium and placed him there on a platform so that he could be seen by everyone. On his head they spread out a piece of papyrus for a diadem and clothed the rest of his body with a doormat for a robe; and someone who had seen a small piece of native papyrus lying on the street, gave it to him for a scepter. And when, as in a theatrical mime, he had been dressed up like a king and received the insignia of kingship, young men, bearing sticks on their shoulders as if they were carrying spears, stood on either side of him in imitation of bodyguards. Then others approached him, some as if to salute him (*aspasomenoi*), others as if to plead their cause before him (*dikasomenoi*), again others as if to petition

[39] Alston 1997; van den Horst 2003: 18–34; Blouin 2005.
[40] 36–39, trans. van den Horst 2003 with minor modifications.

him (*enteuxomenoi*) about the affairs of the state. Then there arose a strange shout from among the multitude of those standing around him: They called him "Marin" – which is said to be the word for "Lord" in Syriac – for they knew that Agrippa not only was by birth a Syrian but also ruled as a king over a great part of Syria.

Like Gellius' account of Hadrian, this too should be read as an attempt to make sense of a moment of judgment. But here the context is different: rather than express their understandings through written texts, the Alexandrians recreate, as a public spectacle, the external trappings of royal judgment to highlight their defective content. Their "king" is not a king but a madman; his clothes are not royal but ragged; his scepter is not granted but found. Nonetheless, they make a point of greeting him, submitting cases to him, and petitioning him about the affairs of their community. On Philo's telling, the stagecraft required the efforts of a significant number of members of the community, all in on the act: the bodyguards carrying sticks, the petitioners, and the multitude who shouted to him in mock Syriac. All colluded in crafting a scene of the inversion of royal jurisdiction. No doubt such a performance was also designed to engage an audience, and to send a clear message to anyone who might have been either indifferent to, or perhaps even pleased by, the imminent arrival of Agrippa.

Whereas Gellius focuses on the substance of the decision reached (and the process for reaching it), the Alexandrians focus instead on the "frame" which makes jurisdiction possible. Such a frame, of course, would have been immediately understandable to anyone living in the Roman provinces: the advent of the emperor or the governor, accompanied by formalized greetings, was an affair similarly symbolized by the hearing of cases. To submit to the jurisdiction of another meant to acknowledge the other's superiority and sovereignty. For the Alexandrians, with their wry spectacle and linguistic play, the point was to use this scene to mock Agrippa's ambitions to sovereignty more generally, and to highlight that any Jews who welcomed him as a monarch needed to be put in their place. On their logic, handing a petition to a Jewish monarch was essentially the same as handing one to the local derelict. Moreover, the very presence of such a person in their city – even in spite of his close connection to the emperor – was an affront to their dignity, and to the dignity of *their* governor (Aulus Avilius Flaccus).

Jurisdiction thus came to serve as a potent locus for thinking about the nature of community, and the nature of the hierarchies within a particular community or between particular communities (in this case, an Alexandrian community on top, Jews and others on the bottom). To rephrase my claim just slightly: enacting a story – a myth – about law through the degraded body of Karabas was, for the Alexandrians, a way of enacting their understandings of the ideal relationship between imperial sovereignty and local communities more generally. By a performance of jurisdiction, a political problem was laid bare and made tangible. In this case it was done through play, a ludic act binding together the Alexandrians *as* a community, producing the very thing it depicts and absorbing the participants and audience within it. As they play, the participants are absorbed in the moment and engaged pre-rationally; the experience is cathartic, even transcendent. It is also pedagogical, teaching a moral lesson – and offering a threat – to those not in on the act. If nothing else, law here comes to be thick with meaning.[41]

It might be objected that in pairing Gellius' Hadrian – thoughtful, learned, and fair – with the riotous Alexandrians, I compare apples to oranges: that there just is a difference between the substantive ruling of an emperor and the frenzied mockery of sovereignty, and that the one *really* is law (a formal ruling on a particular case) and the other *really* is not. To be sure, one (the ruling of Hadrian) was written down and placed in some sort of an archive. The other was, by its nature, ephemeral. But while this may be, the broader objection – that combining the two texts makes an

[41] On legal performances more generally, see Peters 2008. On play, see Gadamer 1989: 112: "This gives what we called transformation into structure its full meaning. The transformation is a transformation into the true. It is not enchantment in the sense of a bewitchment that waits for the redeeming word that will transform things back to what they were; rather, it is itself redemption and transformation back into true being. In being presented in play, what is emerges. It produces and brings to light what is otherwise hidden and withdrawn." As for the Alexandrians, it might be that in so playing they were engaged in the identical process that emperors themselves engaged in. If one accepts the account of Tuori 2016, the constitutional foundation of imperial jurisdiction came not through formal grants, but rather through narratives of their jurisdiction that circulated through the empire. The claim has proven initially controversial, but it aligns well with the fundamental study of Peachin 2015, who raises important questions about the slow process by which Augustus himself "discovered" his jurisdictional powers.

error of categories – privileges, a priori, a definition of law that is coterminous with what the state says it is, and in so doing begs the question. As I shall argue in what follows, the locus of legal creativity – of what Robert Cover once called *jurisgenesis* – was nowhere near as secure, in the first three centuries AD, as jurists, ancient or modern, might wish it to be. Like all pre-modern states, the Roman Mediterranean was prolific of sovereigns.[42]

Finally, what is "real" is not the same as what is "official." The Alexandrians, at least, were quite aware of this. Others were as well. In a world suffused with official documentation, and where official documentation often made claims about reality, there were nonetheless voices of doubt about the potential for mismatch. Thus Lactantius, in describing the last days of the emperor Valerian, could make a sophisticated critique of the mismatch between reality and official documentation:[43]

> [the emperor Valerian], having been captured by the Persians, lost not only the power (*imperium*) which he had used so badly, but also his liberty – the very thing he had taken from others, living in the most vile slavery. For when Shapur, the Persian king who had taken him captive, wanted to mount his chariot or his horse, he would order the Roman to bow before him. He would then use him as a stepstool, and with a smiling reproach say, "*This* is true, not what the Romans paint on walls or tablets."

But one could go further and say that, insofar as it resides in and is expressed through language, law has to be understood as sitting in relation to a broader world of rhetoric and narrative. To recognize something *as law* relies upon stories, often unarticulated or enthymematic, about the history of government, the nature of power, and the conditions of legitimacy that make a ruling recognizable.[44] Hadrian may be framed as making a statement of law, a simple claim about what will be accepted as true, *ceteris paribus*. But to know that it is law requires understanding him within a historical genealogy of imperial power in Rome and being able to hear his statement about the possibilities of parturition as being spoken within a register that

[42] Cover 1992b. Cf. the perceptive comments of Edwards 2011: 585. On empires more generally, see Burbank and Cooper 2010. For a rich comparative study, see Hulsebosch 2005.

[43] *Mort. Pers.* 5. [44] Constable 2014; Bryen 2014a.

renders his reading binding and decisive. To hear him making law, in brief, requires that we see him emplotted within a broader, historical, political and *ethical* narrative that enables us to make sense of his behavior as introducing a sensible reform rather than malignly barking imperatives.[45] The Alexandrians, of course, had their own narrative – a similarly political and ethical story about the nature of community and sovereignty and justice, and about the relation between monarchy and local communities. Such a story had its own cast of heroes and villains, and contained its own understanding of the relationship between sovereign power and community consent. For the Alexandrians (and many others besides, as I will argue), law did not consist in sovereign commands or rulings. Law rather *emerged* through dialogue between subjects and rulers. And to engage in dialogue with a man like Agrippa was to engage in dialogue with a lunatic off the street; like wrestling with a pig, nothing redeeming could come from such an interaction.

Accordingly, if we choose to elevate to the status of law one (Hadrian) and not another (the Alexandrians), then we have acquired the burden of explaining this choice. To explain it on the grounds that one narrative is "official" and the other not is, to my mind, an exercise in circularity. It also does violence to the sources (for Gellius himself makes no claims to report "official" acts). Perhaps more to the point: both of these texts deserve to be paired, since they are both acts of legal exegesis that seek, through their narratives, to comment on what they took to be the decisive texts of the law: the decision of Hadrian, in one case, and the person of the (purported) sovereign, in the other.

What counted as "legal" was a moving target in this age. There was no single text, only commentary. Or rather, there was a proliferation of acts of deixis that pointed to some texts and tried to persuade others to raise them to the status of *the* texts that deserved commentary. I mean for this to be taken in the strongest, most anti-foundational sense possible. When we seek to write the legal history of the Roman provinces in the first few centuries AD, we are faced with a world that is radically decentralized in comparison to modern systems of law (which are anyhow nowhere

[45] Herz 2025.

near as centralized as people might hope), a world in which there was no universal consensus on what ought to count as law, and no Ur-texts. It was commentary all the way down, as competing understandings of law pressed against one another, animated stories and myths, and produced a struggle over institutions and their meaning more generally.

***

With that said, people nonetheless were keen to make claims, and to try to find foundations. This leads to a further point: any account of how law operates has a theory of political order at its base. Arguing about the nature of law, at least at this level of generality, raises foundational questions of political order: who are we, who are you, and what rules guide the interactions between us? These questions of politics emerge from questions about law and will be a fundamental part of what follows.

The inhabitants of the Roman world were divided as to what answers they should give to these basic questions, and through their storytelling they engaged in what deserves to be called political debate. Over the course of the first four centuries AD, they imagined law according to four major groups or patterns, four ways of conceiving "law as."[46] To conceive of "law as" involves a way of imagining the foundations or anchors of the legal action more generally; it involves a commitment to a particular vision of politics. But it also involved the sort of deixis that I flagged earlier: a set of assertions that there were, in fact, foundational texts that ought to be raised to canonical status. These stories often echoed one another, even when they did not overtly acknowledge competing viewpoints. But the echoes are sufficiently closely patterned that, when we can identify them, we ought to take them as salvoes in a broader political conversation.

In what follows, I identify four such patterns. In the Roman world, law could be imagined as documents, dialogue, ecstasy, and books. The first two groups (documents and dialogue) for imagining

[46] In framing this problem, I owe a debt to the symposia organized by Christopher Tomlins. See the papers collected in the symposia "Law As ... (I–IV)" in the *UC Irvine Law Review* 1 (2011), 4 (2014), 5 (2015), and *Law Text Culture* 21 (2017).

law sought to embrace its potential: for those who imagined law as anchored in documents and dialogues, legality offered a rhetoric – a repertoire of ways of speaking – that enabled speakers to imagine themselves in some sort of better future. (Rhetoric, as Aristotle reminds us, is always about what we *should* do, and how we *should* understand; even when explaining the past, it always smuggles in normative claims about the future.)

Part I (Text) begins with the world of archives and documentation and their relation to civil litigation. What I will call, *faute de mieux*, a "subaltern" class of provincial subjects, believed that law was founded upon the text of official documents that could be recovered from local archives. For these litigants, law was not so much a rationalized structure as a running list of privileges and disabilities, each of which could be expanded or contracted to fit the needs of a given occasion. The consequence of such a belief, however, was that it produced a politics of archival knowledge, one which the Roman government had difficulty controlling. Archival knowledge was highly localized and heavily dependent upon modes of reasoning advanced by subjects themselves. Those who saw law as anchored in documents conceived law as a running list of privileges and disabilities; activating those privileges depended on provincial subjects offering to imperial officials an account of how best to use and read archival sources. Through these readings, they argued that the state could be bound by the quotation of language. They negotiated rulership in the same way that they sought to bind gods and neighbors through incantations and curse tablets, except that in the legal arena they had an advantage: the sources from which they quoted were local in nature.[47]

While the litigants of Part I were skeptical of the idea that law was a rationalizable structure, others disagreed, especially when confronted with the high-stakes world of criminal judgment. Thus, in Part II (Dialogue) I turn to the criminal courts, the most highly visible acts of Roman justice in the provinces, and institutions designed to impress upon provincial consciousness the power of the Roman state. However, such acts by the Roman state were not simply deemed virtuous or not; rather, by writing about criminal trials (and re-writing

[47] See now Nasrallah 2024.

the stories of such trials), provincial populations reimagined these rituals of sovereign justice as moments of dialogic encounter between subjects and governors. By framing law as a dialogue (rather than simply an act of sovereign will), subjects demanded that, as a condition of its legitimacy, law's violence be founded upon *logos* – upon reasoning, expressible through language, rather than upon acts of spectacular violence.

The face-to-face encounter might provide a testing ground for provincial ideas about legitimacy, but it might also be adapted to other purposes as well. Thus, stories began to circulate about other characters who confronted the powerful through the same rhetorical moves they had developed in the courtroom. Thus, in Chapter 5 I turn away from the courtroom to show how dialogue – the testing of the judgment of the powerful in face-to-face confrontations – became a way of thinking through claims about domination more broadly. Chapter 5 pays the most attention to trying to pick apart this very subaltern political theory.

In response to these claims, counter-ideologies emerged, which I discuss in Part III. Some members of both Jewish and Christian communities began to experiment with escapist ideologies of legality, imagining a world in which genuine legality – and a properly ordered polity – might be constructed independently from the administrative machinery of the empire (Chapter 6). The courtroom similarly terrified the elites of the empire (Chapter 7). It could easily reveal that they were, in fact, no better than those whom they dominated: both could bleed, and governors often took pleasure in showing that certain elites were, in fact, capable of suffering punishment and degradation. Accordingly, these urban elites sought to avoid law's judgments by crafting an ideology of elite male sociability that encouraged the avoidance of such spaces. They argued instead that conflicts ought to be resolved through extra-legal practices, and in particular through the use not of the legal register of speaking, but of a different register altogether. The elegant speech that they generated – in reaction to legal speaking – was, in turn, connected to a package of techniques of the body, which marked men as sharing in elite culture, or *paideia*.

Paideia was a category that enabled such elites to judge others simply by observing their bodies, and to determine whether they were noble or base, worthy of punishment or deserving of sociability. In short, *paideia* denoted not just "education," but a system of physical and mental training by which such men could settle disputes, negotiate with imperial powers, and discern the character of those they dominated. Hence, among a number of urban elites – and among some sub-groups of Jews and early Christians – we find emphasis on law as a practice that demanded *ekstasis*, in the sense of the Greek word: as requiring transcendence, an ability to stand apart from the quotidian.[48] For such men, this transcendence would constitute "real" law, something that necessarily differed from law as practiced in the quotidian administrative paper-pushing that otherwise characterized the Roman world. These ideas of law as ecstasy, however, were not *sui generis*. They emerged as a reaction to a world where the courts hummed with business.

These elites additionally began to outline a concept that would compete with the broader provincial understandings of the nature of legal rationality: *thauma*. We might provisionally define this as "wonder" or "amazement." As is fitting, such a category sits uncomfortably with legal traditions, which almost universally prize transparent, easily reconstructed chains of reasoning. *Thauma*, by contrast, is an affective category: someone experiencing *thauma* is placed outside of the space of everyday reasoning, and brought, as it were, to a higher plane. The wondrous, like its cousin, the sublime, transcends the normal experience of reasoning and marks itself as operating in a space apart, governed by unique rules. According to the ideology of these elites, achieving this affective state would suspend the normal administrative functions of a bureaucratic state and bring men, otherwise in conflict, into a state of deep, affective interconnection. As such, "amazement" came to operate as an extra-legal, if not anti-legal category – one that was, by virtue of its capacity for emotional supercharging, *superior* to law itself. It came to be a model for how an empire ought to work more generally.

One important takeaway from the distribution of these legal ideas across the landscape is that their use does not map easily onto many of the normal axes of analysis through which we divide the population

[48] In adapting this category, I owe a debt of gratitude to the work of Laura Nasrallah (2003).

of the Roman Empire as a whole. That is to say, it is not the case, for example, that Christians only thought of law as documents, whereas Jews only thought of law as dialogues; or that urban people thought of law as ecstasy, while rural people thought of law as documents, and so forth. The way one imagines law, I shall suggest, is best taken not as an index of some sense of class, religious, or ethnic belonging, but as a mode through which one imagines one's *relation* to empire, government, and community more broadly. Thus, I shall show that we can find Christians and pagans, wealthy and weak, all imagining law, for instance, as dialogue; we can likewise see a convergence between Greek hyper-elites and rhetoricians, thinking about law as ecstasy, with some trends among early Christians, who made similar imaginary moves (albeit to different ends). Thus, my terms "elite" and "subaltern" must be taken with a sharp qualification: I use them not to refer to *actual* social status (many of my "subalterns" were, in fact, quite wealthy, and of high status), but to the ways in which individuals and communities imagined themselves in relation to imperial power – whether they felt themselves fundamentally insiders or outsiders.

Parts I–III of this work are devoted to explaining the ways in which claims about law served a political function. The diachronic arc of my story picks up primarily in Part IV. Roman jurists and later on Roman emperors, starting in the late second and early third centuries AD, came to be increasingly interested in thinking of law primarily *as books*. This was not an effect of the quality of jurisprudence, or even of the growth of bureaucracy or the spread of citizenship. It was, rather, a *reaction* to the challenge of governing a diverse and fractious populace with multiple and diverging commitments to, and understandings of, law and its foundations – the protagonists, that is, of Parts I–III. Jurists and emperors reacted to the claims of such people by trying to monopolize hermeneutic authority over law. In collaboration with jurists, emperors reimagined law not as a set of practical solutions to problems that emerged from concrete interactions with subjects, but instead as something ideally abstract, codified, and certain, a finely textured, self-replicating web capable of an increasing scope of constraint. They also imagined it as something fundamentally distinct from, or even superior to, politics.

It was through this process of pushing back against local understandings that the Roman state transformed itself from a diverse and heterarchic polity into something more rationalized and hierarchical – into something that we would recognize today as a bureaucracy, accompanied by a rule of law. This process, while hardly linear, was substantially completed by the end of the fourth century. In other words, to the extent that the Roman state moved in the direction of making law a codified and rationalized "system," it did so not because it had any intrinsic preference for such a thing, but because it sought to place limits on the number of voices that could contribute to the body of law as a whole.

As a result, beginning with the legal revolutions of the Severan period (AD 193–235), and extending until the late fourth century, we see not the great opening up of the Roman system (by granting citizenship to all of its inhabitants, or by rationalizing provincial administration), but rather its great closing. It was a moment – or rather a succession of moments – in which the state tried to monopolize authority to create and enforce law, to achieve hegemony over legal interpretation, and to put an end to political argument.[49]

The effect of this government reaction, I shall argue, is an important historical horizon not only for the Roman state, but for the way that we conceive law more generally. In this act of seeking to close off alternative modes of imagining law, the Roman state developed the kernel of a distinction that haunts us today, namely, the distinction between law "in the books" and law "in action" – the latter always a derivative and defective enactment of something ideally possessed by experts.[50] Two outcomes resulted. First, this process ensured that the voices that had previously *constituted* law could only now be seen as *reflecting* it. The second result was a fetishization of legal knowledge and with it, a perverse form of lawyer-worship that casts a long shadow over legal history even today. Namely, the belief that jurists, in the words of Ulpian of Tyre, are uniquely placed to "attend to justice, profess knowledge of the good and the fair, divide the fair from unfair, and separate the permitted from the illicit, inclining to make men good not only by making them fear punishments, but

[49] My chronology substantially coincides with that proposed recently by Letteney 2023, although our accounts of causation are substantially different.

[50] The distinction was originally drawn by Roscoe Pound in the early twentieth century.

also by urging them towards rewards – practicing, I should say, true philosophy, rather than the imitation of philosophy." For Ulpian, this special talent made the jurists not just learned men, but rather something like priests. It also earned them a place close to imperial power.[51] The historical roots of this vast and arrogant claim shall be taken up in what follows, with attention to the historical processes – and their attendant acts of violence – that made it not just sayable but also convincing.

[51] *Dig.* 1.1.1.1 = Ulp. 1 *Inst.*, Frg. 1908 Lenel: *cuius merito quis nos sacerdotes appellet: iustitiam namque colimus et boni et aequi notitiam profitemur, aequum ab iniquo separantes, licitum ab illicito discernentes, bonos non solum metu poenarum, verum etiam praemiorum quoque exhortatione efficere cupientes, veram nisi fallor philosophiam, non simulatam affectantes.*

THE RHETORIC OF INCLUSION

PART I

LAW AS DOCUMENTS

2

Becoming the Roman Provinces

The great bulk of this book will be about acts of imagination and rhetoric. It might therefore seem dissonant to start in a different vein – under the sign of Marx, as it were – by foregrounding some aspects of the material, administrative, and political transformation of the world of the eastern Mediterranean.[1] It is nonetheless essential. The rhetoric of legality – and the broader provincial legal imaginary – emerged from particular moments of historical transformation, from particular practices of exploitation, and from particular challenges of governance. The goal of this chapter is to begin to map these material conditions. I will come, at the end of it, to explain how legalism arose at the historical junction that it did. The provincial experience of legality was not rooted in some essential, trans-historical eastern Mediterranean tendency towards litigiousness, but in the collective experience of Roman rule.

Yet, to say this only complicates matters. Roman rule was an evolving historical phenomenon, and this evolution took place over a lengthy period of time. Rome had become entangled in the politics of the eastern Mediterranean starting in the third century BC. It began a halting process of extending formal control over parts of peninsular Greece and Macedonia in the middle of the second century BC. Conquests of Pompey and Caesar in the first century BC acquired more territory; Egypt was added in 30 BC; Judaea flitted

[1] Chakrabarty 2000.

haltingly between direct and indirect control until the death of Julius (Herod) Agrippa in AD 44; and Lycia was only added in the reign of Claudius. The process of territorial acquisition (much less governance itself) might only be said to be complete with the annexation of Arabia by Trajan in 106 AD or even of Mesopotamia. Within such broad chronological bookends there were dramatic developments in the culture and government of the metropole, to say nothing of well-documented shifts in political, institutional, economic, and military capacities. What is more, in the provinces themselves the particular institutional, political, and cultural forms that Roman rule produced continued well into the fourth, if not until the fifth century AD, and they themselves evolved.[2] What, then, justifies speaking of "provincial culture," much less its material foundations and its relation to legality, over such a long period?

It would be hard to overstate the diversity of territories that made up "the eastern provinces." The expanse of territory starting in peninsular Greece, ranging across the Anatolian landmass and the Taurus mountains to Syria, then south through Judaea and Arabia and back west to Egypt and eventually Cyrenaica, contained a bewildering number of different cultures, languages, trade and agrarian regimes, and population densities (see Figure 1.1). The advent of Roman control affected the conquered in highly variable ways. We might just take two examples. *Grosso modo*, we might say that those peoples deemed "Greek" who lived in *poleis* tended to be treated as acceptable if periodically quirky interlocutors, while those deemed "other" tended to be looked at askance; accordingly, "Greek culture" came to thrive in the east as normative, and the Greek language became a privileged medium of self-representation.[3] But such a picture is still highly imperfect. For one thing (quite apart from the breezy acceptance of the category "Greek culture"), it neglects the

[2] There is lengthy debate concerning the transformation of the late antique city: for a survey, see Humphries 2019.

[3] E.g., Bowersock 1969; Bowie 1970, 1982; Swain 1996; Goldhill 2001a; Whitmarsh 2001; Borg 2004. Yet recent work by some of these same scholars has begun to raise important questions about these claims: e.g., Whitmarsh 2013, challenging the easy acceptance of canons; or the various works of Simon Goldhill (e.g., Goldhill 2002; Conybeare and Goldhill 2021), detailing the complex processes through which "our" canons of Greek literature have been formed.

fierce rivalries between Greek poleis.[4] These rivalries often resulted in the destruction of some communities in favor of others and the incorporation of the territory of the disfavored community into the territory of the favored one. It similarly involved the reclassification of certain disfavored groups as juridically non-Greek, even when they shared a common language and history with juridically "Greek" cities.[5] This view similarly neglects the divergent ways in which non-prestige linguistic and ethnic groups thrived, declined, or vanished: thus while a number of local languages largely died out (especially in the western Mediterranean), others (like Aramaic/ Syriac or Egyptian/Coptic) persisted, and emerged or re-emerged as literary languages in late antiquity.[6]

Similar things could be said of agricultural and economic diversity. *Grosso modo*, the growing interconnectedness of the Mediterranean seems to have been generative of prosperity, or at least generative of the sorts of public conveniences that we might, rightly or wrongly, take as indices of prosperity: densely built cityscapes with public conveniences and monumental architecture, extensive trade, banking and manufacture.[7] But not all people prospered, or prospered equally. At a most basic level, the Roman Empire was extractive, relying on moving wealth from one region to another.[8] Even within regions, growth often promoted exploitation – especially of free but disenfranchised peoples, but sometimes even simply of those who were politically inconvenient.[9] Sometimes this was spasmodic and catastrophic (as, for instance, when Aemilius Paullus opened Epirus to looting to reward his soldiers in 167 BC, resulting in the enslavement of some 150,000 people), at other times it resulted in the creation of

[4] E.g., Robert 2007 [1977]; Alcock 1993; Heller 2006; Ando 2010b: 31–40.

[5] This was especially the case in Egypt: see Mélèze Modrzejewski 1970, 1988; and on the persistence of ethno-juridical assumptions even when this system was notionally overturned, Bryen 2016a.

[6] On language death, see Adams 2003: esp. 289–96. For a survey of extant literatures, as well as valuable methodological reflections, see Selden and Vasunia forthcoming. For an important case study on the development of Coptic, see Fournet 2020.

[7] On the question of growth, see Saller 2002; in general, Scheidel et al. 2007; Wilson and Bowman 2017. On urbanization and art as indicative of general prosperity, see Mayer 2012. On other ways to measure prosperity, note Harper 2016: 107: "Thanks to their imperial ecology, the Romans were rich but sick." Important cautions: Morley 2011; Bowes and Grey 2021.

[8] E.g., Hopkins 2018 [1980]. [9] Rizakis 1998.

exploitative structures that persisted over the *longue durée*.[10] The temporal and geographical unevenness of exploitation similarly had ramifications for the social structures that pre-existed Roman control. In some areas, ancient, pre-Roman aristocracies were broken up (by design or by neglect) and replaced with new ones; in others, entrenched power groups thrived; and in yet others, groups of powerful Roman citizens, either deliberately settled in the territory or simply doing business there, came to dominate the landscape (more on this last group presently).[11]

***

It would thus be easy to think of the eastern Mediterranean as a world characterized by fundamental and insuperable diversity if not radical fragmentation, for the reasons above and for many more besides.[12] Yet in spite of these indices of diversity, it still makes sense to think of the extension and consolidation of Roman control as part of a single, continuous historical process, replicated at various times over the landscape as a whole. At the heart of this process were acts of violence.

At times, this violence was highly localized. Cities might be besieged and plundered, as Athens was by Sulla (87–86 BC) or as Jerusalem was by Vespasian and Titus (70 AD). Regions, too, might be opened to looting (as in Epirus). Perceived acts of dissent or rebellion were treated harshly: not only were the Jewish populations of Judaea savagely punished for their rebelliousness, but during later outbreaks of rebellion under Trajan a number of diaspora Jewish communities

[10] Epirus: Plut. *Vit. Aem.* 29. Structural problems in agricultural exploitation in Egypt: see the nuanced discussion of Haug 2017, and Blouin 2014 on the Mendesian nome in the Nile delta. On the place of devastation in the imaginary of Roman intellectuals, see Lavan 2020.

[11] On the persistence of local aristocracies, one might note the attention paid by Roman administrators to questions of marriage and inheritance, for instance in Aemilius Paullus' regulations for Macedonia (Livy 45.29.10) or in the *Gnomon* of the Idios Logos (*Sel.Pap.* II 206). On the importance of concepts of citizenship in creating or maintaining aristocracies, with special reference to Roman citizenship, see Lavan 2021. Valuable regional case studies: Goodman 1988 on Judaea, Monson 2012 on Egypt. Powerful groups of Roman citizens: Cyrene edicts (*FIRA* I 68), and below, p. 57–58; see also Thonemann 2011: 99–109, on the community of Romans at Apamea/Celaenae, seemingly becoming rich on the basis of the slave trade.

[12] The most important study is Horden and Purcell 2000; their final chapters, however, raise questions about the nature of commonalities at the level of culture.

were singled out for harsh treatment.[13] That rebels were punished should not surprise, although such acts of punishment were, like rebellions themselves, relatively infrequent. But the salience of such spectacular acts of violence was that they had to be repeated only infrequently to be an effective reminder to the inhabitants of empire that they were, in fact, subjects. Periodically cities or groups might forget or push too hard at a boundary; they might then be subjected to violence both as punishment and *pour encourager les autres*. Thus as late as the third century, Caracalla might vent his rage on the citizens of Alexandria, butchering them en masse in the center of the city on account of their jesting at his expense.[14] By contrast, the inhabitants of Antioch were surely relieved when, in the late fourth century, the emperor Julian forbore from spectacular violence under similar circumstances, choosing instead to mock the Antiochenes (and himself) in a pamphlet, and to strip them of certain privileges. Julian's forbearance was, however, a deviation from the normal pattern: the inhabitants of Thessalonica would be massacred with imperial permission only a generation later under Theodosius I.[15]

Such a list could of course be extended, but the gist should be clear enough: it was a structural feature of Roman rule that Rome reserved for itself the right to deploy violence against those it deemed problematic or rebellious. Rome was, moreover, perhaps unique among its contemporary Hellenistic rivals in its ability to muster the institutional capacity to deploy such violence at an exceptionally high level of intensity.[16] To be sure, spectacular, overwhelming violence

[13] For an overview of the destruction of the Jewish communities of Egypt and Cyrenaica, see Mélèze Modrzejewski 1995: 198–225. The Jewish revolts are only the most conspicuous; other regions, for purely local reasons, dealt periodically with revolts and instability: note, e.g., the case of the "bandit" Lydius who occupied Pisidian Cremna, a Roman colony, in the late third century (Zos. 1.69–70, with discussion and reconstruction in Mitchell 1995: 177–217; cf. Zimmerman 1996); or the Boukoloi "revolt" in Egypt, convincingly connected to Roman fiscal policies and their interaction with a local environment by Blouin 2014: 265–96.

[14] Cass. Dio 78.22–23; Hdn. 4.9. For an overview of the relevant sources, see Rodriguez 2012.

[15] On Julian in Antioch, see Elm 2012: 269–335; on Theodosius, McLynn 1994: 315–30.

[16] Corinth and Jerusalem might serve as examples. Reassessing the "abandonment" of Corinth, with careful distinctions between political and material discontinuities, but noting its much-reduced state: James 2014; on Jerusalem: Rives 2005.

might only be enacted periodically, and those who used it might be (later) denounced as vicious tyrants, unworthy of their office. But violence was an important tool nonetheless, and no less effective for being rare. (As Christian rhetoricians have long since proven, the frequency of acts of violence is no bar to the power of violent acts, real or imagined, to constitute communities.[17]) What is more, the ideology supporting such violence proved durable in directing governance more generally, and assumptions about the importance of anchoring sovereignty in acts of violence permeated the Roman approach to criminal law in the provinces more generally, albeit at a smaller scale. Similarly, throughout the provinces, subject cities themselves adapted this ideology of pacification, imbuing in their elite young men a militaristic ethos notionally directed against the "bandits" that dwelled in their hinterlands.[18]

Having highlighted the common experience of violence, we ought nonetheless to draw distinctions, both typological and chronological. Typologically, we might suggest that the acts described above might be imagined as examples of *ordered* violence: the sort of violence that subjects would recognize, or were supposed to recognize, as involving a claim of sovereignty.[19] This does not mean, of course, that in practice subjects agreed that the claim was rightly made, only that they were construed as obliged to recognize that such a claim *was* being made. The claim was relatively straightforward: that there was indeed a locus of sovereignty superior to any other, and that, because of local behavior, those who were sovereign were angered and decided to punish. However messy in practice, these periodic violent interventions operated to integrate diverse territories: should one imagine stepping out of line, one would not need to look geographically too far to be reminded of the nature of Roman sovereignty.[20] This tendency towards acts of spectacular violence even came to be imagined as an essential part of the character of Roman people. As Polybius noted, "generally speaking, the Romans rely on force (*biai*) for everything. They feel obliged to finish anything they start and regard nothing as impossible once they have made up their minds."[21]

[17] Sizgorich 2009. [18] Brélaz 2005, 2020.
[19] Rives 2005 is illuminating in this regard. [20] E.g., Plut. *Praec.* 813d–f.
[21] 1.37, trans. Waterfield 2010.

Polybius immediately conceded that they do often fail, but the point was clear enough – the Roman tendency towards violence was imagined, from an early period, to be an innate national characteristic; those who were on the receiving end of it, like Polybius, might expend great amounts of energy developing a theodicy capable of explaining it.

In addition to a common experience of acts of ordered violence, Roman rule similarly brought acts of disordered or merely opportunistic violence. It would occupy too much space to catalogue the many acts of cruelty and greed done by Roman generals, soldiers, and hangers-on, both under color of law and not. A quick perusal of Cicero's speeches against the incontinently greedy governor of Sicily, Gaius Verres, will suggest that the opportunities for cruelty abounded, as did the opportunities for self-enrichment at the expense of others. Ancient sources amply detail the transfer of movable wealth from provincial communities to the metropole, be it in the form of *objets d'art*, slaves, or cash.[22] But scholars have only recently come to better understand the impact of conquest on patterns of ownership in the provinces more generally. Aside from movables and cash, substantial commercial concerns were siphoned into the hands of Roman citizens.[23] In addition, great amounts of land also changed hands. The process was similar to the case of movable wealth: the Roman state took large amounts of land in the process of provincial organization, but individual Roman aristocrats and ambitious Italians (to say nothing of the family and associates of the emperors) also ended up with extensive estates and choice tracts.[24] A non-trivial segment of this wealth came simply from confiscating it from local elites, both officially (as punishment) and unofficially, through processes that, while often historically unrecoverable, were

[22] In general, Harris 1985. The main evidence is collected in Frank 1933.

[23] Eberle and Le Queré 2017.

[24] E.g., Mitchell 1993: I:149–54, 163–64, on Italian acquisitions in Galatia and Pisidia, respectively. On imperial estates in Phrygia and on Italian acquisitions in the Maeander valley, see, respectively, Thonemann 2011: 113–115, 251–253. For a fascinating case study of two small cities, Blaundos and Nacolea, see Dalla Rossa 2020, and for Phrygia more generally Thonemann 2013a: 35 (suggesting a disjuncture between an ideological "culture of urbanization" and the prevalence of actual urbanism). The question of acquisitions by the imperial family and their friends in Egypt remains vexed; for a variety of perspectives, see Parássoglou 1978; Kehoe 1992; Tacoma 2015; Broux 2019; and for the emperor more generally, Dalla Rossa 2014.

surely also degrading and unpleasant.[25] These new, often absentee owners devolved control over their lands and tenants to their slaves, freedmen, and agents in the countryside, instructing them to extract resources – a process that likely ended up de facto devolving upon their agents a set of quasi-feudal powers.[26] Importantly, these sorts of takings would under other circumstances have raised complex problems of legal title, transfer of ownership, and conflict of laws that would have kept jurists quite busy. Except, of course, these takings were done across such a steep gradient of inequality, and with such a significant threat of violence looming in the background, that they mostly failed to generate court cases, much less juristic rulings, in the first place.[27] In fact, they barely register in the sphere of learned law at all.[28]

This process of violent extraction ebbed and flowed in intensity. The period from the late second century BC through the civil wars of the mid to late first century BC might represent the apex: a mix of ordered, official pillage, supported by a ruthlessly extractive taxation system, with the messy ebb and flow of ad hoc demands generated by the immediate needs of commanders in the field and hostile factions.[29] Even Plutarch, no enemy of Roman order, remembered hearing from his grandfather a story that might be taken as representative of the misery of the period: towards the end of the civil wars, his

[25] On republican period confiscation, see Rizakis 2015; on acquisition under dubious color, Eberle 2016. Prominent citizens in the provinces always risked losing their status and along with it their massive holdings. Note the case of Claudius Hipparchus, the grandfather of Herodes Atticus: Oliver 1989: no. 92; or *P.Oxy.* LXII 4337 (c. AD 178), which may relate to confiscation as a criminal penalty.

[26] Procurators in charge of imperial property were formally granted jurisdiction from the age of Claudius (Brunt 1990 [1966]: 163–87), and we are given hints that they abused it (*CJ* 3.26.3); it takes no great feat of imagination to think that the agents of other senatorial landholders acted in a similar fashion. Compare the abuses of the *conductores* on the Saltus Burunitanus (Hauken 1998: no. 1), or the quasi-feudal punishment of the villagers in the Kemaliye inscription (Hauken 1998: no. 4).

[27] See in particular Eberle 2016, on one of the rare exceptional cases. Cf. the case of the jurist Cascellius, who refused to create a formula for praetors and governors to ratify the various transfers of ownership made under the Triumviri: Val. Max. 6.2.12. The result was to place all of their "benefactions" *extra omnem ordinem legum*, thus ensuring that they could never ripen into civil law ownership.

[28] For what evidence there is (largely from the *gromatici*), see Grelle 1963.

[29] For a sense of how cataclysmic these ad hoc demands might be, see Magie 1950: 418–26 for a narrative of the exactions of the "liberators" in Asia Minor.

grandfather and his fellow citizens were forced to carry grain to fill Antony's ships; anyone too slow to keep up would be whipped like a common slave.[30]

Of course, some cities or local power brokers profited from this era of political disorder: cities such as Aphrodisias kept their freedom or enlarged their territory; loyal henchman like the naval captain Seleucus of Rhosos were offered Roman citizenship and other special privileges that set them apart from their fellow citizens. But in densely populated parts of the world, one city's territorial expansion necessarily came at the expense of others – even, at times, at the cost of the erasure of preexisting political communities. It is certain that Aphrodisias' neighbors envied its success, and that Seleucus' fellow citizens detested him.[31] And sometimes even the winners were left in a precarious state, as Menippus of Colophon found as he shuttled back and forth to Rome to protect his city's autonomy from its violations by Roman governors.[32] Still, at least Menippus was successful. Others fared worse. A substantial proportion of our epigraphic documentation concerning the rights of cities can be explained as a reflection of this process: cities advertised their status and privileges in permanent media precisely because they were, in practice, insecure.[33]

The frenzied violence of the first century BC came to an end with the end of the civil wars and the rule of Augustus. From this point on, the absence of intra-Mediterranean warfare would allow the eastern world to breathe, as the extraction of resources came to take a more predictable form.[34] Government too became more predictable

30 *Vit. Ant.* 68.4. On Plutarch in his Roman context more generally, see Jones 1971.

31 Reynolds 1982: no. 13 = *IAph2007* 8.32; Raggi 2004, 2006.

32 *SEG* 39 1244; Cf. the attempt of the otherwise undistinguished polis of Naryx to preserve its rights, presumably against another city that sought to encroach upon them: *SEG* 51 641.

33 Compare the arguments about the "epigraphic habit" raised by Woolf 1996.

34 Scheidel 2015, who emphasizes that the aims of the imperial state were satisficing, rather than maximizing, but allowing for the fact that corruption existed at various points throughout the system. Note, however, the recent study of Bowman 2017, suggesting that even while satisficing, the normal rates of taxation were considerably higher than normally supposed. The evidence for corruption, or at least for claims about corruption, is vast and overwhelming. See the following paragraph. Note, e.g., *P.Princ.* II 20 (133–37), two edicts of an unknown governor forbidding *telōnai* from illegally exacting taxes, and detaining people who questioned their tax estimate with the result that the people would have to bribe the *telonai* to be released early.

and, theoretically at least, more accountable.[35] But "predictable" and "accountable" should not be mistaken for "favorable" or "enjoyable." For all that the end of the civil wars meant the end to cataclysmic disorder, when the Roman state appeared in its extractive capacity it was widely loathed.

The right to extract rents or taxes was indissociable from the right to use violence in so doing. "Nobody is unaware of the extent of the audacity and insolence of cliques of tax farmers," thundered Ulpian in his commentary on the praetorian edict.[36] Not to be outdone, the lexicographer Pollux offered an extensive list of names one might call such people: "burden, pack animal, garrotter, sneak-thief, shark, hurricane, oppressor of the downtrodden, inhuman, nail in my coffin, insatiable, immoderate, shameless greedyguts, violator, strangler, crusher, highwayman, strip-Jack-naked, snatcher, thief, overcharger, reckless, shameless, unblushing, pain in the neck, savage, wild, inhospitable, brute, dead weight, obstacle, heart of stone, flotsam, pariah."[37] It mattered little, in practice, whether collectors were local officials, their imperial overseers, or tax contractors (*publicani*), or whether free or enslaved. All possessed the right to use violence in the name of the state. In the eyes of those who were obliged to pay, it was beyond doubt that these men of privilege were sadists who relished the opportunity to take from their lower-ranked neighbors.[38]

Backstopping this system of extraction was a system of borrowing and credit that was no less potentially destabilizing. In an agrarian world where taxation was extracted in the form of staple crops and cash, borrowing was a necessary and unavoidable part of life: crops were only ready at a certain moment during the year and cash followed shortly thereafter, while expenses came year-round. Harvests might fail, leading to more borrowing.[39] Papyri from the province of

35 Brunt 1961. 36 Ulp. 38 *Ed.* Frg. 1072 Lenel = *Dig.* 39.4.12.pr.

37 *Onom.* 9.30, translation with valuable discussion from van Nijf 2008.

38 Cf., e.g., *BGU* II 515 = *W.Chr.* 268 = *Sel.Pap.* II 286 (AD 193), tax collectors assault the mother of a man in arrears (but who claims he has paid 9/10 of the grain taxes he owes) and confiscate her cloak. Philo, *Spec. Leg.* 3.30 for similar acts of distraint of family members by tax collectors. In general, Corbier 1990.

39 Garnsey 1988. Horden and Purcell 2000 have emphasized that Mediterranean agriculture is optimally designed to be flexible and adaptive; they allow, rightly, that pressures from the state to raise cash crops to meet tax and rental burdens make it much less so.

Egypt amply demonstrate a world of debt and debtors; and while a number of these credit relationships moved along the lines of families, we would be remiss in thinking (a) that such relationships were always marked by fairness and forgiveness, or that (b) they might not move quickly from being marked by generosity to being downright exploitative.[40] These relationships of credit, moreover, might quickly turn into acts of violence, since the procedures for distraint common in the provincial world were often indistinguishable from acts of strong-arm robbery.[41] It would only be later on, and then only if the parties chose to go to court, that the justifiable claim over property and the act of illegitimate force might be sorted out. Taken as a whole, it seems reasonable to suggest that the pressures of this system were a substantial factor in producing litigation.

***

While the reign of Augustus might have made certain aspects of life more predictable, it also brought a dramatic shift in the demographic structures of the east, with a massive program of military demobilization. Veterans of the civil wars were settled in Roman colonies throughout the Mediterranean basin starting in the middle of the first century BC, but the process expanded dramatically under Augustus.[42] The scope of colonization was such that it transformed the landscape. New communities of Roman citizens, drawn from a combination of Roman civilians, veterans, and select locals, sat alongside ancient and venerable places – a reminder of the nature of

40 As a general treatment of the potentially exploitative nature of these arrangements, see Graeber 2011. For a late antique example of elite lending on the basis of tax debt, see *C.Th.* 11.28.10 with the discussion of Corbier 1990: 233, correctly insisting that *evidence* for such a practice would necessarily be rare in earlier centuries. Cf. the offer of "good" patronage from landlords, made by Libanius (*Or.* 47.19): offers of remission of debts, offers of grants, and offers to settle cases between dependent villagers.

41 E.g., the tangled web of debt and distraint evident in *P.Fam.Tebt.* 37, 38, 40 (AD 167–73/4). Of course, authorities tried to limit this: note, e.g., the *decretum* of Marcus, *Dig.* 4.2.13 (= Call. 5 *Cog.*, Frg. 37 Lenel) with duplicate in *Dig.* 48.7.7, assimilating repossession without a court order to *vis*; or the first preserved chapter of the *Lex Coloniae Genetivae* (*RS* 25). In the future I hope to return to this topic in an essay tentatively entitled "Confiscation of Property in the Roman Empire."

42 For an overview, see MacMullen 2000. On colonies in the east, see Brélaz 2017, and on Philippi specifically, Brélaz 2018.

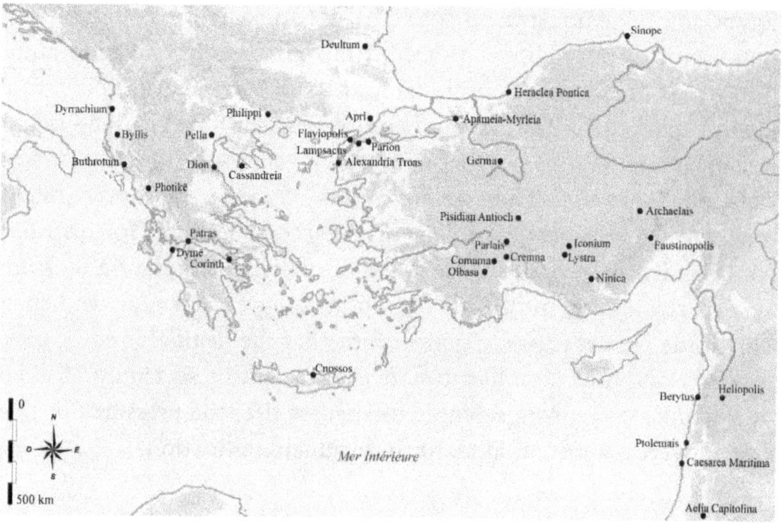

FIGURE 2.1 Map of Roman colonies in the Eastern Mediterranean. C. Brélaz, *Philippes, colonie romaine d'Orient. Recherches d'histoire institutionnelle et sociale*, Athens: École française d'Athènes (Bulletin de Correspondance Hellénique, Supplément, 59), 2018, p. 353 (some place names translated by author).

the new regime (see Figure 2.1).[43] The land upon which they sat was "purchased" (with compulsion) or confiscated from local inhabitants and redistributed, leaving most of them in the status of mere "residents" (*paroikoi*) without formal rights in the new city.[44] The land was then repopulated with Roman citizens, drawn predominantly from the ranks of veterans. And because Roman citizens were prone to marry only Roman citizens, colonies came to attract yet more Roman citizens as inhabitants, not least those retiring from a life of military service, flush with their discharge bonuses.[45]

Aside from formal colonies, the landscape came to be dotted with other types of settlements of Roman citizens, placed in strategic locations.[46] In Syria and Judaea there were, compared to Greece and Asia Minor, comparatively few colonial foundations – although

[43] On the ideology of veteran colonies, as expressed through coinage, see Katsari and Mitchell 2008. For a valuable case study of processes of integration, see Blanco-Pérez 2015 on Apamea/Myrleia. Cf. also Bowden 2011.

[44] Rizakis 1998, 2015; Gagliardi 2015.

[45] Eck et al. 2020. [46] Broughton 1935; Levick 1967; Mitchell 1979; Brélaz 2016.

the foundation of Aelia Capitolina on the site of Jerusalem was an important gesture of Roman domination, and the foundation of Berytus (Beirut) brought a vast territory under the control of a single urban center.[47] But the effects were nonetheless largely the same, if not felt even more acutely: large numbers of cities were simply garrisoned.[48] Egypt remains something of a puzzle: it hosted no colonies, and the role of the Roman army and its veterans in Egyptian society remains debated.[49] Still, these demographic changes – and their associated programs of road building and infrastructure creation – dramatically reoriented the channels through which power flowed.[50] It needs hardly to be added that the reorientation was designed at least in part around the need to organize and tax this world. It is a feature of Roman rule that we ought to keep constantly present in our minds.

In brief, the scale of the changes that Roman rule brought to the eastern Mediterranean was staggering. These changes took their origin in acts of violence and were stabilized and regularized through acts of control, not least the system of taxation and a new demographic and infrastructural regime.[51] Control of territory and its taxation – and attendant acts of intimidation or even terror, by both imperial and local collectors – served as the foundations for what would eventually emerge as a new, distinctly provincial culture. This change would take time, as one would expect. But to some – among them the aristocrats who benefited most from this regime – the change was welcome. As they reminded their audiences at every turn, pre-Roman systems of government were in no sense benevolent. Roman rule, they insisted, may have been founded in violence, but it was a sort of rational violence that was eminently predictable.[52] Such men knew that they were making the best of a complicated situation. Others would have waited patiently to see if the system would remain stable. After

47 Bowersock 2003; Millar 2006 [1990].

48 On soldiers in the near eastern context, see Isaac 1990; Pollard 2000; and on the social impact of soldiers more generally, Fuhrmann 2011.

49 Alston 1995, with further discussion in Bagnall 1997.

50 Ando 2017; Ma 2024: 301–33.

51 For a much more optimistic vision of the changes occurring in the period, at least in the city of Ephesus, see Kirbihler 2016.

52 E.g., Aristid. *Or.* 26.15–27. On the defects of the pre-Roman interstate system, see Eckstein 2006.

the disruptions of the first century BC, stability was hardly a foregone conclusion. And in point of fact, the coming of Roman domination did put internal pressures on communities.

***

It is well known, if the details are nonetheless still poorly understood, that one long-term effect of the Roman conquest of the East was the transformation of local political institutions. In some exemplary cases, such as Alexandria, the most important organ of local government – the council or *boulē*, composed of local elites – was simply denied to the city until the early third century AD. In other cases, Roman officials were quick to alter constitutions if they perceived local or regional disorder, or to snatch away any privileges that a city might otherwise have. To adopt a contemporary parlance, we might say that this produced something of a "chilling effect" on the conceivable possibilities for how any particular collective might be internally organized.

These broad changes also placed subordinated communities under tremendous pressure, which destabilized them and, in a number of cases, led to civil war. The internecine strife that the Roman presence produced in Judaea, for instance, is well known. But it is remarkable primarily because it serves as an unusually well-documented instance of a broader pattern. Not only did some cities or peoples crumple under internal pressures, but the particular contours of their collapse are interesting for what they might teach us about the emerging legal cultures that Roman domination generated. Specifically, courts and mechanisms for dispute resolution came to be the sites of struggle, if not outbreaks of civil war.

Thus, the Jewish zealots, in rebellion against Rome, organized sham trials of their political enemies alongside their larger campaign of terror.[53] But while perhaps exceptional in their violence, there were analogous events throughout the provincial landscape. The "Lovers of Rome and Caesar" (*philorhomaioi kai philokaisares*) in Lycia, for instance, might dedicate to Claudius a statue while heaping upon him their blessings for "delivering us from civil war and lawlessness and banditry," and restoring to them "concord and equal justice

[53] Jos. *BJ* IV 334–44.

(*isēn dikaiodosian*) and their ancestral laws of their constitution." Their dedication, however, could only hint at the more disturbing history that had preceded: their constitution had to be restored, they insisted, because they had suffered at the hands of the "indiscriminate mob" (*akriton plēthos*). The "mob," we learn elsewhere, seems to have been a popular movement that gained control over the judicial apparatus, such that a number of local worthies fled and a number of Roman citizens were put to death – presumably through formally legal processes, but also likely out of anger and spite. This was not unheard of, but it was also a red line for Rome: though in some aspects formally independent, local communities were not welcome to sentence Roman citizens to death.[54] Accordingly, Claudius revoked Lycia's former autonomy, incorporated the previously free territory as a province and placed the dedicators into power. A group of "councilors recruited from the best of the citizens" would now hold the line against the popular mob.[55] Claudius also sent a trusted man, Quintus Veranius, to supervise a massive campaign of road building to stave off any future turmoil.

The story of the "Lovers of Rome and Caesar" is a story of civil war, told from the point of view of the victors. In this case the precipitating factor was precisely the material and political interference that came from sitting at the edge of an expanding empire. Though Lycia was formally independent, Roman citizens were still there, and were probably hated for good reason.[56] They had a tendency to snap up the best properties, and therefore to put communities under pressure,

[54] Cf. Cass. Dio 54.7 (Augustus enslaving Cyzicus for whipping and executing Roman citizens); 60.24 (Rhodians impaled some Roman citizens).

[55] *SEG* 51 1832; Cass. Dio 60.17. On the inscription and its context, see the helpful discussion of Aitor Blanco-Pérez: www.judaism-and-rome.org/honours-claudius-stadiasmus-patarensis, (4/28/21, accessed 11/10/21), and the reconstruction of Thornton 2001.

[56] On civil disorder in the Hellenistic world more generally, see Gray 2015. A book (in progress) by Emily Mackil will add important detail to our understandings of the relations between civil war, property, and political stability in the earlier periods; see, for now, Mackil 2023. On Romans abroad, see Purcell 1990; Eberle 2014; Ramgopal 2016. Note also the various attempts to exterminate them during political vacuums: most obvious of these attempts being that of Mithridates in the first century BC, but also the massacre of Roman colonists in Heraclea by Adiatorix during the Triumviral period, who claimed to be acting on behalf of Marcus Antonius (Strabo 12.3.6).

even when – or perhaps especially when – they were not formally operating as agents of the state. Accordingly, as resentment built, the population reacted against them and sent into exile the local aristocrats most likely to have colluded with these unwelcome interlopers. From the perspective of the local aristocrats, this might be described as "civil war and lawlessness and banditry," but it likely looked very different from the perspective of the popular party. Control of the courts was an essential part of this process. According to the victorious aristocrats, not only must the courts ensure "equal justice," they must prudently be steered away from a path of legal maximizing – that is, they must avoid interfering in any case that might affect the optimal distribution of power in society, at least as seen from the perspective of a local aristocracy and an empire desirous of stability. As I shall detail in what follows, one of the most important effects of the advent of Roman control was a series of disputes about the place of adjudication in society and its relationship to individuals and communities. It is worth emphasizing, for now, that these discussions over courts and adjudication emerged from a material basis – from the actual and at times bloody struggles over power that came *pari passu* with the extension of Roman control.

Perhaps the most telling example of how Roman advances affected local distributions of power comes from a story set in the first century BC, but which could just as easily reflect the circumstances of the first century AD, when it was told, or even later. The story is recounted by the scholar Plutarch, and relates to the history of his hometown, Chaironeia. In the course of wintering near Chaironeia, Plutarch reports, a Roman army commander developed a lust for a beautiful but orphaned aristocrat, a youth named Damon. Unable to successfully woo the young man by gifts or entreaties, the unnamed commander decided upon rape – but before he got the chance, Damon and a group of friends covered themselves with soot, and, fortified with quantities of wine, snuck up on the commander as he was performing a sacrifice in the center of the city. There they murdered him along with a number of his guards and associates. Terrified of what were to be certain reprisals, the council (*boulē*) of Chaironeia immediately convened and, it seems, without the benefit of any judicial procedure at all – much less one where Damon might mount a defense – condemned Damon and his associates to death. Damon's reprisal was immediate: that night, as the city councilors were dining, Damon and his associates broke into their dining hall, murdered them, too, and escaped for the nearby hinterland where, like a bandit, he harassed his hometown.

At this point it happened that the Roman commander, Lucius Lucullus, was passing through the region with his own army. Hearing of the emerging civil war in Chaironeia he immediately intervened to broker a compromise. Realizing that the fault lay neither with Damon nor with the city magistrates, but with Roman misconduct, he brought the parties to the negotiating table. The city was to conciliate Damon for its mistreatment of him – namely, the death sentence passed in absentia – and, in contrition, to make him the head of the city's gymnasium (not in charge of government, per se, but a high honor, and a position of authority with respect to the city's youths). Despite these formal ceremonies of reconciliation, resentment still burned among at least some members of the city: a short time later, Damon was murdered as he was anointing himself in the baths.[57]

If this were the whole story, it would serve as a useful example of how opportunities for selfish enrichment on the part of a Roman government agent served to destabilize local communities. But the story continues, for Chaironeia's neighbor and rival, Orchomenos, decided to use these internal dissentions as an opportunity for aggrandizement. They hired a Roman informer (*sukophantēn*) to bring murder charges "against the whole city as if it were a single individual."[58] Luckily, the Chaeroneans wrote to Lucullus, who verified their account in the trial. His testimony cinched their victory, and they erected a statue of Lucullus in the agora as a token of gratitude.

In recounting the intricacies of local politics, Plutarch allows us to see at a level of detail to which we are rarely otherwise privy how communities can fall apart: the civil war starts with sex, or at least the pressure for sex, when an arrogant Roman commander abroad feels entitled to help himself to things or bodies otherwise off limits. The desires of the commander provoke violence, but also local divisions; as private desires come to have public repercussions, local organs of

57 Plut. *Vit. Cim.* 1. For discussion, see Jones 1971: 6–7; Blamire 1989: 80–84; Goldhill 2002: 255.

58 Plut. *Vit. Cim.* 2.1–3.

justice are brought into the process – in a fashion akin to the events in Lycia a century later. Courts become a weapon of politics, while at the same time they serve as a venue for advertising to others, in this case neighboring Roman commanders, that the city *qua* institution wished to put space between its corporate acts and the acts of one of its inhabitants. Yet the cost of such a declaration is to abrogate normal procedures, leaving the council open to the charge of perverting the course of justice. The echoes of the complaint of the Lycian aristocrats are thus visible, *mutatis mutandis*, in the acts of the magistrates of Chaironeia. In the Chaironeian case, of course, the city's magistrates are slain immediately thereafter.

But the tit-for-tat murders have another aspect as well: internal dissension allows one's neighbors in on the game. Using a novel legal strategy, the Orchomenians go to the court of the governor in the hopes that they, having won, might help themselves to the city's territory and resources. Though we are not privy to the details of their complaint, it seems that the governor of Macedonia was in fact prepared to entertain the charges (proffered, as they were, by a pliant Roman plaintiff), and even contemplated condemning the city, as a corporate unit, for the murder of Roman citizens. As in comparable cases where cities were punished for killing Roman citizens, the penalty would likely be not just the end of autonomy, but the withdrawal of recognition as a corporate unit – that is, the reduction of the inhabitants of Chaironeia to mere *paroikoi*, subject to the control of Orchomenus.[59] Only the virtue of Lucullus (a good Roman, compared to the others) managed to save the Chaironeians: they remembered him on a regular basis, by viewing his statue in a prominent place in the city, and by retelling the story of Damon.[60]

It would be easy to dismiss the story of Damon or of the Lycians as a symptom of the pressures of the moment of provincialization, or, in the case of Damon, to blame them on the well-documented failures of Roman government during the first century BC. Periodically, however, we get glimpses of the sorts of pressure placed on societies that were *already* incorporated into the Roman provincial system. The ethnic riots that occurred in first century Alexandria might be taken as an instance of this, for example (see the Introduction, and

[59] E.g., Cass. Dio 54.7. [60] Jones 2011.

Chapter 4). But we might also note a comparable case from the province of Cyrenaica, one that came to the attention of Augustus himself. Responding to a complaint by some Cyrenaic cities, he declared:[61]

> In the Cyrenaic part of the province the total number of Romans with a census of 2,500 denarii or more, from whom the jurors come, is, I find, 215 of all ages. The embassies from cities of the province have complained that among these very jurors there exist certain conspiracies, which victimize the Hellenes in the death penalty cases, the jurors allegedly taking turns in bringing accusations and in supporting each other with testimony. And I myself have learned that some innocent persons have been oppressed in this way and have been brought to the ultimate penalty.

To be certain, the goal of this edict was to try to rein in such behavior, and accordingly Augustus laid out, in the remainder of the edict, a list of reforms to the local jury system designed to mitigate such abuses. But it is worth noticing three things. First, this privileged class of Roman citizens in Cyrenaica must have always been tempted to oppress its neighbors through means both fair and foul – that is, both directly and through insinuating itself into organs of justice to commit selfish acts under cover of law. Second, these Romans were not extraordinarily wealthy men. The census for jurors at Rome, for instance, was 100,000 sesterces: a jury census of 2,500 denarii in the provinces meant that one only needed to have 10 percent of the wealth in Cyrenaica as one did in Rome to decide the fate of others. It was cheap to be abusive. Too cheap, it seems, for to stop these conspiracies, in addition to changing the structure of the courts, Augustus also raised the minimum property qualification to 7,500 denarii, though he conceded that this might leave an inadequate number of Roman jurors.

Third and finally, this group seems to have been sufficiently protective of its corporate identity that when the "Hellenes" of the province chose to complain, they identified themselves to Augustus precisely *as* a group. In other words, the source of the oppression was clear enough to the preexisting community. So much so, it seems (from the third edict on the same stela), that some of these "Hellenes" sought to acquire Roman citizenship themselves, so that they could divest themselves of local responsibilities and join the

[61] *FIRA*² I 68 = Oliver 1989: no. 8, who also provides the translation.

class of people that was in charge. Augustus put an end to this, too, but from their abortive attempt we might learn something of the ways in which Roman control put pressure on provincial societies. It provoked hatred of the oppression done at the hands of cabals of privileged men. It also provoked envy – that is, a longing to join the ranks of the oppressors oneself, to sever oneself from one's native community whose status (Hellene) previously enabled its domination of others. Such a mixture of resentment and envious desire is not surprising. This was, after all, a colonial encounter. Finally, we note, again, the implication of courts, and especially criminal courts, in all of these processes.

The behavior of the Romans and Hellenes in Cyrenaica might help us to understand the broader transformation of society in the provinces and the dramatic shifts in the channels through which power flowed. In the case of Cyrenaica and Lycia, and, one suspects, Chaironeia too, the presence of Roman citizens in the provincial landscape was destabilizing. The matter was not made any less complicated as provincials themselves started to gain Roman citizenship – especially those provincials at the apex of local communities. In a number of subordinated cities (though certainly not all), the Roman government's desire for stability and its innate conservatism tended to upend local systems of government and authority and to place control in the hands of trustworthy and compliant men, upon whom they often conferred Roman citizenship. This meant, in turn, that such men were strongly disincentivized from making local marriage alliances and had to look to places other than their own communities for political support – in turn furthering political divisions within communities.[62] We might take, as an example of such a phenomenon, a man like C. Julius Eurycles, the tyrant of Sparta: promoted during the civil wars, he was eventually brought down by local Spartan aristocrats who had not been given Roman citizenship.[63] A similar pattern seems to have prevailed in Athens: not only did some four families – Roman citizens all – practically monopolize high offices, they also tended to

[62] Lavan 2021.

[63] Eurycles: Strabo 8.5.5; Plut. *Apophth. Reg.* 207F, with Bowersock 1961. Jones 2011 sees a parallel between the eventual downfall of Eurycles and that of G. Julius Nikanor in Athens.

cause grief among their fellow Athenians. One can only imagine, for instance, how satisfying it must have been for the Athenians to receive the olive groves confiscated from Claudius Hipparchus, which they were permitted to cultivate at a favorable rate. The Athenians' dislike for Hipparchus' grandson, Herodes, was similarly famous (and will be discussed in Chapter 7).[64]

It is hard, in these cases of political disorder, to have a sense of their precise causes. Complex and overlapping personal relationships surely served as catalysts. When men like Dio Chrysostom or Aelius Aristides railed about the dangers of *stasis* in communities, they betrayed little knowledge of the particulars of any given case, and tended to think in moral, rather than sociological, terms about the problems of civic disorder. But there is no necessary reason to think that the societal pressures caused by the incorporation within the Roman empire were simply or naturally outgrown over the course of a century or two. In some cases, of course, the pressures were successfully managed. The peace dividend of the first century AD (in some areas) and the second (in others) certainly allowed at least some conflicts to be managed and a large number of places to thrive.[65] The common devotion to the cult of the emperors – which emerged in this period as a reaction to these sweeping political changes – might similarly have served to channel some tensions over hierarchy and status.[66] Similarly, over the course of the first three centuries AD, the colonies themselves – the most tangible symbol of Roman difference and interference – gradually came to look more and more like Greek *poleis* (though without changing their juridical status) rather than disturbing and alien impositions on the landscape.[67] As elites came increasingly to share culture and education, a number of gaps were bridged that allowed them to maintain control over their home cities and regions.[68] But the structures of power had changed decisively,

[64] Hipparchus: *SEG* 15 108 = Oliver 1989: no. 92; Herodes: see Chapter 7. On offices at Athens more generally, see Camia 2014; Rizakis and Zoumbaki 2017.

[65] The arguments of Sherwin-White 1973 that the inexorable spread of Roman citizenship caused integration (and vice-versa) have been called into question, to my mind decisively, by Lavan 2016. On the consequences of this historiographical shift, see the perspectives collected in Lavan and Ando 2021.

[66] Price 1984. On the images of the emperor himself as encouraging unity, see Noreña 2011.

[67] Katsari and Mitchell 2008. [68] Woolf 1998; Lavan et al. 2016.

and institutions to mediate or naturalize these changes had to be, in many cases, dramatically reanimated or devised wholly anew.

The stories that local communities told to explain the changes of this violent era persisted. In fact, the closest analogue to Plutarch's story about the disorders that Roman rule caused in Chaironeia is found at the tail end of our chronological horizon. When seeking to explain the destruction of Jerusalem, Palestinian rabbis explained the causes as stemming from a deeply personal feud. The explanation comes from a midrash, *Lamentations Rabbah*:[69]

> There is a story about a certain man in Jerusalem who made a feast. He said to his slave: "Go and bring to me my friend, Qamtza." [The slave] went and bought him Bar Qamtza his enemy and he came and sat down among the guests. He saw him between his guests and said to him: "You are my enemy and you are sitting in my house! Get up and leave my house!" [Bar Qamtza] replied to him: "Do not shame me and I will return to you the price of the feast [i.e., what I have eaten]." He said to [Bar Qamtza]: "You must not recline." [Bar Qamtza] said to him: "Do not shame me and I will return to you double of what I eat." He said to him: "You must not recline." [Bar Qamtza] said to him: "Do not shame me and I will return the cost of this entire banquet." He said to [Bar Qamtza]: "Get up and go!" Rabbi Zechariah son of Eukolos was there and it was in his hand to stop it and he did not stop it. [Bar Qamtza] left from there and said to himself: "They are reclining and feasting extravagantly and I am going to go and press charges against them."

Though the story is told by late antique Rabbis, we are not far removed from Plutarch's account of Chaironeian society under pressure: in both accounts, the possibility of being shamed – whether socially or sexually – leads to escalation, and to the intervention of political powers into purely local disputes. In this case, Bar Qamtza ran to the court of the governor with a manufactured accusation that the Jews reject the animals that the governor offers them for sacrifice. This was a claim that the Jews as a collective (rather than just the host as an individual) rejected the bonds of reciprocity that the Romans offer them. After initially hesitating, the governor sent Bar Qamtza

[69] *Lamentations Rabbah* 4.3, trans. sefaria.org; cf. *BT Gittin* 55b–57a. The story is stitched together from a series of pieces, some of which reflect actual historical memories (though transformed in this context), others probably folktales. For help with this text I thank Amit Gvaryahu. See also Tropper 2022.

back to Jerusalem, accompanied by a "governor" (*eparchos*) and a group of sacrificial animals to test the veracity of Bar Qamtza's claim. At night, however, as the governor slept, Bar Qamtza rendered all of the animals impure, ensuring that the animals could not be offered as sacrifices and that his lie would appear true. When they arrived in Jerusalem, the governor saw that the Jews refused to sacrifice the animals, leading the governor to believe Bar Qamtza's claim:

> [The governor] sent and said to the king: "The whole issue of the Jews is exactly as it was said." Because of this he came to the Temple and destroyed it. See! Because of this story they say: "Between Qamtza and Bar Qamtza the Temple was destroyed."

This rather dismal harvest of stories about internal dissension and civil wars might serve to make two points. First, despite a tendency among scholars to see the eastern world as thriving, there were nonetheless real pressures on provincial societies. This does not mean that societies did not or could not thrive. Many did: they expanded economically, became seats of culture and learning and art, and avoided violent catastrophes. But to do so meant developing a modus operandi within the structures of an empire. Such a balance always threatened to become upset, sometimes over circumstances that seem trivial but which nonetheless were deeply implicated in local systems of honor, status, and hierarchy. In such a world, it made sense to continue to promote ideologies of concord (*homonoia*) that might keep interpersonal disputes from escalating into politically dangerous events. Second, these tensions were exacerbated by processes of taxation, colonization, and demographic transformation: as Rome extruded a privileged population of settlers and veterans across an already densely urbanized landscape, there were bound to be additional conflicts and tensions. Finally, when these interactions became heated, they turned on questions of adjudication, dispute management, and jurisdiction.

***

One effect of these profound shifts was the development of a culture of legalism. This is perhaps paradoxical. Rome was not the first empire to rule over large parts of the eastern Mediterranean, yet earlier empires provoked nothing like the interest in law that emerged on the scale it did over the first four centuries AD. Yet the challenge of governance, and specifically, of governors, opened up a pathway for legalism and legal complaint.

Governors had an ambivalent relationship to their provincial subjects, Roman or otherwise. Starting in the age of Augustus, the possibilities for a governor of a province to win distinction through military conquest began to be sharply constrained. Save in a few places, all peripheral and all carefully supervised, governing a province no longer brought the possibility of military distinction. Governors were to be primarily administrators, and self-aggrandizing improvization through acquiring territory was frowned upon.

There was nonetheless a great deal of work to do. The primary task of a governor was to provide for safety and security: these instructions were enclosed in his *mandata*, his formal instructions from the emperor.[70] But they were also common sense. To provide for safety, in practice, that the governor was to make certain his province was militarily secure and safe from organized banditry. It also meant that, with some specific exceptions, the governor was in charge of all capital jurisdiction and a great deal of lesser criminal jurisdiction. This would constitute a large amount of work, but it hardly exhausted the governor's portfolio: governors were also expected to hear disputes between cities and a great number of civil cases between individuals, as well as to periodically supervise the internal workings of a large number of cities in the provinces to ensure that public funds were not wasted or embezzled.

The job was monumental. It was also almost totally undertheorized, and instead presented as a largely moral endeavor. (I describe Roman *thinking* about governance, as opposed to the practice of governance itself, in Chapter 8.) It was made more complex because the governor carried out his work by riding circuit on his annual assize (*conventus*, *dialogismos*). The press of paperwork would have posed remarkable challenges even when government was organized hierarchically and bureaucratically. Egypt, for instance, comes closest to having a system of this sort; yet even here we know that the amount of work handled by a governor at a stop on his assizes was overwhelming. One papyrus gives the crucial number: at one stop on the

[70] *Dig.* 1.18.3 = Paulus, 13 *Sab.*, Frg. 1854 Lenel.

governor's assize, over the course of a few days, a whopping 1,804 petitions were processed. Even considering that (a) the governor had a staff to help manage this litany of complaints and that (b) the vast bulk of these cases would be sent back to local officials, this was a crushing amount of work.[71] It was likely even more work in other provinces, characterized by less integrated administrative frameworks and a greater diversity of subordinate political structures.[72]

Even the most diligent administrator would have had a hard time doing this sort of job effectively. And despite what must have been the emperor's careful efforts at thinking through which man would be the right fit for which job, plenty of administrators were simply unsuitable. Among the members of the equestrian order, where it must have been the most likely to select for talent, there were simple structural challenges that made this difficult: many men, each with many and varied capacities, and many voices making suggestions of their favored candidates. To select talented and responsible senators as provincial governors was yet harder, since the pool of available talent was smaller and emperors had to be concerned with the optics of appointment and the politics of gift-giving.[73] Even if a potential governor (senatorial or equestrian) seemed promising, other considerations might make him problematic or ineffectual – illness, love affairs, a taste for drink or art, poor advisors, or a fall from grace in the metropole.[74] By contrast, he might be *very* effective, and need to be quickly transferred to a more pressing position. (The city of Rome presented no lack of management problems that required diligent oversight, as did the frontiers of the empire.) Turnover might thus be either a blessing or a curse, with little way to predict in advance.

To one extent or another such structural problems might be mitigated by ensuring continuity at the level of staffing, by the

71 *P.Yale* I 61 (208–11 AD). See further, Lewis 1981; Horstkotte 1996. On the system for processing all the paperwork generated during the assizes, see Haensch 1994. The manifold duties of the governor, with special attention to his fiscal duties, are surveyed by Jördens 2009. For attempts to manage the complexities of the *conventus*, note *P.Oxy.* XXXVI 2754 (AD 111); *P.Oxy.* XLII 3017 (AD 176–77). In general, Kokkinia 2004b.

72 Burton 1975; Haensch 1997.

73 On equestrians, see Brunt 1975; Saller 1980; on senators, see Talbert 1984: 396–402; Lendon 1997.

74 Jördens 2020.

employment of trustworthy imperial slaves, and by filling the governor's *consilium* (his close circle of advisors) with talented men of experience – and even by preventing the governor from selecting all of them himself.[75] What is more, within provinces there eventually developed a bar of assessors who might be counted on to have institutional knowledge of what was appropriate to a particular situation and how a given problem had been handled in the past.[76] But the structural issues remained: there was too much work, too few possibilities for oversight, and too much leeway for local actors to take advantage.

This placed the governor in a tenuous position. Serving a relatively short term in office, he would arrive in his province to find a complicated cast of characters upon whom he might understandably look with suspicion: local aristocrats bent on feathering their own nests, by turns toadying and quarreling amongst themselves; groups of soldiers and state officials notionally involved in the business of commerce or extraction; slaves and freedmen of emperors and senators in charge of the exploitation of vast demesnes in the distant and unpoliceable countryside; Roman colonies, peopled by the descendants of veterans, that were notionally free but nonetheless required supervision. All of these, and more, wanted by turns to be left alone and to be granted favors elevating them above their rivals and neighbors – insistent upon their rights when it suited them, and insistent that identical rights be changed, adjusted, or abrogated when claimed by their enemies. They were a difficult, obstreperous, and needling lot, and the governor was both reliant upon them and charged with controlling them.

Failure to attend to their desires, much less their actions, might quickly end up jeopardizing the governor's prime directive to preserve the province's safety and security. This meant that the governor had to have something of a double relationship to his subjects, and his most privileged subjects in particular, because he relied upon them to keep the peace and to collect taxes. To manage this effectively, governors had to make a constant show of deferring to such subjects, making them feel honored. They also had to concede to some of these subjects the right to use certain amounts of violence,

[75] Kantor 2017b.
[76] On the development of the bar in North Africa, see Dolganov 2020b.

at certain times, and under certain circumstances, in the name of the state: otherwise, those subject to taxation would not part with their valuable resources. Yet allowing these local authorities the right to use violence unchecked was a terrible option: non-elite subjects needed to know that their local betters *could* avail themselves of violence but *would* refrain from it so long as those who owed managed to cough up something approximating a reasonable sum. It was a most delicate balance, and I return to the questions it provoked among jurists in Chapters 8 and 9.[77]

The problem of managing violence and extraction was adequately complicated in theory, but more so in practice. Taxation implicated governors in local relationships in which they would be periodically allied and periodically in tension with identical groups of people – and in ways that one might not necessarily predict based on the social status of the parties.[78] We might take as an example the problem of slave managers of senatorial property. We ought to assume, for instance, that the slave *pragmateutai* who administered the estate of the Ummidii in the Kibyratis did at times lord their authority over their tenants, though the latter were free men. These slaves protected the interests of a powerful senatorial family; that gave them great authority to ensure the orderly administration and exploitation of a series of massive tracts of land. They also likely had close connections to groups of Roman businessmen (*pragmateuomenoi Rhōmaioi*) throughout the region more generally.[79] The governor, in turn, was likely connected to the family of their owners and also at other times responsible for detailing soldiers to help these slave procurators perform their extractions.[80] But to be shaken down by a slave was degrading, and the tenants on these estates, had they decided one day to be bold, might have filed a complaint, one that the governor would be morally obliged to hear. Alternatively, they might flee, abandoning their lands in the hope of finding less degrading circumstances

77 E.g., Plin. *Ep.* 9.5.
78 For a set of examples from the late republic, see Eberle 2016.
79 On the estate of the Ummidii and its relation to the "demos" of the Ormeleis (which was, it seems, actually just a group of villages), see Corsten 2005: 6–17. Compare the more famous petition of the *coloni* of the Saltus Burunitanus in Africa (*ILS* 6870 = Hauken 1998: no.1, or the *SC de Pisone Patre*, ll.85–90.
80 E.g., Plin. *Ep.* 10.27–28; Hauken 1998: 188–96.

elsewhere, leaving the governor a different problem to solve.[81] Worse yet, they might simply lynch the offending slaves and clam up about it during a subsequent investigation.[82]

These would be extreme measures, but they were not unheard of. Villagers who bore the brunt of official extraction might normally grumble and hand things over, but their compliance was in no way guaranteed.[83] At times, processes of extraction could spin out of control politically: thus the historian Herodian describes how, during the turbulent period after the end of the Severan dynasty, an imperial procurator in Carthage decided to engage in a campaign of maximizing profits from the numerous imperial estates surrounding the city. He not only stepped up his exactions from among the various tenant farmers on these estates, he decided to use the courts connected to the imperial treasury to extort money from local aristocrats as well. The local aristocrats and tenant farmers quickly made an alliance, and together they marched to the procurator's house where they collectively murdered him. Realizing that they would soon be punished, they then marched to the residence of the provincial governor, an old man named Gordian. At sword-point they offered him a choice: accept being declared emperor or be murdered on the spot.[84] He accepted, only to rule for less than a month.

To be sure, the sort of violence that took place in Africa was an extreme response to unusual pressures: the end of a dynasty, the pressure to pay warring armies, and the advent of a period of empire-wide chaos. But, as with the case of the complex interpersonal dramas discussed above, there was always the threat that a local drama might escalate into a political problem that would eventually jeopardize a governor's career – or even his life. Not for nothing did the people of

[81] Note, e.g., the edict of M. Sempronius Liberalis (*W.Chr.* 19), on which see Strassi Zaccaria 1988.

[82] Cf. Phil. *VS* 517–18 (Scopelian), where Cytherus, the freed slave of Scopelian's father, is assaulted while trying to collect money from what is presumably his tenant farmer.

[83] E.g., *P.Col.* VIII 242 (AD V). Similar is *P.Oxy.* XLVIII 3409 (AD IV), from the archive of Papnuthis and Dorotheus. Cf., e.g., *PSI* III 222 (AD III–IV), where the collector of the tax on wild animals and birds meets armed resistance from local hunters; *P.Stras.* V 401bis (= *P.Stras.* IV 242, AD 123), a weaver beats up a tax collector.

[84] Hdn. 7.4–6.

Lampsacus rise up against Gaius Verres when he was but a governor's lieutenant, threatening to burn him alive in the home in which he was staying.[85] They failed, but Cicero, at least, understood the nature of their complaint. At some point, people could only be pushed but so far.

***

Finding the proper balance between exploitation and optimal levels of extraction might be difficult. But governors were also faced with a second, perhaps more difficult problem. The official powers of the Roman state might also be *laundered* through the numerous para-state actors who were at times responsible for carrying out the commands of Roman governors and their agents. Many of such people were Roman citizens moving throughout the provincial world. Citizenship could be a boon: Romans considered their own citizens as something of a privileged caste in a landscape otherwise destined for exploitation.[86] Proximity to such remarkable amounts of state power led those who were not, officially, engaged in state business to engage in exploitative acts themselves. And in a patrimonial empire where interpersonal relationships were often substituted for bureaucratic lines of authority, it could be hard to distinguish between what was and what was not official.[87]

Governors worried a great deal about this laundering of state power and tried to maintain a distinction between official needs and mere opportunism. Finding that a broad cast of characters was requisitioning transport wagons from the town of Sagalassos, the governor, Sex. Sotidius Strabo Libuscidianus, tried to crack down on the practice. In an edict, he declared that only the imperial family, senators, and active-duty-military could requisition ten wagons; equestrians could requisition only three, centurions only one. But "those who transport grain or anything else of that sort either for their own use or to sell" should not be allowed to requisition anything at all.[88] These last two groups of people were obviously his target. Grain merchants and transporters were not members of the Roman administration, but they

85 Cic. *Verr.* 2.1.63–70. Cicero also reports that the people of Africa had recently done the same to their governor, Hadrianus. On the events in question, see Steel 2004.

86 E.g., Cic. *Verr.* 2.5.167. 87 Lendon 1997.

88 *SEG* 26 1392 (14–21 CE) = Mitchell 1976, who provides the translation. My debt to Mitchell's study will be evident in what follows.

must have imagined themselves as having analogous privileges. They engaged in public law contracts with the Roman state, and their services were essential for keeping the peace in Rome and in the major cities. Accordingly, they were arrogating to themselves privileges analogous to those deserved by other members of the state. The second group, merchants who were simply transshipping other goods (that is, not *frumentum* but things for their personal profit and use – *quaestus sui caussa vel usus*) helped themselves to the same privileges as well.[89]

Such laundering of power seems to have been consistent enough that, at least in one case, the emperor was forced to worry whether these sorts of abuses would lead to something like a right acquired by prescription. Thus, in a letter to a procurator in Syria, the emperor Domitian warned that "until now an inveterate custom (*sunētheia*) survives, and it will gradually become law (*nomon*) if it is not vigorously prevented from gaining strength. So I enjoin it upon you to take special care that no one, unless he is provided with my diploma, seize an animal."[90] But distinguishing between those acting in official and unofficial capacities was often no easy task. The governor of Egypt found himself in a similar situation, finding that many of the soldiers travelling through the country while not officially deployed were corruptly requisitioning boats and animals, essentially paying off local officials to look the other way. As a result, the governor insisted that "private persons are subjected to violence and abuse and the army is reproached for greed and injustice."[91]

Soldiers were by far the worst offenders.[92] But there are hints that they were not the only ones and that others – private persons presumably somehow affiliated with the army – piggybacked on their privileges. Thus, in an inscription from Syria, the governor confirms that "if anyone – either a soldier or a private person – lodges with you against your will (*biaiōs*), send him to me and I will judge him."[93] In

89 Note a series of similar cases preserved in rescripts relating to *navicularii*: *Dig.* 50.6.6.3–6 = Callistratus, 1 *Cog.*, Frg. 8 Lenel).

90 Text and translation from Oliver 1989: no. 40. Cf. *SEG* 38 1244 (part of letter of Pertinax and an edict of the governor prohibiting soldiers from wandering off the main road and demanding *supplementa*).

91 *PSI* V 445 = *Sel.Pap.* II 221 (133–137 CE), trans. ed. with modifications.

92 Note the inscription recently published by Reger 2020, detailing not just abuse by soldiers, but their use of (quasi-judicial) torture. Cf. Lib. *Or.* 47.33.

93 *IGR* III 1119 = *MARE* 113 = Hauken 1998: 180–87.

all of these cases, then, the concern was not only with abuse by officials but additionally with abuse by private people who in some fashion attached themselves to officials. Thus, a similar situation seems to prevail in an inscription from the area near Kibyra, where a group of local villagers complained about abuse by "Hedistus, whom you appointed tabularius, and the two Crispi and Zosimus, Cassius, Chrysogonus and Sabinus" for making "supplementary exactions" from the local peasants (*paroikoi*). This odd mixture of Greek and Latin names in an area filled with senatorial estates suggests that a group of leaseholders and their slaves or agents, confident in their power, used it to shake down the local peasants, expecting that they would be treated as acting in an official capacity.[94] The peasants disagreed and complained to the emperor, who in turn instructed the governor to investigate further.[95]

In this case, as in the one discussed above (the letter from Domitian), it is the emperor or emperors, rather than the governor, who is brought in to respond to local problems of disorder. Indeed the emperor was as often as the governor the preferred recourse for quotidian unfairness and exploitation – on the rare occasions, that is, that he could be reached.[96] It is worth remembering, however, that insofar as governors and emperors tended to agree on the optimal means of dealing with exploitative actors, the attention of the emperor to the affairs of a particular province might be unwelcome. Not all oversight was benevolent, nor were all the emperors doing the overseeing. Imperial intervention was yet another factor that governors would have to balance.

***

The preceding discussion only begins to scratch the surface of the challenges that governance posed to governors themselves – indeed much more evidence could be adduced to show that the challenges of

94 *SEG* 59 1556 (prev. *SEG* 48 1583) = Souris and Haensch 2009, with further discussion (esp. 361 on the identity of the malefactors).

95 To this we might compare *BGU* XVI 2258 (= Hagedorn and Jördens 2006), an edict of 22 BC forbidding anyone other than soldiers from wearing the *paenula*. Presumably, the presence of state actors wearing such a garment inspired others to try the same thing, with the goal of shaking down their neighbors.

96 The literature on imperial justice is massive, but for a useful study of the court of the emperors (on the basis of the *Codex Hermogenianus*), see Connolly 2010. On imperial attempts to ensure justice in the absence of an emperor, see Peachin 1996.

controlling powerful people in a province were massive. I have not, for instance, discussed any of the challenges posed by the *internal* politics of cities – though such evidence certainly exists, and will be discussed further in Chapter 7.[97] But I should like to just note, on the basis of the sources above, a few salient points.

First, in the world of the eastern provinces, sharply unequal individuals sat cheek-by-jowl with one another. Governance was done by a loose confederation of imperial/state, local, military, and parastate individuals. In such a world, sorting legitimate from illegitimate authority or exactions was necessarily a complex if not totally inscrutable affair. There was no clearing house, like the office of sheriff or bailiff, designed to ensure that at the end of a particular transaction/exaction the right property ended up in the right person's hands. As a result, there might often be multiple and competing claims on a particular person, a piece of property, or a particular obligation. That is, throughout this landscape, power was pluralistic in the least morally attractive sense of the term. This is not to say that there was necessarily anarchy or quasi-anarchic predation – though at times it probably depended on one's perspective – but in the "structural dysfunction" of the Roman provincial system there was always a tendency in that direction.[98] In any given poorly managed corner of this world powerful individuals might be tempted to increase their own margins at the expense of the structurally weak. To sort out who had a legitimate claim and who did not was a complicated, expensive, and time-consuming affair that the Roman state was poorly equipped to handle because its only means to do so was through litigation, done by the governor and his relatively few delegates, during the course of his assizes.

Second, since litigation was the only solution on the table, it was the threat of litigation that served to protect those who felt they were on the wrong side of a transaction.[99] Thus we see emerge, in the

[97] Note only the case of Dio Chrysostom: Jones 1978, 2012, and more generally, Heller 2006.

[98] I borrow "structural dysfunction" from Brélaz 2020: 180.

[99] Quite obviously I am aware that litigation is more often threatened than completed – and that the threat of litigation leads to a great deal of "bargaining in the shadow of the law." Such bargaining was both common and essential to the smooth functioning of the system. Nor is there any doubt, as is evidenced by the profusion of arrears, that in many cases when it came to successfully extracting what they wished, many officials were simply impotent (or that they were collusive in letting the debts of

world of the provinces, a tendency on the part of subjects to complain about the acts of their notional superiors. Though there had certainly been complaints in the pre-Roman period, the volume of such rhetoric and the extent to which it came to permeate provincial society as a whole is indeed new, and a strong reason for thinking that a common language of complaint emerged in this world as the result, a generation or two later, of processes of incorporation within Roman domination. What is more, because the nature of power in this world was overlapping and pluralistic, such a rhetoric of complaint could come to play such a dominant role. In communities that are under pressure structurally, complaint emerges because one *cannot* trust local or neighboring sources of authority to deal with a problem responsibly. Hence, not only did people in the Roman world develop a rhetoric of legality, the point of that rhetoric was to gain the attention of powerful individuals like governors and their entourage, a level of power removed from the intimate and oppressive politics of local communities themselves.

It is here, specifically, that we are to look for the origins of provincial legal *cultures*. The plural is important. The impulse to fight over the terms of material exploitation through the language of law and the threat of litigation might be shared – but the shared nature of a particular idiom did not, at the end of the day, lead to all parties valuing its existence in an identical way. Ideological commitments to the nature of governance, legitimacy, and legality varied substantially among various groups of people. I shall trace patterns in these various responses over the course of the following chapters. But I should like to turn, in what follows, to those who perceived themselves, or at least presented themselves, as occupying the lowest level of the hierarchy. (Whether that perception is justified is another story, of course.) How did they claim their rights? And can we be more precise about the particular rhetoric of legality that emerged to cope with the world of material exploitation as it was practiced in the world of the eastern provinces?

some favored parties go uncollected). On litigation and the tendency to bargain or settle, see Harries 1999, 2001; Kelly 2010.

3

Arguing from Archives

In the middle of the second century AD, the satirist Lucian of Samosata (c. AD 125–180) composed a text known as the *Bis Accusatus* ("Twice Accused") in which he describes a day of judgment. It begins with Zeus complaining to Hermes about the onerous nature of running the universe:

> In the first place, I have to supervise the work of the other gods who have responsibilities under my regime, to make sure they don't slack in their duties. Then I have a million tasks to perform myself, scarcely manageable because of their complexity. It's not as though I simply have the major administrative tasks to perform, I mean managing and organizing the weather – rain, hail, wind, and lightning – before I can simply sit down and take a break from my assigned worries. I've got to do all this and keep a watch in all directions and supervise everything as though I were that herdsman at Nemea: people stealing, people perjuring themselves, people sacrificing. Has someone made a libation? Where's the sacrificial smell and smoke coming from? Who has called for me in sickness or at sea? But the most onerous task of all is being in so many places at the same time: Olympia for a hecatomb. Babylon for a battle, with the Getae to hail, with the Ethiopians to feast ...
>
> Take an example. We're so damned busy, we've got an enormous backlog of old lawsuits not dealt with. They've been stacked there so long, they've fallen apart with mildew and they're covered in spider's webs. I'm thinking in particular about the ones taken out against certain individuals associated with the intellectual arts and crafts. Some of them are absolutely ancient. The litigants themselves are bawling on every side, grinding their teeth, calling for justice and accusing me of tardiness. What they don't realize is that it's not through contempt that these decisions have passed their sell by date.

It's because of the state of bliss that they think we live in. That's the name they give to our complete lack of spare time.[1]

Hermes concurs with Zeus, though without failing to point out that the legitimacy of his rule is, unfortunately, predicated on keeping up with this enormous pile of paperwork that governs the lives of the cosmic empire. To clear the desk, Zeus and Hermes decide to set up a "market for lawsuits" (*agoran dikōn*), a standard Greek translation of the Latin *conventus* or assize. They locate their assize prominently beside the Athenian acropolis, allowing everyone to come, for the day, to plead their old cases before the lord of the universe. And come they do. In short order the acropolis is thronged with petitioners, who fill to capacity even the sacred precincts at its foothills. So numerous are the litigants that immediately Zeus and Hermes realize their mistake in announcing a general session and decide to place a limit on the kinds of cases they plan to hear.[2]

The vast amount of business that Zeus complains about would not have been news to Roman emperors or governors.[3] The courts of the eastern provinces hummed with activity. As noted earlier, one governor of Egypt "heard" (or at least processed) a total of 1,804 petitions over a three-day period in AD 209. Even assuming a ten-hour workday and support staff, such complaints would be processed at the rate of about one per minute.[4] This was hardly divine justice. But the litigants themselves were undeterred, lining up at the governor's assizes or waiting for him at his more permanent residences.

Emperors hoped that governors would do this part of their job at least competently, for effective provincial governance would prevent litigants from clogging the courts of the emperor himself, or attempting to chase him down en route to other, more pressing (or more enjoyable) business. Thus, the emperor Julian once counted himself

1 *Bis accusatus* 2–3, trans. Sidwell 2004.

2 *Bis accusatus* 13. Cf. the attempt of a Roman governor to limit the sorts of cases he would hear in the first instance to a relatively circumscribed list of criminal offences: *SB* XII 10929 (AD 133–37).

3 On the emperor's paperwork, see Millar 1992: 213–52; on the workload of governors, specifically with reference to petitions and litigation, see Lewis 1981; Haensch 1994; Kokkinia 2004b, and on the governor's responsibilities more generally, with a focus on Egypt, Jördens 2020.

4 *P.Yale* I 61. On the rate of work, see Lewis 1983: 190; Horstkotte 1996.

especially clever: confronted at his court in Constantinople with a gaggle of Egyptians ("a contentious race of men, by custom always delighting in intricate litigation") intent on pursuing their private lawsuits, he sent them off across the strait to Chalcedon to await his presence. He then banned the local ferrymen from giving any Egyptian passage back to Constantinople. Having stranded them there, he could safely ignore them and attend to other business.[5] Such a nasty trick was hardly in keeping with his duty to be responsive to his subjects, but certainly in keeping with his penchant for dark humor. Some subjects, after all, were more deserving of imperial attention than others.[6]

To explain the emergence and persistence of this culture of litigation one needs to look towards the central tension in Roman government outlined in the previous chapter: the ambivalence of emperors and governors towards the privileged populations of the empire upon whom they also relied for the keeping of peace and the extraction of resources. This tension opened a space for Rome's imperial subjects to attempt to deploy local interpretations of law to claim their rights. Over the course of the first two centuries AD, provincial populations developed a language that resonated with emperors and governors: a mode of arguing, through the language of law, that they were indeed subjects, but not abject ones. They argued that they, too, had rights – against their neighbors, against the notional elites of their communities, and against the state and its representatives. At the center of these rights claims were broader understandings of the nature of law, and more specifically, understandings of the ways that legal *documents* allowed provincial subjects to vindicate their claims. In the everyday business of courts in the eastern Roman provinces, documents came to sit at the center of provincial understandings of law, constituting the nature of subjecthood and mediating the relationship between a subject and his or her rights.

***

To explain the emergence of this culture of litigation we should begin not with the work of the courts themselves, but with the

[5] Amm. Marc. 22.6, trans. Rolfe, LCL.

[6] Cf. Julian's attitude towards a group of litigants in Ancyra: Amm. Marc. 22.9.8–11. On the tendency of lawsuits to get backed up, see Suet. *Vesp.* 10.

culture of recording that emerged alongside the transformation of provincial society with the advent of Roman rule. As explained in the previous chapter, the process of conquest and provincialization was violent, thoroughgoing, and periodically traumatic. But it had another side as well. It brought along with it – though always at a lagging pace – a process of imperial knowledge production, of the mapping and reorienting of material concerns and responsibilities, and the fixing of populations with respect to their legal and fiscal status.[7] This process had two key aspects: the fixing of the status of territory and institutions, and the fixing of the status of people. Both revolved around documents, kept in archives, which came to be a source of fascination and political struggle. I shall return to these presently.

Any attempt to govern a particular territory involved determining what sorts of political units were contained within it and what the responsibility of those units was to the imperial center. At the bare minimum, Roman generals, governors, imperial procurators, and emperors had to make decisions as to which unit was responsible for which taxes, and the means by which they would deliver those taxes. The rights attached to any particular unit of empire could take on a bewildering variety of forms, based on legal status, previous history, relative prestige, operative treaties, or imperial grants. They were also constantly subject to negotiation or revocation.[8] Roman emperors and administrators often changed statuses simply by fiat: the heartland of Africa or Cisalpine Gaul, for instance, remain even today marked by the ruins of cities and territorial markers imposed by dint of imperial will upon the landscape, each one the deliberate erasure of a previous history and a complex tangle of rights.[9] The wave of Roman colonization in the eastern Mediterranean

[7] Nicolet 1991; Ando 2010b. For doubts, Cf. Jördens 2010, who emphasizes the role of documentation in creating legal certainty. The two positions do not seem to exclude one another. Lagging pace: Burkhalter 1990.

[8] These exemptions could be picayune indeed: in the third century the jurist Papinian might make a special note that real security over the property of a deceased debtor might still be claimed in Antioch on the basis of its local law (*Dig.* 42.5.37 = 10 *Resp.*, Frg. 646 Lenel); similarly, the citizens of Troy were exempt from taking on tutelage of children who were not Trojans (*Dig.* 27.1.17.1 = Call. 4 *Cog.*, Frg. 24 Lenel).

[9] Africa: Caillemer and Chevallier 1954; Cisalpine Gaul: Purcell 1990.

operated similarly.[10] But unlike in Gaul or Africa, in the densely populated areas of the eastern Mediterranean, it took ages to work out, in practice and in usable detail, what was to be the relationship between imperial authority and the local landscape. It was less an act of imposition than a process of negotiation that called on all the parties involved to craft narratives justifying their particular rights.

These processes of negotiation can be seen most clearly in cases where communities dealt with questions of immunity from taxation – obviously a highly valuable commodity in an extractive empire. We might take as an example the problems posed by the lands connected to the temple of Zeus at Aezanoi in Phrygia. In the third century BC, king Attalus I decided to settle a group of soldiers on lands belonging to the temple of Zeus, dividing the land into allotments (*klēroi*); the settlers' rights were confirmed later by the Bithynian king Prusias I (228–182 BC), but, it seems, the *klēroi* were never properly surveyed – or if they were, the evidence of such surveys had long ago vanished or been made to vanish. Without any physical markers marking the divisions of property, the settlers and their descendants had ceased to pay to the temple whatever rents they were supposed to have paid. Accordingly, the families of this privileged class came to enjoy their land without making any contributions to the common weal. This vexed the chief political unit in the area, the city of Aezanoi (distinct from the temple), which, probably in the late first or early second century AD, decided that these lands should be classed as subject to *vectigal*, that is, that they had ought to be taxed at the customary rate for public lands farmed by private individuals. This would have served to offset the total tax burden for which the city of Aezanoi was responsible.

The holders of the allotments protested, refused to pay, and ended up in the court of the governor of Asia, Mettius Modestus, in AD 119–20. In no mood to complicate his life by declining a good source of revenue, Modestus ruled that the land was indeed subject to such payments. Still, the landholders refused to relent: how, they asked, could they be made to pay, if the boundaries of their allotments had become obscure – that is, if it was unclear in what amount each of them was to be taxed? Accordingly, they ended up in the court

[10] E.g., Romano 2003 on Corinth.

of a subsequent governor, Avidius Quietus, some five or six years later. Though Quietus grouched that the dispute "has dragged on for many years" and had caused a great deal of consternation (the social and political ramifications of which on the community are not to be underestimated), he agreed to write to the emperor Hadrian for a determination and to an imperial procurator, Hesperus, for a survey. Hadrian eventually replied, as did Hesperus: if it was impossible to figure out the original dimensions of the allotments, then a survey should be made of the area in question, as well as surveys of neighboring territories, to determine "what are the largest and smallest dimensions of a *klēros* in the neighborhood and in that region itself." Once those dimensions were determined, by the grace of the emperor each possessor would be charged the average from that point on. And yet the story has a further twist: a series of boundary stones from two years after the decision of Quietus have since been found, in which Hadrian claims to have "restored the territory given to Zeus, the founder, and the city of the Aizanitai by the kings Attalus and Prusias ... according to what king Prusias established." In other words, the emperor might pretend that the ad hoc decision to tax according to the local average allotment size was, in fact, based on a specific decision of a Bithynian monarch made in the late third century BC – some three hundred or so years beforehand.[11]

The dispute at Aezanoi gives some sense of just how hard it was, in practice, to generate and verify this very imperial form of fiscal knowledge. When faced with a group of subjects committed to withholding from their fellow citizens and from Roman administrators any evidence or knowledge they might have had of how things "really" were, the best Roman administrators could do was to use the law of averages and call it history. It thus gives a sense of how committed local actors might be to blocking attempts at being

[11] The texts concerning the dispute are gathered in *MAMA* IX, P.A–D; the boundary stones are *MAMA* IX 8–9. I rely heavily on the reconstruction of the editors of *MAMA* IX (xxxviii–xliii); see also the valuable overview by Blanco-Pérez (www.judaism-and-rome.org/hadrian-and-zeus-aizanoi), who also provides the translation of the boundary stone. See also Kantor 2013: 164–66, and on the constructed nature of this history, see further Kantor 2017a: 72–73. For the ideological insistence on the continuity of local history as expressed through boundary stones, compare the case of the Bargylioi of Macedonia, as discussed by Arnaoutoglou 2020.

known (and taxed), as well as to their commitment to make the court of the governor (and by extension, the emperor) into a site for the negotiation of local histories and claims of right. Second, though the result of the case was something of a mixed bag for the litigants (they had to pay taxes going forward, but not arrears), the decisions were inscribed upon the temple of Zeus, potentially forestalling other claims in the future. Third and perhaps most importantly, the dispute at Aezanoi reminds us that fiscality itself was productive of litigation: the modes by which the imperial state claimed its right to take were constantly contested and negotiated. In this sense they became the subject of a new provincial politics. And they were repeated with stunning regularity across the landscape: no fewer than eighty-eight such boundary disputes are known, each potentially as fraught as the situation at Aezanoi.[12]

People were as important as land, and they produced similar arguments over classification. The operation of Rome's fiscal engine depended on having near to hand an account of the people who lived under its rule. The census of course had a lengthy pedigree: developed in Rome and in Italy primarily as a way of assessing political rights and military manpower, the Roman government continued to count its own citizens, whether in Italy or abroad, throughout the period of its rule. In an important sense, this marked Roman citizens as holders of privilege at the same time that it subjected their persons and property to complex regimes of taxation and surveillance (the inheritance tax, regimes of guardianship, and the complex paperwork of registering, in Latin, the births and deaths of all Roman citizens).[13] The same was broadly true of provincial populations. While we know less than we might like about how individual (non-Roman) cities outside of Egypt carried out their census-taking duties, at the

[12] See Burton 2000, who is more optimistic than I about the finality of these sorts of imperial solutions. A more extensive catalogue (which includes Italian boundary disputes) can also be found in Campbell 2000: 454–67. With additional attention to republican precedents, see Israelowich 2019. Cf. the numerous petitions for *asylia*: Tac. *Ann.* 3.60–63. See Rigsby 1996: 540 for the reminder that, for the Romans, unlike for prior Hellenistic monarchs (save the later Ptolemies), *asylia* meant exemption from laws.

[13] For a valuable overview of the census more generally, and with further bibliography, see Dolganov 2021.

very least they kept records of who was a local citizen, and of what each citizen's property holdings consisted.[14]

The case of cities to one side, provincials in general were subject to a robust apparatus of information gathering and recording at least shortly after their incorporation into the empire, and on a periodic basis thereafter – and certainly so if they wished to claim a privileged or protected status.[15] Egypt is, unsurprisingly, the best-documented case, with scores of papyri attesting to the state's interest in gathering fairly intimate knowledge of its population on a regular basis through a relatively intrusive regime of documentation and surveillance.[16] It remains a matter of controversy how representative the Egyptian case is compared to that of other provinces, but it seems reasonable to guess that, perhaps second only to the annual harvest or to the periodic motions of the military, the census was the major cause of human mobility, travel, and upheaval, with all its attendant dangers, miseries, and discomforts:[17]

> In those days a decree went out from Emperor Augustus that all the world should be registered. This was the first registration and was taken while Quirinius was governor of Syria. All went to their own towns to be registered. Joseph also went from the town of Nazareth in Galilee to Judea, to the city of David called Bethlehem, because he was descended from the house and family of David. He went to be registered with Mary, to whom he was engaged and who was expecting a child. While they were there, the time came for her to deliver her child. And she gave birth to her firstborn son and wrapped him in bands of cloth, and laid him in a manger, because there was no place for them in the inn.

Yet the recording of the empire's inhabitants was more than just an attempt to map and count the population. It was also an exercise in ordering and ranking the population by status and privilege, and as such, it attempted to put imperial power on display by instantiating,

14 On the Egyptian status declarations, see Nelson 1979; Kruse 2013.

15 Though the relationship between the census and provincialization lagged: see Claytor and Bagnall 2015. For an overview, see Le Teuff 2012.

16 Hombert and Préaux 1952; Bagnall and Frier 1994.

17 Luke 2:1, trans. NRSV. On the administrative and chronological problems posed by the conventional translations of the Lukan account, see Huebner 2019: 31–50. On the harvest, see Shaw 2013. On other opportunities that the census offered for emptying cities of "undesirable" lower-caste inhabitants, cf. *W.Chr.* 202 (104 AD), *P.Giss.* I 40 (AD 215).

through processes of writing and recording, a vision of how society ought ideally to be ordered. By creating, at least in writing, a tableau of optimal social organization, the emperor and his representatives might imagine that they had ensured a form of order that was ultimately transcendent. The logic was, ultimately, no different than the logic of other forms of imperial display – such as capital punishment. Supporting this vision of a well-ordered society was a suite of civil and criminal penalties for evading registration and for attempting to blur or transcend the categories into which one was placed.[18] But since these status determinations also ranked people with respect to their neighbors, they were hotly contested, as the inhabitants of the empire sought to acquire privileges and statuses that they might deploy in local conflicts.

Backstopping these processes of imperial knowledge creation was a wealth of documentation. Local and province-level archives were developed and were enlisted in the cause of documenting, recording, and storing all of the many facts about personal and territorial status that Roman governance generated.[19] Copies and summaries of information gathered at the local level were forwarded to other officials and made available for examination. Not by accident was Augustus, in dealing with the problems posed by the Roman community in Cyrene, able to state unequivocally that there were "215 Roman citizens with a census of more than 2500 denarii" present in the province.[20] Control of land was especially well documented in local archives from throughout the empire, and transfers of land – because they had fiscal implications – were registered with local authorities.[21] But land ownership was only a small piece of the total volume of documentation: a wide variety of transactions, privileges,

[18] The most important is the *Gnomon* of the *Idios Logos*, which specified in great detail a harsh regime of property confiscations especially in cases where people sought to move property between these classes (Roman citizens, Alexandrians, or Egyptians among them). *BGU* V 1210 = *Sel.Pap*. II 206; a partial copy can be found in *P.Oxy*. XLII 3014 (on the date of which see Dolganov 2020a). Similar things could be said of the so-called *fiscus iudaicus*, the 2-denarius tax that represented the contributions that Jews made to the Jerusalem temple, now re-routed to the god Jupiter Capitolinus as punishment for the revolt of AD 66–70. On penalties for evasion of the census more generally, see Hombert and Préaux 1952: 97–99.

[19] See esp. Ando 2000.

[20] *FIRA* I 68. I owe this point to Nicolet 1991: 132.

[21] Moatti 1993.

and memberships were subject to registration.[22] What is more, the extensive records of these transactions, preserved on papyrus, seem to indicate that the population was comfortable with or at least resigned to using these systems, and, by extension, consented to be known in such a way by the state itself.

***

We should pause here to make two, if not three points. The first is obvious and might be dealt with briefly: while it is certainly true that sources, especially from Egypt, document a huge variety of transactions, demonstrate the recording of a great number of life events, and supply a steady drumbeat of instances where taxes were paid and where subjects made themselves legible, there must nonetheless have been a great deal that escaped the gaze of the Roman state. This is true in all social contexts, but especially so in the premodern world.[23] In the Roman case, the state placed tremendous ideological weight on the act of recording, but devoted relatively little administrative capacity to building or maintaining systems of surveillance.[24] What enforcement there was – and there *was* enforcement – came when transactions fell apart, when jealous neighbors or family members sought to claim something that would not have been theirs but for a defective registration, or when family members or fellow villagers were held responsible for something that should

[22] On the Egyptian evidence for archives, and the items they recorded, see Cockle 1984; Burkhalter 1990; Keenan et al. 2014: 62–83 for useful surveys; for discussion of the archives of governors, see Haensch 1992.

[23] For important comparative studies, see Richardson 2012, 2017.

[24] Dolganov 2021: 192 proposes something like a surveillance state in the high Roman Empire. Hers is a useful statement of what one might call a "maximalist" perspective on the importance of documentation, but attention to social context is obviously important. Indeed, only some people – some *kinds* of people – are ever asked to "show their papers." This leads in contexts both modern and ancient to errors that have to be naturalized after having been allowed to persist over long periods of time – e.g., as in the case of Claudius and the Anauni (*CIL* V 5050 = Sherk 1988: no. 52), or in numerous cases in which slave status might be conveniently "forgotten" (e.g., Plin. *Ep.* 10.29–30; *CJ* 10.33.2; *Dig.* 1.14.3 = Ulp. *Sab.* 38, frg. 2842 Lenel). One might also note the perhaps quixotic attempt to "fix" a local archive in a state of deterioration, *P.Fam.Tebt.* 15, 24. Cf. *SEG* LXII 917, a decree of the first century for an Attalos who, among his other achievements, cleaned up the city's archives and "restored the tax register and returned it to the people" (ll.20–24). On the increasing centralization of archival practices in Egypt, see Claytor 2018.

have been another person's problem.[25] Such problems are amply documented, but we must operate from the assumption that consenting to participate in certain forms of official documentation was only one strategy among many. It probably varied according to the extent to which someone thought that he himself – or his local enemies – would be eventually subject to serious consequences. Such a calculation would probably depend on one's social class, position in a town or village, and proximity to agents of state enforcement – to say nothing of one's capacity to ignore or beat such agents senseless if they ever attempted enforcement.[26] The choice of whether or not to subject oneself – or to what extent to subject oneself – to any particular aspect of a system of imperial registration and documentation likely involved a careful casuistry: a hard look at the local landscape of power at any particular time.

Second, it is tempting to take the perspective of the state and to conclude that the things that we can see in the documentary record are in fact *all* the things that mattered. They were not. The Roman government never sought encyclopedic or panoptic knowledge of its subjects. Rather, it sought primarily *fiscal* knowledge, that is, knowledge of the things that it wished to tax. As a matter of regulation, this also involved making interventions in other places. For instance, given that a huge proportion of ancient wealth was transferred not by sale in a public marketplace but through inheritance, prudent lawmaking also meant making interventions in the nature of family and inheritance law.[27] Similarly, considering how much wealth and prestige

[25] E.g., *P.Oxy.* XLVI 3274 (AD 99–117), where an estate is denounced to the Idios Logos because of a problematic provision in the will, with the result that half the estate is confiscated. On the fiscus, see further below, Chapter 9.

[26] Choosing to use official channels for solving problems: Kelly 2010. On following official requirements for the registration of real property, Jördens 2010: 168–70. On resistance of powerful people to quotidian demands, cf. *BGU* III 747 = *W.Chr.* 35 (AD 139); to demands of the governor, *CJ* 1.40.2 (AD 328), 9.39.2.1 (AD 451); on the resistance of groups of villagers to the tax collection demands of the council of Antioch (because the villagers were under the "protection" of soldiers), Lib. *Or.* 47.1–10. The existence of persons totally beyond the reach of the state is imagined, e.g., in Apul. *Met.* 9.35–38; cf. Shaw 1984.

[27] Although in certain aspects of family law Roman administrators were perfectly happy to use or adapt Indigenous practices: see Alonso 2013. I look forward to the publication of Nicholas Purcell's book on sale in the Roman world, which hopefully will give a more robust account of these issues. Inheritance badly needs a general, comparative treatment; in the interim, see Champlin 1991, on Roman inheritance

were tied up in the ownership of land, and how important it was as a fiscal category, Roman administrators looked especially carefully at any attempts to change the status of land. Thus, when the inhabitants of a group of Macedonian villages sought to prevent a group of people called *eparchikoi* (possibly former Roman officials) from encroaching upon their community's lands, they first sent a draft of their proposed law to the provincial governor, Junius Rufus, to ask his blessing, since changing the status of *who* could own might affect the imperial coffers.[28] Fiscal knowledge might in practice have been extensive (although the question is fundamentally comparative – extensive as compared to *what*?). But it was not encyclopedic, much less panoptic. The Roman state was notoriously disinterested in a great many things.

Indeed, the best evidence of this disinterest comes from provincial voices themselves. Regarding the *archontes* ("the rulers," here broadly conceived), the apostle Paul might urge his followers to "pay to all what is due them – taxes to whom taxes are due, revenue to whom revenue is due, respect to whom respect is due, honor to whom honor is due," as well as to refrain from any sort of predation that might occasion punishment. This might be a prudent policy, but could nonetheless offer a wide scope of space for early Christian communities to design for themselves the modes of social and quasi-political organization that they deemed optimal (see further Chapter 6).[29] Similarly, when the Pharisees, wishing to bait Jesus of Nazareth into saying something revolutionary, asked him whether it was lawful to pay taxes, the answer was an emphatic yes:[30]

> "Whose head is this, and whose title?" They answered, "The emperor's." Jesus said to them, "Give to the emperor the things that are the emperor's, and to God the things that are God's." And they were utterly amazed (*ethaumazon*) at him.

Jesus' statement was, crucially, more restrained than Paul's claim (for it said nothing about honor or respect). It was "amazing" because it opened the possibility for his audience to conceive a relationship

strategies, and Lavan 2021 on Roman marriage strategies; for an excellent comparandum, see Hartog 2012.

[28] *SEG* 30 568. On Roman attempts to encourage production in marginal lands in the east, cf. Quass 1996; Rizakis 2004.

[29] Rom.13:7. On such forms, see Meeks 2003. [30] Mk. 12:17, trans. NRSV.

with imperial government in radically diminished and contingent terms – as a matter of *mere* fiscality. It left open a huge space in which meaningful social or religious action might take place. This restraint is the source of its radicalism.

***

Jesus of Nazareth was, of course, an aberration. It was much more often the case that it was precisely because imperial documentation contained an authoritative statement about one of a range of matters impinging on normal social action that interested parties sought to harness the state's fiscal interests to fight with their friends, families, and neighbors.[31] This was in some respects simply a straightforward convergence of interests, since a great deal of everyday fighting and litigating already overlapped the concerns of the state, even narrowly defined. This was especially so in fights over matters pertaining to property – the vast array of disputes over who owns what. At one level, ownership and possession are the elementary building blocks of fiscality and imperial extraction, and the Roman state took a strong interest in documenting ownership and possession.

But fights over property were also fights over the material conditions of existence – who would be able to produce enough crops to eat, to stave off the tax collector, and to turn into cash to provide for other necessities of life. And quite apart from state and material interests, fights over property were also subjectively important, raising questions about family and community harmony more generally. They tended to be fights over where one sits, and with what degree of dependence or independence, in a world of potentially hostile kin and neighbors.[32] It was here that legal documentation tended to insert itself into local matters of hierarchy and dignity. It was similarly through such litigation that provincial subjects might begin to imagine law as *emerging from* local systems of documentation. This law, however, would never simply emerge autonomously: it would need the voices of provincial subjects to help bring it to life.

We might take as an example the protracted litigation of a woman named Gaia. The case is interesting, in large part because we learn about it not through official documents, but through a personal

[31] Ando 2020. [32] See the excellent discussion of Kantor et al. 2017.

letter. As such, it reveals what we might take to be evidence of the ways that law was imagined to operate at a local level, and by the choices of litigants, rather than simply in obedience to some dictate by the imperial state.

Writing to someone who was presumably her relative in Oxyrhynchus, Gaia detailed her struggles at various courts in Alexandria in order "to receive the interest on her grant (*charitos*) of maintenance." This was either a sort of gift (*donatio*) or usufruct of the interest from an endowed fund (or rents from land that such a fund had been set aside to purchase) that would offer her an income. If she was at the margins, such a grant might enable her to live in dignity; if she was better off (as we might suspect), it might have still been substantial enough to justify her efforts, to say nothing of having symbolic importance.[33] Though she does not explain precisely who was withholding this income from her, one might reasonably suspect that such a gift was tied to family. Similar gifts came as part of a dowry; Gaia's might have come as part of an inheritance.[34] Whatever the case, the identity of her opponent(s) would surely have been obvious to the recipients of her letter.

In her letter, Gaia details a process whereby, in order to receive her money, she initially approached the provincial governor, Heracleitus; he subscribed her petition, and his subscription likely enabled her to pursue her case by instructing a subordinate official to hear it. With the subscription in hand, she approached an official named Agrippa. Agrippa, however, ruled unfavorably. Infuriated, Gaia insisted that this was a "lawless judgment" (ἄ̣ν̣ο̣μ̣ο̣ν̣ ἀπόφασιν). Undeterred, she approached the governor on appeal (at that moment L. Valerius Datus), and the governor sent the case back to Agrippa. Under pressure from the governor, he agreed to hear the case again. But he was hardly happy about it, and, it seems, he began to stall. Accordingly, Gaia brought a further appeal to the incoming governor, Julius Basilianus. To this, she attached "the order criticized by Agrippa and

33 *P.Oxy.* XLIII 3094 (c. AD 215–18). Cf. *P.Oxy.* VI 899 (AD 200), the petition of Apollinarion asking to be released from the mandatory cultivation of lands. Like Gaia's petition, it too is a complex mélange of earlier documentation made to secure a right. Apollinarion's petition demonstrates that such modes of using documentation were not a post-AD 212 phenomenon.

34 Gifts in general: Taubenschlag 1955: 399–401.

other orders and the whole of the petition to Heracleitus and the subscription and the petition to Agrippa, complaining that he had delivered a judgment contrary to the laws (*para tous nomous*)."[35] (She also blamed her lawyer for what she perceived to be his incompetence.) Basilianus conceded that Gaia was on the side of right, and he returned her petition with the order, "exercise your rights" (*tois nomimois...chreisasthai*). In theory, this was a clear victory for Gaia; she, however, felt that his order was ambiguous (*amphiloxōs*), so she petitioned him once again, to ensure that the governor intended her to use the rights conferred by the original subscription of Heracleitus. Again, he agreed. Finally satisfied, Gaia wrote to her friends or family to detail the intricacies of her case, and to inform them of her victory. Whether the decision would ever be enforced would be an entirely separate matter.

What are we to make of this case, with its dogged protagonist willing to sacrifice vast amounts of time pursuing her case in Alexandria (or, alternatively, a shrill and disingenuous protagonist with a potentially weak case engaged in gamesmanship)? To begin with, she was hardly alone. Numerous letters, preserved on papyrus, attest to litigants awaiting the governor, normally at Alexandria, as they pursued litigation against their local enemies, neighbors, and families.[36] Gaia may have been more dogged than most, or the stakes here might have been especially high. Either way, she was hardly far outside of the norm.

Nor should we be surprised by the responsiveness of state officials in cases regarding these transactions. Making certain that all property was properly accounted for – ending up in the right hands – was a central preoccupation of government. Were funds to get lost or wrongly assigned in the course of normal transactions or (in particular) in the process of intergenerational wealth transfers, they would be hard to pin down later when it came to assessing

[35] Ll. 18.24, trans. eds.

[36] A partial list, drawn just from two major collections, would include: *P.Mich.* VIII 493 (AD II); *P.Mich.* VIII 507 (AD II/III); *P.Oxy.* II 294 (AD 22); *P.Oxy.* VII 1070 (AD III); *P.Oxy.* VIII 1158 (AD III); *P.Oxy.* VIII 1160 (AD III–IV); *P.Oxy.* XII 1479 (I BC); *P.Oxy.* XXXI 2597 (AD III–IV); *P.Oxy.* LV 3813 (AD III–IV); *P.Oxy.* LV 3820 (c. AD 340); *P.Oxy.* LVI 3855 (AD 280–81); *P.Oxy.* LIX 3992 (AD II); *P.Oxy.* LXXIII 4960 (AD II); *P.Oxy.* LXXV 5062 (AD III).

people's various fiscal burdens. Hence, no fewer than three governors were ready to handle Gaia's claims. We know not, however, why Agrippa, whatever his position, was keen to have the matter quashed or delayed. Perhaps he was simply uninterested. But we ought not to forget the chronological parameters of the case: the litigation dates to shortly after the universal grant of citizenship in AD 212. It may well be that the grant (*charis*) whose interest was set aside to maintain Gaia took something of an unusual form, and the status of that form under Roman law might have raised questions. Either way, the assiduousness of governors in protecting Gaia's rights is noteworthy, especially at a time when pre-existing legal arrangements might be imagined to have been placed in jeopardy by a (potentially) radical act of imperial intervention.

We should similarly notice how important documentation is for Gaia and how intently she fixates on it to advance her various claims. At the core of these acts of paper pushing sits an understanding of legality, one not unique to her. Whatever the nature of the "grant" that Gaia sought to have enforced, she was insistent that no fewer than three governors assent to her claims. The fact that the first governor, Heracleides, had assented, she imagined – or rather, she insisted – justified a *particular* outcome at the court of Agrippa; any deviation from that outcome is, in her telling, "lawless." It seems to have mattered little that, by Gaia's own admission, the form of the governor's subscription was vague.[37] Perhaps a better sense of her tenacity can be gained from the subsequent interactions. Having received a second subscription from the governor Basilianus, she judged it ambiguous and asked for and received a third subscription specifying precisely which rights she was able to use. We should remember, in this context, that only a very small number of litigants, and normally only those of elevated status, might expect to receive so much attention from the chief executives of the province. We should also note that in each of these cases – and certainly in the final two – the governor surely thought the matter closed with the mere fact of his subscription. But each subscription led to further petitions, negotiations, and clarifications – further dialogue, and further documentation. Subscriptions,

[37] On the problems posed by this form of subscription, see Foti-Talamanca 1979: 218–32.

which on one theory operated to *settle* matters of law, were in practice *invitations* to further exchange; what might, on one theory, constitute a definitive ruling, on another theory produced an *entanglement* – a relationship between two parties going forward.[38]

While preternaturally tenacious (or merely a nudnik), Gaia did not differ substantially from the great majority of litigants in the Roman world. How, then, might we explain the results of her complaints? We might begin with a "state-centered" or positivist explanation. On this line of reasoning, the governor simply ensures that *pre-existing* rights are being enforced. As a general matter, Roman government permitted particular subjects or citizens a broad package of property rights. When others obstructed them, it was the job of the state to make sure that the rights previously vested in particular subjects were preserved. In the rare cases where two rights were in conflict, the job of the state was to decide which party's rights prevailed, and to what extent. The job of imperial subjects, on such a theory, was to find a right, and tailor their presentation of "the facts" of the case such that it fit squarely within its boundaries.[39]

On such an understanding, the status of subjects operates in a clearly defined way, with clearly delineated capacities, rights, and obligations attached to each particular status. The empire was as a whole characterized by a bewilderingly complex system of grants of right that might be attached to a specific community, city, or individual. The system was so convoluted that emperors had to employ freedmen to oversee, define, and operationalize the various perquisites that had been given to subjects over the years.[40] Rights might even be extended to the inhabitants of the empire as a whole. The emperor Caracalla, for instance, imagined that he was doing precisely this when, in AD 212, he gave Roman citizenship to the entire free population of the empire. But more often they took the form of highly localized grants to individuals and communities. They could similarly take the form of highly localized impositions of *disabilities*, such as when one city or community fell out of imperial favor, or a particular individual committed some sort of prohibited act.

38 I take inspiration here from the work of Dietler 2005.

39 On the nature of these fact/law distinctions among the Roman jurists, see Cornu Thénard 2020.

40 Scarano-Ussani 1981.

On such an account, the business of governing entailed determining the status of particular subjects, determining whether they held a specific right by general or personal grant, and then holding them responsible for their respective obligations while protecting their particular rights.[41] Backstopping these arrangements was the system of documentation outlined above. The role of subjects, in turn, was to understand the nature of their status, and thus to become *conscious* of law's requirements or to be held *liable* for acts of boundary crossing. (Note that in such an account of law, consciousness is treated as a simple binary: one either is or is not conscious of a particular right or requirement. I shall return to this.)

But this state-centered account is inadequate, and not only for the reasons that I outlined in the Introduction (i.e., that such claims about state-centered power are more reflective of the ideology or aspiration of rule than they are an empirical description of it, and that to confuse the two is to commit an ontological error). Such a theory of state-centered legal order gives an inadequate description of Gaia's own actions. If Gaia inhabited a world where legal order was constituted by a straightforward process of linking "the facts" (her grant of maintenance) to some pre-existing right, then why be unsatisfied with one positive answer from the governor? Why insist that, when the governor instructed her to "exercise [her] rights," that he should have to review a further petition to which Gaia appended "all of the foregoing, and asking him if he wanted me to make use of the subscription of Heracleitus"? That is, if it were the case that the state was merely recognizing her (pre-existing) rights, presumably this degree of specificity would be unwarranted, as would the obsessive copying and recopying of petitions, responses, and affiliated documentation.

One might rescue the "state-centered" account by offering some possible responses. Perhaps Gaia was paranoid or compulsive, and, soured by a set of bad experiences at the court of Agrippa, she insisted on overdoing things by demanding subscription after subscription – by engaging, that is, in a sort of hyper-compliance.[42] Basilianus, irritated or bemused, might simply have signed to get rid of her, even temporarily. Perhaps the legal system, in her case, worked sub-optimally, leading her to insist upon specificity. After all, plenty of judges, bored or

41 E.g., Yiftach 2020. 42 Cf. Czajkowski 2020 on *P.Dura*.

irked by the parade of litigants before them, take personal umbrage at overly assertive plaintiffs. Sometimes a judge takes pleasure in screwing a party who irritates him personally, knowing that the consequences for the judge himself are normally minimal. Unless we fetishize state power, we are not entitled to assume that minor officials in the Roman provinces were necessarily decent or even competent people. We might finally remember that any litigation in Alexandria during the years of Gaia's case took place along a backdrop of political instability: not only might the grant of universal citizenship have complicated a range of pre-existing transactions, the emperor Caracalla himself appeared in the city in AD 215. An imperial visit is often a complex affair, but the visit of Caracalla to Alexandria was an unmitigated disaster, leading to a wholesale massacre of a large number of the city's residents, to say nothing of the punishment of provincial officials. Gaia's complaints came, one might say, at an interesting time. We might forgive her for being assiduous in the midst of such disruption.

Such diagnoses may well be accurate. But we should also attempt to take her rhetoric seriously. When she went to Heracleides and explained the fundamentals of her case, he offered her a subscription that allowed her certain forms of recourse. When she recopied her petition, his subscription, and the "lawless" judgment of Agrippa, she insisted that another governor decide upon the truth of her account and preserve her rights. When she went again, to Basilianus, and again attached a thick dossier of documentation, she asked not if the facts of her case fit the law, but whether when he said "exercise [your] rights" he meant the rights contained in the entire pile of documents upon which he wrote his subscription.

In other words, rather than a situation in which Gaia "fit" a set of facts to a pre-existing right, her rhetoric and her actions – the spectacle of paper-pushing, copying, and resending that she describes to the recipients of her letter – describe a collaborative process where subject and governor alike use writing to construe or establish a particular subject's rights. That is, the fact of a petition and the fact of a response is not just the evidence that pre-existing rights got recognized. *It is the process of acquiring rights itself.* On Gaia's account, her rights emerged first from private arrangements and then from direct encounters with imperial authorities – and from the assent, by those authorities, in writing, to the things that she claimed as hers. And here it is important that the process is described by Gaia not in a petition, but in a letter: she describes to an audience of private people, not public officials, a process in which she and the authorities *collaborated* in the creation of rights by using, and then producing, documentation about those rights.[43] Law, on such a theory, is generated precisely in these sorts of intimate encounters between petitioner, paper, and public power. To refuse to accede to the results of such a process – as she grumbled that Agrippa did in dismissing her case – was not just a failure to enforce a particular right, but rather illegality itself.

Once we are open to the possibility that Gaia's rhetoric is not just *reflective* of a law about which she is or is not conscious, but in fact *co-constitutive* of law itself, several important conclusions follow. First, the claim that the state establishes rights to which subjects bring facts collapses upon itself. On the provincial theory, the state no longer has a monopoly on lawmaking powers. It can of course grant or withhold rights, but it most commonly collaborates in determining them in the course of a dialogue with provincial subjects. Second, and consequentially, we must imagine that a far wider array of voices participated in the creation of legal orders in the provinces generally, by participating in the annual, and sometimes continuous, process of initiating lawsuits, making complaints against their neighbors, and lining up at the courts of the governor describing to him the rights that they thought they had. Third, we come much closer to an understanding of how it is that the number of rights attached to subjects might have expanded over the course of the first four centuries AD. At the heart of this story is also a story about documentation, and about archives. It is also a story of how provincial subjects learned to tell stories about how to interpret them to access the rights they imagined they deserved.

***

In Gaia's legal imaginary, her rights emerged as the governor assented to her various *narratives* about her right to an endowed fund, and from the *documentation* about the fund – including the documentation of the previous "illegal" judgment – that accompanied her

[43] For guidance in thinking through this problem, I thank Justin Richland. See further Richland 2008; Jacoby and Ochs 1995.

repeated petitions. In her case, Gaia herself generated a great deal of the relevant documentation. Some of this documentation would have been returned to her (in copies, so she could present the relevant subscriptions to anyone who challenged her rights). But it would also go on to be archived. And in creating such a paper trail, Gaia's legal acts created a documentary record that was available to public scrutiny.

The provincial archives not only operated as storehouses of various important "facts" about subjects who were governed (who they were, what they owned, what they mortgaged, what they owed), but also a vast record of the transactions they engaged in with both private parties and state officials. At times, of course, subjects generated this paperwork as they argued over the "facts" themselves. Thus, as governor of Pontus-Bithynia, Pliny wrote to Trajan regarding a case in which an individual's personal status came under scrutiny. Was it the case that a potential juror, Flavius Archippus, was disqualified because he was actually a criminal, condemned to the mines for forgery some quarter century ago, who had subsequently escaped his sentence? Or had he been freed from his sentence and had his status restored?

Parties on both sides brought documents to prove their cases: Archippus' accusers brought a copy of the original sentence. Archippus and his supporters brought the response of Domitian to a petition of Archippus's in which Domitian conferred upon him a *beneficium* of some 600,000 sesterces worth of land, a letter of Domitian recommending Archippus to a friend, edicts of Nerva proclaiming that Domitian's acts valid, and a decree of the people of Prusa in Archippus' favor. Yet Archippus could not produce any proof that his sentence had been revoked. Pliny thus wrote to Trajan for a ruling. Trajan admitted that it was possible that Archippus had managed to escape from prison and then mislead Domitian and others into granting him benefits, but concluded that it nonetheless seemed reasonable to presume that the sentence had been revoked – not least since some of the people granting Archippus honors would have been privy to the initial criminal sentence (and therefore would have presumably known not to give honors to a condemned criminal).[44]

[44] Plin. *Ep.* 10.58–60. On the problem of documenting the end of punishment, see Plin. *Ep.* 10.31. On the conflicts between Archippus and his community, see Kokkinia 2004a.

In the case of Archippus, two scenarios are possible. Either the archives themselves were faulty and for some reason could not establish that an otherwise important person had indeed had his sentence revoked. Or Archippus' local enemies were right – he had in fact escaped from prison, and after doing so, somehow convinced powerful people to grant him a series of honors. Both scenarios are plausible, and both speak to the ways seemingly stable questions of knowledge fundamental to the operation of the state (the status of a particular – and highly visible – person) might be decided not by reference to stable imperial categories backed by authoritative documentation, but on the basis of a set of rhetorical claims constructed to explain a pile of paperwork.

Were it the case that Archippus' sentence had been remitted, we might imagine that he would have clung tightly to any such documentation. After all, documents conferring status were copied, recopied, and registered with great frequency by the great bulk of the population, and sometimes even beautifully memorialized (like the many military diplomata given to discharged veterans that conferred upon them the status of Roman citizens, or the elegant bronze plaque recording the grant of Roman citizenship to a certain Julius of the Zegrenses and his family).[45] It may well be that Archippus' enemies were right: that he did escape from custody and managed to start building a documentary record that could potentially re-establish him as a citizen in good standing. (It might be worth remembering that Archippus was originally condemned for forgery.) Alternatively, even in otherwise functional documentary regimes things slip through the cracks, and in this case would have needed to be reconstructed through other sources that might inadvertently shed light on a question.[46] Finally, we might also note that, in the case of

[45] *Tabula Banasitana*: Seston and Euzennat 1961. Among the Egyptian elites, surely a great deal was learned about the power of archives to produce privileges during the process of *epikrisis*: Kruse 2013: esp. 324. Kruse 2013: 309 also reminds us that the process of *epikrisis* was similarly an occasion for celebration. Official document freeing someone from a sentence: *SB* I 4369 (AD 209); reproduced as Figure 3.2 below.

[46] Note, e.g., *P.Oxy.* XXII 2340 (AD 192), from Alexandria, where the status of a professional is unclear (either a weaver or a perfumer – the former would involve a liturgical exemption).

particular important documents, they were often *presumed* to exist in an archive, even if no one had actual access to them.[47]

Whatever the truth of the matter, we might note two things. First, in this case technically unrelated documents (i.e., a decree of Prusa in his favor) might be made to have force if they could be pressed into the service of a reasoned claim. Thus, while Archippus' enemies might have had the governor's original sentence, rhetoric allowed Archippus to bring proxy evidence to bear on the question of his status. Second, Archippus quoted not only a general edict of Nerva, but a section of a communication that Nerva sent to the former governor Tullius Justus that might bear upon his case. That is, documents from imperial archives were relevant to more than just the people whose personal or fiscal status they might have originally been intended to document. Just as Archippus manipulated documents relating to him personally to make a claim about his status, so too might documents related to other people be adapted by third parties and appropriated to their particular cases. Once the document was joined to the power to explain and convince, it could be pressed into the service of very different "facts."

The inhabitants of the eastern provinces were assiduous gatherers of documentation, and they adapted it to press their various claims. The documentary record of Egypt in particular preserves the traces of such document gathering. "Remember the man – you know who I'm talking about – in the archives," writes one letter writer, in the midst of reminding his addressee to send on some cheeses, "the man knows what you want in the archives. Search from year 1 of Alexander to year 9, and if you can get an endorsement from our other relatives you'll be right to do so."[48] These writers were hardly alone. "Legal sources" of all sorts – from imperial and gubernatorial edicts to reports of proceedings – were fervently sought in local archives, and at times in archives that were less than local.[49] As

47 E.g., Marc., 1 *Iud. Pub.*, Frg. 184 Lenel = *Dig.* 1.18.12: although no statute prohibits people branded with *infamia* from serving as assessors, there is nonetheless some imperial decree (*alio quoque decreto principali*) – that Marcian cannot find – that prohibits this.

48 *P.Mert.* II 85 (AD III). Cf. *P.Col.* X 252 (AD I).

49 E.g., *P.Oxy.* XVII 2104 (AD 222) is an edict of Severus Alexander to Bithynian Greeks prohibiting people from illegally forestalling appellants that made it into *commentarii*

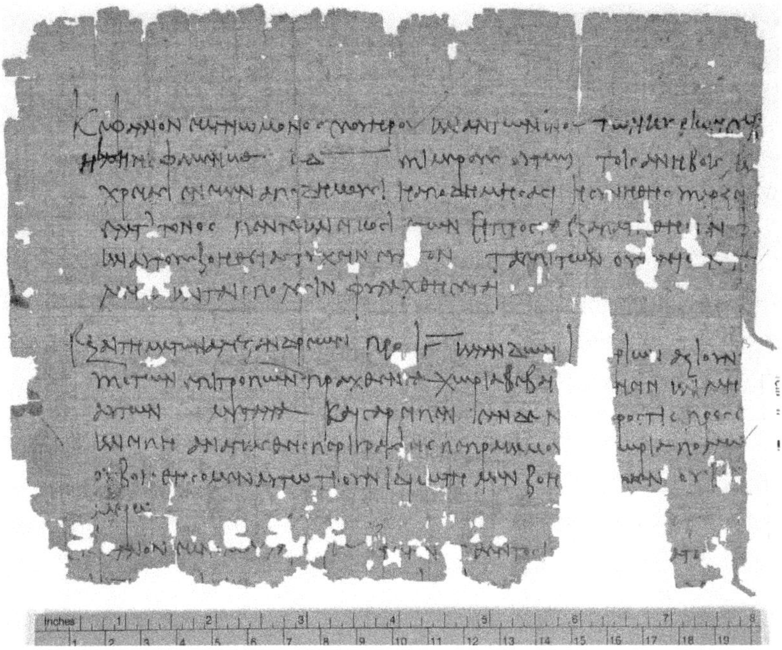

FIGURE 3.1 *P.Oxy.* LXIV 4435, Collection of rulings on the legal rights of minors, presumably from a private compilation. Courtesy of The Egypt Exploration Society.

in Archippus' case, these varied and various "legal compilations" were attached to a particular petition or submitted in support of a particular litigant's case. Thus, in many cases, we know the broader arguments that such authoritative documents were meant to support (I shall return to one such case presently). But it is worth noting that a large number of these case collections are simply acephalous – they exist simply as collections of legal sources without any accompanying complaint or case (for instance, Figure 3.1). It is tempting, of course, to imagine that they were specialized compilations, made by skilled attorneys, and to divine from their contents the broader question of import in a particular case.[50] If we were to engage in such an

of the governor, and also into *Digest* (49.1.25): on the process, see Kantor 2009: 256–58. van Minnen 2016 proposes an analogous process in the case of *P.Giss.* I 40.

50 In dealing with cases that concern reports of judicial proceedings, I owe a debt of gratitude to Anna Dolganov, who is endeavoring to collect and re-edit the entire body of such materials with the aid of a grant from the Austrian Research Foundation. I look forward to the final publication of this project's results.

exercise, we might note compilations that touch on issues like inheritance,[51] ownership and possession,[52] the legal status of soldiers and their marriages,[53] liturgies and privileges,[54] and civil procedure.[55] Such matters are central to a state concerned in particular with the exaction of resources. Still other collections defy easy description.[56] What is more, documents that appear at first glance "official" may in fact be private copies as well. There is reason to suspect, for instance, that a great many texts preserving edicts of governors and emperors were private in nature.[57] Without question, a great many such texts that are preserved epigraphically were inscribed on initiative of a local community; what is more, the papyri that seem to be the original or official versions of edicts are marked by a degree of elaboration and care that is lacking in most other papyri that contain edicts (see Figure 3.2).[58] Finally, we might also note that, at a broad level, provincial documents seem keen to conform, at least outwardly, to what subjects imagined to be legally "required" for their documents to be efficacious.[59] In brief, the extant material from Egypt, at least, provides us with a granular view of a vast economy of documentation and with evidence that provincial subjects engaged it at the level of both content and symbol.

But even without knowing the context of a great many of these discrete acts of legal engagement, the behavior itself is indicative of a broader horizon of provincial expectations. To begin with, we should

51 *BGU* I 361 (post AD 184); *P.Oxy.* XLII 3015 (AD II).

52 *P.Stras.* I 22 = *M.Chr.* 374 (AD III).

53 *P.Catt.* recto = *M.Chr.* 372 (AD II); *P.Harr.* II 202 (AD III), edicts on marriage rights of veterans.

54 *P.Phil.* I 1 (AD 103–24); *SB* VI 9040 (AD II); *PSI* IV 293 (AD III); *P.Oxy.* XLII 3018 (AD III).

55 *P.Hamb.* I 29 (post AD 94); *PSI* IV 281 (AD II).

56 *P.Oxy.* XXXVI 2757 (post AD 79); *P.Oxy.* XVII 2111 (c. AD 135), copies of judicial proceedings, written in a literary hand; *BGU* IV 1085–86 (post AD 170); *P.Amh.* II 63 = *M.Chr.* 376 (AD 200); *P.Amh.* II 65 = *SB* VI 9050 (AD II); *BGU* II 628 r = *Ch.L.Ant.* X 415 = *M.Chr.* 371 (AD II–III).

57 E.g., *P.Mich.* IX 522 (AD 142–43); *P.Oxy.* LXIV 4435 (formerly *P.Oxy.* VII 1020) (AD 198–201), two rescripts of Severus concerning *restitutio in integrum*; *P.Oxy.* VIII 1100 (AD 206), private copy of edict of Subatianus Aquila; *P.Oxy.* VIII 1155 (AD 104), private letter in which the author forwards the recipient the text of a governor's edict. Citations of governor's edicts more generally: Haensch 1992: 298–306. On accuracy, Eich 2009.

58 *SB* I 4639 (AD 209); *P.Oxy.* L 3577 (AD 342).

59 See esp. Cotton 1993; Meyer 2004; Czajkowski 2020.

FIGURE 3.2 *SB* I 4639 (AD 209), a document in a calligraphic hand freeing someone from a sentence to the mines, accompanied by additional writing documenting bureaucratic processes. Staatliche Museen zu Berlin – Ägyptisches Museum und Papyrussammlung, Inv. No. P 11532. Photo: Berliner Papyrusdatenbank.

not rule out the possibility that any particular group of "legal" texts might have been compiled simply out of interest, or in anticipation of a case that had not yet arisen. That is, while some of this activity of compiling is surely the work of skilled experts, we have no grounds to conclude that *all* of it was. Just as literary texts that engaged legal themes circulated among a comparatively wide readership in the Roman East (see the following chapters), so too did legal documents. We would do well to remember, in this context, that a great deal of knowledge about law and about the operation of courts emerged simply by the fact that the *conventus* was by design a public affair.[60] People arrived from all around to complain, but also to watch their

[60] E.g., Dio Chrys. *Or.* 35.15–17, trans. Cohoon, LCL: "And what is more, the courts are in session every other year in Celaenae, and they bring together an unnumbered throng of people – litigants, jurymen, orators, governors, attendants, slaves, pimps, muleteers, hucksters, harlots, and artisans ... So it is, you see, that the business of courts is deemed of the highest importance toward a city's strength and all men are interested in that as in nothing else."

FIGURE 3.3 Military diploma conferring citizenship and rights on discharged veteran Dasmenus Azalus, c. AD 149. Metropolitan Museum of Art.

neighbors make their cases, using their (or their lawyers') finest rhetoric. Audiences in Egypt in particular would have watched the *epikriseis* (the formal selection/confirmation process) of the "better" classes of the towns and metropoleis, or perhaps of priests or veterans, wherein their families submitted copies of authoritative documents to secure their positions. Others would have watched guilds of Dionysiac artists secure their rights by making similar presentations of documents, or observed discharged Roman veterans presenting their handsome military diplomata to guarantee their rights as citizens (Figure 3.3).[61] That is, given the amount of public legal activity that structured the everyday patterns of life in a provincial town or

[61] Dionysiac artists: e.g., *P.Oxy.* XXVII 2475 (AD 289).

city, it should not be surprising to think that any provincial subject who was competent in Greek and moderately literate might take an interest in law – and especially so if that meant securing his or her rights against a neighbor or irritating family member.[62]

This genre of legal engagement has a remarkable chronology: it begins in earnest in the first century AD and continues well into the third if not the fourth centuries AD.[63] That is, this particular manner of interacting with legal texts is an effect of empire and a part of a provincial legal culture that, though ultimately *caused* by state action, nonetheless came to operate *independently* from state-based determinations of personal status. This is true even with respect to the massive reclassification of nearly all the empire's subjects by the universal grant of Roman citizenship in AD 212. The grant of citizenship did not change the culture of gathering and using documentation to obtain rights. It was not a significant chronological horizon for legal practice, in the sense that it does not seem to have changed the behaviors or expectations of provincial litigants in any meaningful way. It simply encouraged subjects (and now citizens) to attempt to claim more privileges on their own behalf. As such, state action, even along what is potentially the most meaningful axis of legal belonging (personal status) was capable of being encompassed within this local system of rights claims. We are far indeed from an account of provincial law wherein the state determines legal status, and provincial subjects make attempts to fit "facts" to "law."

Egypt may provide the best evidence at the granular level, but the pattern is broadly eastern provincial. The papers of Babatha, for instance, from the province of Arabia, are similarly marked by a deep engagement with law and its documents.[64] But the pattern extends beyond individual acts of collation to the behavior of whole cities and communities. Thus in the middle of the third century, the city of Aphrodisias in Caria repurposed a wall by decorating it with a series of inscriptions attesting to the privileges of the city (Figure 3.4). These

62 For a comparative study of the ways in which knowledge of law might emerge from participating in public fora, see Edwards 2011.

63 For possible changes in record-keeping in the middle of the first century AD that might have a causal relationship to the development of provincial legal culture, cf. Haensch 1992: 235–37.

64 Cotton 1993; Czajkowski 2017.

FIGURE 3.4 Section of the Aphrodisias "archive wall." New York University Excavations at Aphrodisias (M. Roueché).

ranged from a *senatus consultum* of the first century BC, letters of various emperors, and subscriptions to petitions. Crucially, in at least one case, the subscription was not directed to Aphrodisias itself, but to Smyrna, denying to the Smyrnaeans privileges that were given to Aphrodisias. It is hardly clear how the Aphrodisians got their hands on such a document, but they enjoyed their possession of it mightily and were happy to display it.[65]

Still, perhaps the most remarkable example of such archival endeavors does come from Egypt: the massive petition of Dionysia, dating to AD 186. This remarkable text – no fewer than eight whole columns (of which three remain unpublished due to poor preservation) – represents the final stage of Dionysia's lengthy conflict with her father, Chairemon, a member of the local elite of the town of Oxyrhynchus. In a dispute of this length, and one so amply documented, we can see how provincial subjects managed to combine legal documents and rhetoric to make claims of right. At the heart of their strategies were claims about law as something ideally generated by the forms of discourse that emerged from explaining the documentary record to those in positions of power.

The petition also introduces a series of issues that will be explored in greater depth in the chapters to follow. Two things, in particular, deserve attention. First, from Dionysia's petition we begin to get an account of *logos* – speech, but also reason. As we shall see, this was a hugely loaded word, and communities in the provinces struggled fiercely over its meaning. Claims that certain actions and interpretations were in accordance with *logos* – in accordance, that is, with rational principles – suffuse the evidentiary record. In Dionysia's case (and others besides), the struggle over *logos* was also a struggle not just over the reasonableness of claims but struggles over *whose* speech is deemed authoritative – hence its double meaning. Second, and in that context, Dionysia's petition reminds us that, in these struggles over whose speech was to "count," provincial litigation could easily lead to socially disruptive outcomes. That is, litigation, in this case between an elite father and his disobedient daughter, might undermine

[65] The relevant sources are collected with commentary in Reynolds 1982. On the "archive wall" at Aphrodisias in the context of similar collections of imperial documents, see Ando 2000: 94–95; Kokkinia 2015–16.

the sorts of social and familial hierarchies that the Roman state otherwise sought to preserve. Combined with the authority of archival documents, claims about *logos* might emerge as a powerful tool of the subaltern against the dominant.

As in all family disputes, the true origins of Dionysia's family drama are impossible to reconstruct. The fight came to center on the question of property that Dionysia had inherited from her mother. Dionysia claimed this property was hers, since, she claims, she was given it as part of her dowry. Chairemon similarly asserted a claim over it: he had a usufruct in it and had mortgaged it to another man.[66] When she and her father locked horns over this piece of property, he tried to force her to divorce her husband in order to reclaim her dowry, bring her back under his control, and extinguish her claims. Dionysia and her husband, Horion, vigorously objected.[67]

The legal issues raised by this petition are interesting and important but have largely been dealt with elsewhere.[68] I should like to focus, in what follows, on the ways the litigants construct their claims on the basis of documents and interactions with representatives of the Roman state. There are three aspects of her petition – three phases of her dispute with her father – that deserve attention. First, a series of contracts that Dionysia and Chairemon made at an earlier phase of her dispute, as part of an attempt to mediate their disagreements over the possession of the property, and the litigation that followed; second, Chairemon's attempt to void these agreements by introducing a petition accusing Dionysia and her husband of using violence against him, such that he could, as a consequence, terminate her marriage; and third, Dionysia's citation, in response to Chairemon's petition, of a series of records of proceedings in her petition against her father (the case for which she prepared the extant document). In all three of

66 Dolganov 2019: 52 plausibly suggests that this "mortgage" might actually have been a covert sale: Chairemon does not seem to have had any interest in paying back the loan that "his" property secured.

67 *P.Oxy.* II 237.

68 In general, Yiftach-Firanko 2003; on Dionysia's legal claims specifically, see (with further bibliography) Dolganov 2019. I find her account persuasive, and in her willingness to revisit foundational questions her treatment of the petition should set the parameters for future investigation. A future publication (in progress) by José Luis Alonso and Jakub Urbanik promises to shed further light on the papyrus and the associated dispute.

these moments, the relationship between father, daughter, and state institutions was mediated by appeals to a documentary record. In this case, as in the others, the documentary record was more than the static *reflection* of legal arrangements. It was rather a constitutive element in deciding how, precisely, litigants imagined that law ought to be made to conform to and build upon local claims. In this respect, I hope to show, a documentary archive is not simply a repository of facts to be respected, it is also *a repository of arguments to be made*.

We begin with the contracts. As the relationship between Dionysia and Chairemon fell apart, over the course of a set of exasperating negotiations the parties made a series of contracts – three, it seems – dealing with responsibility for her mother's property and with the consequences of Chairemon's borrowing against said property.[69] The contracts (*homologia*, *homologēma*), on Dionysia's understanding of the case, were significant: because they were recorded in the city's archives, not only did they represent evidence in favor of Dionysia's case, but, because Chairemon had agreed to them too, they represented a shared truth – literally, a common *logos* – within a strained relationship. These truths were guaranteed by institutions, being deposited in the town record office.

The importance of these contracts to the structure of Dionysia's relationship to Chairemon comes fully to the fore when, despite the various agreements, the case entered litigation. When their contractual arrangements fell apart, Chairemon initiated litigation by a petition to the governor, Longaeus Rufus. In Dionysia's opinion, this failure to abide by the prior agreements was a remarkable act of chutzpah; the only basis for his complaint, she maintained, was a lie.[70] Accordingly, she counter-sued in the governor's court, attaching not only the most recent contract she had made with her father, but also (as "the best sorts of precedents" – *kallistoi*[*s*] *para*[*deig*]*mas*[*i*]) an order of the former governor Sulpicius Similus regarding marital property and an order of the former governor Mettius Rufus concerning the requirements for registering real property.[71]

69 Contracts: ὁμολόγημα: iv.6, iv.13, iv.26, iv.36, v.11; ὁμολογία: iv.33; ὁμολογοῦντα: iv.15. Exasperating: πάλιν: iv.12, 13, 26, 31.

70 iv.34: τ̣ε̣τ̣ο̣λ̣μηκέναι̣ αὐτῷ γράψαι τὴν ἐπιστολὴν πάν[τα] τὰ ἐ̣ν̣ τῷ πράγματι ἐψευσμένον.

71 Similis' order circulated fairly widely among litigants: *P.Mert.* III 101 contains a copy, and *P.Iand.* VII 145 makes a reference to it.

Dionysia had made the right move: through her countersuit, she convinced the governor to restrict the case to an investigation of the series of contracts made between her and her father. Rufus subscribed her petition, wrote to the local *strategos* (the chief executive of the *nomos*, essentially an administrative subdivision of the province), and instructed him to see to the affair and to forward the complaint back to him if there were issues that could not be solved at the local level. The strategos then held a hearing with both Dionysia and Chairemon present. Though caution is necessary because the papyrus is fragmentary, an important detail is concealed in Dionysia's narrative (v.8-16):

> Having received this subscription I delivered the petition in year 26 in the month of Thoth in the presence of my father Chairemon, asking the strategos to write a request to the record-keepers, and having them report to him all the details of the ... of my father ... of the agreements and reports made in common between us over time ... to not be any impediment to the inquiry now taking place by him according to ... He, being present at the reading of the petition, fell silent (*esiōpēsen*) before the tribunal, capable of saying nothing in reply ... because of the truth of the things that were written in the petition. Accordingly, the strategos followed the order of the governor precisely, not allowing the inquiry to be into anything other than the report of the record-keepers.

Though the papyrus is fragmentary, several details are noteworthy. First, though Chairemon had initiated the litigation, it was Dionysia who managed to get the governor's reply to the strategos first. Accordingly, Chairemon was brought to the strategos' court for a preliminary hearing, one that would answer the question of the scope of the inquiry. Second, once both parties were present, the strategos read aloud Dionysia's petition and the governor's reply. This provoked an emotional reaction in Chairemon: language failed him, and he fell silent.

We should linger on this detail, as the politics of language and *logos* will feature prominently in chapters to come. The word *logos* is notoriously vague. *Logos* means *both* speech and reason – and it is undergirded by a strong presumption that they are the same. In the minds of imperial subjects, to speak was to expect to be understood, both linguistically but also logically and, when necessary, ethically. It was to insist that the realm of two individuals speaking to one another, under the sign of reason, was ideally walled off from a world of pushing and shoving – a world of violence. The distinction between language and violence was fundamental to subjects living in the Greek world, and it remains one of the most important and humane intellectual legacies of the era.

To move outside the shared language of agreement (contract, Greek *homologia*), according to Dionysia's rhetoric, is to exit the community of shared *logos*. The crossing of the boundary is indicated by the failure of language, and the shame and humiliation that come from having this language fail in the public sphere of litigation. A number of contemporary legal documents refer to "silence" (*siōpē*) and related words. Here "silence" occurs most often in the part of the petition that explicitly asks for justice: petitioners claim that they are unwilling to "be silent" about something that has happened, and that they need to speak up about an injustice. Thus, in a petition of the fourth century in which a man details a verbal attack on his wife, he claims that since it is "not possible to pass over in silence (*siōpēi paradidosthai*) the things said by her (*sc.* his wife's assailant) contrary to the laws ... I hand over to your excellency this petition."[72] Likewise, in describing a conflict over the ownership of a slave, a man claims that his mother, "not being able to be silent (*mē siōpē[sa]sē*) about this crime" sent a petition to the governor.[73] Furthermore, this particular usage of "to be silent" is restricted primarily to the Roman period.[74] It renders quite well a particularly Roman provincial understanding of legality and of the role of legal interactions in daily life: that law allows those within its ambit to speak, providing them a space for validating the truth of the claims written on their petitions.[75] There is also a corollary: that those who are outside of the law cannot.

72 *P.Flor.* III 309.5 (= *P.Lond.* III 983, AD IV).

73 *P.Oxy.* XII 1468.27–28 (AD 253). Similar usages: *CPR* XIV 48.13 (AD 506); *P.Ammon* II 47.5 (AD 348); *P.Berl.Frisk* 4.19 (AD IV/V); *P.Giss.Univ.* III 27.16–17 (personal letter, a refusal to be silent at a tribunal, AD III); *P.Mert.* II 92.18 (AD 324); *SB* XX 15036.31 (AD II–III). Possibly connected is *P.Mil.Vogl.* VI 287 (AD II), part of a trial transcript.

74 Only two Ptolemaic uses are extant, one too fragmentary to render sense (*P.Köln* X 412), the other part of an official letter (*P.Dryton* I 33).

75 Cf. Bryen 2016b: 21. There are earlier if imperfect parallels from the world of high rhetoric in Athens: Montiglio 2000.

Dionysia's usage of *siōpē* to describe her father's affective state thus makes more sense. Chairemon cannot muster a reply, it seems (though here caution is necessary because of the poor preservation of the text), because of "the truth of what is written in the petition."[76] In accepting and subscribing her petition rather than his, the governor, she claims, assents to and authorizes her account of the truth. This truth is contained in the contracts that have been deposited in the public archives. Any attempt to reach beyond these contracts is therefore something that will not be accepted as legally speakable in court.[77] That Chairemon unwillingly assents to this truth as well is evidenced by his silence.

Dionysia's language is revealing of a set of deeply embedded assumptions in the broader provincial world. She is not just stating a fact (that Chairemon could not muster language); she is describing what would have been read as a terrible experience for her father. The tribunal was a high-stakes place. Officials – even local officials – determined one's well-being and did so in a public place in which one was judged by the persuasive elegance of one's speech. To stand there and be *dumb-founded* – without speech, incapable of articulation – was deeply humiliating, but also the embodied consequence of his failure to keep his word. Again, the text is fragmentary, but this line of reasoning would seem to be confirmed a few lines below: Chairemon tries to get in a last word, but in vain: all he can do is mutter to himself (*pros heauton legein*), because he is aware that his own agreements have undermined his case.[78]

We might draw two conclusions from this preliminary legal battle. First, the struggle between competing litigants is not only over what is legally "correct," in the contemporary lawyer's sense of the term, but also over who can use argument to animate the documentary record in such a way as to avoid finding oneself speechless. Second, to speak through and about legally valid documents can provide a means of binding or neutralizing a powerful opponent. In this case, it can even bind Dionysia's own father – a man especially threatening because of his privileged status, his gender, and his long

[76] πρ̣ὸ̣ς ἀ̣[ληθ]ῆ̣ ὄντα τὰ τῷ̣ βιβλιδίῳ̣ ἐνγεγραμμένα.

[77] On the importance of official archives in determining legal truths, see Ando 2020.

[78] v.25: τὸν δὲ πατέρα μηδὲν ἕτερον ἢ πρὸς ἑαυτὸν λέγειν καὶ τὰ ἑαυτ̣ο̣ῦ̣ [γρ]ά̣μ̣μ̣ατα πα̣ν̣[…].

history of having already dominated her. Legal documents, on this reading, are more than just a tool, or a framework, or a set of facts *about* Dionysia but ultimately external to her. Instead, they offer her a means of exposing who sits within a shared community of legality. Only those firmly within this community have the means to speak – only they possess the power of *logos*.

Dionysia's victory came by generating moments of collaborative writing: with the reports from the record keepers in hand, Dionysia wrote again to the governor, asking him to write again to the strategos, to affirm her property rights and to allow no further action on the case. This he did, and Dionysia sent it along to the strategos. The *strategos*, in turn, wrote Chairemon, instructing him to "keep quiet" (*hēsychian agein*) and not to further irritate (*enochlein*) the governor or to threaten Dionysia.[79] If this was a contest over who got to speak authoritatively about a problem, Dionysia had won.

* * *

Having lost the first stage of the dispute, Chairemon changed strategies. He claimed that Dionysia sought to attack him and harm his property at the behest of her husband, Horion. As a result of this behavior, Chairemon sought to force Dionysia to divorce her husband and return to his house. Accordingly, he sent off a petition to a subsequent governor, Faustianus, which Dionysia quotes:[80]

> Lord Governor, my daughter, Dionysia, has, at the instigation of her husband, Horion, often treated me impiously (*asebōs*) and illegally (*paranomōs*). Accordingly, I sent a letter to his excellency Longaeus Rufus, asking that I be able to lawfully take back what I had given her, thinking that by doing this she would stop her violence against me. He wrote to the strategos of the nomos on Pachon 27 of year 25, appending copies of what I had written, so that he (the strategos) would examine them and do what is fitting. Therefore, Lord, since through her rebelliousness she continues her violence against me, I ask, since the law gives me the power – and I attach below the section of it so you can see it – to take her, even if she is unwilling, from her husband's house, and that no harm come to me at the hands of Horion or his agents, since they continually threaten it. I have attached below a few of the many (relevant) cases, for your information.

[79] vi.3–4. [80] vi.13–20.

FIGURE 3.5 *Phthoneros* choking himself. Terra cotta from Egypt (British Museum).

Dionysia was furious. As to the facts alleged by Chairemon, "he could produce no act of violence nor any other wrongdoing against him for which he could blame me." To the extent that Dionysia has accurately copied his petition, she seems to be right. Egyptian litigants tended to be exquisitely precise about how they had been injured, while Chairemon's specific accusations are vague in the extreme.[81] His accusations, she alleged, came from envy (*phthonōi*) – that dark impulse that made one hate another for her happiness and success. They were also slanderous abuse (*loidoroumenos*).

These were strong words. Verbal abuse (*loidoria*) is a category of speech whose speaking is prohibited or punishable. The envious (*phthoneroi*) are normally depicted as choking on their own hate (as in Figure 3.5).[82] That is, Dionysia describes Chairemon's petition as being built out of language that was *unspeakable* in both a literal and an institutional sense. As for the complaints about her husband, they were yet more "worthless."[83] To write such a petition was to "mutilate" (*ēkrōtēriasen*) all of the salient facts of the case and to shamelessly attempt to deceive (*planēsai*) the governor himself.[84] Quite apart from such vague accusations of misbehavior, was the case not closed? Upon what ground could Chairemon ignore the extensive litigation that had just recently concluded?

[81] vi.20–22. Cf. Bryen 2013. [82] Dunbabin and Dickie 1983.

[83] The editors of the papyrus print καινότερον ("strange"), but given an analogous iotacism in vii.36, it may also be read as κενότερον, "more worthless, empty, without substance."

[84] vi.7–8.

Dionysia's proposed answer to this question is telling. To write such a petition, Chairemon had to "silence" (*siōpēsas*) "the letter of Rufus and the circumstances under which he wrote it, and my complaint, and the subscription of Rufus, and the inquiry of the strategos, and the testimony of the record-keepers, and the letter written to you by the strategos concerning these things, and the subscription which was given by you, lord, at my request, as well as the letters to the record-keepers about this."[85] Here "to silence" takes the active sense, and a proper translation into English would be "to suppress" or "to disregard." It is relevant that the Greek word is the same one she uses to describe Chairemon's affective state in the hearing before the strategos. On Dionysia's reading, such speech is illegitimate not only because it ignores the many times that governors and local officials had assented to her claims, but also because it is only *her* claims, arguments, and reasons that can provide the proper interpretive framework for making sense of the archival evidence that *does* exist. As for Chairemon's claims that the law will back him up in his complaint – and he did attach sections of it – "not even Rufus considered them comparable precedents."[86]

To defeat Chairemon's efforts, Dionysia argued that they were based in the so-called "Law of the Egyptians" – that is, that they were nothing more than appeals to a local but defective legal tradition.[87] To counter his claims, she copied into her petition a series of "precedents" – decisions in earlier cases that, she insists, prove that, if there was such a law permitting fathers to take daughters away from their husbands, Roman governors had long since overruled it in a number of instances. We shall turn to her use of precedent presently, but to fully understand it we should begin with a fuller understanding of Chairemon's legal strategy. What was he hoping to achieve by citing what Dionysia calls, the "Law of the Egyptians"?

There is reason to think that Chairemon and Dionysia were at odds not only over the proper structure of their relationships, but over their concepts of what anchored legality more broadly. The appeal to customary law is at the heart of this divergence. Historians of law tend to think of customary law, at least in imperial encounters, as something that is fundamentally continuous throughout

[85] vi.8–11. [86] vi.26. [87] Dolganov 2019.

time. Yet there is something unmistakably new about the references to the "Law of the Egyptians" that start to emerge in the second century – so much so that some historians have posited that Roman authorities engaged in a massive – or at least deliberate – project of codification of local rules, especially regarding family and personal law.[88] That is, though we may see few references to the "Egyptian law" in the papyri of the first century, we ought nonetheless to presume that people were living according to a more or less uniform set of principles of verification, contract, dowry, and so forth. This is in some sense surely true, and it would have been sustained by a Roman tendency to respect, to the degree possible, preexisting and functional local arrangements and practices. But it is nonetheless worth asking why, at a certain point in time, *ideas* of customary law – rather than just customary law itself – get reintroduced into a conversation with authority.

The evidence permits no certainties, but several clues emerge. The second century is the age of Gaius, the age when Roman jurists begin to think systematically about the connection between natural and civil law, and the connection between people, citizenships, and bodies of law, systematically expressed. The pithiest summary of this principle is found in the opening of Gaius' *Institutes*, written around 161 AD: "All peoples who are governed by laws and customs use law which is partly theirs alone and partly shared by all mankind. The law which each people makes for itself is special to itself. It is called civil law (*ius civile*), the law peculiar to that state."[89] In the world of Gaius, law is linked to the historical record and emerges from it. At the very least there seems to be a link between the "laws of the Egyptians" and this relatively new way of thinking about law that arises contemporaneously: law is linked to discrete peoples and "their" history *as discrete peoples*. The Egyptians are a discrete people. It follows that they must have had their own *ius civile*.[90] And if they did not, one must be found for them, and it must be agreeable to a community of powerful local actors like Dionysia's father.

88 Taubenschlag 1955: 6–7; Yiftach-Firanko 2009: 555. On the Greek roots of the "laws of the Egyptians," see Mélèze Modrzejewski 1988.

89 1.1.

90 Cf. the discussion of Julianus (84 *Dig.* = *Dig.* 1.3.32.1), well-analyzed by Alonso 2013: 379–86.

The pressure to create a body of "Egyptian" law likely came from below as well. Men like Chairemon were jealous of their prerogatives and wished to build for themselves space to act in ways that protected their power. In this respect, their interests aligned with Roman juristic thinking to produce a remarkable harvest of legal creativity among provincial populations in recopying, commenting upon, and in some cases monumentalizing pre-Roman artifacts of law. Thus, from second century Egypt we see not just claims about the "Law of the Egyptians" but also the recopying of – and perhaps the first attempt at translating – a massive, third century BC legal code.[91] In the city of Gortyn on the island of Crete (itself a provincial capital) a fifth century BC law code (the so-called "Great Code") was re-erected sometime between the first century BC and the first century AD. The massive inscription was written in an archaic phase of the Greek language possibly no longer comprehensible in Gortyn, and furthermore, it was written in a nonstandard hand that alternated between writing right-to-left and left-to-right, prescribing monetary penalties in a denomination no longer current at that time.[92] Finally, a series of late antique sources claim that in Athens, the emperor Hadrian revised and restored the archaic laws of Draco and Solon. (Such claims were, of course, baloney.) Nonetheless, Hadrian was credited in Athens and elsewhere with being a "lawgiver" (*nomothetēs*), and there is ample evidence that he did revise a number of Athenian laws. It would not be hard to imagine that, as a point of local pride, the Athenians might envision themselves as living under a freshly revised version of their very own ancient constitution.[93]

The second century thus marks a significant horizon in Roman and provincial thinking about law and its relation to local history and custom. This might have important practical consequences in structuring

[91] *P.Oxy.* XLVI 3285 (AD II). The editors argue that the original translation was Ptolemaic, and this document represents a recopying of the Ptolemaic version. This is possible, yet the argument for a Ptolemaic original is based on extremely slender evidence (that the papyrus uses αὑτοῦ instead of ἑαυτοῦ in some places, and that the usage of the former dies off in the first century BC). *P.Fay.* 22 = *M.Chr.* 291 might represent a similar case. Cf. also *P.Oxy.* LXXVI 5096 + 5098 (AD I), a collection of Ptolemaic laws on the recto, and the speech of an advocate on the verso. A non-Egyptian parallel might be *P.Dura.* 12 (AD 225–50), possibly a recopying of a Hellenistic inheritance law.

[92] Note also the second century reinscription of the Pergamene Astynomic law (*OGIS* 483, with commentary and discussion in Saba 2013).

[93] Cortés-Copete 2018: 110–15.

the relationships between Roman governors and local men of importance like Chairemon. It is one thing for governors to monopolize the right to issue edicts and decide who gets to make rulings on cases. This is the privilege of rulers, and no matter how cruel or unjust a particular ruling may have been, the legal system would still have been in a constant state of development. But coping with this sort of system is made in key respects easier when governors could also be counted on to respect and support an "official" and static body of local law, authoritatively interpreted by local intermediaries who represented powerful constituencies. Governors themselves (and the emperors to whom they were ultimately responsible) might also be relieved at the prospect of not having to continually renegotiate basic categories of family and property law. To the extent that they might imagine the law of a particular community as being static, rather than developing, the task of extraction would become more regular.

Such, at least, might be the desired outcome of a system of local law. But there were countervailing forces. At a certain level, it is not clear that Roman administrators were ever completely comfortable with this new tendency, not least because local intermediaries could not always be trusted (see further Chapters 8 and 9). Here a certain vulnerability in the system is exposed, one through which we can explain the interest in precedent by a woman like Dionysia. Her use of precedent emerges as a reaction to a larger movement in the second century to place and keep people within discrete ethnic frameworks, and to prevent them from accessing Roman justice and Roman courts. When she cited her precedents, her strategy was directed at just the sort of high-ranking local person who began, in the late first and early second centuries, to articulate a claim to knowing the "right" interpretations of law and tradition at imperial behest. The citation of precedents deliberately marginalized the appeal to custom and customary law – precisely the sorts of justification capable of being manipulated by powerful local actors. Precedent, as it emerged through the manipulation of documentary artifacts, was a firmer justification than tradition, and one capable of protecting structurally weaker parties like Dionysia.[94]

[94] The legal salience of precedent has generated a substantial bibliography. See, inter alia, Katzoff 1972; Anagnostou-Canas 2004; Metzger 2004. Alonso 2013 proposes a broader theory, but his attention to the category of "binding" is important more generally.

Precedent could thus serve as an important resource for the weak when facing off against the strong.

Dionysia cites four precedents, each a case in which governors and others had overruled fathers in their attempts to remove daughters from their marriages: a decision rendered by the governor Flavius Titianus; a decision of the *epistrategos* (regional sub-governor) Paconius Felix; a decision of the *iuridicus*, Umbrius; and an opinion of a legal expert (*nomikos*), Ulpius Dionysodorus, concerning the consequences of particular local forms of marriage. She further attaches two governor's edicts and a further extract from a trial, as well as a memorandum. To review the contribution each one makes to her rhetorical and legal strategy would take us far afield, but it is worth taking a single example:[95]

Extract from the minutes of Paconius Felix, epistrategos. Year 18 of the deified Hadrian, Phaophi 17, at the court in the upper division of the Sebennyte nome, in the case of Phlauesis, son of Ammounis, in the presence of his daughter Taeichekis, again Heron son of Petaesis. Isidorus, advocate for Phlauesis, said that the plaintiff therefore, wishing to take away his daughter who was living with the defendant, had recently brought an action against him before the *epistrategos* and the case had been deferred in order that the law of the Egyptians might be read. Severus and Heliodorus, advocates (for Heron), replied that the late governor Titianus heard a similar plea advanced by Egyptian parties, and that his judgment was not in accordance with the inhumanity of the law but with the choice of the daughter, whether she wished to remain with her husband. Paconius Felix said, "Let the law be read." When it had been read Paconius Felix said, "Read also the minutes of Titianus." Severus the advocate having read: "Year 12 of Hadrian Caesar the Lord, Pauni 8, etc.," Paconius Felix said, "In accordance with the decision of his highness Titianus, they shall find out from the woman," and he ordered that she should be asked through an interpreter what was her choice. On her replying, "To remain with my husband," Paconius Felix ordered that the judgment should be entered on the minutes.

There are several layers to this extract. The case in question, which took place before the *epistrategos*, refers to a still earlier case, this one taking place six years earlier at the court of the governor Titianus. Titianus' decision was juxtaposed, by the advocates for the husband, to the law of the Egyptians. All were stacked together with additional

[95] vii.29–38, trans. Rowlandson 1998.

precedents to support Dionysia's arguments. This complex stacking of stories contains a theory of law: its origins are not in timeless traditions connected to a particular people, such as "Egyptians." Instead, law consists of a historically generated body of rules, based on dialogue, and emerging from archival sources.

These secondary uses of documents, like the "casebooks" discussed earlier, represent an active relationship between individuals and the world of documentation that claimed to know them. Litigants like Dionysia (or Gaia) constructed their arguments through a process of bricolage, which assembled past instances to articulate the outlines of a specific claim. They were an invitation to discuss in court, an invitation to the governor or the judge not only to confirm the value of previous decisions, but to confirm them with additional language that itself will come to make new law. By inviting the presiding magistrate to offer judgment, more law emerged; the more law that emerged, the more it was understood clearly by petitioner and magistrate alike that legal traditions are alive and shifting, that history is a guide to the present and future. Tradition, by contrast, represented only one point of view, and not a particularly useable one at that.[96]

***

We should finally ask, what account of legal and political being underwrites these claims about the importance of documents? How might we characterize the relationship of a person like Dionysia – and many others besides – to the state that governed her? We would do well to be cautious here. Accounts of legal being nearly always work from static categories – for example, if one is a citizen of Rome (static category), one has, for example, the right to marry and pass property to one's children, or the obligation, for example, to pay a certain tax on receiving an inheritance. Such an account thus presumes a fullness of legal being – one either is or is not a Roman citizen, and the relationship of a person to her status is presumably total and all-encompassing. Such accounts, moreover, have tended to smuggle

[96] Cf. *P.Oxy.* LXXVII 5111 (AD II–III), the attempt of a group of temple personnel to have an imperial procurator confirm the privileges they hold as an "ancient custom." However, it seems that such a custom had already been overruled in court, leaving the temple staff to scurry towards a different official in hopes of reinstatement. The text is, unfortunately, fragmentary.

in claims about other forms not just of being but also of *belonging*: to inhabit a certain legal category is to subjectively *feel* oneself a part of a particular community.[97] Such an account of legal being undoubtedly works well for certain populations in the provinces – not least among which were communities of Roman citizens themselves.[98] It is also an account of political being: it sees the world as composed primarily of *communities of peoples*, each possessing a discrete history and some internal coherence that enabled them to operate *as* communities – that is, to govern themselves internally, as best as they might wish.

But such an account does little to explain the strategies of someone like Dionysia. Her strategy before the governor relied upon rhetoric, performance, and the creation of interpretive strategies that allowed her to speak through authoritative documentation. It relied on a theory of *logos*, shared by all who agreed to participate in legal community. Yet in contrast to Chairemon's claims, it also operated on a theory of *shared living traditions*. Dionysia was not in a static relationship to a pre-determined category of legal belonging. She was rather seeking to cultivate an evolving relationship with agents of the state. Her rights were not guaranteed; they were instead contingent and operationalized when she asked to exercise them personally. The documents that she mustered in support of her desired legal outcome evoked a historical relationship to the law that was continually emerging.

At the core of Dionysia's strategies was also a theory of political *subjecthood*. Provincial subjects knew their places. They were inscribed in an imperial hierarchy, and accepting that basic fact of subordination – with its attendant obligations to hand over things they deemed valuable and to obey imperial requirements to make themselves known to the state – was part of a larger bargain well known from other contexts: the trade of obedience for protection.[99] But subjecthood is a useful term because, unlike legal "status," it also evokes an ongoing *relationship* of dependence. As with all such relationships, the particular rights that a dependent could negotiate for him or herself would necessarily ebb and flow, depending on the

97 Sherwin-White 1972, 1973. For fuller discussion, see Bryen 2021a.
98 See esp. Lavan 2021 on such communities.
99 See the helpful overview of Muller 2017.

temper of the dominant partner and the persuasiveness of the dominated. But subjects also knew two other things: that they were not slaves, and that they were not barbarians. That is, though they may have had fewer rights than a privileged caste of imperial masters, or even than a number of their neighbors, they nonetheless could not be exploited at will. Emperors promised as much, both explicitly and implicitly, and governors repeated these promises.[100] Provincial populations sought to protect their persons and property accordingly – not just from exploitative fathers, but from neighbors and agents of the state as well.[101] The end result of this process of arguing for the preservation of one's personal security was the cultivation of a particularly imperial form of belonging.

Though structurally weaker, provincial subjects had a sense of rights, or at least a set of provisional but testable hypotheses about what they deserved.[102] However, the rights themselves do not simply and unproblematically flow from a given legal status. We might venture to say, instead, that these rights were imagined to be *quasi-contractual*: they attached to subjects to the extent to which subjects could use the documentary record of empire as the basis for a rhetoric of desert. The acceptance of provincial claims about how best to interpret and operationalize the rights potentially latent in the archives created a relationship between subject and governor that would emerge historically, as various micro-rights, given as *beneficia* by powerful patrons, came to be respected as part of legitimate government.[103]

There is a final element to this understanding of subjecthood. At its heart sits the belief that, should the right documents be found, and the right rhetoric developed, then both governors and fellow subjects ought to feel obligated to accept the claims of a subject, since such claims are anchored in human rationality, or *logos*.[104] We have seen, in the petition of Dionysia, that her emphasis on rationality (*logos*)

[100] Explicit promises: *SB* XII 11012 = Oliver 1989: no. 39 (letter of Nero?); *PSI* V 445 (edict of Mamertinus).

[101] E.g., *P.Bacch.* 19.11–17 (AD 171), reporting official abuse from a dyke inspector; *BGU* I 45 (AD 203), interpersonal violence; *PSI* IV 292 (AD III), invoking imperial law to keep his body "free from violence and abuse"; *SB* XX 14401 (AD 147).

[102] Welch 2019.

[103] I thank Sam Erman for the phrase "micro-rights."

[104] Ando 2000.

sits at the heart of her initial complaint against her father. We have similarly seen, in the letter of Gaia, that failure of a subordinate official to follow the subscription of the governor is understood as simple illegality. This language of *logos* penetrated deeply into provincial society. Thus, we hear one man complain to another about the collection of taxes, presumably in contemplation of formal action, "don't you know that they have illegally exacted money, and that they have violated the rights of our people? This is completely without reason!" (*ouk estin eulogon*).[105] In another case a man complained that he was nominated for a liturgy "not according to reason" (*ouk ana logōn*).[106]

This vocabulary of reasonableness eventually spread, and reached relatively far down the social scale: thus a group of Phrygian peasants might, in the mid third century, complain to the emperor that "we are being extorted beyond even what is unreasonable (*para to alogon*) and are being shaken down by those who ought to be preserving the common good."[107] We even see the vocabulary of irrationality being reflected in the *answers* given to petitioners by emperors themselves. Thus Antoninus Pius, responding in Greek to a petition from a group of hunters, would insist, "It is completely unreasonable (*ouk estin eulogon*) for you to hunt on the property of other people!"[108] Similarly the emperor Pertinax might write, echoing the language of a petitioner: "Even if the number of one's children does not normally release fathers from all civic obligations, since you have demonstrated, in your petition, that you have *sixteen* children, it is not irrational (*ouk estin alogon*) for you to be allowed to be relieved from civic obligations and to be at leisure to rear your children."[109] As I shall demonstrate in what follows, a political struggle emerged, throughout the eastern world, over the nature of *logos* and its relation to legality. This struggle did not emerge *ex nihilo*, but rather from the attempts of litigants, in the civil courts in particular, to explain to governors the nature of their rights and their basis in the documentary record.

105 *P.Michael.* 26 (AD II). 106 *P.Oxy.* XII 1405 (early AD III?).

107 Hauken 1998: no. 6, ll.13–14. Cf. *TAM* V.1 419.

108 *Dig.* 8.3.16 = Callistratus, 3 *Cog.*, Frg. 15 Lenel.

109 *Dig.* 50.6.6.2 = Callistratus, 1 *Cog.*, Frg. 8 Lenel.

PART II

LAW AS DIALOGUE

4

Criminal Justice and the Challenge of *Logos*

In spite of its importance in structuring people's material lives, Roman civil justice was not something that tended to goad provincial subjects into a flood of discourse and comment. Roman criminal justice, by contrast, captured the provincial imagination. This was by design. The business of civil courts moved at a steady hum; the great mass of business was done on paper, involving lengthy waits and verdicts that were difficult to enforce. Criminal justice, by contrast, operated in public spaces, in face-to-face confrontations between the accused and the authorities, and with dramatic acquittals and convictions. Add to this the Roman taste for spectacular and gory public punishments, and it takes no stretch of the imagination to understand why the Romans put such emphasis on the practice of criminal justice as a technique of rule.[1] When subject populations came to tell stories about law more generally, it thus was criminal trials and punishments that they turned to for making sense of the nature of Roman rule, and of their relation to it.

The practice of criminal punishment was of particular importance to subjects not (or not only) because of the tremendous violence involved, but also because criminal trials staged dialogic encounters between ruler and ruled. The criminal court was a space where structurally unequal people might be forced to speak to one another and to construe one another as partners capable of mutual, rational understanding

[1] Coleman 1990; Shaw 2003.

structured by rules of law. This, at least, was the ideal. Whether there actually could be a rational search for mutual understanding, whether these encounters were capable of being framed by rules of law, whether the courts provided a space for more than simply venting imperial rage on provincial bodies – these were always open questions.

In asking these questions about criminal punishment, subject populations also raised a set of broader and more basic questions about the boundaries and legitimacy of imperial rule. For them, the scene of criminal punishment demanded some form of answer to the question, "what gives you the right to do this to me?".[2] In asking such a potentially politically fraught question, subjects might also make a corollary demand: that the person asking the question be given an answer *in the form of reasoned language* (rather than, as will become clear in what follows, through gesture or through violence).

This emphasis on reason and language – on *logos* – is key to unpacking these understandings of legality. We have already seen how *logos* raised questions of legality and responsibility in Dionysia's petition. The texts that structure this chapter build on Dionysia's account, emphasizing the importance of *logos* in guiding provincial and imperial legal practice and channeling imperial violence. In making these arguments, provincial populations echoed a key ideological claim of the Roman state itself: that it operated in accordance with rational principles.[3] But provincial subjects went further than official Roman ideology. They raised *logos* to a central test of Roman state action, contrasting it both to violence, and to a category of acts that they indict as being *irrational* (*alogon*). In other words, the practice of criminal law – and the provincial texts that reflect upon it – introduce us to a *politics* of language and reason by asking a series of questions about *logos*: Who has it? Who should have it? What responsibilities does it entail? And what ought its force to be in a legal encounter? We shall see, in chapters that follow, that the struggle over *logos* was hardly restricted to discussions of criminal law. It came to inform all sorts of attempts to understand oneself in relation to legality, administration, or even domination more broadly.

[2] Williams 2005: 1–17 calls this a "basic legitimation demand." See also Walzer 1987, or in a different vein, Tilly 2006.

[3] Ando 2000.

Provincial subjects raised these questions continually, often coming to different answers. The texts that record these various answers were written in conversation with one another, as populations throughout the provinces struggled to define the boundaries and content of imperial law and imperial authority more broadly. What we see when we analyze these stories, then, are not just foundational myths about (or critiques of) criminal justice per se, but a genre of political theory in narrative form.[4] That is, though these texts are telling stories of the punishment of "criminals," and sometimes preserve important details about the operation of provincial courts, the purpose of telling these stories was to reflect on what their respective authors took to be the foundations of legitimate acts of power. These stories seek to describe what legitimate state violence *should* look like, and what the relationship of that violence ought to be to provincial claims.

Additionally, the interest in these dialogic moments – these episodes of confrontation between ruler and ruled – may have originated in attempts to explain criminal law and practices of punishment, but it soon was adapted to think through other elements of provincial life. Specifically, *logos* and dialogue came to be important not just to *individual* interactions between a subject and his government; they also developed into a system of ethical and political axioms that might be adapted to understand relations of hierarchy within the empire more broadly. "What gives you the right to do this to me?" is a question that, once asked in the context of a confrontation in a provincial courtroom, can quickly be adapted to situations far beyond it. In a pluralistic empire, this question is often asked in light of the relationships between one community and its neighbors: "What gives you the right to do this to me, *but not to them*? Why are we treated as different or less honorable than others?" What is more, the shape of the question means that the person asking it can occupy many roles: he can be a provincial subject, but he can also be a slave. The question

[4] I just note here that claims about "the end of dialogue" in antiquity (Goldhill 2008) strike me as unpersuasive, even on the basis of the evidence assembled in that volume. Apart from not engaging the sorts of evidence laid out in this chapter and the next, the framework laid out by Goldhill tends to obfuscate the distinction between dialogue per se and dialogue as a literary form, leading to confusion about the relationship between dialogue and the character of political institutions. For additional objections to these sorts of claims, see Cameron 2014, and more generally Lim 1995. For an attempt to engage a similar question through the perspective of Talmud, see Boyarin 2009.

can be asked of a governor or an emperor, but it can also be asked of anyone who insists upon the right to dominate another. Simply to ask the question was to insist that the roles that people played were not natural; they required justification.

***

To recast an act of punishment was a political act. It was an attempt to transform a *Gestalt* of images, assumptions, flesh, blood, and screams into something essentially apprehensible – something with a narrative arc that interpreted events by locating them in time and space, allocating praise, blame, and responsibility. To make a particular act of punishment "make sense" meant that one was required to discover an underlying logic, something which could be submitted to the judgment of reason – and be deemed, if necessary, unreasonable. We thus might distinguish between what acts of punishment achieved or sought to achieve, and the subsequent attempts at understanding provoked when a system that was thought to be stable or obvious was declared not to be so.[5] And while Roman administrators might have been successful in reducing audiences in the moment into exclamations of approval or disapproval, they exerted no such control over subsequent attempts at interpretation.

We might begin with a series of texts that were produced and circulated in Christian communities, the "Acts of the Martyrs" (martyr – from the Greek *martys*, or "witness," being an inherently legalistic category). Among these, the *Martyrdom of Polycarp* might be singled out for its engagement with questions of legal procedure. The text, a letter from the church of Smyrna to the church of Philomelium in Phrygia, describes the events connected to an outbreak of anti-Christian sentiment in Smyrna in the mid-150s AD. The date of the text's composition is harder to pin down: it was certainly written before the early fourth century, when it was epitomized by Eusebius in his *Ecclesiastical History*, but more specificity is impossible.[6]

[5] See Daniel-Hughes and Kotrosits 2020.

[6] In general, Bowersock 1995. On the dating of the early *acta*, see esp. Barnes 1968b. On the legal rhetoric of the martyrs, see Liebs 2002. On Polycarp, Dehandschutter 1993; Hartog 2013: 165–203. Moss 2010 proposes a relatively late date for the text; her arguments are intriguing but not decisive. Moss 2013 makes a persuasive case that there is no evidence that *Polycarp* was read until the third century.

The text begins by noting a pattern of persecution emerging in Smyrna, culminating, at least initially, in the execution of some Christians in the amphitheater. These Christians had initially been interrogated and forced to swear oaths to the emperor, refused, and were put to death after being publicly tortured. Others, the text claims, volunteered themselves for martyrdom, but then recanted when placed under pressure. Still, these rituals of death or defeat only served to whet the appetite of the assembled crowd, who, eager to purge their city of "atheists" (*atheous*), demanded the arrest of the elderly Bishop Polycarp. Polycarp was quickly hunted down by armed guards who delivered him to the local eirenarch (an official in charge of local security). The eirenarch in turn brought him to the city stadium to be interrogated by the proconsul. The stadium was packed with an angry crowd eager to see the old man square off with the governor.

At stake legally was whether Polycarp would swear by the *tychē* or *genius* of the emperor. But the text is equally concerned with the dynamics between the governor, the accused, and the crowd (described as "lawless pagans" – *anomōn ethnōn* – assisted by Smyrna's Jewish population). Read against the grain, one might conceive of their interactions as enacting a scenario that was likely relatively common in the provinces: a source of social dysfunction is identified by the populace as a whole, who pressures the governor to act; the governor then indulges their desire for vengeance and purification.[7] Governors, especially in long-pacified provinces, would have little in the way of abilities to placate a mob genuinely bent on violence. The author of *Polycarp* is of course unsympathetic to the governor's predicament in controlling the mob. To paint his acts as illegitimate, it focuses on his relationship to the crowd, and through that, on the question of trial procedure more generally:[8]

> But the proconsul persisted, and again said to Polycarp: "Swear by the emperor's genius." Polycarp responded: "If you are deceived into thinking

[7] Angry mobs: *Mart. Pionii* 7.1; Apul. *Met.* 10.6. Compare the permission given by Flaccus to the Alexandrians allowing them to plunder the houses of their Jewish neighbors: Phil. *Flacc.* 54, discussed further below. It does seem that there was a tendency, in moments of rage or panic, to converge upon the theater. Cf. Acts 19:29; Phlegon, *Mir.* 1.14, on a ghost-sighting.

[8] *Mart. Polycarpi* 10. Text from Rebillard 2017.

that I will swear by the emperor's genius, then you pretend not to know me, and who I am. So listen while I speak freely (*meta parrhēsias*). I am a Christian. If you wish to learn the rationale (*logon*) of Christianity, set aside a day and listen." The proconsul said: "Persuade the people (*peison ton dēmon*)." But Polycarp said: "I thought that *you* were worthy of an account (*logou*) – for we have been taught to pay honor to the offices and powers set up by god, provided they do not harm us. I do not think that *those* people [i.e., the crowd] are worth our giving them a defense speech (*apologeisthai*).

The "trial" procedure in *Polycarp* is unusual, even by the standards of other texts. Normally there were hearings before local officials (such as eirenarchs), and then an additional set of hearings before the governor. In *Polycarp* there is only a brief conversation between the bishop and the eirenarch, one that takes place in the eirenarch's coach on the way to the stadium. Likewise, though there is a conversation between Polycarp and the governor, there is no "trial" per se: there is just the demand that Polycarp swear by the genius of the emperor. Whether this is an accurate portrayal of what happened in Smyrna is beside the point. The text is crafting the interaction as illegitimate by focusing on violations of procedure. Accordingly, Polycarp insists that the governor conduct a formal hearing ("set aside a day" – *dos hēmeran* – a translation of the Latin term, *diem dicere*). Though the governor alone would have been empowered to do such a thing, he instead chooses to forfeit his legitimacy by placing the decision in the hands of the assembled crowd – the *demos* – whom Polycarp must persuade if he is to have his chance at a trial.

Placing the decision of whether or not to have a trial in the hands of the crowd would have been in some ways a shrewd strategy on the governor's part. Though assemblies persisted in many Greek cities in this period, their *formal* powers were much constrained. Governors were free to overturn any legislative initiatives that struck them as problematic or repugnant, which meant, in practice, that few such initiatives were raised in assemblies in the first place. What is more, though the text refers to the crowd as the *dēmos* (the citizen body as a whole), assemblies did not have judicial powers in the first place. Though they could not try particular malefactors, their decisions could sometimes serve as de facto sentences (i.e., they could give or withdraw particular honors), or pass legislation within their ambit intended to punish individuals or classes of people.[9] Despite these formal disabilities, the governor might nonetheless find opportune moments to pay honor to the Hellenic tradition of self-government – and it might be especially useful to do so at moments when the populace was enraged. Forcing Polycarp to appeal to the crowd for the ability to make his case would thus have been politically useful. But this is precisely the problem: rather than hold a proper trial, with all due formalities, the governor simply lets the assembled people make the crucial decision. According to *Polycarp*, the governor instead should listen (*akoue*) and convene a formal hearing. Only in that context could Polycarp make a formal defense speech (an *apologia*).

But the text makes arguments that are substantive as well as procedural. It emphasizes that Polycarp is prepared to give an "account" or a "rationale" – a *logos* – of Christianity itself, but only to the governor. Still, even to claim that Christianity *had* a *logos* was, in the second century, rather bold. Pliny, for instance, seems to have thought quite the opposite: Christianity, he declared, was nothing more than "a depraved and extravagant superstition" – hardly the stuff of reason. Similar charges were made in the late second century by the pagan Celsus, who crafted a treatise (in the form of a dialogue) to prove that Jesus was a fraud: in fact, Celsus claimed, Jesus was a country bumpkin (from a village, rather than a proper *polis*), the

[9] On the continued legal productivity of councils and assemblies in the cities of the east more generally: Lewin 1995; Fernoux 2011; Kantor 2015; Ma 2024: esp. 348–53. The evidence of legislation is collected in Rhodes and Lewis 1997. There are odd exceptions to the rule that assemblies did not have judicial powers: thus, in Hadrian's oil law, the Athenian assembly could judge especially egregious cases of misappropriating oil (over the amount of 50 amphoras) "along with the council": *IG* II^2 1100 = *MARE* 90 = Oliver 1989: no. 92, ll. 47–50. Some sense of the ways that councils and assemblies might act as quasi-judicial organs can be found in the orations of Dio Chrysostom: *Or.* 31 (the Rhodians repeatedly vote to have statues of honorees taken down or reinscribed) – Dio insists (31.71) on the distinction between the assembly choosing to do this because it is parsimonious and a magistrate doing it because the honoree was found guilty of a crime; *Or.* 7 (the assembly in an unnamed Euboean city votes to punish the poor peasant who is the protagonist); cf. the fragmentary *Or.* 47, where Dio defends himself before the assembly on charges that his collaboration with a "wicked proconsul" resulted in people being tortured, banished, or put to death. Note also *Or.* 37, probably by the sophist Favorinus, who complains that the Corinthians ordered a statue of him removed "without a trial, and actually without any reason at all" (37.16). On legislation concerning the use of land (and in particular barring disfavored classes of people from owning land in a community) note the law of Gazoros (*SEG* XXX 568).

offspring of an adulterous liaison between a spinning woman and a Roman soldier, who then worked as a laborer in Egypt where he learned not the rational habits of a philosopher, but rather how to do magic. Christianity, in his view, was *anti-rational*. Accordingly, he proposed to correct such nonsense by writing a book entitled *The True Logos* (*alēthēs logos*).[10]

Logos was on the minds of Christians as well. (And on the minds of others – Christians were not in this respect unique.) We need not, in the present context, review the manifold claims made concerning the nature of *logos* in early Christian theology or its relationships with earlier philosophical traditions or Jewish traditions.[11] It will suffice to note that, in *Polycarp*, the proper venue for *logos* is the courtroom – that is, in a formally constituted setting in which accounts of truth and falsehood are hammered out by engaging in articulate speech. To beg an angry crowd is a different thing entirely.

To be sure, courtrooms might be imagined as venues that tend to be institutionally agnostic towards the sort of language that plaintiffs and defendants use. In many cases, it was simply expected that defendants would lie and deceive, and, if those strategies failed, beg forgiveness.[12] But *Polycarp* urges us in a different direction, if only to mark the contrast between what a trial is *supposed* to do, and the sort of popular justice that the governor was urging in Smyrna. Courts, in this text, were institutions to be classed among "the offices and powers set up by god" – institutions to which Christians agree "to pay honor." But not all offices or powers were deserving of honor, nor was it the case that, because an institution was constructed by a person with formal power, it was thereby worthy of respect. In the present context, merely providing official sanction to a lynch mob did not thereby render it a legitimate extension of the governor's power. This, I take it, is the logic that underlies the condition that Christians

10 Plin. *Ep.*10.96.8: *nihil aliud inveni quam superstitionem pravam et immodicam*. On Celsus, Origen, *C. Cels.* 1.6, 27. On Celsus' status, Frede 1999: 147–48. In general, cf. Luc. *Per.* 13 (Christians accept doctrines and practices without any serious arguments for them).

11 On *logos* theology in Jewish contexts and its ultimate rejection by Rabbinic authorities, see Boyarin 2004. On *logos* in Justin Martyr and Philo, see Goodenough 1923: 139–69; Chadwick 1967. For the claim that Justin's theology of *logos* operates independently of pagan traditions, see Edwards 1995.

12 Cf. Cohen 1995: 107–9.

pay honor to the powers that God has set up provided that "they do not harm us."

Faced with such a challenge, the governor can only resort to violence: "I have wild beasts, and I will throw you to them, if you do not change your mind." With Polycarp unmoved by such threats, the governor additionally threatens to burn him alive. "Bring out what you want," Polycarp responds. The text thus moves a claim about law's potential as a way of providing space for provincial *logos*, to a duel pitting force against resistance. Two things are important to note here. First, the text does not begin with this sort of resistance, but rather holds up resistance as the correct response *only* when attempts to prove one's point through reason are ignored – or, put slightly differently, when it finally becomes clear that one party has reason, while the other party has only force. Second, it follows that acts of government are legitimate only to the extent that they might be anchored in a respect for *logos*. This does not preclude the use of violence. No one would seriously question the right of governors to punish. It means, rather, that the right to punish was, ideally, conditioned on the use of, and respect for, *logos*.

This claim is made explicit in Justin Martyr's *Second Apology*.[13] Purporting to tell its addressee about "the things that happened in your city yesterday and the day before" in the court of the prefect of the city, Quintus Lollius Urbicus, Justin goes on to tell the story of two Christians, Ptolemaios and Lucius, whom Urbicus had sentenced to death. The sentences, Justin explains, are emblematic of a larger problem, one "happening everywhere," where governors have "irrationally" (*alogōs*) condemned Christians to death.

Justin's specific complaint begins with domestic drama. An unnamed man and woman both lived "licentiously" together until the woman converted to Christianity. Her new religious orientation convinced her that it was "irreligious to sleep any longer with a man who tried, wrongly and against the law of nature, to make use of every opening for pleasure."[14] Accordingly, she eventually sent her

[13] For full discussion of the problematic relationship between the *First* and *Second Apologies*, see the recent edition of Minns and Parvis 2009, from whose text I work. On the imperial legal context of the work, see Cline 2016.

[14] 2 *Ap*. 2.4, trans. Minns and Parvis.

husband a notice of divorce. Enraged, the husband denounced her as a Christian. She prevailed in the legal wrangling, however, getting an imperial dispensation to delay the criminal proceedings while she got her financial affairs together (one imagines that, like Dionysia, this unnamed woman was of a rather high status). Finding himself stymied by his wife, the husband went after her "teacher in Christian doctrine," Ptolemaios. The husband connived to have Ptolemaios arrested by a centurion and thrown into prison. After a long while, Ptolemaios obtained a hearing before the city prefect, Urbicus, but it was perfunctory at best: Urbicus simply asked if he was a Christian, and Ptolemaios responded affirmatively; Urbicus immediately ordered him to be led away for execution. But this otherwise routine task was interrupted by a bystander:[15]

> When Urbicus ordered him to be led off to execution, a certain Lucius, who also happened to be a Christian, saw that the sentence had been so irrationally (*alogōs*) handed down, and said to Urbicus: "What is the charge (*aitia*)? Why did you punish this man here? He has not been proven to be a pimp or a prostitute or a murderer or a clothes-stealer, indeed, he hasn't been shown to have committed any wrongdoing at all – he just agrees that he calls himself a Christian. Urbicus, you judge him in a manner ill-befitting the pious emperor or his son the philosophical Caesar or the sacred senate." But Urbicus could offer no response to Lucius other than to say, "It seems to me that you're the same sort of person." Lucius responded, "Indeed I am," and Urbicus ordered him too to be led off to execution.

At stake in this interaction is the charge that Urbicus, and other governors besides, judge "irrationally." Following *Polycarp*, we might begin by noting that the judgment is "irrational" in the sense that the matter is fundamentally open-and-shut: Urbicus merely asks a question, receives an answer, and uses force – he does not make a formal charge (*aitia*). Ptolemaios was not so much given a trial as he was, in modern parlance, *processed*, and from there moved on, assembly-line style, to his execution. From the perspective of Urbicus (undoubtedly a busy man), Ptolemaios' guilt was obvious and so was the need to punish.

But Justin's account is richer than that of *Polycarp*. The intervention of Lucius operates to raise a set of questions about the substantive

[15] 2 *Ap*. 2.15–18.

law itself. If Ptolemaios was guilty, then guilty of what? Lucius rattles off what we might think of as classic charges in criminal law: immoral debasement of oneself or others (the Romans were not libertarians on this point), the violation of property, and the taking of life. The challenge, implicit in Lucius' complaint, is that the (comparatively recent) prohibition on Christianity cannot be squared with the existing body of criminal prohibitions.[16] One might go further: the prohibitions that Lucius details are fundamentally ancient and venerable prohibitions: prohibitions of these sorts were part of most if not all of the bodies of criminal law found throughout the ancient Mediterranean. One might consider them akin to a sort of natural law. At the very least they probably seemed intuitively obvious to most people. The prohibition on "being a Christian," whatever the legal form it took, was of relatively recent vintage. To the extent that it ought to count as a valid, "rational" prohibition, it must be able to fit within the structure of the older prohibitions. Christian apologists, Justin among them, argued vigorously that it did not. Romans, like Urbicus, of course disagreed. In a "rational" world, the matter would have to be settled through discourse, debate, and intersubjective understanding, rather than through the arbitrary violence of the strong.

If at one level irrationality is manifested both by the hurried nature of the hearing and by the inability to provide rational grounds for the prohibition on Christianity, it is compounded by the fact that Urbicus cannot provide Lucius a substantive answer: "He could offer no response" – other than to resort to violence. Though there is no evidence of any relationship between the *Martyrdom of Polycarp* and the *Second Apology*, the parallel is striking: just as the governor in *Polycarp* cannot muster a response to Polycarp's challenge and instead threatens him with beasts, so too Urbicus substitutes violence for reason, and in so doing, proves his actions illegitimate. A similar pattern may be discerned in a text from the western Empire, though one written in Greek and sent to the churches of Asia and Phrygia: the *Martyrs of Lyon*. In that text, a "distinguished" Christian, Vettius Epagathus, attempts to plead the case of the Christians before the governor, unable to tolerate the "irrational judgment given against

[16] On legislation, see Barnes 1968a.

them." Rather than listen to him, those surrounding the governor's dais shout him down, preferring violence to reason and dialogue.[17]

***

A conspicuous feature of these interactions in court is that they focused on moments where the persons in charge were dramatically shown that their violence was so little grounded in reason that they simply fell conspicuously silent. The silence of the violators was no innocent trope: in a world where the ability to articulate oneself distinguished the worthy from the debased, to fall silent in the face of criticism was to admit that there was, in fact, no *right* to punish – there was only the empirical fact of power, without any necessary relationship to legitimacy. As with so many fundamental truths, the power of both *logos* and violence were made manifest at a physical level – they both registered in the body. Their force was thus public and undeniable.[18] Like in the case of Chairemon (above, Chapter 3), the inability to speak – the inability to share in the register of *logos* – makes clear that one sits outside the community of those whom the law is designed to protect.

Perhaps the most elaborate exploration of these themes comes in the *Martyrdom of Pionius*. Written probably shortly after the death of Pionius in Smyrna in 250 AD, in the wake of the emperor Decius' edict of universal sacrifice, it chronicles the extensive pre-trial hearings among local officials and, eventually, the trial and execution of Pionius before the governor of Asia.[19] The author is unknown, but clearly has read other accounts of Christian martyrdom, the *Martyrdom of Polycarp* in particular. Like *Polycarp*, *Pionius* starts with distinctions between the demands of obedience to the dictates of the state, on the one hand, and the necessity of giving provincial defendants space to speak and to defend themselves on the other. From there it moves quickly into an episodic series of verbal duels where Pionius manages to get the better of a large cast of local elites.

The action begins with Pionius being summoned to give sacrifice at the temple of Nemesis, where the proceedings are presided over by

17 On the lack of relationships between the two texts, see Moss 2013. Vettius Epagathus: *Mart. Lyon* = Euseb. *HE* 5.4 (Rebillard 2017). See also Rivière 2004: 169–203.

18 On extemporaneous speaking as a marker of authority, see esp. Brown 1992: 35–70; Gleason 1995. On aphasia, Gleason 1999, 2001.

19 For *Mart. Pionii* I work from the text and commentary of Robert 1994.

Polemon the temple warden. The Christians approach having draped themselves in chains to remind the excited crowd that they were being forced, rather than persuaded to appear at the temple – a clever piece of political performance art. Confronted by Polemon, the discussion immediately turns to obedience, if not submission: the emperor has issued his edicts (*diatagmata*); will the Christians obey (*peistheisesthe*)? As in *Polycarp*, force is very much on the table: the expectation is that the Christians will obey authority like everyone else, or else be punished.[20] Unlike *Polycarp* or the *Second Apology*, however, in *Pionius* the accused gets to speak, and to speak extensively. When pushed by Polemon, he makes an extensive defense speech (*apelogēsato*) in a particularly bicultural idiom, citing Homer for the Greeks of Smyrna before launching into an anti-Semitic diatribe laced with biblical allusions for the Jews in the crowd. The assembled crowd and even the local officials themselves are astonished both by the content of Pionius' speech and by his audacity in giving it, and fall so silent (*hēsychian*) that no one makes a sound.[21] Once again, the truth of the righteous person's speech is so self-evident that it registers in the bodies of those who observe it.

The local officials then move Pionius into the center of the marketplace, where he meets his next set of interlocutors, a group of local lawyers or case-pleaders (*agoraiōn*).[22] In so doing, *Pionius* raises an issue that was only implicit in other texts: social status. As a provincial elite himself, Pionius is expected to respect the wishes of men of similar station and make a token gesture of obedience to prevent raising a fuss. To do otherwise would provoke the interference of the governor. It would also reveal to the assembled crowd that their supposed "betters" were punishable just as they were.[23] Accordingly, the lawyers appeal directly to his "virtue and distinguished character" (*ēthous ... kai epieikeias*). Such a discourse was deeply resonant among elites, but it was also a discourse based solely in affect, rather than reason. (I shall return, in Chapter 7, to the ideology of affect among elites.)

20 4.1. 21 5.1.

22 Robert 1994: 63 dismisses this translation, but the text frames the interaction with these *agoraioi* in the context of a series of interactions with other local elites; it would on this ground seem reasonable to accept the more specialized "case-lawyer" or "pleader" as preferable to the more general, "la foule, les habitués de l'Agora."

23 Potter 1993.

Pionius rejects this offer of elite bonhomie. But at least one of his interlocutors, Alexander, tries to bring him back into the fold. His attempt quickly unravels:[24]

"Listen to us, Pionius." Pionius replied, "You should try to listen to me, since I know the things that you know, while you are ignorant of the things that I understand." Wishing to mock him, Alexander asked him ironically, "What are these [sc. the chains] for?" Pionius said, "[We are wearing] them so that, as we walk through your city, we will not be suspected of having come to eat sacrificial meat, and so that you understand that we do not seek to be questioned, but have instead decided to go not to the temple of Nemesis but to go to the prison, and so that you do not drag us off by force, like you did with the others, but allow us simply to go, since we are already chained. And it is the case that with these chains you did not bring us to your temples." And thus Alexander was shut up (*ephimōthē*).

If these sorts of verbal duels are a contest of *logos*, then to be "shut up" is emphatically a loss. Alexander does not merely stop speaking, but is actively "stopped up" – *ephimōthē*, (from *phimos*, a muzzle for a dog or a cow). To "shut someone up" was not simply to verbally best them, but to do so with sharp elbows. Thus Jesus "shut up" the Sadducees when arguing with them about the nature of the resurrection; Lucian's Peregrinus, the cynical huckster, similarly "shuts up" those seeking to prosecute him for murder by shamelessly giving away money to his home community.[25]

Humiliated, Alexander makes a last-ditch effort: "What use to you are these words (*logōn*) of yours, when it is impossible for you to live?" It is both a threat and a pathetic admission. Alexander makes his living not just speaking, but from arguing cases in public – speaking, that is, in the name of the law. He is thus forced to concede that his profession operates essentially in bad faith. Rather than using language to check violence or even to divert it from himself and his clients, as a lawyer might claim, he must admit that in fact language only works as a complement to, or an extension of, raw power.[26] This is worse than merely acknowledging material reality. It operates

[24] 6.1–4. [25] Matthew 22:34; Luc. *Per.* 15.
[26] For this sort of claim made for the power of rhetoric, cf. Lib. *Or.* 1.2, trans. lightly modified from Norman, LCL: "My family was one of the greatest in a great city – in education, wealth, the provision of shows and games, and in the oratory which opposes itself to the power of governors" (λόγοις, ὅσοι φοραῖς ἀρχόντων ἀπαντῶσιν).

as an admission that those who pose as relatively independent local worthies are actually just faking it; they are just cogs in the imperial machine, and subordinated ones at that.

The humiliation of local authorities had an effect on the onlookers. Excited by this verbal combat, the assembled populace demanded that the proceedings be moved to the theater – to hold not just a hearing on whether the Christians will or will not sacrifice, but a proper assembly (*ekklēsian*). The prospect was terrifying to the local officials, and in particular, to the officials in charge of the city's food supply: they approached Polemon and urged him to get Pionius to stop talking, "lest they [the people] go into the theater and create a disturbance and a bread riot."[27] To head off the disturbance, Polemon urged Pionius merely to enter the temple of Nemesis – to make, that is, some sort of conciliatory gesture, even if its content is ambivalent. Such a strategy would have allowed all involved to save face and, in theory, prevent a more generalized riot where the populace ceased to defer to the authority of local leadership. Pionius naturally refused: "You have been ordered either to persuade us or to punish us: you're not persuading us, so punish us (*ou peitheis; kolaze*)."[28] This was a taunt. Knowing that these local worthies were powerless to punish, the authorities instead did precisely as required: they held a formal inquiry with an official scribe, and got Pionius on record as confessing that he was a Christian. Then they dragged him and his companions off, as violently as possible, to the prison (harming them "incidentally," rather than "punishing" them).

Even these improvised acts of violence did not manage to quell the public disturbance. The crowd became increasingly disorderly. Some insisted that the local officials punish Pionius (perhaps a jibe at the officials as well, since they were unable); others seemed interested in hearing more. Still others were perplexed that Pionius, previously

[27] 7.1: ἵνα μὴ … θόρυβος καὶ ἐπιζήτησις περὶ τοῦ ἄρτου γένηται. Robert 1994: 67 follows Jones 1990: 72 in translating "an enquiry about the bread," which is both correct and too literal. The assembled people were interested in an "enquiry" in the sense that the social disorder provoked by Pionius' undermining of local worthies now empowered them to complain about a subject dear to them; from the perspective of the local officials, this would have been most upsetting and probably would have invited the (unwelcome) attention of the governor.

[28] 8.1.

one of their distinguished fellow citizens, might act in such a fashion: "So much education, and yet he acts like this!" Others were merely confused at his failure to conform to his role as a leader: "But you starved alongside us!" (presumably a reference to a recent famine). Even in the prison "many pagans" approached Pionius and his companions, seeking to persuade them to sacrifice and save themselves, but when they hear the responses of the imprisoned Christians they were "astonished" (*ethaumazon*). Through his performances, Pionius undermined the ritual. Rather than punishment (or the threat thereof) producing social cohesion and orderly administration, the actions of the local officials undermined both.

The local officials tried again, this time changing the frame of the interactions: instead of trying to convince Pionius to avoid a full-scale legal proceeding, they threatened imperial judgment. Pionius responded legalistically. When asked again to obey the orders of the emperor, Pionius argued that "those put into prison should await the arrival of the governor – why are you infringing on his prerogatives?"[29] Finding themselves again exposed as powerless, the local officials resorted to a trick: Theophilus the hipparch (another high-status local official) told Pionius that the governor has ordered him transferred out of Smyrna to Ephesus. Pionius called his bluff: if the governor had really sent someone to do this, the person he sent is welcome to come and take him away. The ruse exposed, Theophilus burst into rage and wrapped his cloak (his *maphorion*, which he wore to display his office) around Pionius' neck and choked him until he could no longer breathe. The target was intentional: the battle is, in a sense, between force and reason. Just as Pionius has silenced others, so too do the local officials attempt to silence him. That they did so by force rather than by application of reason only proves the author's point about their legitimacy.

Even this failed to achieve the desired result: Pionius and his companions physically resisted being dragged to the temple of Nemesis and had to be carried by armed guards. Thrown before the altar in the temple, the dialogue changes character. No longer interested in convincing the Christians to sacrifice, the local officials now merely vent their anger. "Why won't you sacrifice?" asked Lepidus, whose

[29] 15.2.

position is not named but who clearly was of similarly high status. Given the standard Christian answer, Lepidus and the others mocked Pionius and cursed him. Pionius refused to take their bait, instead drawing attention to their violations: over their laughter he cried out, "respect piety, honor justice, recognize humanity, and follow your own laws (*nomois*): you punish us on the grounds that we do not obey, but you yourself are disobedient! You were ordered to punish us, not to violate us (*kolazein ekeleusthēte, ou biazesthai*)."[30]

Besides explicitly complaining about the lawless behavior of his tormentors, one might note the important assumption of the text about punishment: that it was, ideally, a law-governed activity, distinct from a mere orgy of violence wherein a vengeful sovereign vented his rage. Whereas Roman administrators were often content to vent their rage on those who were horrid or obstreperous (and local officials, to the extent that they were able, might imitate them to the extent they were permitted), those who perceived themselves as being in a position of subordination vis-à-vis state authority saw the matter with greater nuance. They distinguished punishment from mere violence, and allotted legitimacy to the former only on the condition that punishments conformed with a law that was rational and apprehensible to all involved.

The wrangling with local officials finishes with a final episode, where Pionius was confronted by Rufinus, "one of those considered to excel at rhetoric." Unlike a mere lawyer, a rhetorician was not merely a pleader of cases or a public speaker; he was, rather, a master of language who might be expected to represent the city in public, to communicate with officials or even emperors in Rome, and even to serve, periodically, in the various imperial bureaux devoted to communication. More shall be said about such men in Chapter 7. In this case, Pionius' interlocutor seems to have been a well-known individual: two men named Claudius Rufinus, probably father and son, are attested at Smyrna. The elder Rufinus even earned the approbation of Septimius Severus and Caracalla.[31] A man like Rufinus commanded a

30 16.6.

31 *MARE* 127 = Oliver 1989: no. 255, with discussion in Robert 1994: 96–97. On the importance of rhetoricians more generally, see Bowersock 1969; the relevant epigraphic evidence for rhetoricians and their careers is collected in Puech 2002. See now, in general, Janiszewski et al. 2015.

great deal of local respect, and, through his influence at the imperial court, could prove important to the city in times of need.

Unlike the others, Rufinus was imperious. He insisted that the nonsense come to an end:[32]

> "Stop being a fool, Pionius." Pionius said: "So this is your rhetoric? And these are your books? Socrates didn't suffer such things from the Athenians, but now everyone is an Anytus or a Meletus. Would you say that Socrates and Aristides and the others were fools when they practiced philosophy and justice and perseverance?" At this, Rufinus fell silent (*esiōpēsen*).

A lawyer, a temple warden, a hipparch, a rhetorician, and, of course, a mob: these were the faces of local authority, de iure or de facto. With each character, Pionius manages either to disabuse them of their pretensions to power through appeals to legality (Theophilus and Lepidus), or to astonish them into silence through his answers (Alexander, Rufinus, and the crowd). In each case he manages either the better argument, which his interlocutors acknowledge through their silence (in this case using identical language to the petition of Dionysia), or he provokes them into acts of violence that exceed their station. In so doing, Pionius dramatizes their inability to engage at the level of reason and dialogue.

***

These Christian texts emphasize the gap between violence and reason: in each case, the accused possesses reason, while those in charge possess only force. Those who possess the means of violence are, moreover, incapable of providing a rational explanation for the application of it, thus proving that they use it illegitimately. All of these texts thus accept that there *could* be a rational account of imperial violence – just not in the case of persecuting Christians. That is, they accept that the government was entitled to use violence *in particular circumstances* – but not in general or whenever a particular individual so chose.

Yet while this particular line of reasoning is on vivid display in these early Christian martyr acts, this is not an exclusively Christian discourse but a broadly *provincial* one. It emerged not because of a

[32] 17.1–4.

particular group's theology, but rather from the ways in which subordinated peoples perceived themselves – and whatever group they imagined themselves a part of – in relation to imperial power and authority. To put the matter slightly differently, these provincial ideologies about law emerged as an *effect* of power. Of course, the particular effects that perceptions of subordination had within particular groups were coded within particular local discourses, histories, theologies, and experiences – and as such it makes sense to group together Christian, Jewish, and Pagan accounts of the nature of law, punishment, and dialogue. But the broader focus should be on the provincial experience writ large.

While the focus of the early Christian martyr acts was on the ways that law structured the relationship between the state and the individual, other texts extend that reasoning to think of the courtroom, and its attendant practices of criminal punishment, as a space that could also mediate between the state and entire communities. This was true in two senses. First, that representatives of particular communities might find themselves negotiating their community's position vis-à-vis Rome in settings that functioned as criminal trials. But also, second, that the criminal trial might serve as a place in which the *relative* status of particular communities was negotiated. That is, some communities in the Roman world might have existed in a purely dyadic relationship to Rome, but in some other cases different communities lived side by side. In some cases, members of these communities imagined the courtroom as the ideal mode for settling questions of community priority – who, that is, was to be ranked higher than whom.[33]

***

We might in this context turn to two bodies of literature, one by the Alexandrian Jew, Philo, and the other, known as the *Acta Alexandrinorum*, a pagan literature preserved exclusively on papyrus.

[33] For the ways in which cities imagined ranking and hierarchy amongst themselves, see Robert 2007 [1977]; Lendon 1997: 76–77; Heller 2006. On communities within communities (with special reference to Roman citizens abroad), see Purcell 2005; Eberle 2014; Ramgopal 2016. Particularly in Egypt the various citizen statuses were imagined to be ranked: cf. Plin. *Ep.* 10.6–7. I look forward to the dissertation of Rafail Zoulis (Yale, in progress), which hopefully will take on the question of law and community relationships at a broader scale.

These two groups of sources share a common point of origin: the social tension that turned, eventually, into an anti-Jewish riot in Alexandria in AD 38. Mention has already been made of the events leading up to the riots: the visit of the Jewish Tetrarch, Agrippa, to Alexandria, which threatened to upset the balance of power between the city's Greek, Egyptian, and Jewish denizens, leading to the eruption of political protest among the Alexandrians, who mocked Jewish pretensions to sovereignty by dressing a local lunatic, Karabas, as a king and petitioning him in the gymnasium. Protest and mockery soon turned to violence, when mobs of Alexandrians and Egyptians assaulted the Jews (first with the indifference and then with the eventual support of the Roman provincial government).[34] In the wake of the violence of AD 38, though not because of it, the Roman governor of Egypt, Aulus Avilius Flaccus, was recalled by Gaius to Rome, tried, and exiled (then later executed). A further outbreak of violence in Alexandria followed, one that resulted in both the Alexandrian Greeks and Jews sending embassies to Rome. The Jews initially found an audience before Gaius, who in the meantime had begun plans for installing a giant statue of himself in the Jerusalem temple. The experience of the Alexandrian Jews under Flaccus, and the subsequent embassy to Gaius, are the subjects of Philo's two extant historical works. The Alexandrian Greeks likewise sent at least two embassies to Rome, one to Gaius and then a subsequent one to Claudius after a further outbreak of violence in Alexandria after the death of Gaius.[35] In these embassies the Alexandrians sought both to complain about the behavior of the Jews and to try to secure rights that they had lost under previous emperors. The experience of the ambassadors provided the initial impulse for the composition of the *Acta Alexandrinorum*, a highly fragmentary literature found exclusively on papyrus.

As one might expect with such conflicts, the details of "what actually happened" are confusing and contradictory.[36] I am less concerned with the actual historical details, but rather with the ways that these perceived acts of unfairness – and unfair punishment, in

[34] See Introduction, pages 21–24.

[35] Depending on which documents are reckoned as part of the *Acta Alexandrinorum* proper, there may have been additional embassies as well.

[36] In general, see Modrzejewski 1995: 161–83; Gruen 2002: 54–83; Blouin 2005; Gambetti 2009; Alston 2020.

particular – provoked attempts at interpretation revealing of provincial legal ideologies more generally.

We might begin with Philo, who deals with the riots and their aftermath in two extant texts, *Against Flaccus* and the *Embassy to Gaius*. These were likely part of a lengthier series of what were likely historical books, perhaps five in all.[37] The goal of such writing was not just to recount the experiences of the Jews in Alexandria, but more broadly to use historical experiences to demonstrate god's providence and his special relationship to the Jewish people. Both texts lean heavily on questions of law and legality, and both focus in particular on trials as moments that reveal crucial truths about the nature of empire. Both might similarly be read as engaging, albeit in a distinct idiom, themes present in the Christian martyr texts – even though there are no signs of direct borrowing between the traditions.[38] Furthermore, both of Philo's texts transcend the traditional areas of criminal law. In so doing, they demonstrate that thinking provoked by imperial practices of punishment could come to inflect transactions that we might instead think of as diplomatic.

In Philo's telling, the governorship of Flaccus (32–38 AD) began auspiciously. Unlike many governors, Flaccus was a quick study of Egyptian and Alexandrian affairs.[39] Equally important, Flaccus was a fair judge: "He used to judge important cases in cooperation with the magistrates, he pulled down the arrogant, and he always prevented a motley crowd of people from all quarters from conspiring."[40] He even managed two further groups of disruptors. First, he suppressed the Alexandrian "clubs" and "organizations" – groups of thuggish loafers who, according to Philo, later participated in the riots against the Jews. Second, he reined in the military – a source of frequent misery in the countryside (and likely in the cities as well) whose requisitions

37 The question is summarized in van den Horst 2003: 5–6.

38 Eusebius' engagement with Philo was probably mediated through Origen and Clement: see Inowlocki 2006: 139–49 in general and Inowlocki 2004 on the *Legatio*. Much ink has been spilled on the question of whether Justin Martyr read Philo's work; the better argument seems to me that he did not, or if he did, that his knowledge was confined to questions that did not touch on the politics of legality. See Runia 1993: 97–105.

39 On the question of in-country experience of Egyptian governors, see Brunt 1975.

40 *Flacc.* 4. All translations of *In Flaccum* come from van den Horst 2003. On Philo more generally, from differing perspectives, see Berthelot 2011; Niehoff 2018.

proved burdensome even when legal, and which were more often just a semi-organized and unprosecutable form of theft.[41] On Philo's telling, Flaccus' dutiful administration managed to fill the province with *eunomia* – good order and lawfulness. This *eunomia* came precisely because Flaccus was able to transcend popular sentiment and to bend local interests to his will.

This period of good governance began to fall apart starting in AD 37 with the accession of the emperor Gaius, whom Flaccus feared. The death of the praetorian prefect Macro, Flaccus' friend and ally and an important restraint on the young emperor, was similarly terrifying, and left Flaccus without a powerful friend in Rome. Fear caused a change for the worse in Flaccus, who, in Philo's telling, began to lose his capacity for reasoning – his *logismos*.[42] Rather than his normal advisors, he brought in people who flattered him but whose intentions were nefarious. Of these, Philo singles out three Alexandrians, Dionysius, Lampon, and Isidorus, whom he disparages as seditious popularity hunters and, in the case of Lampon, a "tamperer of documents" – a man who perverted the course of justice by changing the documents that recorded the verdicts of cases. These men, he claims, took advantage of Flaccus' turn for the worse by turning him into their plaything: "they put him (Flaccus) on stage as no more than a mute dummy with the title 'government' (*archēn*) inscribed upon it."[43] These three new councilors also slowly turned Flaccus against the Alexandrian Jews.

Notably, the initial signs of his injustice appeared in the course of litigation: when one of the parties was Jewish, Flaccus inclined towards the opposing party. Similarly, he refused the petitions and requests of Jews: when they approached him with their requests Flaccus would turn away in disgust, refusing to grant them the right to speak on terms equal to that of others (*isēgorian*).[44] The gravamen

[41] E.g., *PSI* V 445 = *Sel.Pap.* 221 (AD 133–37). On requisitions, see Mitchell 1976; Souris and Haensch 2009.

[42] 16. On *logismos*, cf. 4 *Maccabees*.

[43] 20. I have lightly modified van den Horst's translation.

[44] 24. The text does not state explicitly that Flaccus refused the Jews when they were delivering petitions, but the mention of *isēgoria* seems to necessitate such a conclusion: Jews were approaching Flaccus in order to make requests of some sort, and he denied them the right to make their cases.

of Philo's complaint is similar to that of the Christian authors discussed earlier: that the governor has, in siding with a mob, structured legal interactions to exclude the speech of certain groups of subjects. Philo's complaint, however, is even more general. Whereas the Christians complained specifically about the administration of criminal law, Philo speaks of being excluded from litigation more generally – from the venues in which subjects competed with one another over resources both material and symbolic, and where subjects sought to make claims upon their rulers. Philo's grievances provide us with an aperçu into the Christian texts as well. While criminal punishment (to which *Against Flaccus* will soon turn) may have been the most conspicuous practice of sovereignty and the one that drew the most attention from provincial commentators, it was important not just per se – that is, not just because it was a violent practice that demanded legitimation through dialogue. It was important because it served to bring into focus key assumptions about law, and therefore about governance, more generally.

From this initial refusal to acknowledge Jewish speech, things rapidly took a turn for the worse: the arrival of Agrippa in Alexandria gave Flaccus' new counselors the opportunity they sought to vent their rage upon their neighbors. With Flaccus' blessing or studied disinterest, they first mocked Agrippa in the gymnasium by creating his effigy, Karabas, whom they hailed and to whom they submitted their mock disputes (all the more poignant, since Flaccus refused to hear them). This served to enflame passions further, leading a crowd to assemble in the theater. There they insisted, through acclamations, that statues of the emperor be installed in synagogues. This was, according to Philo, "an entirely novel and unprecedented violation of the law (*paranomēma*)."[45] Flaccus agreed, conceding to the assembled mob the right to overturn longstanding imperial dispensations to the Jewish community. But worse was still to come: shortly after the meeting in the theater, Flaccus proceeded to the destruction of the Jewish community *as* a community:[46]

For only a couple days later he issued a decree in which he stigmatized us as foreigners and aliens and gave us no right to plead our cause (*mēde logou*

[45] 41. [46] 54.

metadous) but condemned us without trial (*akritōs*). What could be a better promise of further tyrannical behavior than this? He himself became everything: accuser, enemy, witness, judge, and executioner (*katēgoros, echthros, martys, dikastēs, kolastēs*). But he then added to the first two (crimes) a third one, namely, he gave permission to those who wanted to plunder the Jews, as at the sacking of a city.

Aspects of this account are perplexing, and we have no independent witness for Flaccus' decree(s). But even putting aside the question of historical reconstruction, we might note that, in Philo's telling, two things are essential. First, the decree(s) of Flaccus represent, in effect, the withdrawal of Jewish legal personhood, both individually and collectively. Prior to these decrees, Jews had a *politeia* – a collective political organization that enabled the Jews to worship, to petition for their collective needs as a corporate group, and to judge their own members in particular sorts of cases. (Philo seems to use the word *politeia* in a slightly different sense than our "citizenship," which is also a possible translation.[47]) After the decrees, Jews quite simply no longer "count" among the residents of Alexandria who have rights that are worth protecting. Rather, they are mere "foreigners and aliens" whose individual property can be plundered at will. Second, when Philo seeks to describe the outcome of these decrees he reaches, perhaps ironically, for legal metaphors. "If someone were to call the excessive sufferings that our people underwent 'violence' (*hybrin*) or 'outrage' (*aikian*)" – two words well known from the papyrological record as reflecting grave civil offenses – "he would not be using these words in their proper sense."[48] The better metaphor, he insists, is that of a criminal court: through excluding and stigmatizing the Alexandrian Jews, Philo acts as "accuser, enemy, witness, judge, and executioner."

Worse yet, in usurping these roles for himself Flaccus refused to allow the Jews to mount their own defense: he "gave us no right to plead our cause" (*mēde logou metadous*) – that is, no right to speak in court. The mention of *logos* is key: Philo normally avoids speaking

[47] The question of what kind of collective organization *politeia* denotes is a vexed issue. Perspectives are summarized in van den Horst 2003: 155–56. On the Jewish *politeuma* in the Ptolemaic period, see Sänger 2019; Czajkowski 2019.

[48] *Flacc.* 59. On *hybris* and *aikia*, see further Bryen 2013. Mascellari 2016 argues that these terms have relatively specific valences, rather than overlapping ones.

of *logos* in either the *Against Flaccus* or the *Embassy to Gaius*. In Philo's larger philosophical system, *logos* has a specific meaning: it was the intermediary power that effects the work of God in the intellectual and material spheres.[49] This sense would be impossible in this context. Here, Philo expresses his outrage over Flaccus' injustice by using the term in a normal, provincial vernacular: at stake is the simple right to speak in court, which is in turn a metaphor for the right to be treated as full members of society with rights that deserve to be protected.

After Flaccus' decrees, synagogues were sacked and defiled and the Jews pushed from their normal homes in the city into a single city quadrant, which was soon packed beyond capacity.[50] Any Jews caught in the other parts of the city were clubbed, stoned, or set aflame. As bad as this may have been, it was capped with an incident that drew further ire from Philo. The birthday of the emperor took place during the riots, so to celebrate the occasion Flaccus thought it appropriate to punish some criminals in public.[51] Accordingly, he had thirty-eight members of the Jewish council of elders arrested, paraded through the city bound or chained, and then forced to stand nude in the theater to endure humiliation. Treating them as if they were incorrigible criminals rather than local notables, he had them publicly whipped in front of their Alexandrian enemies. Worse still, he whipped them with the sorts of scourges that were typically used for "rustic Egyptians" (Alexandrians were supposed to be beaten with the flat side of a blade – such distinction in punishment being a common means of marking difference in status). The councilors were then tortured and put to death. This display, Philo notes, went on from "dawn till the third or fourth hour"; this macabre production was followed with another, featuring "dancers, mimes, flute-players, and all the other forms of amusement in theatrical competitions."[52]

In Philo's telling, the total destruction of the Alexandrian Jews at that moment was averted only by god's providence. But though the

49 For an overview, see Niehoff 2018: 209–24. 50 See further Alston 1997.

51 Flaccus was somewhat *avant la lettre* in using the occasion to punish; perhaps more importantly, this does not seem to have been punishment of the Jews by condemning them to fight with beasts or with gladiators, a practice that would become more common later.

52 *Flacc.* 84–85.

emphasis on providence was part of Philo's project of historical interpretation, we might nonetheless note how deeply enmeshed his story is in broader, provincial discourse about the importance of *logos*, and the importance of being able to articulate one's claims before imperial authorities. Without the ability to speak on one's behalf, nothing except divine providence can stand in the way of a governor committed to a campaign of violence and degradation. Put differently: legal procedures, anchored in *logos*, are imagined to operate as a shield to violence. Such procedures are of especial importance in a world in which even a virtuous governor can easily be swayed to the side of vice – and, to generalize from Philo, *every* governor is at risk of such corruption. That a governor – or even an emperor – might choose not to recognize these legal impediments to his own violence was a standing threat.

***

The outbursts of violence in Alexandria led to a series of attempts by both Jewish and Alexandrian elites to try to restore or rectify their respective statuses. I shall turn, momentarily, to the odd local literature that documented the "Alexandrian" perspective on these embassies. But it is worth returning, for the moment, to Philo's telling, articulated in a separate historical text, the *Embassy to Gaius*.

The *Embassy* is a complex text with many strands, but these are subordinated to the book's main action: the encounter of the Jewish embassy with the emperor Gaius himself. Rather than greeting the delegation under traditional, formal circumstances, Gaius offered them only a perfunctory hearing, one that took place as he was supervising renovations to some of his properties:[53]

> As soon as we came into Gaius' presence, we realized from his appearance and gestures that we were standing not before a judge (*dikastēn*) but before an accuser (*katēgoron*) more hostile to us than our actual opponents. For the duties of a judge are as follows: to sit with assessors chosen on their merits during the investigation of a vital question affecting many thousands of Alexandrian Jews, which had not been raised for four hundred years and was now being brought up in court for the first time; to let opposing parties stand on either side of him; and to listen first to the accusation and then to

[53] *Legat.* 249–50. Text and translation from Smallwood 1961.

the defense (*apologias*) for the allotted time; and finally to retire and discuss with his assessors what would be the fairest judgment to pronounce. His actual conduct, however, was that of an implacable tyrant with a scowl on his despotic brow.

The obligation of a judge, on Philo's telling, is simply to be neutral and respectful of provincial speech *on both sides*. Such a claim should be relatively uncontroversial. However, in an echo of Philo's complaint against Flaccus, Gaius had already predetermined the outcome: he was giving the Jews a "hearing" in order to accuse them, rather than to hear their case, and in so doing he combined the role of judge and accuser. Despite the biased nature of the proceedings, the Jewish delegation nonetheless tried to put the proceedings back on track: they bowed immediately, and while greeting the emperor as "Augustus Imperator." This display of obeisance and politeness, however, yielded nothing. Gaius simply smiled at them and asked, "So you are the god-haters, the people who do not believe I am a god?" With this, Gaius raised his hands towards the sky and "he uttered a name which it is a sin even to hear, let alone to pronounce" – presumably the tetragrammaton.[54] This shocking act of blasphemy was presumably a key part of Gaius' strategy: it raised, in pointed fashion, the question of who or what was really a divinity, and what relationship, more generally, divinity had to sovereignty. It is, in that sense, akin to the question raised in the Christian texts discussed earlier. In the case of Gaius, the problem was that he asserted that the two things to be one and the same. It is here that the "charge," such as it was, became clear to the Alexandrian Jews: if this was a trial (rather than an embassy), it was a trial about the emperor's *maiestas* – his majesty and his superiority.[55]

[54] *Legat.* 353.

[55] In general, see Bauman 1967; on early Augustan developments, see Mantovani 2011; Peachin 2015; on the *SC de Pisone Patre*, see the discussions of Eck et al. 1996; Cooley 2023. See also the discussion of Smallwood 1961: 319–20, *ad loc.* It is interesting to note that, if we take ἀσέβειαν at *Legat.* 355 as a statement of the "charge" against the Jews and as a translation of *maiestas* (on the basis of Cass. Dio 57.9), then it is put into the mouths of the Alexandrian ambassadors, rather than the emperor. This would mean that the Alexandrians were proposing what was, in essence, a novel theory of *maiestas*, using the Jews as something of a test case. This would be very much in accordance with the model proposed by Peachin 2015 on the basis of the second Cyrene edict (*SEG* IX 8 = *FIRA* I 68). Crucially, this was *not* an understanding of *maiestas* that caught on.

Gaius' initial performance, though terrifying to the Alexandrian Jews, sent the embassy of the Alexandrian Greeks, also present, into paroxysms of joy. "They waved their arms about, danced up and down, and called him by all the titles of the gods."[56] The scene is structurally similar to the scenes in the Christian texts: the judge (here the emperor, there the governors) has taken the side of a mob, or of the leaders of a mob, eager for blood. Isidorus (the same Isidorus who played a role in the *Against Flaccus*) goaded the emperor yet further: the Jews, he reminded the emperor, were the *only* nation who refused sacrifice to Gaius. This prompted a temporary showing of courage from the Jewish embassy: "Lord Gaius, we are being slandered!"[57] The Jews insist that they had sacrificed – quite a lot, at that. The difference, however, was obvious to Gaius: they had sacrificed, but they had not sacrificed *to him*. At this the Jews began to despair, and affairs seemed only to get worse: Gaius may have been their judge, but he was far from passive. He moved throughout his property, inspecting various rooms and ordering improvements and decorations, all while keeping the hearing going. "The whole affair was a farce (*mimeia*)," Philo insists – a grotesque parody of the thing that it was designed to be.

Gaius, however, was far from through with his questioning. Moving from anger at the Jews' failure to sacrifice, he took the path of ethnographic inquiry: "Why do you not eat pork?" he asked. This produced further howls of laughter from the Alexandrian Greeks. Even serious issues, Philo contends, were treated mockingly: Gaius asked, "We should like to know what political rights (*peri tēs politeias dikaiois*) you enjoy?" Taking the bait, the Jews attempted to reason with their inquisitor:[58] "We began to give an explanation, but as soon as Gaius had a taste of our pleading (*dikaiologias*) and realized that it was not easily dismissed, even before we had produced our strongest arguments he cut us short." As in the Christian texts, so again here the proof of illegitimacy comes not only from the emperor siding with a group perceived to be a mob, but similarly from his refusal to engage with his subjects through the medium of rational argumentation. We similarly get a sense of the potential threat that

[56] *Legat.* 354. [57] *Legat.* 356. Translation slightly modified.
[58] *Legat.* 364. Translation slightly modified.

such an argument might pose: finding that the Jewish arguments were not easily dismissed, Gaius took active measures not to hear them, instead cutting the Jews off, lest he be forced to show, in public, that his policies could not withstand rational argument. As a political matter, this marked them as people who simply did not count; it also marked him as an emperor who failed the most basic test of leadership: listening to his subjects.[59]

The only solution left, on Philo's telling, was miraculous intervention: the Jewish embassy accordingly began to pray to God, who heard their prayers and softened Gaius' heart. His verdict was insulting, but ultimately favorable – or at least not overtly harmful: "He became gentler and merely said, 'I think that these men are not so much criminals as lunatics in not believing that I have been given a divine nature.'"[60] As in *Flaccus*, for Philo, providence is necessary when confronted by the possibility of an unjust emperor refusing to engage on a rational basis with his subjects.

***

Much more could be said about Philo as a legal and political thinker. The great bulk of his tremendous oeuvre deals, in some sense, with law – from his exegeses of biblical texts to his treatises on specific aspects of Jewish law. Similarly robust is his treatment of the importance of *logos*. Both of these strains of his thought, though, operate either at a high level of abstraction or upon the plane of narrative exegesis (or both simultaneously): they seek to explain, through a philosophical lens, the fundamental structure of the universe and the place of Jews, Jewish law, and Jewish religious practices within it.[61] But when Philo chooses to talk about his contemporary world and to identify concrete practices of governance as problematic, he is very much of his provincial milieu: like his non-Jewish contemporaries, he focuses on the courtroom.

The *Embassy* contains a further lesson as well: the idea that legality is tested, or even generated, in face-to-face confrontations and

59 The foundational problem in the classic account of Millar 1992.

60 *Legat.* 367.

61 The relatively small number of other passages where Philo makes reference to his contemporary world were initially collected in Goodenough 1938; recently, however, the importance of his contemporary world has been profitably reinvestigated: see Niehoff 2018; Berthelot 2011.

dialogues with those in authority does not only apply to the governor at work in the provinces. It can be applied to the emperor as well. To be sure, the actual amount of time that provincial subjects would have spent litigating before the emperor must have been extremely limited. Though as an ideological matter emperors sought to be accessible to litigants (and in practice they often went to surprising lengths to hear the cases of relatively unimportant people), obtaining a hearing before the emperor must have normally been a function of mere luck unless one was a member of, or somehow connected to, a narrow elite.[62] However, even if one was unable to obtain access to the emperor, one could nonetheless *imagine* what such a trial would have consisted of, and how it ought ideally to operate.

Further, to the extent that law and *logos* operate to forestall violence, it must be admitted that, on Philo's telling, these are weak shields indeed. All that was necessary was for a person in a place of authority to choose to ignore the relevant procedures. This is, I take it, something of a dismal verdict on the position of subjects more generally. For all that one might hope that legal procedures could forestall violence, one would be unwise to wager on them – even if that was, in fact, all that one could do. Philo says this directly in the *Embassy*:[63]

> What heavier burden could a slave have than a hostile owner? Subjects (*hypēkooi*) are the slaves (*douloi*) of an Emperor, and even if this was not the case under any of Gaius' predecessors, because they ruled reasonably (*syn epieikeiai*) and lawfully (*meta nomōn*), yet it was the case under Gaius, who had cut all humanity out of his heart and made a cult of illegality; for he regarded himself as the law (*nomon*), and broke the laws of the lawgivers of every country as if they were empty words.

Legality, on this telling, is intimately connected to history: the status of the Jews had initially been protected by the Ptolemies; Augustus and Tiberius similarly preserved and protected it.[64] These kings had

[62] On "everyday" litigants before the emperor in the tetrarchic period, Connolly 2010. Of course, there were periodic exceptions, such as a chance imperial visit. The most important documentation of which is *P.Col.* VI 123 (AD 200), listing decisions of Septimius Severus in Egypt; *SEG* XVII 759 (AD 216), a hearing before Caracalla memorialized in an inscription.

[63] *Legat.* 119.

[64] The various edicts compiled in Josephus' *Jewish Antiquities* provide evidence at least for the proposition that *some* Jews thought they possessed a suite of privileges in the Hellenistic and Roman world. On these, see Pucci ben Zeev 1998; Pont 2022.

ruled "reasonably" and "legally." They understood that law was connected to a historical trajectory that, barring exceptional or rebellious behavior on the part of the people whom they regulated, set parameters for future interactions. Law was also able to give structure to, and to alleviate, what was in fact a relationship of simple domination – conceived here in its purest form, slavery (see further the discussion of the next chapter). Gaius departed from the parameters set up by law and history, but also, and perhaps more problematically, attempted to change the ontological status of law itself: no longer something that emerged as part of an evolving negotiation or dialogue between ruler and subject, it was now proclaimed to be vested in the ruler himself. Everything else was just "empty words" (*kenas rhēseis*). Changing the status of legal rules (from agreed upon external constraints to mere positive impositions of imperial will) negated the protected status of the Alexandrian Jews and allowed their persecution. The result is similar to the result of Flaccus' decrees: rather than being subjects – a tolerable position of subordination that entailed both responsibilities *and rights* – Gaius' innovations, and his attempt to change the nature of legality more broadly, resulted in the reduction of subjects to slaves.[65]

Finally, both of Philo's texts speak to the importance of the criminal trial for the ways provincial populations imagined their place in the empire. In the case of the Jewish embassies, collective self-representation was imagined to best be articulated in face-to-face encounters, bound by *logos*, that eventually produced authoritative declarations about their community's status. It is here worth remembering that the Roman world had well-developed diplomatic procedures by which cities and groups negotiated their status, procedures that did *not* normally turn on questions of crime and punishment.[66] That is, there was an extensive vocabulary for, and a lengthy tradition of, sending embassies to Rome to negotiate one's political rights, and this tradition did not imagine that judgments about a particular group needed to be rooted in the procedures of criminal law.

[65] For another instance of this sort of provincial legal ideology, see Bryen 2014a: 356 on *SB* IV 7464 (AD 248). For the ideology of subjecthood, see Bryen 2021a.

[66] For an overview, Millar 1992: 375–447. On the ways in which the language of diplomacy inflected Christian concepts of community, see Rives 2009.

For such interactions, the traditional language of diplomacy would normally have sufficed. In Philo's narrative, however, we are dealing with something different: the imagined insertion of the language and practices of criminal law into a set of different practices – purely, it seems, to make the stakes so readily understood. In Philo's case, whether the emperor chose to conceive of the Jews as members of a broader imperial order or mere slaves was, in his eyes, a matter of life or death. It was also a matter that turned on the question of whether the emperor was prepared to engage in rational dialogue.

***

Yet questions of the nature of community, and the proper institutional venue for articulating concepts of community, were in some cases still more complicated. The "trials" recounted in Philo's *Embassy* might have answered the question of the nature of the relationship between Rome and the Jews of Alexandria (or beyond); there was nonetheless also the question of the relationship between Rome, the Alexandrian Greeks, and the Jews more generally. How, specifically, were these three communities to relate to one another?

These questions animate a body of literature from the province of Egypt preserved exclusively on papyrus, the *Acta Alexandrinorum*. As noted above, the *Acta* take their origin from the same events as Philo's historical works: the outbreak of anti-Jewish violence in AD 38, and then a subsequent outbreak of violence after the death of Gaius in AD 41. These outbreaks led to multiple embassies to Rome of both Jews and Alexandrians. Whereas Philo focuses on the experience of the Jews before Gaius, the *Acta* focus on the experiences of the Alexandrians before multiple emperors: Gaius features in one important text and Claudius in another. Perhaps more importantly, the genre seemed to its authors sufficiently capacious that it came to deal with events unconnected to the riots of the first century AD. Thus, *Acta* stories came to be composed about interactions between Alexandrians and later emperors (Trajan, possibly Hadrian, and Commodus). For the Egyptian readers of the *Acta* the action of the courtroom – and its attendant practices of punishment – came to serve as a more general framework for interrogating the legitimacy conditions of the empire. Most importantly, in this body of texts, the courtroom is framed as *the* central institution through which one could make collective claims about one's political status in the empire (and, in particular, one's political status vis-à-vis others who might coexist nearby).

Unfortunately for such a promising body of sources, their analysis is fraught with scholarly controversy. To begin with, nearly all of the papyri containing copies of the *Acta* are fragmentary, leaving scholars to hazard guesses about how to make sense of them and whether and how their various lacunae might be restored. Inquiry has been further dogged by questions of historicity. Like some of the early Christian martyr acts, a number of the extant texts are designed to look like official documents, leaving the question of where to place the line between fiction and history. Similarly fraught is the date or dates of the texts' composition: they may have been composed anytime over the first three centuries AD.[67] With relative certainty we can say that the Alexandrian embassies were an important locus of collective identity in the second and early third centuries; presumably they were a locus of concern (if not a goad to literary elaboration) when the events were still fresh in people's minds. It may be, as the most recent editor of these texts has suggested, that stories of Alexandrian ambassadors circulated orally.[68] More we cannot say: memory can be continuous or recently recovered or even wholly concocted; in no case is its effect at a present moment any less strong. What we have, in any case, is a series of narratives about embassies from Alexandrians to emperors in Rome clustered around a series of themes: the dignity of

[67] The early editions of Musurillo (1954, 1961) have now been totally surpassed; still useful are the edition and discussions of Tcherikover and Fuks (1957–64: vol. 2); Chris Rodriguez has given new editions and discussions of individual documents (e.g., Rodriguez 2010b) and has composed a doctoral thesis (*non vidi*) that appears to offer a new edition of the complete corpus. It awaits publication. In the meantime, a comprehensive new edition has appeared, the product of a Cologne PhD. thesis: Vega Navarette 2017. This most recent edition sets the standard, and in what follows I work from its numbering of the texts. There remains substantial controversy about the date of composition: Vega Navarette does not accept two first century AD documents (*PSI* inv. 123 and *P.Oxy.* XLII 3021) as part of the *Acta* proper, thus confining their production to the second and third centuries AD. (She accepts *P.Oxy.* XLII 3021 as part of the historical background to the corpus, document 2.3 in her edition.) On *PSI* inv. 123, see Rodriguez 2010a. Other important recent studies of the *Acta Alexandrinorum* include Harker 2008; Magnani 2009; and Gambetti 2009 (the latter two confined to the trial of Isidorus, discussed below, and the reconstruction of the AD 38 riots and their outcome).

[68] Vega Navarette 2017: 59–60.

Alexandria, the relationship between the Alexandrian elites and the emperor's ability to reward and punish communities, and the relative hierarchy of Alexandrians vis-à-vis others in the empire. All of these are raised within a series of face-to-face confrontations between the emperor and the ambassadors.

It might be useful to imagine the *Acta Alexandrinorum* as a cycle of stories about Alexandrians and emperors that circulated throughout the province of Egypt. The text that speaks to the earliest of these interactions (though it is not necessarily the earliest of the compositions) is known as the *Gerousia Acta*. It recounts an embassy on behalf of the 173 members of the Alexandrian Gerousia (council of elders) to Rome in the age of Tiberius.[69] Presumably the issue is strife between the Alexandrian community and the Jews, similar to that which will be recounted in texts that deal with the events of AD 38 and beyond.

The inclusion of a story set under Tiberius changes the entire frame of the interactions of these two communities. By posing an alternative chronology of the relationship between Alexandrians and Jews, this text locates the origin of their dysfunction *not* in the riots of AD 38 (and therefore not with the visit of king Agrippa or Flaccus' misconduct), but earlier. Arguing for an origin in the age of Tiberius situates the dysfunction in Alexandria in the larger context of imperial action against the Jews more generally. Thus in AD 19, Jews were expelled from the Italian peninsula on the grounds that they were converting Roman elites and causing them to waste their resources on lavish gifts to the Jerusalem temple. Similarly, Jews appear to have been targeted by Tiberius' praetorian prefect, Aelius Sejanus, prior to his death in AD 31.[70] As such, the *Gerousia Acta* start by emphasizing that the Alexandrians are acting in accordance with, rather than at variance to, broader Roman policies towards a problematic and dangerous minority.

The *Gerousia Acta* are a story of Alexandrian victimization. The otherwise distinguished Gerousia has been accused by Jews, a nation

[69] Crucially, we know very little about what role, if any, this council played in the Alexandrian political structure of the first century AD. See Vega Navarette 2017: 66–67.

[70] See discussion of the relevant sources in Smallwood 1956; Philo's first "historical" monograph probably dealt with the persecutions planned by Sejanus. Another attempt at reimagining the history of relations between Rome and Alexandria might be *P.Oxy.* XXV 2435 (AD I?).

settled in Egypt for some 630 years (since pharaoh Psammetichus II stationed a garrison in Elephantine), but never formally members of the city itself.[71] The nature of the accusation is unclear, as is the identity of the accuser (he is just called *katēgoros*, i.e., "accuser"). But whatever its specifics, it provokes the response of the Alexandrians, who collectively sail to Rome. After disembarking in Ostia, they make their way to the city, only to find that Tiberius has died and Gaius has succeeded him. Undeterred, the embassy, led by two men named Areios and Eulalos, attempt to plead their case before Gaius.[72] Areios' speech begins respectfully, and by emphasizing that the Alexandrians are willing to accept precisely the issue later contested by the Jews: "You (i.e., Gaius) are the god of the universe and you have taken rulership of the city." (We might also notice here a common effect of the politics of polarization: to the extent that the Jews of Alexandria detested Gaius, so to a similar extent the Alexandrian Greeks embraced him.[73]) The text indicates that the new emperor is also ready to listen graciously: Gaius greets both Areios and Eulalos, and they waste no time in addressing the issue at hand. "Hear me," Areios insists, "for I am ready to give my defense (*apologian*) to the accusations against the Alexandrians." The Alexandrians, he explains, derive from the community of Macedonians settled in Alexandria; they are ethnically pure. The same cannot be said of his accusers.

Accordingly, Areios asks Gaius for permission to interrogate his accusers. Gaius grants it, and through dialogue the truth rapidly emerges: "Glaring at his accuser, Areios said: [do you hear?] what he says? What is this? ... You [accuse?] my fatherland, but perhaps I should [accuse?] yours!" He continues: "This man is a foreigner who is usurping (Alexandrian?) citizenship: in point of fact he is registered elsewhere!" This, it seems, is sufficient to prove the point: "Thus," the

71 Gambetti 2009: 135. In making sense of this text, the edition of Stephens in *P.Yale* II 107 is highly valuable.

72 3.1. In what follows every reconstruction of the texts is provisional. In many details I follow the insights of Vega Navarette 2017, but for the sake of the reader I have minimized repeatedly calling attention to the fragmentary and uncertain nature of the texts.

73 There is a long history of picking one's totem to distinguish oneself from the other team: this is a central insight of Boyarin 1999. We might note, in this context, the Jewish embrace of Nero, who in *BT Gittin* (56a) becomes a proselyte and the ancestor of Rabbi Meir.

narrator of the text explains, "the accusation was proven to be without justice, and Gaius Caesar ordered the accuser to be burned alive." To ensure that the communities remained apart, and that the Jews remembered their subordinate position relative to the Alexandrians, Gaius further produced a letter (*epistolēn*) that the text then proceeds to quote (though the letter itself is scarcely preserved). Some fragments at the end of the text might refer to the subsequent events of AD 38: perhaps back in Alexandria, one group falls upon another, and a large number of people are gathered together and beheaded. It is possible that the text endorses the subsequent anti-Jewish riots, framing them as a continuation of the work done in Gaius' courtroom.

The extant fragments of the *Gerousia Acta* raise a series of questions about the nature of interactions with the emperor that will define the action in the other *Acta*. To begin with, these texts are concerned with the nature of community – they seek to define who is in and who is out, as well as to bring clarity to the sorts of hierarchy that are desirable. In the case of the Alexandrian ambassadors, this means never permitting a situation in which the Jews rank higher than the Alexandrians in collective honor. Roman sovereignty is always acknowledged but made bearable precisely because the Alexandrians have their integrity reaffirmed and are acknowledged to be superior to their Jewish counterparts. In this sense, the *Gerousia Acta* articulate an idealized model of state-community interaction. The emperor allows the ambassadors to speak in court, listens closely to their complaint, and sticks to the topic at hand. The Alexandrians, for their part, get not only to speak, but even to subject their accusers to the test of reason (interrogation). The Jews, as the party encroaching upon the privileged status of the "better" community, get punished (never mind that they seem to be plaintiffs, rather than defendants). Gaius, undoubtedly the hero of this tale, uses violence instantly and without apology as soon as realizes their trickery.[74]

The *Gerousia Acta* thus operate as an example of what we might call an "inverted" martyr act. They lay out a model of proper respect for provincial *logos* and condition the emperor's use of violence upon respect for it. In this case, the emperor performs his task with aplomb, deploying violence when the Alexandrians prove, through

[74] Various suggestions have been mooted for why in this case the *accuser* gets punished: see Gambetti 2008.

their interrogation, that the recipient is deserving of it. Such violence is to be celebrated precisely because it follows the paths laid out by provincial *logos*. This vision of the relationship between legitimacy, violence, and *logos* is, moreover, essentially consistent with that articulated by the Christian martyr acts, even as the moral worth of the particular actors is differently evaluated.

***

The rhetorical target of the *Gerousia Acta* is Gaius' successor, Claudius. Claudius famously restored a number of the privileges of the Alexandrian Jews and threatened to punish the Greeks of Alexandria if they continued their harassment of the Jews.[75] He also punished individual Alexandrians for their participation in the riots. In particular, his punishment of Isidorus (the same Isidorus who appears as the accuser of the Jews in *Against Flaccus*) is the topic of one of the most extensive preserved *Acta*. These *Acta* are preserved in what most likely are two recensions, the relationship between which is unclear. Similarly, we have two copies of one recension which shows only relatively minor differences. If nothing else, this gives some sense that the *Acta Isidori* was a text that circulated at least among some limited circles.[76] As in Philo's *Embassy*, the Alexandrian delegation, headed by Isidorus, has come to Rome to litigate their interactions with the Jews. Specifically, their goal was to place the blame for the disorders of AD 38 on Agrippa – presumably, since Agrippa's visit had occurred several years before the most recent outbreak of violence, by making a sort of "they started it" type of case.

The text begins with a hearing in Rome, and a discussion between Claudius and the senators Tarquinius and Aviola. The senators appear to be sympathetic to the Alexandrians: as the senators recognize, the ambassadors are in Rome on behalf of their homeland (*hyper patridos*) – an admirable trait. This conversation sets the stage for the appearance of the Alexandrian ambassadors: they are brought in, and Claudius postpones their hearing until the next day, thus ensuring them a full and proper measure of time to make their case. (It will be recalled that this "setting aside of a day" is precisely

[75] *P.Lond.* VI 1912 = *CPJ* II 153 (AD 41). He was also quite happy to threaten the Alexandrian Jews.

[76] 3.3.1.1 and 3.3.1.2 in Vega Navarrete's edition.

what Polycarp requests and is denied.) In other words, the text begins by emphasizing procedure. The Alexandrians are similarly portrayed as being invested in respectful formalities. The next day they enter the emperor's court, and greet him and his *consilium* respectfully. Isidorus begins by addressing the emperor: "My lord Caesar, I beg at your knees: hear me (describe) the sufferings of my fatherland." The emperor approves, as do the senators assembled as his *consilium*, because "they saw what sort of man Isidorus was."

From its initial scenes emphasizing procedure and mutual respect, the text shifts sharply. Rather than allow Isidorus to speak, the emperor interjects:[77]

> Claudius Caesar: "By the gods, say nothing against my friend (i.e., Agrippa). For you have already destroyed two other friends of mine, Theon the *exegetes* and Naevius the governor of Egypt, the former head of the praetorian guard at Rome – and now you pursue this man." Isidorus: "My lord Caesar, what does this threepenny Jew Agrippa matter to you ..." Claudius Caesar: "What [do you say]? You are the most [contumacious?] of all men."

From procedure and consensus, the text pivots dizzyingly towards hostility and censorship. The Alexandrian ambassadors are told that they are held to be responsible, at least in the eyes of the emperor, for the deaths of Theon (whose identity is disputed) and Naevius – that is, Naevius Sutorius Macro, the praetorian prefect and counselor of Gaius, who had been given the position of governor of Egypt but was forced to commit suicide before taking it. They are furthermore not welcome to accuse the very person whom they intended to accuse: Agrippa. The text echoes Philo's portrayal of the Jewish ambassadors before Gaius who, when finally offered an opportunity to explain their "political rights," are quickly cut off by the emperor. Here, though, the emperor forecloses the possibility of discourse in advance.

A lacuna of indeterminate length prevents us from knowing what precisely transpired in the aftermath of this prohibition on speech, but it is certain that the results were not good. When the text resumes, the emperor and Isidorus are in a full-fledged shouting-match:[78]

[77] 3.3.1.2, ll. 11–20.

[78] 3.3.1.1, ll. 3–12. There is controversy over the proper translation of "dancing girl" (*mousikē*), but it is surely a low insult; see the discussion in Vega Navarette 2017 *ad loc.*

> Claudius Caesar: "Isidorus, you have killed many of my friends." Isidorus: "I obeyed the king who at that time ordered it. As for you, tell me whom you would like me to accuse." Claudius Caesar: "Surely you are the son of a dancing girl, Isidorus!" Isidorus: "I am not a slave or the son of a dancing girl, but a distinguished man, the gymnasiarch of the city of Alexandria. And you are the cast-off child of the Jewess Salome! And this is why (...)"

As the discussion degenerates into insults, the Alexandrian ambassadors know that the tables have been turned. One of them, Lampon, declares that he has foreseen his own death. Turning to Isidorus, he asks in despair, "What can we do but yield to a deranged king?" Claudius, however, will not put up with being insulted. He quickly orders the execution of both Isidorus and Lampon – who were, again, plaintiffs rather than defendants.

The ambassadors' mission may have been doomed, but despite imperial censorship they manage to reveal the truth: the emperor is controlled to an unacceptable degree by the Jews, Agrippa in particular; the only way to keep this unpleasant truth from public scrutiny is to limit the right of people to speak it. In other words, what makes this text a martyr act is precisely that it comes from the problematic world of a pluralistic empire, where the proper relations that ought to hold between particular communities are imagined to be distorted or inverted. In this case, the normal hierarchy – Romans, then Alexandrians, then Jews – is perverted by the proximity of the Jewish king Agrippa to Claudius, thus enabling Agrippa to put his own community in a place of unearned privilege vis-à-vis more deserving communities of the empire.[79] So far as legality goes, this rearrangement of political hierarchies is predicated on particular acts of punishment and prohibition: the murder of the ambassadors for revealing the truth about the nature of political community, but also the prohibition of violence between communities as they jockey for relative position.

These texts thus use the courtroom, and its attendant practices of discourse, dialogue, and punishment, to bring to the fore the question

[79] I work from a relatively capacious understanding of what it is that constitutes "martyrdom." I hope to pursue this point in greater detail in a future study. On this sort of accusation about disordered community relations more generally, see Nirenberg 2013. For alternative formulations of what constitutes a "martyr" text, see Bowersock 1995; Boyarin 1999.

of the relative ranking of communities. In doing this, the authors of these texts developed something like a model for imagining events that stretched well beyond those of AD 38 and its immediate aftermath. Thus in the *Acta Hermaisci*, likely set in the context of a violent revolt of the Jews of Egypt under Trajan, the Alexandrian Hermaiscus goes to Trajan's court only to find that Trajan's wife Plotina has urged his councilors to take the side of the Jews.[80] Accordingly, Trajan greeted the Jewish ambassadors in a friendly way, but took umbrage at the greeting offered to him by the Alexandrians: "Do you greet me as if you are worthy of my greeting," Trajan thunders, "after you have done such terrible things to the Jews? Go off ..." Later in the text, when in discussion with Hermaiscus, the accusation that the emperor is merely a pawn of his subjects is made explicitly:[81]

> (The Emperor Trajan said) "... Though you scorn death, you are approaching it when you respond to me so defiantly." Hermaiscus said: "But we are aggrieved that your council is filled with the unholy Jews." The Emperor said: "I will say to you again, Hermaiscus: trusting in your descent, you answer defiantly." Hermaiscus said: "How, O Greatest Emperor, am I answering defiantly? Show me." The Emperor said: "Since you caused my council to be composed of Jews." Hermaiscus: "Is not (even) the name 'Jews' difficult (to hear)? You should moreover help your people and not advocate for the unholy Jews."

The situation, in the case of Hermaiscus, seems to be totally hopeless: the emperor has been captured by an inferior community and cannot be dissuaded. More speech, more reasoning, more argument – these will not budge the person who is committed to injustice.

Still, it appears that in the case of Hermaiscus, Trajan's conduct was so unfair that the heavens itself could not bear it. "When Hermaiscus had said this, the bust of Serapis which the Alexandrian embassy had brought suddenly started to sweat. Seeing this, Trajan was astonished (*apethaumas*[*e*]*n*). A panic soon arose in Rome, with multitudes screaming and shouting as everyone ran to the highest parts of the hills."[82] As in Philo, divine intervention succeeds but only *after* reasoning fails: realizing that Hermaiscus has reason and cosmic

[80] For an overview, see Mélèze Modrzejewski 1995: 198–214.

[81] 3.5, col. III ll. 3–13.

[82] 3.5, col. III ll. 15–18. On the legal and political importance of *thauma*, see Chapter 7.

forces on his side, the emperor is struck dumb, and reveals, in an echo of *Pionius*, that he cannot engage with provincials on a rational basis.

***

Though pagan texts, the *Acta Alexandrinorum* use the courtroom scene to highlight a similar set of concerns to Philo and some of the Christian martyr acts.[83] Whereas Christians emphasized the demand that Christians be treated in a way similar to other subjects, and Philo emphasized that the Jews have to be treated *as a community*, the Alexandrians adopt the mode of the courtroom narrative to argue that they ought to be treated as a *privileged* community. In failing to do this – that is, in failing to see how the city of Alexandria ought to be distinguished because of its relative importance, antiquity, connection to Alexander the Great, its collective learning and its institutions – emperors reveal that they are not, in fact, excellent judges. They are, rather, boors who just happen to have control over the means of violence at that particular moment. They can rule only by forcing distinguished subjects to refrain from stating, in a space normatively governed by free discourse, what ought to be an obvious truth: that the emperors have been captured, institutionally, by an inferior people.

These texts echo one another because they came from groups of provincials with *shared* perceptions of their relationship to imperial governance. Still, there were others among the dominated who did *not* share these perceptions. That is, this is not simply a story of the divergence between imperial and subaltern perspectives on rule. It is in fact far richer.[84] Accordingly, we might expect to find, among Christians for example, that some Christians found the idea of law as dialogue meaningful and generative, and others who, because they imagined their position in the empire differently, did not. And this is what we do find: some Christians took the position that the pagan state was not deserving of legalistic engagement, much less dialogue. Perhaps the classic statements of this position come not from the eastern provinces,

[83] An analogous set of claims might be made about a minor literature produced in Rome itself: the so-called *exitus virorum illustrium*. See, e.g., Plin. *Ep.* 5.5, 8.12 and the survey of Ronconi 1966.

[84] On analogous processes of negotiation occurring in texts emanating from Sassanian contexts, see Gross 2018, 2024. It would be a fruitful exercise to compare the imperial structures that animated these analogous processes.

but from Africa: from texts like the *Passion of Perpetua and Felicitas*, where Christianity is treated as an all-encompassing identity, or from Tertullian's rejection of the institutional and cultural frameworks of the city in the pamphlet *On Spectacles*.[85] Analogous things might be said for Jews, and for others as well.[86] In other words, the categories of persons (Jews, Christians, polytheists) that have traditionally guided historical analysis (and which I have replicated here for organizational purposes) are in fact not especially useful for explaining the rich and varied conceptions of law in the Roman world and the claims that people made about it. We should start, instead, from communities and commonalities of perception. From there, we can also begin to explain the ways that some provincial subjects, regardless of their theology or ethnic or regional identity, reacted against this emphasis on *logos*. We shall turn to these reactions in due course.

Finally, one might add that the cumulative effect of these attempts at making sense of punishment eventually came to transcend mere questions of criminal law and trials, important though these may have been. What these provincial writers did when they wrote about criminal law was to begin to construct the underpinnings of a separate, larger claim: that legality and legitimacy were generated, and tested, in moments of face-to-face dialogue more generally – that is, that law could be generated in places other than the courtroom merely by dint of sovereign power engaging in the practice of explaining its orders to people who were expected, by virtue of their position, to obey. This set of questions will occupy the next chapter.

[85] On Perpetua, see esp. Shaw 1993; Heffernan 2012.

[86] E.g., Boyarin 2004. For an example of using similar forms to come to the opposite conclusion, cf. Bryen 2021b on *P.Aktenbuch*.

5

Law among the Degraded

For subjects of the Roman Empire, the confrontation in court emerged as an archetypal scene. The courtroom focalized broader concerns about power, punishment, position in an empire, the nature of community, the desirable or legitimate use of violence in society, and the ability of *logos* to constrain sovereign authority. To be sure, as I shall argue in Part III, for some provincial populations, insiders in particular, this was precisely the danger of the courtroom – and a good reason that these sorts of confrontations should be avoided. But for numerous others, confrontations in court took on mythical status. Provincial subjects returned to such scenes repeatedly, using them to tell a wide variety of stories about what, in the end, actually mattered to their communities.

The emphasis on dialogue was transposable. Confrontations in the courtroom were important, but those confrontations taught a larger lesson: that power was mediated not through abstract categories or even through the written record but through face-to-face interactions. In the course of a face-to-face interaction, subjects might advance arguments that could bind a powerful person or work to constrain his temper or his innate tendency towards violence. Dialogic engagement thus came to be a mode of negotiating power more generally, even without the institutional guardrails of legal process, however scant they may have been in practice. Dialogue came to sit at the heart of a broader, distinctly provincial, social and political theory. This theory will be at the heart of this chapter.

The provincial theory had three aspects. First, it offered a dramatic and visually coded portrayal of the operation of power. Little has been said so far on the importance of imagining dialogue not just as an exchange of language, but as a visual spectacle as well. Roman governors relied on aesthetics to convince their audiences of the right ways to "read" the bodies of the condemned. As we shall see in Chapter 7, Greek elites similarly imagined their excellence to manifest itself physically, in beautiful bodies and beautiful speech – speech which *protected* their bodies from the violence of the law's operations more generally. It is thus striking that, in the texts that structure this chapter, powerful individuals are always faced with an interlocutor marked as somehow deformed, abnormal, or stigmatized. These texts staged the confrontation between the sovereign and subject also as a confrontation between power and *ugliness*. Yet this ugliness was more than a visual coding to the nature of power differentials. It also entailed a claim that *logos* ought to be a weapon of the structurally weak or aesthetically repellant.

Second, in framing these confrontations, provincial thinkers did more than portray the weak as merely problematic or ugly; instead, the characters that reoccur in this line of thinking are grotesque – comically misshapen and exaggerated, they are disruptive presences meant to provoke laughter and ridicule. Yet these characters also blend important claims about legality into their absurdity and low humor, in a mix of registers that bears some resemblance to the ancient category of the *spoudogeloion* – the "serio-comic."[1] We should not miss this humor, often delivered deadpan. This low-comic aspect allowed certain claims about law to be put into the mouths of supposedly problematic or stigmatized people. This is especially important when those claims were radical, for they were made, in a sense, in the subjunctive – that is, where the speaker is not, or not necessarily, committed to the propositions that he advances. But by speaking in this register – by evoking or even winking at some of the more radical claims that one *could* make about power, were one so motivated – one could raise questions of great seriousness while also retaining some sort of plausible deniability about whether one was ultimately committed to the radical answers that might emerge.

[1] I have benefited much in thinking through these categories from Branham 1989 and Boyarin 2009.

The serio-comic register was also combined with a sharp eye towards the third aspect of provincial social theory: a fixation on the nature, boundaries, and limitations of power, political or otherwise. The question, "What gives you the right to do this to me?" was not restricted to asking about the violence of punishment. It could be taken outside of the courtroom, and into less public and more intimate – and therefore more institutionally unstructured – social spaces. This lack of institutional structure posed a standing threat: in the courtroom, with its relatively clear scripts and defined roles, there were rules of the road – a set of moves that one knew one could make that fell within the boundaries of what was and was not acceptable. A trial may have been, in practice, unfair or conducted in bad faith, but those conducting it had at least to gesture publicly towards fairness and consistency. If nothing else, those gestures would remind onlookers that these sorts of imperial rituals were supposed to operate under the sign of reason.[2]

Far less clear was how to handle someone with power in a private setting. Here any rules were vague, the power differential vast, and the setting neither ritualized nor especially conducive to publicity. The answer, for at least some provincial subjects, was to *legalize* the interactions to the extent possible – to imagine extralegal applications of power as being normatively bound by the same basic principles that operated in a more formal setting. As I shall argue in subsequent chapters (8 and 9), this was both a shrewd strategy and one that came to have resonance with a particularly influential group of Roman jurists, who adopted it in their own attempts to imagine the regulatory structures that ought to obtain in the provinces. These jurists, in turn, came to juridify numerous aspects of provincial life – that is, to claim a new and increasingly large space for the territory in which law ought to operate.

This chapter is structured around two texts featuring grotesque characters: the slave Aesop, and the Midrashic hunchback, Geviʿa ben Psisa. Both characters were capable of being put to subversive ends, mocking both themselves and those who held power over them. They were subversive because they might adapt the language of law and of courtrooms to raise foundational questions about the operation of

[2] Ando 2000.

power in society: whether it operates in good faith, whether and under what terms it can be constrained, and whether rules themselves have any inherent value. This is a different position than the subaltern voices that we have previously encountered, who tended to assume, at least rhetorically, that systems of rules were in general things of value – that law did ultimately matter. What follows thus focuses less on law itself than it does on the system of power relations in which law exists, or from which law emerges. The reason for this is that these texts urge us to ask a basic set of questions: where is law within these relationships, and what power ought it to have as compared to *other* modes of power or domination? That is, in a violent world, how much does law actually matter? In raising these questions, the characters in this chapter anticipate those of the next part (Part III) of this book: people who sought to find alternatives to day-to-day law in an empire.

***

One thing that provincial subjects and Roman administrators shared was a common metaphor for understanding domination: slavery. It is perhaps a truism that the Roman world was a "genuine slave society" in that slaves made up a significant part of the broader population (though admittedly they were unevenly distributed).[3] Perhaps most importantly, the everyday practice of slavery produced, in Mediterranean elites, a particular sort of violent habitus. Raised to expect deference, elites in the Roman world expected it; they lashed out when they did not receive it, especially when the disrespectful party was servile – or in some cases, even merely humble.[4] Sometimes this violence would be careful or considered, as some philosophers urged it to be. Just as often it was not.

It was thus easy to imagine a link between the government of provinces and the government of household slaves. To begin with, the men who governed provinces derived their "habit of command" from their earliest years and from their experience with the quotidian violence of the home.[5] As despite the fact that provincial populations

[3] Though see Lenski 2018, who rightly suggests that such a category misleads more than it explains, and argues that a more robust model needs to be developed.
[4] In general, MacMullen 1974; Lendon 1997.
[5] I take the phrase from Genovese 1965: 33.

might hope that relations with governors would be conducted under the sign of *logos*, much governance was done by summary violence, with little interest in hearing from the party being violated. Slavery, then, was not just a legal status; it was also a way of imagining political and social relationships of domination more broadly: it gave articulation to categories of personal status, to modes of ordering society, as well as to ways of imagining property.[6] It so predominated as a mode of imagining the social landscape that it occluded a great number of fine (or even less-fine) distinctions: there were many ways to be poor, humble, and semi-free in the Roman world, and in many cases it was easy enough to categorize such people as merely servile and thus deserving of violence. Thus when Apuleius depicts the protagonist of his *Metamorphoses* losing his privileged position in society, he can only describe this fall from privilege as a transformation into chattel.[7]

The equation of domination and slavery passed, in turn, into political theory. For some, the mere possession of sovereignty sufficed to render those subject to sovereign authority slaves. "Whenever another has the power to have a man scourged or imprisoned or put to death, or have anything else done to him that he wishes, then that man is the slave of the other," insists an imaginary interlocutor in Dio Chrysostom's fourteenth *Oration*, channeling what was undoubtedly a popular understanding.[8] Slavery thus also became part of the larger metaphorical vocabulary for understanding the structure and operation of empire. Both subjects and elites availed themselves of metaphors of enslavement for understanding their particular political situation.[9] We will similarly do well to remember Philo's claim about empire: "What heavier burden could a slave have than a hostile owner? Subjects are the slaves of an Emperor." In Philo's telling, only law stands between a subject who deserves

[6] The literature is vast; Bradley 1987 is helpful for the practice of slavery and its connection to everyday acts of violence; see also Patterson 1985 on the ways that slavery can come to be generative of other modes of theorizing domination. Slavery as a (largely inadequate) category for the co-construction of the category of freedom: Wirszubski 1950; Ando 2010a. On the importance of slavery in constructing the Roman imagination of property: Whitman 2025. On slavery and government, Lavan 2013.

[7] Bradley 2000. [8] *Or.* 14.12, trans. Cohoon, LCL.

[9] Lavan 2013. Note also Roller 2001, on the ways in which Roman elites used the vocabulary of slavery to interpret political domination by an autocrat.

respect and a slave who can be handled as one desires. Such a view was likely not unique to Philo.[10]

***

The *Life of Aesop* focuses on the experience of a slave, and as it does, it raises a package of questions about the nature of sovereignty and domination more generally. Aesop is perhaps the most prolific character of antiquity, with a mass of traditions both learned and vernacular constantly circulating throughout the Mediterranean. These traditions substantially predated the Roman Empire and substantially outlasted it as well.[11] But the particular tradition that I focus on in what follows most likely dates sometime between the first and third centuries AD, and, due to the low register of vernacular Greek in which it is written, almost certainly comes from a provincial context.[12]

This version of the *Life* is known as *Vita G* (hereafter, just *Life*). It poses substantial challenges. The only manuscript is dogged with problems and missing pages. These can sometimes be supplemented by a different and probably derivative *Life*, the *Vita W*. This poses dangers, however. The *Vita W* has a rather different agenda; critically, for present purposes, the redactor of *W* tends to miss some of the more subtly legalistic jokes. Internally, the text is wildly varied: as scholars have noted, this particular version of Aesop's life drew from a deep reservoir of stories, sayings, and traditions about Aesop that had been floating throughout the Mediterranean world for centuries

[10] On law as protecting individual people from personal violation akin to being treated as a slave, see further Bryen 2013, 2021a.

[11] Sources are collected and edited in Perry 1952, from whose text I work. I have also checked the text of Papathomapoulos 1990. The study of Kurke 2011, though literary rather than historical in orientation, has been essential in my thinking about this text. Similarly important is Hopkins 1993.

[12] The date of the text is hard to fix. Given the prevalence of Latinisms, it would be hard to place it before the first century AD, and contemporary papyri show that the story was being circulated and rewritten in the high empire. Unfortunately the papyri only provide rough dates, since they are dated paleographically and they show differences from the major recensions preserved in manuscript. For a brief summary of the papyrological evidence, see Papathomapoulos 1990: 21–22. By a similar token, there is no reason to think that the text is late antique: the mention of a *strategos* (*Life* 65) seems to reflect a typical official of the high empire, and there is little further reason to posit a late date. My arguments stand to the extent that the text can be said to be neither Hellenistic nor Byzantine.

at least.[13] Its structure is complex, and it blends a series of styles and registers of speech together into a single unit. Still, like a Gospel (to which it has been compared), the *Life of Aesop* represents a single, particular attempt to claim Aesop, or at least a version of him, within a larger set of arguments.[14] In brief, like Pythagoras, Apollonius of Tyana, or Jesus of Nazareth, Aesop was a figure whose life was told and retold in order to explore social or political issues – and, in the case of the *Life*, more specific questions about the nature of power, law, and *logos*.[15] In that regard, I should like to focus just on the first part of the *Life*, which deals with the relationship between Aesop and his new master, the philosopher Xanthus (a caricature of a puffed-up philosopher, and a wonderfully cruel send-up of the elites who feature in Chapter 7). The relationship between Xanthus and Aesop poses the central conundrum of the first part of the *Life*: how to navigate a world in which sovereignty sits in the hands of someone who was, at best, undeserving of it.

To understand these interactions between slave and master, some context is necessary. Aesop was most famously a fabulist, and in a number of highly learned traditions the telling of moralistic animal fables was his most substantial contribution to literary history. But there was another important tradition about Aesop that circulated, especially in the Roman period: he was something of a poor man's lawyer. As described by the *Suda*, Aesop "became a *logopoios* [storyteller], that is, someone who came up with stories and *responsa* … He wrote the story of what happened to him in Delphi in two books. But others say that Aesop only wrote a single book of *responsa*."[16] As we can tell from the reference, the compiler(s) of the *Suda* had not read these books, but their designation as *responsa* is no less remarkable: books

[13] Ruiz-Montero 2014; Karla 2016.

[14] For the importance of thinking of the individual recensions of these stories as elements in an "open tradition" of composition, see the remarks of Gallo 1996.

[15] In addition to Philostratus' *Life of Apollonius* (discussed in Chapter 7), Apollonius was also the subject of a biography by the governor of Bithynia, Hierocles, who composed a text called, according to Eusebius, the "Lover of Truth" (*Philalēthēs*) as a response to Christian stories of Jesus. Similarly, a certain Soterichus produced what was probably an epic poem on Apollonius (*FGrH* IV 1080).

[16] Suda, s.v. Αἴσωπος (= Perry 1952: T 3): ἐγένετο δὲ λογοποιός, ὃ ἐστιν εὑρετὴς λόγων καὶ ἀποκριμάτων … ἔγραψε τὰ ἐν Δελφοῖς αὐτῷ συμβάντα ἐν βιβλίοις β'. μᾶλλον δέ τινές φασι τὸν Αἴσοπον ἀποκρίματα γεγραφέναι μόνον.

of *responsa* had been a mainstay of juristic literature from the height of the Principate.[17] The "right to give *responsa*" was similarly a coveted status of jurists.[18] Aesop, however, was in many respects an *inversion* of the jurists: while they were staid and scholarly, detached men of high status who practiced a mandarin craft, Aesop was the paradigmatic *humilis persona*: ugly and misshapen, a slave, and a foreigner. As the *Life* introduces him:[19]

> The *logopoios* Aesop, the great benefactor of mankind, was a slave by status and by birth a Phrygian from Amorion in Phrygia, repugnant to behold as an attendant, worn-out, potbellied, pot-headed, snub-nosed, swarthy, black, stunted, crooked, weasel-armed, squint-eyed, liver-lipped – almost a proclamation that something had gone wrong.

Outwardly horrifying and socially degraded, Aesop could only navigate his world through the manipulation of *logos*. Roman jurists would have bristled at being called *logopoioi* (storytellers); Aesop's "jurisprudence" was inseparable from his ability to wield *logos* in a particularly tense situation. This skill, however, consisted not of setting out axioms of law and exploring their boundaries. Rather, it consisted of being a shrewd interpreter of language and, especially, of rules.

In the *Life*, sovereign power is violent indeed. Xanthus the philosopher is imagined as a leader of his community. But while his students fawn on him (and also constantly plot to upstage him), Aesop has no patience for his puffery. Accordingly, Aesop takes every opportunity to deflate his owner, to expose his pretension, and to undermine the seeming naturalness of his domination. Xanthus, in turn, continually reminds Aesop that his power is founded in violence and threatens to beat Aesop. These threats do nothing to change Aesop's behavior. Aesop's sharp tongue gets Xanthus in trouble with his shrewish wife,

17 See Schulz 1946: 223–42; Bryen 2019b. On Aesop as a jurist, see Bryen 2016b: 14–22.

18 On the vexed question of the *ius respondendi*, see now Tuori 2007.

19 1. The passage is corrupt in the manuscripts; Perry reconstructed from "crooked" (*blaisos*) on, improving the manuscript text substantially; Papathomopoulos follows this reconstruction, but makes a series of emendations to the earlier descriptors that strike me as highly plausible. In some details the translation of Daly (in Hansen 1998) is also useful: from him I take "liver-lipped" as the best translation of the unusual *mystakōn*. Little trust can be placed in the specific descriptors; the point nonetheless stands that this is a visually stunning portrait of a grotesque.

and eventually begins to upstage him in the lecture halls, managing to answer, with ease, the sorts of philosophical questions (*zētēmata*) posed by students to Xanthus himself. In each case, Aesop bests Xanthus by drawing not on the artificial learning of the schoolroom, but on a sort of folk wisdom combining the close observation of the everyday with a studied disinterest in cultural assumptions. To take but a single example, from Xanthus' lecture-hall: "'What would be the greatest disaster that could befall mankind?' one of the students asked. Standing up behind Xanthus, Aesop said: 'If the dead should rise and ask for their property to be returned.'"[20]

Realizing that his slave was eroding his image as a highly composed man of learning and wisdom, Xanthus started to rein Aesop in. His first attempt came in the form of a command: "Do not harm me by doing anything less or more than what I command you."[21] Such a command is typical of sovereign thinking. In formulating such a rule, Xanthus proposes that the problem in managing his subordinate comes not from the nature of the interaction (i.e., that "bad" behavior is just an inherent part of a relationship of absolute domination), but from the deficient interpretive capacities of his subordinate. The solution, according to this line of thinking, is to limit the subordinate's interpretive freedom. If Aesop would just do exactly as he was told, Xanthus would face no further embarrassment.

Xanthus' instructions, however, bring forth a series of interactions inherent in all attempts to reduce legal interpretation to something mechanistic or algorithmic. Instructing Aesop to accompany him to the bath, Xanthus orders him to "bring the oil-flask and the towels." To teach him a lesson, Aesop does precisely this:[22]

> Xanthus took off his clothes, handed them to Aesop, and said, "Aesop, give me the oil-flask." Xanthus took the oil-flask and tried to pour it, but found it empty. "Aesop, where's the oil?" he asked. "At home," Aesop said. "Why?"

[20] 47. One wonders if this passage doesn't hint at the prevalence of debates, taking place in the provinces, concerning the resurrection of the dead. See the remarkable discussion of Shaw (2011: 212–14) to get a sense of this debate as it took place in Africa in the fourth century.

[21] 38. The page prior to this instruction is lost; for the reconstruction of the text as a command, see Perry 1936: 5. The context is probably something like, "[I order you] not to harm me by..." (...⟨ἵνα μὴ⟩ βλάπτῃς).

[22] 38.

Xanthus said. Aesop said: "Because you told me to 'bring the oil-flask and the towels.' You said nothing about oil itself. And I was supposed to do nothing more than you said, and if I diverged from your law (*nomou*) I would find myself liable to a beating." At this, Xanthus fell silent (*hesychasen*).

This model of interaction is repeated throughout the first section of the *Life*. Thus, Xanthus orders Aesop to make for his student lentil soup, Aesop embarrasses Xanthus by producing a soup containing only a single lentil (Xanthus, he protests, should have ordered him to make *lentils* soup); similarly, when Xanthus sends Aesop to deliver a gift to his wife, he uses a periphrasis – "send it to the one who loves me (*eunouousēi*)" – so Aesop gives the gift to the family dog; and so on.[23]

We might note just a few features of these interactions. First, the command of a master to his slave is imagined to take the form of a *nomos* – an act of legislation. From the perspective of the master/sovereign, such a law was designed to smooth social interactions between ruler and ruled by making the instructions – the wish of the sovereign – perfectly clear. From the point of view of the master, the law, so long as it is clear, is also self-interpreting: good legislation, in other words, comes down to questions of draftsmanship. But this is also what makes Xanthus' enactment so ill designed. On the reasoning of the author of the *Life*, a particular order will always involve interpretation. There is no perfect and gapless law, and any attempt to design such a thing is doomed to failure precisely because it denies the importance of interpretation – that is, because it refuses to imagine subordinates as co-creators of law's content. Xanthus, then, enacts a master's fantasy of sovereignty over his slave. Aesop, in turn, undermines the performance by following the law so literally as to render it monstrously inefficient.

Second, though these particular interactions take place in the baths or the home rather than in the courtroom, the means of demonstrating the shortcomings of this particular vision of legality are identical to those on display in the texts discussed in previous chapters. The slave and his master argue, face-to-face and through the medium of dialogue, over the proper interpretation of the command. When the slave has the better argument, the master can only blush and fall silent. In this respect, the interaction follows the pattern laid out in

[23] 39–41; 44–49; cf. 51–55 (the best and worst of foods).

the petition of Dionysia and the *Martyrdom of Pionius*. Unlike in the *Martyrdom of Pionius*, however, here an effective argument successfully forestalls violence.

Defeated in these interactions, Xanthus takes a different tack. Rather than searching for a better rule, he becomes determined to find a pretense for giving Aesop a beating. So when Aesop is cooking a dish of pig's feet for Xanthus and his students, Xanthus steals one of the feet so that Aesop would come up short and embarrass Xanthus, thus giving Xanthus a reason to beat him. Aesop nonetheless detects Xanthus' attempt to find a pretense for violence, and manages to defuse the situation by finding an "extra" pig's foot for the pot. The solution is grotesquely violent: Aesop goes to the garden and amputates one foot from the pig living there, and thus avoids being beaten. Similarly, to placate his enraged wife, Xanthus again agrees to find a pretext for beating Aesop; Xanthus thus invites his students to dinner with the goal of humiliating and then beating Aesop. When asked to serve "the best" of foods, Aesop serves piles and piles of pork tongues, until the students become ill; when asked to serve "the worst" he does the same (on the grounds that speech can be both wonderful and horrid). His strategy is again both grotesque and successful: swollen and ill, neither the students nor the master can muster the energy to punish him. Finally, when Aesop finally gives in to his urge to vent and calls one of Xanthus' students a "busybody" (*periergon*), Xanthus insists that Aesop will receive a beating if he cannot produce someone who is *not* a busybody (*aperiergon*) – which Aesop manages to do.[24]

The individual interactions are highly amusing, but we need not detail them here. More important are the presumptions about violence and its relationship to rules and laws more generally. The author of the text assumes that the goal of the master/sovereign is, in fact, to use violence – that is, that the use of violence sates some particular desire on the part of those who are in charge. Therefore, any reason offered for the use of violence is *always* pretextual: when the goal is to inflict pain on one's inferiors, a pretext can always be found. A further and

[24] There is a major difference between the ways that *Vita G* and *Vita W* tell the story of the "man who is not a busybody" (56–64). In *Vita W*, Aesop initially fails to find such a man, and gets beaten; in *Vita G* he does not.

more radical thesis follows from this: no matter what masters may proclaim, in such a system violence is never – and can never be – *corrective*. And if violence is never corrective, individual rules are not worthwhile in and of themselves; they are rather snares designed to trap foolish subordinates.

The only way to avoid degradation and violence, on this logic, is to take a page from Aesop's book: to deploy reasoning whenever possible, but also to be willing to cheat – for the other side, the sovereign himself, is always operating in bad faith. (We might note how dismal a verdict this is on the role of law in society, compared, at least, to Philo's claim that legality is ameliorative of the most unpleasant aspects of domination.) Finally, the only way to get to the heart of these matters of control and punishment is through face-to-face confrontations with the master/ sovereign himself, through the medium of dialogue, and by treating the command of a master exactly as if it were the command of a governor, and susceptible to the same modes of interpretation and scrutiny. At the very least, such careful scrutiny might manage to make a violent person blush and refrain from violence, if only for a single occasion.

With these theses in mind, we might also consider Aesop's advice to Xanthus about how he ought to have treated his slave. "You should not have made such a law for me, or I would have served you better, master."[25] On its face it appears conciliatory: if only the master would have made different laws, or no laws at all, he would have gotten better results. This might seem to square poorly with the propositions just articulated. But this is part of the text's humor: in order for Aesop to be an ideal slave to Xanthus, what he needs is freedom to decide how to serve. This is precisely what he does not have. He cannot choose to serve or not to serve, or how best to serve. The argument is absurd: to make me a better slave, free me. By such "logic" Aesop manages to trip Xanthus up: he gives him the *image* of a rational or at least a moral argument, but one that collapses upon scrutiny. Yet it works on the learned professor, because even though he has sovereign power, he is nonetheless a simpleton. The humor is deadpan, but brutally effective.

***

[25] 43.

I should like to adduce one further anecdote from the *Life of Aesop* that sheds a somewhat different light on the ways that provincial populations thought about the challenges of legal interpretation. This anecdote is, in important ways, structurally different from the ones above; in it, Xanthus and Aesop are forced to collaborate to solve a legal problem. The target here is less Xanthus the abusive sovereign (though he is undoubtedly *a* target), but rather, experts in legal interpretation more generally. So far, comparatively little has been said about the class of men who counted themselves *iuris periti*, or experts in the law. Of these, the Roman jurists are of course the most famous. But the legal profession held attractions for provincial up-and-comers more generally, offering an important path to social mobility. And though we know little about the content of legal education, starting in the second century individuals in the provinces begin to commemorate themselves as legal experts.[26] We might be justified in suspecting that such men copied the sorts of claims about their privileged status in society that their counterparts in Rome made: that they were masters of a particular, arcane branch of knowledge, that such mastery marked them out as deserving of privilege and veneration, and hence, that their mastery of legal interpretation justified their domination of others. And though we can see traces of their existence across the landscape (including in the legal judgment by Ulpius Dionysodorus included in Dionysia's list of "precedents"), it remains a fact of some consequence that whatever work they *were* doing manages to resonate not at all in the preserved works of Roman jurisprudence. I shall return to this problem in Chapter 8.

The story in question begins with a betrayal. Despite his elevated social status as a philosopher, the *Life* makes clear that, like Xanthus himself, Xanthus' students were neither an especially clever lot nor an especially loyal one. While perhaps happy to lavish attention upon him in public, they were also eager to defenestrate him and take his position for themselves. Accordingly, they laid a trap for him: at dinner one night, they waited until he was good and drunk, then made him commit to an extravagant claim:[27]

[26] Dolganov 2020b on North Africa; Cf. the debate between Furstenberg 2023 and Rosen-Zvi 2023 on whether a similar paradigm might apply to rabbis.

[27] 69.

One of the students (*scholastikōn*), seeing that Xanthus had gotten carried away, said, "teacher, is Man capable of all things?" Xanthus replied, "Who has begun to speak of Man? How clever he is, and capable of all things!" The student quickly pressed the argument into absurdity: "Is it possible for any man to drink the sea dry?" Xanthus replied: "It's easy. I'll drink it down myself." The student replied, "And if you don't drink it down, what then?" Xanthus, overcome by the quantity of neat wine, said, "I stake my fortune on it. If I don't drink it down, I will have nothing left." They thus deposited their rings and formalized the agreement (*ekyrōsan tas synthēkas*).

Despite his constant abuse, Aesop tried to deter Xanthus; yet despite Aesop's best efforts, Xanthus committed to the bet. The next morning, returning to sobriety, Xanthus immediately regretted it and begged Aesop to find a way to get him off the hook for his foolish behavior. Note also that again we are in the realm of the grotesque: to even try to win his bet, Xanthus would have to stuff himself beyond all conceivable limits – a sort of *Cool Hand Luke* feat of human capacity stretched into the realm of total absurdity.

Scholars have noted that this particular riddle is not original to the *Life*; a similar version shows up in Plutarch's *Banquet of the Seven Sages*, as a challenge issued by the Ethiopians to the Egyptian king Amasis, and eventually solved, by Bias of Priene, in a similar way.[28] However, the version in the *Life* puts an unusual spin on the scenario. Unlike in Plutarch's version, in the *Life* this bet is framed explicitly as a legal question: Xanthus and his student make a formal contract (*synthēkas*), each depositing their rings with a third party (a *synthēkophylax*). The emphasis on legality is hardly accidental, and speaks to the *Life*'s focus on legal interpretation more generally.

It also evokes a particular context. At roughly the same time, there was what we might call a standing controversy among Roman jurists: how to deal with impossible conditions in stipulations (unilateral promises) and in wills. The controversy over these questions of impossibility was substantial enough that it ended up producing a dispute among various juristic "schools." In his *Institutes*, directed at law students, the jurist Gaius explains the conflict:[29]

[28] Kurke 2011: 217–18.

[29] 3.98, trans. Gordon and Robinson 1988, with minor modifications. On the nature of the school dispute, with reference to this passage, see Leesen 2010: 176–86.

Again, if someone stipulates subject to a condition which cannot be fulfilled, for instance, "if he touches the sky with his finger," the stipulation is ineffective. But where a legacy is left under an impossible condition our teachers hold it to be due, as if it had been left unconditionally. The authorities of the other school think the legacy is as ineffective as an impossible stipulation. And certainly it is hardly possible to give a satisfactory reason for the distinction (*et sane vix idonea diversitatis ratio reddi potest*).

In other words, the *Life* is gesturing not only at a sort of "canonical" problem of wisdom, but also of a particular legal problem that was of roughly contemporary interest, at least among a certain class of legal mandarins.

But there are hints that the problem was disputed more widely, even outside of juristic contexts: thus, when discussing impossible conditions in his commentary *On Urseius Ferox*, the jurist Julian, writing in the second century, notes that "an *impossible* condition is deemed to be unwritten" (*quod* ἀδύνατος *condicio pro non scripta habetur*). The insertion of the Greek word is a linguistic clue to the contexts in which the problem was debated: impossible things were to be done in Greek-speaking rhetorical schools; for hard-nosed jurists, writing in Latin, they simply did not count.[30] Another Roman jurist, also in the second century, when confronted with a case of impossibility, responded with a similarly bilingual snarl, "this question is one of the *impossible cases*, styled *a deception* by dialecticians (*dixi* τῶν ἀπόρων *hanc quaestionem esse, qui tractatus apud dialecticos* τοῦ ψευδομένου *dicitur*)." He refused to be baited into attempting an answer that would leave him in this sort of intellectual trap.[31] In other words, like the rule against perpetuities in American law schools, the question of impossibility was both a substantive legal issue *and* a shibboleth for testing the capacities and boundaries of juristic reasoning – and *a fortiori*, their ability to defend their particular, privileged status. It also marked the jurists as a particular class of people: distinct from those who prattled on in Greek about silly things, jurists did serious things, and did them in Latin.

[30] *Dig.* 30.104.1 = Frg. 888 Lenel.

[31] *Dig.* 35.2.88 = Afr. 5 *Quaest.*, Frg. 52 Lenel. Cf. Aul. Gell. *NA* 9.15, a similar story about the rhetorician Julian dealing with a question of impossibility; *BT Bekhorot* 8b (Rabbi Yehoshua debates the sages of Athens on questions of impossibility).

By telling this story of impossibility, the *Life* raises the specter of contemporary juristic reasoning, but it also ups the ante. The very issue of impossibility is in some sense what is at stake: Xanthus has already conceded (and he is, of course, an expert) that the condition of the bet is not, in fact, impossible, and his counterparty agrees. Such a foolish concession obviously puts Aesop in a harder position than that of his juristic contemporaries. In this context, it is worth remembering not only the notice of the *Suda* (that Aesop was known for giving *responsa*, like a jurist), but also that, in the popular imagination, his ability to solve legal riddles often came at the expense of jurists.

We might consider as an example of this an exemplary Aesop "lawyer" story, told by Phaedrus in the first century AD:[32]

A certain man at his death left three daughters. One of them was a beauty and sought to capture men with her eyes; the second, however, was a spinner of wool, frugal, and a country girl; the third was addicted to wine and exceedingly ugly. Now the old man had made the mother of these girls his heir on condition that she should divide the entire fortune equally (*aequaliter*) among the three, but in the following manner: "Let them neither possess nor enjoy that use of what has been given to them," and again, "As soon as they shall have ceased to hold the property they have received, let them bestow upon their mother a hundred thousand sesterces apiece." Athens was filled with gossip about this. The mother went about diligently consulting jurists (*iuris peritos consulit*). No one succeeded in explaining how the heirs could avoid possessing what might be given them, or reaping the benefit of it; nor, moreover, could anyone explain how heirs who retained nothing were to bestow money.

The story shares with the anecdote about Xanthus the emphasis on a seemingly impossible condition. It is also a send-up of the jurists, and their claims to having the correct hermeneutic keys to solve complex social problems. The mother, on Phaedrus' telling, runs about Athens (always a stand-in for Rome in the imaginative literature of the Empire), consulting jurists whose job it was, in theory, to find a legal means to allow the poor mother not to starve. Their failure is conspicuous, however, and rumors fill Athens.

But just as the mother gets ready to give up her hope of finding a favorable legal opinion, a solution is found. From the perspective of

[32] Phaedrus 4.5, trans. Perry, LCL, with minor modifications. On the politics of Phaedrus' fables, see Henderson 2001. On the problems of his biography and its relation to his poetry, see Champlin 2005.

a jurist it is much worse (I give the words typical of "legal" Latin in parentheses):[33]

After much time had been spent in delay (*mora*), and still the meaning of the will (*testamenti*) could not be deduced, the parent, ignoring the letter of the law (*iure neglecto*), had recourse to equity (*fidem*). For the meretricious daughter she sets aside garments, articles for a lady's toilet, bathing vessels made of silver, beardless eunuchs; for the spinner of wool, the fields, sheep, farmhouse, laborers, oxen, beasts of burden, and farming equipment; to the drinker, a cellar full of casks of old wine, a luxuriously furnished house, and charming little gardens. When she was about to distribute to each the things marked out for them, and the people generally approved, since they knew the girls, Aesop suddenly stood forth in the midst of the crowd and exclaimed:

"Oh, if the buried father still were conscious, how would it grieve him that the men of Athens could not interpret his intentions (*quod voluntatem suam interpretari non possunt*)!"

Shocked that the Athenians cannot understand the intention (*voluntas*) of the testator, Aesop proffers a solution to the will's riddle to ensure that the mother received her share too: he proposes a division that went against the character of each of the daughters' characters (*moribus*), such that they would each immediately liquidate her share. Thus the garments and jewelry would go to the drunk, the farm to the ugly one, and the fields to the urbane beauty. Each would then sell, and that would give them the cash to endow the mother in her old age. In offering this solution, Aesop both undoes the errors of the lawyers (*solvit errorem*) and receives the praise of the citizens of Athens. A final barb, directed at the self-proclaimed *iuris prudentes* is added by the moral of the story: "Thus did the sagacity (*sollertia*) of one man find the answer to a problem that had eluded the inadequate understanding of many (*quod multorum fugit inprudentiam*)."

To return to the story of Xanthus: Xanthus' contract in the *Life* draws on what seems to be something of an empire-wide tradition of Aesop as a legal interpreter. It also invokes Aesop in the context of a highly sophisticated debate on the nature of legality and its relationship to material reality. And, of course, it operates in the context of power: Aesop is not reasoning through the problem in any sort

[33] On Phaedrus' use of legal vocabulary, see esp. Champlin 2005: 111–15, who argues on the basis of such vocabulary that Phaedrus was likely a lawyer.

of official capacity, nor is it referred to him as a neutral arbiter. It is foist upon him by his master, and both master and slave will be dramatically affected by his success or failure in finding a solution. Clever legal analysis, in this context, is more than an idle problem for intellectuals, but a matter of one's own material wellbeing; indeed, the next morning, the students arrive at Xanthus' house to force him to drink the sea or hand over his property, and Aesop is the first item of Xanthus' property that they desire to take possession of.

Being a realist, Aesop recognizes that the bet is unwinnable; it is simply impossible (*adynaton*) to drink the whole sea. Accordingly, he proposes a different solution, giving Xanthus the following instructions:[34]

> When the guarantor of the contract comes with your opponent, telling you to drink down the sea, don't argue, but set out the terms you agreed to while drunk, and with self-control, say: "Get a table, order it to be set and attended by slaves." This will create a spectacle, and the whole populace will come to see you drink down the sea. When you see that everything has been readied, fill a cup from the sea and call over the guarantor of the contract, saying "What did I agree to in the contract?" He will say, "To drink down the sea." Now you say, "Nothing else?" And he will say, "No." Having attested to this, say "Fellow citizens, there are many rivers – both persistent and seasonal – which flow into the sea; I have made an agreement just to drink down the sea, not the rivers that flow into it as well. Let my opponent stop up the mouths of the rivers, so that I can drink down just the sea. For just as it is impossible (*adynaton*) to stop up all the mouths of the rivers in the world, so too is it impossible (*adynaton*) for me to drink down the sea." Thus, one impossibility cancels out the other, and will break the contract.

The solution that Aesop proposes is substantially the same as the one proposed in the banquet of the Seven Sages, but put in legal terms it is clever, perhaps even a sleight-of-hand. Mere impossibility does not itself cancel Xanthus' obligations (for he has conceded that no such impossibility exists). Accordingly, Aesop has Xanthus claim that the *unilateral* obligation that Xanthus has taken on (to drink the sea or to forfeit his property) is actually a *bilateral* obligation: those who wish to see him drink the sea must see to it that *only* the sea gets drunk, and nothing else.[35] And his opponent has to fulfill his side of the contract first.

[34] 71.

[35] To use Bruce Frier's (2021: 84) words, "the stipulation is ostensibly a unilateral promise made subject to the tacit condition that it can be performed." In this case, of course, the tacit condition requires the active performance of the other party.

The trick worked: Xanthus gathered the people in public, insisted on hearing the terms of the contract, and delivered precisely the speech that Aesop prepared. The crowd immediately understood that the situation had been transformed: no longer were they there to witness a grotesque feat of human capacity; instead, they were present at a contest (*agōn* – a standard Greek word for lawsuit): a staged, *structured* standoff between two parties to determine which party was superior. It was, of course, Xanthus. The audience proclaimed: "Xanthus has won (*nenikēken*)! A shout arose from the crowd giving honors to Xanthus." Playing his part, the defeated student "fell before Xanthus' feet, and proclaimed, 'Teacher, you are truly great and you have won – I agree. I beg you, let the contract be voided.'"[36]

What are we to make of this elaborate scene, with its (mock) lawyerly reasoning, and its sagacious slave? To the extent that we might consider it a meditation on the importance of legal interpretation in a situation of domination, we might conclude that it demonstrates that the intellectual ability to engage in legal interpretation is not, or at least not necessarily, located in the hands of the socially dominant. It is a power that is vested in a slave, not only because that slave is preternaturally clever, but also because it is a slave – the dominated party – that has need of such interpretive abilities more often. He is, quite simply, more practiced.

What is more, the slave is perfectly capable of using that power not just to interpret laws in a literal sense, but to interpret them cleverly – sometimes all too cleverly, in the case of Xanthus' contract. In point of fact there is no good reason to assume that a unilateral contract implies a bilateral performance, much less that it would be the obligation of the student (here referred to as a party at law – an *antidikos*) to perform first. Great stretches of Roman juristic writing are devoted to the question of the order in which parties with competing claims must fulfill obligations. Here the solution is just baldly stated, and meets with no protest by the supposedly learned student – who presumably should have known better.

Aesop's "solution" is not so much an act of sophisticated legal interpretation as it is a mockery of it; it is, in a sense, a form of Purim Torah that uses the formal moves of interpretation to mock the pretentions

[36] 73.

of its audience. Those who were formally in power might be easily hoodwinked by such a performance, and if they were, then all the better – they were fools to begin with, and they had done nothing to have earned their particular powers. Finally, we might note that, in proffering his solution, Aesop stages the "performance" of the contract as a public dialogue – precisely the sort of public, face-to-face dispute or test of wills and reasoning that made up the structure of the criminal trial, or the various other agonistic public engagements that constituted public entertainment in the Roman world more generally.[37] In so doing, he made the private agreement into a public contest amenable to legal reason – or at least, a form of trickery spoken in a legalistic register.

I should like to make one final point about the *Life of Aesop*. Aesop eventually earns his freedom and goes on to have a successful career. As soon as he is freed, he becomes the sort of *logopoios* that one would expect: telling animal fables and offering rulers clever solutions to problems. But he becomes much worse at legal interpretation and eventually disastrous at dialogue. After success at the courts of Croesus and of Lygdamis, he eventually travels to Delphi, where he gets himself into trouble by continually insulting the Delphians – on the grounds, no less, that they were the descendants of slaves. The Delphians, as revenge, plant a golden cup in his luggage, and accuse him of stealing from the temples. In precisely the situation that one would expect him to excel (defending himself against false charges), he fails completely and conspicuously. He offers no good reasons for acquittal, only increasingly insulting fables. The Delphians push him off a cliff, as a condemned thief. The power to speak thoughtfully about law and to engage in the sorts of dialogue that reveal its nature, on this reading, does not come from the possession of freedom or a position of power; it is an ability that emerges from, and is bound to, the fact of domination.

***

Aesop – or at least, this particular tradition of Aesop – was perhaps unique in the extent to which he interrogated questions of legality through the persona of a degraded and stigmatized interpreter. But

[37] On other forms of public disputation or tests of ability, see, for medicine, Mattern 2008 and Gleason 2012; for rhetorical performance, Gleason 1995; for criminal justice, Gleason 1999; and for religious truth, Lim 1995: 1–30.

we might point to other traditions of similar sorts of degraded folk heroes who engage in legal interpretation: there is at least a partial analogue in the Gospel of Mark's description of the debates between Jesus of Nazareth and the Pharisees, for instance.[38] And there are traditions about Tevi, the learned slave of rabbi Gamaliel, who carries out an Aesopic performance in *Leviticus Rabbah*. Like Aesop, Tevi traditions circulated through various oral traditions as a folk hero-like character, whose position in society and whose relative virtues were the subject of debate among the Jews of late antiquity.[39]

But there were other Aesopic figures as well. Geviʿa (or Geviha) ben Psisa, or Geviʿa ben Qosem ("son of a sorcerer"), though not a slave, offers an important analogy, as well as evidence that the sorts of legal politics that I have been describing existed outside of traditional "Greek" communities. Like Aesop, Geviʿa is a character who appears in a series of texts from late antiquity: the two scholia of *Megillat Taʿanit* and the Midrashic compilation *Genesis Rabbah* (both from Palestine in the fourth or fifth centuries), as well as in the Babylonian Talmud. The number and diversity of the traditions about Geviʿa, however, suggests that he was a character who emerged, like Aesop, as part of a broader and earlier folk tradition – a person, or at least a character, who might serve as a way to frame crucial problems of power and domination. As his name indicates, he was physically deformed – specifically hunchbacked (*geviʿa*). Although in one telling of his story he is said to be the gatekeeper of the temple, in the other traditions he is a man with no formal position at all: he is specifically called *hedyot* – that is, *idiōtēs* ("simpleton") in Greek.[40] Most importantly, he is *not* a sage or a rabbi. The various traditions about Geviʿa differ in their details, but share two features: he defends the community against an outside threat, and he defends the historical property claims of the Jewish people. The outside threat varies: in the earliest,

38 E.g., Mark 7.

39 *Leviticus Rabbah* 33.1, with the valuable discussion of Wenger 2023.

40 Amit Gvaryahu has generously helped me with these texts and their complicated traditions. Scholion P of *Megillat Taʿanit* and *BT Sanhedrin* 91a (which shows some affinities to it) call Geviʿa *hedyot*; Scholion O calls him the temple gatekeeper. For linguistic reasons I have been unable to engage the study of Noam 2003, who offers an edition of these texts as well as a close reading of this episode. I have nonetheless benefited much from her overview of the text and the scholia: Noam 2006.

Palestinian versions of the story, from *Megillat Taʿanit* and *Genesis Rabbah*, the threat is Alexander the Great himself, who insists upon entering the forbidden precincts of the Temple;[41] in the Babylonian Talmud the threat is a *min* (a sectarian, for lack of a better term) who denies the resurrection of the dead.

It is his status as an inferior, and one visibly – and comically – marked as such, that enables the main action in the Geviʿa stories. These stories share a common narrative framing. In the age of Alexander the Great, or so it is claimed, various communities sought to make property claims before the king that would deprive the Jews of their land. The actors vary in the individual versions of the story, but they include the Canaanites and the Egyptians, as well as the Ishmaelites and the Africans. Worse still, each of these potential threats claims to base its claims to Jewish land on the basis of the Torah itself. The versions of the story seem also to hint at the "greatest disaster that could befall mankind" from Aesop: that the dead should arise and demand back their property.

Though the scenario imagined here is historically unlikely (there is no reason to think that Alexander the Great heard these particular property claims), the text does evoke what must have been a traumatic occurrence in the history of a community, Jewish or otherwise: a moment in which the normal political structure of a region collapsed. These various political collapses happened irregularly but with dramatic results. Taking just the possible points of reference in the history of the Jewish heartland, the conquest of Alexander, the conquests of Pompey the Great, the substantial reshaping of the provincial landscape by Augustus, the destruction of the temple by Titus and Vespasian, and the suppression of the Bar Kochba rebellion by Hadrian might all represent this *type* of moment. Each resulted in dramatic reorganizations of the political landscape. Our text, then, locates its action in a sort of Schmittian moment when preexisting systems of political and legal authority collapsed or were suspended, and before they were reconstructed. Such a moment was pregnant with both danger and possibility – a political chasm would have

41 See further Amitay 2006, who argues that the Alexander of the story is a stand-in for Pompey, and identifies the historical Geviʿa with Kyrtos ("hunchback") the grandfather of Josephus.

opened up to allow in competing claims to property and territory, each justified by particular understandings of history, and motivated by competition for ethno-communal advantage.[42]

One would think that defending against such claims is properly the job of sages or rabbis (supposedly masters of Torah, and self-proclaimed leaders of their communities). But it is Geviʿa who volunteers to go before Alexander and defend the community's claims to its land. In so doing he devises a cunning strategy:[43]

In the days of Alexander of Macedon the Ishmaelites came to dispute the birthright with Israel and they were accompanied by two evil families, the Canaanites and the Egyptians. "Who shall go to plead against them?" it was asked. Said Geviʿa, the son of Qosem: "I will go and plead against them." "Take care not to let the land fall into their hands," they cautioned him. "I will go and argue with them," he replied; "and if I defeat them, 'tis well; while if not, you can say, 'Who is this hunchback[44] to take up our case?'"

In this respect, the various stories are essentially the same. However, when it comes to the defense itself, the stories begin to diverge. In one version (from *Megillat Ta'anit*) the confrontations between Geviʿa and his interlocutors are framed as taking place *prior* to a hearing with Alexander. In *Genesis Rabbah*, by contrast, the action is located in front of Alexander himself:[45]

Said the Ishmaelites, "We are the claimants, and we base our claim on their own laws. It is written, *but he shall acknowledge the firstborn, the son of the hated*, etc. (Deut. 21:17), and Ishmael was the firstborn." Said Geviʿa ben Qosem; "Your majesty! Cannot a man do as he wishes to his sons?" "Yes," replied he. "Then," persued he, "surely it is written, *And Abraham gave all that he had unto Isaac*" (Gen. 25:5).

The basic argument of the Ismaelites might be said to be an inheritance claim: as the first children of Abraham, they are entitled to a

42 Cf. *BT Yoma* 69a, a similar threat involving Alexander the Great, who, at the request of the Samaritans, threatened to hand over and destroy the Jerusalem temple. Unlike in this set of stories, however, the threat is taken care of by the high priest, to whose will Alexander submits. See further Mason 2016: 225–39 on the history of conquest and disruption in Judaea in the Hellenistic period.

43 *Genesis Rabbah* 61.7, trans. Freedman in Freedman and Simon 1983 with modifications. All translations of this text come from Freedman from this edition.

44 Amit Gvaryahu (pers. comm.) points out that the earliest manuscripts of *Genesis Rabbah* here have *geviʿa*; some later editions print something different.

45 *Genesis Rabbah* 61.7

double portion of his estate. But Gevi'a counters with a seemingly legal principle: presumably a man can choose to distribute his estate as he chooses. It should be immediately apparent that no such rule existed in Jewish, Greek, or Roman law – and anyone reading this text would have been intimately aware of this. Gevi'a's appeal to "principle" is thus something of a *trompe l'oeil* – it is more clever than smart, a bit of serio-comic Purim Torah. This is surely the source of its humor. This parody of serious reasoning, moreover, is enough for Alexander the Great, and this is surely part of the joke.

A similar interaction takes place with the Canaanites:

> The Canaanites then pleaded: "We base our suit against them on their own Torah. It is everywhere written, 'The land of Canaan'; let them return to us our country." Said he [Gevi'a] to him [Alexander], "Your majesty! Cannot a man do as he pleases with his slave?" Replied he, "Yes." "Then surely it is written, *A slave of the slaves shall he* [Canaan] *be unto his brethren.* (Gen. 9:25). Hence they are now our slaves." Thereupon they fled in shame.

The Canaanite claim is not so much about legal principles as it is historical and philological: there is a land, the land of Canaan, attested in a text even the Jews deem authoritative, and the complainants are Canaanites. They have therefore presumably been displaced, but the king has the opportunity to rectify this particular injustice. In the eastern Mediterranean, such claims could last a long time indeed: in the third century BC, for instance, king Lysimachus was forced to adjudicate between Samos and Priene over the possession of a tract of land whose possession had been in question since the conquests of king Lygdamis in the seventh century BC. The Prienians came prepared to argue their case on the basis of "histories and other testimonials" as well as various other legal documents that they claimed confirmed their possession. Still, the Samians appear to have prevailed – at least temporarily. The Roman Senate had to intervene in the same dispute on at least two further occasions in the second century BC.[46] Memories in the Mediterranean could be long indeed.

In *Genesis Rabbah* Gevi'a succeeds not only because he can produce other biblical texts that serve to undermine the claims of the

[46] *OGIS* 13 = Welles 1974 [1934]: no. 7; *ARS* 41a = Sherk 1969: no. 10. Cf. the tablet from Esterzili (*ILS* 5947 = Levick, *Government* 53), recording a dispute that lasted from 114 BC to at least 69 AD.

Canaanites, but also because he manages to articulate for Alexander a specific legal principle to guide the reading of those texts. In the case of the Canaanites, the larger principle (that a man can do anything he wants with a slave) explains how to construe the biblical text itself. But the reasoning is again fallacious: in no contemporary society could a man do as he pleased to his slave. Hoodwinked, Alexander nonetheless concedes Geviʿa's point. What is more, he is goaded into accepting the claim that, far from being displaced, the Canaanites should actually *remain* the slaves of Israel. The Canaanites have no choice, under such a reversal of circumstances, but to run away in shame.

In the case of the Egyptians, a similar strategy prevails: the Egyptians claim that the Israelites "despoiled" them when they left Egypt; Geviʿa insists that first the Egyptians need to compensate the Israelites for more than two hundred years of slavery. Only after this reckoning can their competing claim be heard. It is a slightly different but no less legalistic claim: rather than a claim about "substantive" legal principle (i.e., that a master is entitled to his slave's property or that he is sovereign over his son), Geviʿa makes a claim about procedural law – the order in which complaints must be adjudicated. Again, Geviʿa's argument prevails. As the mathematicians begin to work out the bill for the Egyptians, the Egyptians realize that they would be bankrupted long before the process could go forward; like their fellow claimants, they too run away in shame. The move is essentially similar to the punchline in the *Life of Aesop*, where Aesop frees Xanthus from his obligation by insisting on the priority of a particular claim.

The Geviʿa story has a final episode, one that is Aesopic in nature. Presumably impressed by Geviʿa's performance, Alexander decides to go to the Jerusalem temple, and to enter the holy of holies. Geviʿa accompanies him, but also manages to keep him from engaging in a profane act:

He [Alexander] wished to go up to Jerusalem, but the Cutheans told him, "Take heed, for they will not permit thee to enter the holy of holies." When Geviʿa, the son of Qosem, learned of this, he went and made a pair of felt shoes and set them with two costly stones worth twenty thousand silver [*zuz*]. When they reached the temple mount he said to him, "Your majesty: remove your shoes and put on these felt shoes, as the pavement is smooth and you might slip." When they came to the holy of holies he said to him: "Thus far we may enter, but no farther." "When I come out I will straighten your hump," he [Alexander] threatened. "If you do that you would be famed as a great surgeon and receive fat fees," he [Geviʿa] retorted.

The threat of violence against the unprivileged and stigmatized guardian of the community is thus matched with Aesopic wit, which claims that the violence of a superior would actually entail a benefit to its victim. And besides, the dupe (Alexander) has put on a pair or felt shoes, bedazzled by their lavish décor. They would offer him no traction, and thus there would be no kicking (neither, of course, would there be profanation). Told as such, the story is a well-worn folktale: the readiest analogy is the African American tradition of Br'er Rabbit and the briar patch. With Geviʿa, like with Aesop, we are firmly in the world of popular imagination, and among the tricksters.

***

In *Genesis Rabbah* we see a version of the same sort of power scenario as framed in the story of Aesop: in a moment that represents a legal vacuum, where the only certain thing is the pure power of a particular sovereign, the technique of the stigmatized folk hero is to frame the issue at hand as if it were a problem of law. Alexander – or Pompey, or Augustus, or anyone else (including a slave's master) who, through the application of violence, had created such a political and legal vacuum – would not have been under any obligation to listen to such claims, at least not in reality. But at the level of storytelling – that is, at the level of legal mythology and political theory – the assumption was that they would, or at the very least that they *should*, for such was the source of their legitimacy. If one could then take advantage of them while they listened, so much the better.

Yet presumably a sage would have done as good of a job in defending the land – so why is it that a hunchback is the one who is sent forward? We might make several guesses. First, following the model of Aesop, it is precisely because Geviʿa is stigmatized that he can make such arguments in court. He is not expected to make convincing legal arguments, and if he fails in so doing, his notional superiors can deny that he is their representative. Second, within the Greco-Roman context, hunchbacks in particular could be understood to be apotropaic – they warded off threats to the individual and the community, and especially threats that came from *phthonos* – the desire to displace one's enemy from what is rightfully his.[47] This would certainly fit the case of the envious enemies of the Jews, who covet Jewish land and who need to be repulsed. However, it may be that Geviʿa's disabled body evokes more than mere dissonance, producing instead what, in a different context, Ato Quayson has called "aesthetic nervousness": a destabilizing reaction to the presence of the non-normative, who upend normal categories and resist being placed easily within a hierarchy.[48]

Finally, and perhaps most importantly, we should remember that this story – like the stories of Aesop – is meant to be funny. A hunchback getting the better of the enemies of the Jews by being an excellent legal interpreter is absurd and incongruous, especially in a Mediterranean world that presumed a deep link between physical and political excellence. It is similarly amusing that the points he makes about law are not especially sophisticated – they are at best clever, but they work nonetheless because one can count on one's adversaries to be genuine rubes. They are made in the spirit of jouissance. Legal interpretation, in such a world, need not proceed with furrowed brow – it can encompass low comedy and grotesque humor as well. And in this respect we also get a better sense of the ultimate target of this sort of humor: rabbis and jurists might be imagined as humorless men with furrowed brows, and, like Aesop defending Xanthus, might be mocked for their pomposity, only to be saved by their social inferiors.

* * *

I should like to close this chapter, and this part of the book, with two further thoughts. It might be imagined to weigh heavily against my interpretations that characters like Aesop and Geviʿa went on to have very different lives in their later reception histories. Aesop was remembered not as a shrewd lawyer, but as a teller of animal fables that gave relatively straightforward answers to what constituted prudent and thoughtful behavior – especially around the powerful.[49]

47 Dunbabin and Dickie 1983; Clarke 2006; cf. *Life of Aesop* (*Vita G*) 16, and the depictions of *phthonos* in Figure 3.5.

48 Quayson 2007.

49 Though Aesop could always be repurposed: see Monoson 2016.

To the extent that Geviʿa was remembered at all, it is in the relatively limited context of a single section of the Babylonian Talmud. There, he engages in similar sorts of debates with peoples who wish to make claims on Jewish properties, but the frame is entirely different. He features in a lengthy section of tractate *Sanhedrin*, which turns primarily on the justification for the belief in the resurrection of the dead; there he is joined to stories of rabbis (including Rabbi Meʿir, Rabban Gamliel, and Rabbi Judah ha-Nasi) defeating other interlocutors – Roman emperors and Queen Cleopatra among them.[50] What is more, Geviʿa no longer saves the Jewish people from Alexander's threats to their lands (that is, preserving the integrity of the Jewish temple from an outside threat), but rather defeats a *min* (sectarian) in debate. That is, he preserves community harmony in the face of an *internal* threat to disrupt community harmony prompted by mistaken or problematic belief. In this context, the Babylonian rabbis reinterpreted Geviʿa as just another rabbi learned in the Torah, rather than as an unusual and potentially problematic protector of the Jewish people whose presence was a standing threat to the authority of sages themselves.

How did this transformation take place? If these stories operate as meditations on the nature of dialogic interaction in an empire; if they foreground questions of legality; and if they use grotesque, low humor to make their points in the subjunctive – then how did they come to be read as consistent with the values of those in power? How did these characters become unproblematic? Why were these stories read – and re-written – by writers who seem completely incapable of imagining these texts making radical claims?

Some of the answers must be found in a radically changed institutional world. The late antique readers of these texts were no longer committed to the virtues of plurality, and no longer open to the possibility that a notionally degraded or stigmatized person might have something to offer. They wrote in the era in which the historical transformation that this book traces had been completed. These subsequent writers and readers were no longer subaltern. Some of them were Christians in a deeply Christian world; they imagined themselves not as subjects who had to negotiate systems of power that were at times contradictory or inscrutable, but rather as a part of

50 90b–91a.

a sovereign and victorious people whose job was the (re)production of virtue and the prevention of heresy and dissention. Others were Jews in a pluralistic empire, but their particular reaction to life in the Sassanian world was to conceive themselves as a closed community of homogeneous fellow-subjects, knit together by common observance of an exceedingly technical if not picayune law whose major points of reference were located in a world far gone.[51] In both cases, they sought to naturalize these unusual and problematic voices within the structure of a governing class, and in so doing, they lost the ability to appreciate the mockery of the jesters and the sorts of possibilities it invited.[52]

To try to discipline these voices was necessary. Their potential conclusions were too radical. Whereas the bulk of the provincial voices featured in this book so far at least gestured towards the liberatory potential of legalism, these two texts differ in their ultimate conclusions. They might be said to be Seinfeldian. Their humor comes from their absurdity, from their grotesque characters, and from their deadpan delivery. And at the end of the day, they verge on being nihilistic. In their world, sovereign power is always malign, unqualified, and narcissistic. To live in the world in which it operates means finding techniques that succeed in befuddling power, for at least long enough that one can either protect oneself or escape. Rules and law – and the languages through which we discuss and apply them – are ultimately not goods in themselves. They might be useful for protecting the weak, but this is only because the weak can convince the strong that the strong have an obligation to follow them. Under such circumstances, the best strategy is to feign one's commitment to rules, and to treat processes as if they had independent value. Dialogue allowed this to happen, but it had no independent value. It is a grim verdict indeed – a show about nothing.

In the chapters that follow I shall trace a further reaction to subaltern claims about the ultimate value of law. First I shall turn to what became communities of early Christians, who similarly thought that the legal processes of empire offered no ultimate good, and should

[51] On Sassanian pluralism, with reference to Christian experiences in particular, see Payne 2015, and with reference to Jewish experiences, Gross 2024.

[52] Boyarin 2009 is more optimistic.

be avoided in the name of crafting a community that existed beyond, or even above, law's ultimate reach. I shall then trace a fairly harsh and indignant reaction, among elites of the empire, to these subaltern ideas about legality, sovereignty, process, and dialogue. These elites crafted their own understandings of the "true" foundations of imperial law – one based in affect, performance, and the transcendence of the everyday features of administration. Both groups might be said to be "anti-legal" in their orientations. To understand the full landscape of provincial ideas about legality, it is necessary to account for their understandings as well.

THE PRACTICES OF EXCLUSION

PART III

LAW AS ECSTASY

6

The Transcendent Body Politic

When provincial subjects started to question the nature of Roman justice by telling stories about it, they engaged in a form of political discourse. At the heart of this discourse were concerns about the nature of Roman power and the relationship between that power, rules of law, and human reason or *logos*. As I argued in the previous chapter, these stories were not just interpretations of Roman imperial practices; they also advanced several claims: (a) that the most important venue for thinking about the nature of law was the courtroom itself; (b) that the courtroom was the optimal space for communication between ruler and subject; and (c) that the discourse that ought to prevail in the courtroom was, fundamentally, a rational one, whereby subjects and rulers constituted themselves as partners in a dialogue in which each side was, ideally, amenable to *logos*, or reasoned argument. Provincial subjects further insisted that the sorts of guardrails that structured courtroom dialogue – the respect for *logos*, in particular – might be generalized into a broader social theory, where *logos* might channel or parry the tendency of powerful people towards violence. In so far as legality goes, these subjects presumed – and argued, at times effectively – that law was not something fundamentally external to a particular individual or community. It was, instead, immanent, and revealed or negotiated through the process of dialogic encounters with the powerful.

In the previous sections, I argued that such a perspective should be called, *faute de mieux*, a subaltern one: it emerged from the experience of feeling oneself to be on the receiving end of governance. Yet the provinces were diverse, and there was more than one way to process the experience of empire. Two groups of provincial subjects stand out in their opposing theories of the role of legality in society. These are the subjects of this section of the book. One of these, the subject of the next chapter (7), concerned the elites of the empire. Empires could not run without collaboration from local people, and this required buy-in at the ritual, administrative, and even cognitive levels.[1] These members of the empire thus thought of themselves not as subalterns, but as insiders. For them, the subaltern perspective raised problems. The courtroom offered little appeal to the empire's elites. It was, to be certain, a site of imperial power, but it held little attraction as a place to negotiate relationships, even at the level of imagination and fantasy. It was, by contrast, simply a place of administrative processing, and not a particularly attractive one at that. There were, these elites contended, better ways to process problems, and better ways to engage in the practice of *logos*. Their solution was to develop an ideology that might, preliminarily, be called "law avoidance." The alternative that they constructed – a world constituted by the wondrous, based in a shared system of elite male affect – will be dealt with in the subsequent chapter.

At the center of this chapter is a parallel phenomenon: groups of Jews and early Christians who sought to constitute their communities in a different relationship to imperial legality. In contrast to the elites, we may call them "the elect" (fully acknowledging that the term bears baggage from a subsequent era). They were similar to the elites in that they sought to conceive of community as a space apart from everyday legality. Both groups, elites and elect, similarly imagined that law – real law, rather than the stuff of daily administration – came from a process of *transcendence*: a moving-beyond the grubby material world of extraction and paper-pushing, into a space of radical clarity and certainty that enabled the smooth operation of sociability and the solving of problems. While such a space might somehow be emplaced within the material world, it was also off-limits to those who were not somehow initiates into its mysteries. This vision of law – again, a law that was somehow more "real" than the law as was practiced in the

[1] Ando 2000.

empire – was therefore both exclusive and exclusionary. To achieve it required stepping outside of everyday reality: hence *ecstasy* – from the Greek *ek-stēnai*, to stand outside of, but also to be astonished or entranced.[2]

This chapter shall follow one strand of this thinking, in particular as it emerges in the writings of Paul of Tarsus, but also among other communities of Jews in the Roman East more broadly. But it is also a first step in an argument that will emerge over the remainder of this book. As I hope to demonstrate, attempts to remove imperial law and administration from everyday life – to claim that a legal life was possible in a space apart from the practices of empire – also began to entail claims that law was something distinct from daily practice. As such, the ideologies documented in the chapters that follow increasingly came to imagine law – again, "real" law – as something that was ontologically distinct from "what we do" or even "what they do."[3] The distinction between what is "law" and what is "society" would begin to emerge, that is, from these reactions to imperial governance.

***

The Pauline tradition is not normally the fodder for legal history.[4] The texts in this tradition operate with concern for the day of judgment and the possibility of salvation, concerns which are not normally present in traditional legal sources (though legal ideas and practices do often owe a greater debt to such concepts than lawyers might otherwise avow).[5] Paul himself repeatedly and firmly denies that simply following the law can be the path to ultimate salvation. With that said, Paul is vague and contradictory as to whether following law is even valuable in its own right, or if it constitutes some sort of atavism

2 See esp. Nasrallah 2003, to whose analysis I owe a debt of gratitude.

3 Constable 1994.

4 This is true both among scholars of ancient history and scholars of theology. The classic account of Sherwin-White 1963 largely steers clear of the Pauline corpus, preferring to base its account on the Gospels and Acts, only including Pauline material where it bears upon what are imagined to be provincial realia. There is of course an endless bibliography of *Prozeß Jesu* studies; these are not especially relevant for what follows. I look forward to the detailed treatment of Paul promised by Siegert et al. 2023. I also fully endorse the call of Hayes 2015: 140 to attempt to contextualize Pauline thinking within the broader world of Roman legal thinking, even if what follows goes in a different direction.

5 E.g., Whitman 2008.

or perversion. Such denials have major implications for subsequent theology, which need not be engaged here. My goal, instead, is to think about what Paul's claims about lawfulness, legality, and salvation might have meant within the broader legal structures of the Roman Empire, and to what extent we might place them alongside other understandings of legality.

A first difficulty with Paul is assessing his proper context. Though a self-proclaimed apostle to the "nations" (*ethnē*, that is non-Jews), Paul himself was Jewish, and his frame of reference begins with the texts of Jewish scripture.[6] To the extent that the book of Acts is an accurate guide, however, Paul engaged audiences both Jewish and non-Jewish throughout his travels. What is more, he moved across a broad arc of cities and regions between Arabia and mainland Greece. Within his travels, there was a huge range of diversity: the provincial capital of Corinth, a major trading hub (presumably also populated by all the strange and seedy characters that characterize such hubs more generally); the recently settled veteran colony of Philippi; the newly synoecized tribespeople of Galatia; the teeming and diverse city of Antioch; and the Hebrew and Aramaic speaking temple state of Jerusalem (to say nothing of the diversity of rural populations surrounding these cities) (see Figure 6.1).[7] How might one make sense of such a landscape?

Paul preached in a world that had just undergone a century and a half of dramatic changes and disruptions.[8] It was a period in which previous regimes of imperial stability had initially collapsed into a kaleidoscope of cities, statelets, tribes, and warlords which then came under the aegis of Rome. Reviewing the entire complex history would take us far afield. But a few points might be emphasized. For the sake of convenience, it will do to divide the discussion into the effects of this century of disruption into two parts: the effects on the Greek speaking world of Asia Minor (and to a lesser degree mainland Greece), and the effects on Judaea and on Judaism more specifically. In fact, these were parts of the same complex process.

[6] Fredriksen 2017, 2021.

[7] On Galatia, see Mitchell 1993; on Philippi, Brélaz 2018, 2024: 286–87; and more generally Meeks 2003.

[8] Kotrosits 2015.

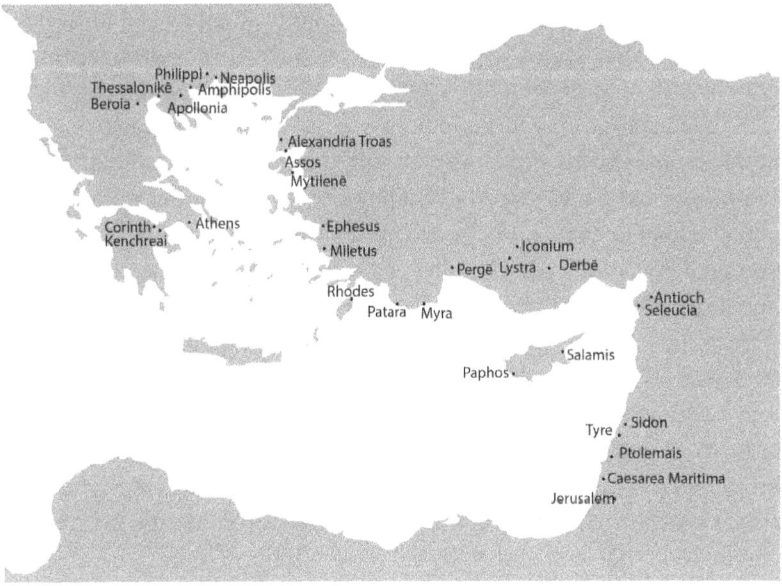

FIGURE 6.1 Map of major cities visited by Paul according to the Book of Acts (not including places that Paul himself says he visited, such as Galatia and Arabia).

The process begins in the early first century BC with the attempts of Mithridates VI, king of Pontus, to extend his rule into the Roman province of Asia. This attempt, which included the massacre of tens of thousands of resident Romans and Italians, led to decades of retaliatory warfare: first under Sulla (who sacked Athens and cities in central Greece in the process), then Lucullus, and then finally Pompey. The campaigns of Lucullus served to widen the actors in the war, which extended into the kingdom of Armenia, which was itself expanding into Syria. The final set of campaigns, led by Pompey, were fought not just against Mithridates and the pirates that had emerged on the southern coast of Asia Minor, but also in Syria and Judaea. This brought Rome into close connection to the Hasmonean dynasty in charge of Judaea, with which it had previously dealt at something of a distance.

The campaigns against Mithridates were destabilizing to Asia Minor. Not only was the territory host to competing armies for some twenty-five years, but in finally subjecting it to Rome, Pompey founded cities and reorganized territories. Veterans and others were settled, and the segments of the territory became enmeshed in Roman fiscal structures. Local tribal systems were reconstructed, leaving a network of semi-dependable client states in charge of the areas that were harder to access (upon payment of tribute, of course).[9] Picking these various client kings also meant picking between a variety of candidates for leadership, as Pompey's legates also did among competing Hasmoneans in Judaea. But Pompeian transformation only presaged the more destabilizing wave of conflicts. Over the subsequent decades, as relationships between the Roman elite deteriorated, Greece and Asia Minor were primary battlegrounds in the Roman civil wars. And while the fighting itself may have been localized, cash was ruthlessly extracted from as far afield as necessary.[10] The subsequent wars between the so-called "liberators" and the Triumviri brought similarly brutal depredations. What is more, the destabilizing effects of the civil wars left an opportunity for a resurgent Parthian empire to invade and occupy Syria, to which they clung briefly if tenaciously, not being entirely cleared out until 38 BC. The final chapter of the civil wars, between Octavian and Marcus Antonius, was similarly destructive.

This series of wars involved not just large armies on the move, but also the subsequent disbanding of such large armies. As a result of such disbanding, a wave of colonial foundations in Greece began during the reign of Caesar; it was continued under the Triumviri and expanded under Augustus. These foundations were part of a broad transformation of the Hellenophone world, one that extended from political geography to demographics to economic structures.[11] But the transformation was not limited to the historical Greek heartland: colonial foundations emerged in peripheral regions as well, and regions in interior Asia Minor and Syria that had previously been under the control of local kings were slowly but inexorably transformed into Roman provinces and urbanized, in a process that stretched well into the first century AD.[12] The process of setting up colonies eventually

[9] Overview in Magie 1950: 368–78. For the urban system that developed in Pontus, see now Madsen 2020.

[10] On Pompeian exactions of money from Syria, see Sartre 2005: 50–51.

[11] For an important study focusing on the province of Achaea, see Alcock 1993; on the colonies specifically, Brélaz 2017.

[12] On the process in central Asia Minor, see Mitchell 1993: I:63.

would reach as far as Berytus (Beirut) and, eventually, by the time of Claudius, to Ptolemaïs/Acco.[13] The process involved not only changes in the political landscape itself, but the extrusion of settlers across it – a process already discussed previously (Chapter 2).

The effects of the violent convulsions of the civil wars and subsequent settlements had effects on Judaism as well, both in the Hasmonean heartland and beyond. To begin at the level of political organization, the conquests of Pompey marked the final stage of the Hasmonean dynasty. In addition to the sack of Jerusalem itself (and an ensuing massacre), a number of Hasmonean conquests were peeled back from the core territories around Jerusalem. The status of a neighboring network of cities (the Decapolis) was raised as a counterbalance. The territory as a whole became subject to the authority of the Roman governor of Syria. These might have been temporary setbacks, but for the subsequent Parthian invasion. The final Hasmonean, Antigonus, had the misfortune of being installed by the Parthians after having been passed over by the Romans. Accordingly, the Triumviri withdrew support for the Hasmoneans and appointed in their stead the Idumean warlord Herod. A short but bloody civil war ensued, as Herod and his family, with the periodic assistance of the Roman army, dislodged Antigonus from Jerusalem, murdered his supporters, and handed him over to Marcus Antonius for execution.

The story of Herod and the transformation of Judaism, like that of the Greek heartland, is likewise best told from the perspective of the aftereffects of the Roman civil wars. Initially a supporter of the liberators (for whom he extracted funds, by force if necessary), Herod eventually found himself on the side first of Marcus Antonius, then Octavian/Augustus. In exchange he was given carte blanche to rule over a territory that included both Jewish towns and Greek poleis.[14] In so doing, he transformed the political and religious landscape. A vast building program – including a massive harbor at his new capital, Caesarea – resulted in both an astonishing new grandiosity and firmer military control of his territory, as well as the reorientation of commerce from

[13] Levick 1967; Mitchell 1993: I: 80–98; MacMullen 2000: 1–29. The process would reach Caesarea only in the wake of the Jewish revolt.

[14] For overviews of the political history, see Goodman 1996, and for the broader region, Millar 1993: 27–56.

its traditional pathways towards the Herodian capital city. Patronage of (and ruthless control over) the Jerusalem temple turned the temple into a gigantic complex, transforming what had initially been small-scale festivals into massive and unruly events that brought in large numbers of Jews from surrounding regions and from the diaspora. As one scholar has put it, Herod's rule transformed "*Judean* institutions into *Jewish* ones."[15] It should hardly be added that such transformations did not come for free: they were backstopped by a large-scale program of taxation, and any hints of discontent were quashed by Herod's armies (normally staffed by non-Judeans).[16]

The Herodian transformation was followed by a period of political chaos. After Herod's death in 4 BC and the brief reign of his successor Archelaus, starting in 6 AD parts of his territory were transformed into the province of Judaea. Governed by equestrians, the area was treated to governance that was inconsistent at best, hostile at worst, and always refracted in complex ways through the various ethno-political groups of the region and their respective elites.[17] Roman troops were introduced into Jerusalem to keep order on holy days. High priests served at the pleasure of Roman officials. A new ruling class emerged, sponsored by Roman governors, and unpopular with the populace as a whole.[18] The subsequent, and temporary, reinstallation of a Jewish monarch (Julius Agrippa, or Herod Agrippa) did little to settle things, nor did the subsequent restructuring of the territory after Agrippa's death. In the course of half a century, a new world – both physical and metaphysical – had taken shape. It was surely a dizzying time for subjects both Greek and Jewish.

The events of the first centuries BC and AD thus brought large numbers of people into contact. They transformed political, economic, and demographic (and in the Jewish case, religious) structures. Thus, despite the rhetoric of later Christian communities, who sought to distinguish a world sharply divided between Jews, Gentiles, and Christians, in the first century AD Paul preached in a world that had shifted dramatically and in analogous ways for people of *all* sorts.

[15] Schwartz 2001a: 45, emphasis original. [16] Girardin 2022: 259–73.

[17] See esp. Mason 2016: 199–280; also Eck 2014 [2011] on the various governors of Judaea.

[18] Goodman 1988.

Paul is a product of this world. A Greek-speaking diaspora Jew from Tarsus on the southern coast of Asia Minor, he grew up in a world that sat at the center of these transformative processes. He could move comfortably between the worlds of Jerusalem and Athens, in large measure because they were not actually radically different: they had all participated in the events started by Mithridates and eventually ended by Augustus.[19] It is a world where Jews often lived in close proximity to non-Jews, moving across the landscape in search of opportunity or to avoid the vicissitudes of Hasmonean rule.[20] Their presence in communities provoked non-Jews to take interest in Judaism (though not always positively).[21] Additionally, Jews of the diaspora had for generations taken interest in non-Jewish forms of culture and expression. Jews – and many others besides – also inhabited a world in which social, legal, and political status might shift rapidly, if not many times over.

As a result, the Pauline letters reveal a rich social world emerging in the first century empire, but also an evolving attempt to grapple with claims being made by the communities of that world about legality and their relationship to it. What did it mean, in such contexts, to imagine law? Under what circumstances, and with what consequences, might one enter a new community, or exit from one? Was law – or liberation from law – an embodied practice, such that to change "laws" one must also change one's physical person? Might it be possible to constitute a community that itself transcended the law – that is, one that operated outside of the normal structures of a Greek *polis* or a privileged ethno-religious community? What might such a community look like, and by which principles would it be organized?

***

Before turning to Paul himself, we might consider some of the ways that these questions resonated within the Jewish heartland. Though a Jew of the diaspora, Paul came from a community that had a history

[19] Mitchell 2008: esp.103–5.

[20] See, e.g., Schwartz 2001b. Inscriptions attesting Jewish presence throughout the eastern Mediterranean are gathered in *IJO*, and in Frey, *CIJ* I. Exiles: Sartre 2005: 15–16. On the Jews of Egypt generally, see Méléze Modrzejewski 1995; on the Oniad community, Piotrkowski 2019.

[21] Evidence collected in Stern 1974.

of asking these sorts of questions and a repertoire of moves for constituting or reconstituting communities in relation to legality. The concern is to put a finer point on this history of Jewish "legalism" in the earlier, Hellenistic period.

At the core of Hasmonean self-justification was their claim that they operated with "zeal" for the Torah and the commandments at its center.[22] This included protection of the temple against outside interference, maintenance of prohibitions on forbidden foods, keeping the covenant of circumcision, and the elimination of idolatry in Jewish territories. This zeal also meant minimizing contact with neighboring non-Jews, or even with Jews who differed with them.[23] Hasmonean insistence on separation extended into their wars of conquest against their neighbors: defeated neighbors were either massacred or forcibly converted.[24] What is more, Hasmonean policies engendered reactions with the community, as documented by the various polemics produced in the (small) splinter group at Qumran. Spokespeople for both groups were in broad agreement that the correct attitude of the people towards the law was that of radical obedience. Obedience produced purity, and purity was pleasing to the lord. These parties only disagreed on the proper recipe for what constituted obedience.

By the Roman period, the politics of obedience had become more complicated. Groups emerged that did not just seek obedience, but who argued that law was a living resource – part of a continuous oral tradition that might expand to take account of an increasing territory of daily life. To what degree this transformation might have started in the Hasmonean period is hard to say; the sources that record it are all from the Roman period.[25] But something might be learned by looking to an episode from the end of the first century BC. Josephus reports that, in Herod's waning days, there was a pair of teachers who were "most learned" (*logiōtatoi*) and who spent their time as "expounders of the paternal laws" (*exēgētai tōn patriōn nomōn*). He further refers to such men as "sophists" (*sophistai*) – part of the broader world of

[22] E.g., I Macc. 2.26, 2.50, 2.58. [23] Baumgarten 1997.

[24] On the vexed question of forced circumcisions, see Weitzman 1999.

[25] It is worth noting that "legalism" does not seem to be intrinsically Jewish, much less even something that emerges primarily as a result of Hasmonean policies. The Oniads in Egypt, for instance, seem much less concerned about quotidian legality and purity. See, e.g., Bohak 1996; Piotrkowski 2019.

non-state, educated actors who made their money by teaching elite children. They were apparently sufficiently popular as "expounders" that, when Herod's death appeared imminent, they convinced their students to purify the temple by removing a golden eagle that Herod himself had affixed at the entrance as a show of loyalty to Rome.[26] Accordingly, they went to the temple and pulled it down; at least forty were arrested as Herod's guards tried to stop them. The remainder escaped.

This sort of popular action, taken at the behest of popular teachers of law, speaks to a difference in both kind and extent from the "zeal" for law of the Hasmoneans or the Qumran sect.[27] Rather than a phenomenon that admits of only limited participation, these teachers found a broad audience for their instruction. Questions of how to live within the law, it seems, were popularized – they were no longer just the stuff of dynastic politics or the preserve of mistrustful sects. Josephus' account suggests that the populace in Jerusalem found these teachers and their students highly sympathetic: popular discontent about the fate of these teachers managed to dissuade Herod from simply executing them and their followers en masse, and instead forced him to punish only the most prominent leaders and offenders.[28]

The legalists of Josephus might serve as the most extreme example of how the populace, in the wake of the civil wars and their various predations and changes, took up legal politics. But there are other, perhaps more controversial, hints in the sources as well, that arguing over the proper way to live according to law came to occupy a more central place in Judean politics. Increasingly, the torah scroll itself seems to have taken on totemic status, and there was increasing popular concern over its desecration.[29] There seems, as well, to have been increasing popular interest in purity, one that perhaps did not begin in this period but accelerated in it nonetheless.[30] In this context we

[26] *Ant.* 17.149–50. Cf. *BJ* 1.648–55.

[27] Furstenberg 2023 makes the case for a much narrower set of legal interests in the first centuries BC/AD, as compared to the more capacious scope of subsequent rabbinic projects. But idolatry remained an important category, even as the demand to destroy idols shifted over time. See Rosen-Zvi 2014.

[28] *BJ* 1.655. *Ant.* 17.163–65 has a rather different account of the punishment, and sets the trial in Jericho.

[29] Schwartz 2001a: 60–61.

[30] Such interest is evident already in the (likely second century BC) book of Jubilees. I thank Ishay Rosen-Zvi for this point.

might note a broad similarity between figures like John the Baptist, who offered a path to individual purity, and the increasing interest of the Jewish "sectarians," such as the Pharisees, in the application of purity laws.[31] This last group is by far the hardest to figure out, but a few points seem to be agreed upon: Pharisees were particularly interested in laws of Temple and individual purity, and on criminal punishment; they accepted and partook in developing a body of oral law (Torah) that complemented sacred texts; and they eventually (but under unclear circumstances) evolved, in the wake of the destruction of the Jerusalem temple in AD 70, into the Rabbis of the second century and beyond.[32] Precisely *when* their legal interests emerged is unclear, but there is good reason to think that they emerged, in part, in the first century BC, *pari passu* with the other transformations that I have already noted – at the very least, evidence for their interest in legalism cannot be recovered for any earlier period.[33] Put differently, while claims to have a unique relationship of obedience to "the law" (the Torah) are a feature of Judaism from at least the Hellenistic period onwards, the increasingly diverse Jewish interests in legal*ism* – in discussing, studying, and arguing about the details of the law as a mode of negotiating political being – was a reaction to complex historical events of the recent past.[34] And in a world of dizzying political and economic changes, taking refuge in the casuistry of individual and collective purity would seem to make a good deal of sense.

Legalism was not, of course, the only option available. As the evidence of the early Christ communities suggests, messianism was also an option for some. (Messianism, of course, is not necessarily opposed to legalism, but there does seem to be an important difference in where one places the accent.[35]) Importantly, this was a theme that stretched across the broader world in question over the first century AD. The names of the multiple charismatic preachers who operated in Jewish areas at roughly the time of Jesus of Nazareth are well-enough known: John the Baptist; Theudas, who led a group of followers to

[31] John the Baptist: Goodman 1996: 766.

[32] The literature is both huge and polemical. For an overview see Cohen 1984; Sievers and Levine 2021.

[33] Schwartz 2001a: 95. [34] Dohrmann 2013.

[35] I thank Ishay Rosen-Zvi for this point.

the Jordan river and tried to reenact Moses' parting of the Red Sea; or the "Egyptian" who prophesied the destruction of Jerusalem.[36]

One might make two points about these groups. First, because they only are known to us through short notices in Josephus (or the book of *Acts*), we know essentially nothing about their particular theologies or ideologies, much less where they might sit vis-à-vis broader questions of legalism. They might have had visions of upturning the legal order, or of reinscribing it in a different and more rigorous way – as did the sect at Qumran. They might, alternatively, have been entirely indifferent to the question as a whole. There is simply no way of knowing. But secondly, it is important also to note that messianism was not simply an internal Jewish problem: after the death of Nero in AD 68 and the end of the Julio–Claudian dynasty at least two and possibly three "false Neros" emerged in the Greek heartland. One of these, a man named Terentius Maximus, gained followers first in Asia and then in the Near East before marching his followers out into Parthian territories, in an interesting echo of Theudas' "exodus" some years before.[37] That is, in the territories most deeply transformed, demographically and politically, by the civil wars and their attendant crises, there was, at least in some corners of society, a shared tendency towards being attracted by those promising a future that was radically different from the present. Such a vision might, in fact, be ruthlessly conservative: to those who had made their peace with Julio–Claudian leadership, and had learned to treat that particular family as uniquely and divinely privileged, a false Nero might promise continuity in a world that was marked by a dismal and intolerably grubby politics of the imperial house. That their vision of success involved defecting to Persia seems more understandable from the perspective of a contemporary world where contemptible and revanchist regimes like that of Orbánist Hungary or Putinist Russia have suddenly become sources of attraction for those in thrall to a cult of personality. Or to put the matter differently: while as a general rule I can accept that human beings can tolerate a great deal of cognitive dissonance, it strikes me that it must have been extremely hard for people having been conditioned, in the wake of immense violence, to show their devotion to

[36] Jos. *Ant.* 20.97–98. 20.6, Acts 21:37–39; Schwartz 2001a: 89.
[37] Champlin 2003: 10–22.

the Julio–Claudian house, to wake up one morning and unproblematically transfer their loyalties to Vespasian and his children (much less Galba, Otho, or Vitellius).[38] This remarkable dissonance, I would suggest, is evident both in the attraction to imitators of Nero and in the near-hysterical public performances of superhuman healing with which Vespasian was credited in Alexandria.[39] These same violent dislocations also go some way towards explaining the turbulent internal politics of Judaea.

Following a charismatic figure was thus one option. But for others, a potential future might be sought from the promise of *changing* one's affiliation entirely. This would not have been inconceivable to the inhabitants of the Greek world: the period from the middle of the first century BC to the end of the reign of Augustus involved wholesale changes of personal status: these might range from a member of a particular political community (a particular *polis*) being incorporated as a Roman citizen within a Roman colony, or being downgraded to a mere *paroikos*, a member of a tributary village subordinate to another city (in which one was not offered membership) or a mere rightless "resident" in a new colonial foundation. Incorporation as a Roman citizen, at least, involved a wholesale change in the laws one was expected to follow, the gods one was expected to worship, the language in which one took oaths, and the relationships between one's parents or the world of potential wives and husbands for oneself and one's children. Throughout the world of Greece, peoples were also incorporated into new foundations by *synoikismos* (the drawing together or smaller polities into a newer, larger polity): this similarly often involved large-scale deportations and, lest one risk the "synoecized" returning to their homelands, the destruction of the temples of a (former) polity's ancestral temples and shrines.[40] In other words, civic membership, in the world that the civil wars made, was increasingly regarded as something potentially changeable, such that it would be possible to wake up one day to find oneself a part of a

[38] For a remarkable comparative case that illustrates, in the modern context, the dizzyingness of regime change, and with what effects for people's individual outlooks, see Gessen 2017. For a sensitive and perceptive study of the process of regime change and religious change, in this case in the province of Egypt, see Rigsby 1985: esp. 284.

[39] Tac. *Hist.* 4.81; Suet. *Vesp.* 7.

[40] See Alcock 1993: 132–45, on Western Greece.

totally new community, constituted by members (veterans, freedpeople, former inhabitants of other *poleis*) with whom one previously had no connection.[41] It might have been a fantasy that *individual* people could change such important axes of belonging at their own will (as opposed to having an imperial state change them by fiat), but it was a fantasy that likely meant a great deal to some.

***

With this in mind, we might turn to two such communities, and the members of those communities who fantasized, in the wake of this era of transformation, about the possibility of radically changing their status.

This involves a methodological warning. What we know of these communities we know only through Paul's letters to them. These are not transparent accounts of historical truth. To begin with, even if Paul himself was seeking to be accurate, there is the real possibility that he did not understand what was going on in communities physically distant from him. There is also the certainty that he distorts things to highlight his own agenda, one which is both urgently theological (since he was convinced that the end of the world was nigh) and internally competitive with other parties who were similarly devoted to Christ.[42] I know no satisfactory way around this problem, other than to flag it and insist upon caution and contextualization.

We might begin with some of the newest provincial communities, those of Galatia in central Anatolia. These ethnic Galatians had recently been moved from tribal organizations into urban nuclei. In the interim, some of the "assemblies" (*ekklēsiai*) of Galatia had been visited by a series of teachers, Paul included, who preached to them the "good news": that the end of times was coming, and that those who chose to follow Jesus of Nazareth would be spared the judgment of God, having already been made righteous. The dead would be resurrected, and a new world would emerge, one radically different from the world they currently inhabited. Some, at least, were attracted by

[41] On freedpeople in Corinth (some of whom, at least, were given a special dispensation allowing them to hold local magistracies), see Spawforth 1996; Nasrallah 2019: 55–67.

[42] As a general guide, I have found especially helpful Fredriksen 2017.

this message. But it raised a major question: in order to participate in this new form of community, would one first have to become Jewish? And to do that, must one follow Jewish law?

For some, the answer was emphatically Yes: those Galatians who wanted to ensure their salvation had to change the community in which they lived and become Jews. This meant following Jewish law, which for Paul, could be expressed by synecdoche as two fundamental things: circumcision and kashrut. That is, they would be required, as a condition of entering the new community, to break from their old community, to inscribe the law upon their bodies (in imitation of the original covenant that God made with Abraham), and to subsequently police their bodies' boundaries. In the case of the Galatian assemblies the mere possibility of being able to be included in a new community by the changing of, and policing of, one's own body, seemed a fair enough price to obtain inclusion in the promises of the "good news." Add to this that there remained, among the Jewish communities of the empire, an anxiety about things like eating and drinking alongside of, or at the homes of, uncircumcised gentiles.[43] People with such beliefs had recently come to the assemblies of Galatia; they insisted upon the Galatians' full conversion to Judaism if they wanted to be treated as full members of the new community. (Paul rails against such people, but that their arguments carried weight was clear enough.) To be included, then, meant to conform to the law in all of its most important details. And this was a source either of great appeal, or at least grudging acquiescence.

The predicament of the Galatians speaks to a basic problem of how communities are legally constituted: they desired a wholesale break with the past, and the adoption of a new tradition along with a new law code. It involved new ways of marking time (sabbaths, festivals), new devotion to a distant cult (the Jerusalem temple), and new principles for the transmission of property to one's heirs. The same would have been true for all those swept up in colonial deductions as well, were they not Roman citizens already. In the Galatian case, those who accepted this new role were willing, as well, to inscribe themselves physically with the evidence of the change.

We should just note for the moment that a change in legal status had further implications for what one could or must do with one's

[43] Fredriksen 2017: 97–98.

body, and in particular, how one must modify and patrol it.[44] In this case, changing communities was very much concerned with the physical person, and with his or her relationship to desire (in this context, it matters that circumcision was largely believed to help men control their sexual urges).[45] We might remember, in this context, the passage from the *Sifra* discussed, above, in the Introduction: "And lest you say: 'They have statutes and we have no statutes' – It is, therefore, written 'My judgments shall you do and My statutes you shall heed to walk in them; I am the Lord your God.' – But there is still 'hope' for the evil instinct to reflect and say 'But theirs are more beautiful than ours!'"[46] In the Introduction, I argued that the experience of empire induced among some conquered populations a sense of inadequacy, and a sense of longing for the prospect of a wholesale change in the body of rules that constitute the person. Changing from one legal regime to another might offer a possibility for alleviating this sense of inferiority. In the Introduction, I suggested that this might be conceived as a sort of *erōs*; it is not surprising, then, that the language of longing and desire might also be central not only to defining the feelings of the Galatians, but to Paul's response as well.

Theologically, the Galatians' attempt to change their status (from Gentiles into Jews) was unacceptable to Paul. But their attempt nonetheless provoked him to articulate some of the first century's most interesting claims about law and legalism. In Paul's explanation to the Galatians, the Galatian assemblies' acceptance of Christ had *already* worked to produce membership in a new community: the Galatians are already "justified" through their faith; following the law would not only not help them, it would actively set them back.[47] To explain why this is, Paul builds a dichotomy that will prove central to his thinking: a distinction between the world of "flesh" (*sarx*) and the world of "spirit" (*pneuma*). The world of flesh is easily apprehensible: it is the world in which one lives, a material world, filled with transparent meanings. It is also the world of human desires. To live in the flesh means not only to inhabit the material plane, but to operate under the sign of unfulfillable longing. Flesh is inherently weak and defective. The world of "spirit," by contrast, is a transcendent

44 On the question of bodies at Corinth, see Martin 1995.

45 Niehoff 2003: 92–102. 46 See above, pages 14–16. 47 2:16–18.

world, accessible only through the acceptance of Christ. By accepting Christ, one dies to the present world – the world of flesh – and one is crucified alongside him; this same act also crucifies one's "flesh," eliminating the problematic desires of the material world.[48] In this respect, it operates as an analogy to circumcision, albeit a more effective one. So why not circumcise oneself, just to be safe? Because, as Paul explains, to begin with spirit (accepting Christ's message) and then turn backwards to the lower plane of "flesh" (following the law) would be tantamount to denying the value of Christ's crucifixion itself.[49]

From this basic dichotomy, a rich structure of thinking emerges.[50] First, and most centrally for our purposes, the presence of the dichotomy allows Paul to relegate legalism – the belief that something is to be gained by acting in accordance with the rules set out by law – to the broader category of "flesh." This demands explanation, not least because, within the broader Roman and Jewish worlds, some claims had been circulating that law might, in fact, be something transcendent – something that reached outside of the everyday work of administration, or even something that might be connected to the divine.[51] That is, even in a world where the great bulk of law on public display might be the quotidian work of administration, there were nonetheless some voices that saw, in legality, a great promise of ascending to a higher plane of being. Pharisees like Paul, not least, seem to have taken such ideas seriously, and in point of fact, Paul never directly says that law itself is fleshy.[52] But Paul does argue that the *desire* to abide by the Jewish laws concerning circumcision (legal*ism*) cannot be part of spirit; it must, accordingly, be part of flesh.

For this he gives two explanations, both based in textual exegesis. First, Deuteronomy (27:26), explains that everyone who does not observe the entirety of the written law is cursed.[53] Presumably, since the entire fulfillment of the law is impossible, the entirety of humanity is cursed. Christ, however, "redeemed us from the curse of the law by

[48] 5:24. [49] 2:21. [50] For a fascinating study of this dichotomy, see Boyarin 1994.

[51] For the Roman jurists, see Schiavone 2012; on ideas of divine law, Hayes 2015.

[52] Fredriksen 2021. Note the language of ascent in Gal. 1:14: προσέκοπτον ἐν τῷ Ἰουδαισμῷ.

[53] Paul adds, "in the book of," an indication that he is considering the law primarily as a written code, rather than as a set of living traditions.

becoming a curse for us" – that is, by dying on the cross (and becoming "cursed" – Deut. 21:23), he allowed people like the Galatians to live, instead, through faith, provided they "crucify" themselves alongside him.[54] Second, Paul argues, there are two relevant moments in Jewish history: the initial promise of redemption, given to Abraham, and the subsequent introduction of the laws of the Pentateuch. The laws were not given in fulfillment of the promise of redemption, but rather "because of transgressions" (*tōn parabaseōn charin*).[55] That is, legality operated on a temporary basis, in order to discipline a population until the redemption of the original promise. That promise has now been fulfilled through the crucifixion. At best, the law was necessary to bring people to the stage of development whereby they could be redeemed; it was, in that regard, at best a teacher (*paidagōgos*), at worst, a pale substitute for actual redemption.[56]

We might note, in this dense and evocative discussion, just a few things. To begin with, Paul accepts the inevitability of human legal regimes. Jews were followers of the law, as they were required to be, even after the introduction of Christ's message. The only question is whether the Galatians were required to be Jews, too. Paul's answer was No. Not only was their remaining Gentiles necessary for the proper fulfillment of the prophecy that the "nations" should "turn towards" Israel (rather than blend into Israel), it was also because of a fundamental belief that the law itself was both extremely limited and extremely limiting.[57] As compared to the transcendent sacrifice of Christ, to follow the law gave access to a much reduced form of being: it could not, he insisted, "give life" (*zōopoiēsai*).[58] To obsess about it, therefore, meant to direct one's energies and desires to problematic ends. In that respect, legalism (rather than law itself) might be considered a perversion, and hence *fleshy*.

Paul's answer might be read as a response to those very imperial longings voiced in the text of the *Sifra*. In the *Sifra*, the Rabbis argue that the path to overcoming the desire to change affiliation is to double-down on the commitment to the individual obligations of

[54] 3:13–14. Translations are based on the NRSV. [55] 3:19. [56] 3:24.

[57] On the *ethnē* turning to Israel, Tobit 14:5–6, with the discussion of Fredriksen 2017: 28–29.

[58] Gal. 3:21. Cf. 2 Cor. 3:6.

Jewish law. Paul, by contrast, urges that the following of Christ allows for a different sort of transcendence of everyday life. By following in Christ, he insists, a new world is made possible: social and legal distinctions are obliterated; there is "no longer Jew nor Greek, there is no longer slave nor free, there is no longer male nor female; for all of you are one in Christ Jesus."[59] Put differently, the proper response to these very imperial longings is not to *change* one's legal status, but to do away with the concept of legal status *tout court*, replacing it with an elect group fully committed to one another that stands apart from the remainder of the world. Legalism, with its obsessive distinctions *between* statuses, could not be farther from this goal. But by *transcending* legalism, a space of perfect equality is made manifest, one that will overcome the distinctions of the everyday world (flesh). This, Paul insists, is genuine freedom (*eleutheria*).[60]

Second, and accordingly, by operating according to spirit, the community is given a new way of interpreting and speaking about things. Most importantly, partaking of the sacrifice of Christ evoked new ways of reading older biblical texts. Thus, in the case of the letter to the Galatians, Paul can construe the sons of Abraham by his two wives, Sarah and Hagar, as an allegory: "One, the child of the slave, was born according to the flesh; the other, the child of the free woman, was born through the promise. Now this is an allegory (*allēgoroumena*): these two women are two covenants."[61] In other words, like the *paideia* of the speaker in Lucian's *de Domo* (below, page 249), accessing the world through Christ's promise holds forth the hope of being able to see things in a text that were previously latent, and to be capable of describing the world anew. If I am right in my broader arguments that the importance of legalism to provincial populations can be explained because it offered a hermeneutic for understanding one's place in an empire, then Paul offers a radically different path forward: a hermeneutic *not* anchored in legalism, but in its transcendence – in knowing a truer and more "spiritual" way to read a privileged text, such that it can embody more than *mere*

59 3:29.

60 5:13. Whether this obliteration of statuses will extend into the age of God's judgment is, however, a different question.

61 4:23–24. The passage has produced tremendous amounts of bibliography. See, e.g., Betz 1979: 238–52.

rules and instructions, and so that it can produce more than mere obedience.[62] In the case of Sarah and Hagar, the goal of such reading is not to derive what one must do at a particular moment in the present, but rather to read the text as pointing towards a potentially liberatory future. Such knowledge is contingent upon entry into a newly liberated community, whose members, Paul insists, are the "spiritual" people (*pneumatikos*) – as opposed to everyone else, whose understanding is defective.[63] Paul's claims, in all of these respects, will be echoed, a century later, by Greek elites (Chapter 7).

Third, accepting Christ is as much a bodily practice as it is a spiritual and intellectual one.[64] Paul insists upon this quite literally, declaring "Let nobody beat me, for I bear the marks (*stigmata*) of Jesus upon my body."[65] The language here is remarkable: in a text that emphasizes the freedom from legal statuses that comes with the acceptance of Christ, Paul reaches for a quotidian metaphor: stigma here refers to the brands placed on slaves, indicative of their disfavored legal status.[66] Paradoxically, it was a visual reminder that they *could*, in fact, be beaten with minimal consequence. This is in keeping with Paul's tendency to use powerful reversals of normal values to better articulate the radical nature of Christ's promise. He does similar things in a letter to the assemblies in the Roman colony of Philippi, where they quote what seems to be an early hymn on the body of Christ:[67]

> Let the same mind be in you that was in Christ Jesus, who, though he was in the form of God, did not regard equality with God as something to be exploited, but emptied himself (*ekenōsen*), taking the form of a slave, being born in human likeness. And being found in human form he humbled (*etapeinosan*) himself and became obedient to the point of death – even death on a cross.

By accepting Jesus, the members of the Galatian were quite literally crucified as well, ridding themselves of problematic desires.[68] This emphasis on the physical body of both Christ and his followers reflects a reversal of normal social assumptions. The elite classes of the Greco-Roman world had for generations sought to portray themselves as perfect physical specimens who embodied Greekness. They

[62] Boyarin 1994. [63] 1 Cor. 2:14–15. [64] E.g., Engberg-Pedersen 2010.
[65] 6:17. [66] Jones 1987. [67] Phil. 2:5–8. [68] Gal. 5:24.

filled their cities with statuary that reinforced what they insisted was a link between physical beauty and political virtue. So too, for Paul, did the followers of Christ use their bodies to demonstrate the superiority of Christ's sacrifice. Yet by inversion: whereas the perfection of the body was coded, by Greek elites, as something aesthetically beautiful, in the Pauline corpus it is coded as physically problematic, even disgusting. Christ's sacrifice is meaningful because he dared to take on the worst form of body, and to subject it to the worst form of punishment. Paul insists, in another context, that they do the same: "I punish my body and enslave it (*hypōpiazō mou to sōma kai doulagagō*), so that after proclaiming to others I myself should not be disqualified."[69]

The images are physical, if not visceral. In their immediacy, they invite aesthetic responses – responses which are, in essence, prerational and incompatible with the normal expectations of *logos*. To contemplate a crucified slave – or even a branded slave – was something that would have evoked little but disgust. But in Paul's hands such disgust was redeemed by the promise of a pure future, after God's judgment, when the crucified slave would be exalted, along with those who followed him. To impress his readers with the gravity of such a scene, he can only revert to a set of concepts generated by quotidian legality. That is, even in language that rejects legalism as a mode of imperial belonging, we can nonetheless still see the imprint of broader imperial processes. At the heart of his thinking there is an account of legal transcendence, albeit one that takes a very different form than the version that would eventually evolve among the Greek elites. But it, too, was a reaction to living with the complex realities of the Roman Empire.

***

Yet when Paul emphasized the changes that take place among those who have accepted Christ's message, he left further questions open: if this is not to be a community constituted by law, but a community that, in its shared abjection, transcends law, then what sort of community might that be? By what principles ought it to operate, even on a temporary basis, as the end of days draws near?

[69] 1 Cor. 9:27.

Some distance away, in the provincial capital of Corinth, another community raised these questions of community regulation, law, and the body in pointed fashion. The import of the "good news" that was being spread around was not that it forced one to enter a new community and obey a new law; it was, rather, a source of liberation from law itself. Here the evidence is extremely exiguous, but among the new followers of Christ in Corinth there was dissension: a community split into factions, each claiming to be partisans of a particular leader.[70] The causes of this dissension are unclear, but given the tone of the letter written by Paul and his coauthor, Sosthenes, to the community, it seems that one source of the fracture was over sexual morality, and it crystallized over one particularly problematic relationship: a relationship between a stepson and a stepmother.[71] What is striking about the relationship itself is that it would have been prohibited under any of the legal regimes from which one might have chosen: Jewish, Roman, or Greek. It seems, then, that the offending parties, insofar as we might ventriloquize them, understood the liberation that came by following Jesus to involve liberation from *all* preexisting legal regimes. It will be added that this is not a problem that need entail any further commitment than simply desiring to have sex with a person of one's choice, one who was previously off-limits. To be antinomian requires little deep thinking. Yet whatever their understanding of their own behavior, their arguments seemed to be grounded in reasoning that was solid enough that it managed to befuddle the community more broadly: that is, if Christ liberated people from the law, then why was such a sexual relationship *not* permissible? The Corinthian community, it seems, had no satisfactory answer other than to rely on their innate sense of disgust. Upset by the practice, they dispatched a letter to Paul.

So how, then, might a community be organized such that an answer might be given to these questions? Such an answer, it would seem, would have to be both political and legal. Politically, it would involve articulating a shared vision of some good that the community shares or towards which it aims. Coming from a rich tradition of Jewish messianism, Paul had ample vocabulary for discussing this good: the imminence of the apocalypse and the coming of God's judgment

[70] 1 Cor. 1:12. [71] 1 Cor. 5:1.

provided urgency for communities to accept Christ. By so doing, they would be properly positioned for redemption at the moment of God's judgment. But how, in the interim, should these communities be organized, not just in terms of their ultimate telos, but with respect to how they manage problems for the present? Are there broad guidelines for behaviors, and if so, from where are they derived? And how might such a community manage conflict? Or, alternatively, to put the question in terms of the problematic Corinthians, was accepting Christ the *only* thing necessary – all other actions or regulations being superfluous?

In rejecting legalism, Paul was far less clear as to what he would prefer to replace it, and how to ensure that that replacement would prove durable. When counseling the Galatians, Paul insists that they are to "walk" the spirit, and not "carry out the desires of the flesh" (*epithymian sarkos*). Of what might such desires consist? Paul was nothing if not convinced of the importance of traditional forms of moral order.[72] Obviously (*phanera*), he insisted, these are "fornication, impurity, licentiousness, idolatry, sorcery, enmities, strife, jealousy, anger, quarrels, dissensions, factions, envy, drunkenness, carousing, and things like these."[73] But we are entitled to ask, where, in the first place, does such a list come from? Is legalism *productive* of such things, such that one must avoid "walking" in its tradition?

The answers are far from clear. One is tempted to think that the list is an attempt to smuggle in a vision of moral society without having to justify it on first principles (or, for that matter, any principles). But the hint remains that legalism is somehow connected to the problematic list of "desires of the flesh." In revisiting the question, a few years later, in the letter to the Romans, Paul would attempt a more robust explanation. Law, he explains, is not the same as sin.[74] Sin preceded law; but law also made sin knowable (*ellogeitai*) *as sin*, and thus managed to increase (*pleonasēi*) the amount of sin in the world.[75] So it is, in some respects at least, suspect, since it gives names to things that might be desirable. At the same time, Paul insists, law itself may even be something positive, something spiritual (*pneumatikos*), but the humans who are supposed to follow it

[72] If not indeed a particularly *halakhic* form of moral order: Tomson 1990: 97–124.
[73] 5:16, 19–21. [74] Rom. 7:7. [75] Rom. 5:13, 21. Cf. Gal. 3:22.

cannot use it to this end, because *they* are fleshy and guided by sin.[76] In other words, a perfect, "spiritual" law might exist, but even if it did, humans would be unable to follow it, and this would lead to the misdirection of desire. By contrast, the sacrifice of Christ has freed them from the problem in its entirety: by accepting Christ the discussion need no longer be had, and the communities of Galatia and elsewhere could structure their lives accordingly. (Whether Jews were still bound to follow these laws is a separate question because of their particular historical trajectory.[77])

Still, this goes only so far in answering the challenge posed by the Corinthians. "All things are lawful for me! (*panta moi exestin*)," some members of the Corinthian community insisted.[78] On what grounds, then, was a *specific* list of acts prohibited? Why, that is, should a community agree to avoid those behaviors? The Galatians who considered converting to Judaism might have been tempted, in no small part, because the precise rules that governed Jewish life could be defended on rational or even metaphysical principles (a defense being prepared, at roughly the same time, by Philo of Alexandria). But this is not the path of reasoning that Paul follows. In fact, even to work out a sufficient reason to avoid going to prostitutes (*porneia*) involves some rather convoluted reasoning: because all members of the Christian community have become "members" or "parts" (*melē*) of Christ, he insisted, and since having sex with a prostitute involves becoming of "one body" (*hen sōma*) with her, sex with prostitutes is to be avoided on the grounds that it profanes the body of Christ.[79] We are entitled to entertain some doubt as to whether such arguments might have convinced a Corinthian. Either way, it does little to explain the other things on Paul's list of prohibitions.

Alternatively, we might simply note that the things that Paul names as problematic are simply *fleshy* – that is, they are linked to desire, and in particular, to incontinent types of desire that are socially problematic at an empirical level. Who but the pathological, after all, ever hopes for more envy in the world? (The modern discipline of economics, which argues that these character defects operate to create broader social value, had not yet been invented.) By naming them,

[76] Rom. 7:14. [77] Hayes 2015: 149. [78] 1 Cor. 6:12.
[79] 1 Cor. 6:16–17. Cf. 12:14.

law only serves to make matters worse, because they become knowable and thus pursuable. And by embracing a law that cannot be fulfilled, the legalists only manage to live in perpetual disappointment, which will eventually encourage rejection of the very principles one holds dear. In this sense, at least, we see a theme that often reoccurs among those excited by the possibility of inhabiting a society without laws: the idea that, if people could just control themselves, there would be no need for formal modes of dispute resolution – put differently, that states or state-like institutions are essentially punishment for incontinent desires. In Paul's version of this theory, the act of "circumcising one's heart" would have made such problematic desires superfluous.[80] In practice, their continued existence proved hard to explain, much less to manage. The avoidance of desire, therefore, becomes central – and is thus a central theme of the letter to the Corinthians more generally.[81]

Paul does not quite give this answer explicitly, but it would be consistent with Paul's general thinking: the reason to avoid these particular behaviors is because they tend, empirically speaking, to put pressure on community harmony. Paul is emphatically concerned with community harmony, of course, and his entreaties not to quarrel make up a healthy proportion of his rhetoric.[82] We will see, in the following chapter, that the identical problem dogged the leaders of the notionally independent Greek city states: how to preside over communities where internal disharmony threatened problematic outcomes – in their case, the possibility of the Roman governor intervening. Like some of his Greek counterparts, Paul expressly rejects the idea that external, imperial systems of jurisdiction should be the preferred mode of solving problems. The Corinthians are to settle disputes amongst themselves amicably, and to avoid, at all costs, the courts of the "unjust ones" (*adikōn*).[83] But failing that, he argues, they are simply to expel any member of their community that they

[80] Rom. 2:29. [81] Cf. 1 Thess. 4:3–12. [82] E.g., 1 Cor. 1:10–13.

[83] 1 Cor. 6:1. Martin 1995: 76–79 speculates that this warning originates in the "Strong" suing the weaker members of the congregation at Corinth. I take it merely as a broader, anti-imperial claim about the value of court avoidance. I similarly find Martin's sociology of the provincial courts unconvincing, for reasons explained in Chapter 4. However, the concern about the "stronger" did occupy a great deal of thinking, just not in the precise way imagined by Martin. See Chapters 9 and 10.

found to be engaged in sin.[84] By what mechanism this might work, however, is opaque (what if someone proclaimed his innocence?); how it might serve to avoid further division, yet more so; and how precisely such a community might relate to the broader administrative structures of the Roman Empire was left almost totally unarticulated (i.e., to what degree, if any, they ought to copy preexisting structures of inheritance and the devolution of property, to what extent they might be permitted to sell or to borrow, etc.).[85]

So how, then, should these communities be organized? This question would vex Paul, and be taken up by his successors, to whom I shall turn momentarily. As is evident from the Pauline corpus more generally, however, it is clear that the problem of internal community relations came as a constant challenge. Paul might have been good at explaining the theology that was necessary for these communities to enter the kingdom of God, but he was not especially good at thinking administratively. With that said, we might nonetheless explore three possible ways that Paul and his coauthors imagine for an "assembly" to organize itself. None, to my mind, is especially compelling or original (theologians may disagree). At the very least, none (save perhaps the last) rise to the challenge of providing workable structures through which the communities might reinvent themselves. All of them, in their different aspects, speak to the challenge of explaining how, precisely, a transcendent community within an empire ought to operate.

To begin with, there is the vocabulary of shared ethical obligation. We might place under this heading the emphasis on friendship or love.[86] Here we see a deep link to the strains of anti-legalism that would be part of the broader political imagination of the elites of the empire more generally: the reduction of political or legal questions (i.e., under what circumstances might one person's wishes prevail over another's?) to *affective dispositions*. In such formulations, fellow feeling can be a powerful impulse to avoid or prevent conflict, or to keep it from spilling into other aspects of life. Such concepts can be especially powerful theologically or even just emotionally, and the

84 1 Cor. 5:5.

85 Save for Rom. 13:1–4, which offers relatively little concrete advice.

86 Unsurprisingly, given their importance to practical theology, such concepts have generated enormous bibliographies, the content of which mostly does not concern us here.

maintenance of fellow feeling (and individual acts of self-control) is a key element in causing the followers of Jesus to be "sanctified" or "set apart" from a degraded, fleshy society more generally. For present purposes, however, it will suffice to note that, in evoking such an ethical/affective vocabulary, Paul frames it as an antithesis to a vision of community anchored in legality and as a way of avoiding legal conflict more generally.

By imagining the "assemblies" of Christ followers as fundamentally affective organizations, Paul is also able to imagine two further things. First, a world of consensual bonds which exists, to some degree, in juxtaposition both to a law-bound community like Judaism and to the normal world of the *poleis* of Greco-Roman citizens. In this sense, a discourse like "love" might be imagined as a counter-hegemonic discourse, at least in the sense that the harmony of a consensus-based community would self-consciously *not* model itself on other forms of political order prevalent throughout the landscape, and furthermore, that such a world might be one that was of no interest to the imperial state.[87] (This proposition would subsequently be tried by Christian communities, only to be found wanting.) But there is a second and perhaps more important aspect to this insistence on fellow feeling. In a world governed by ideas of love – by shared affect – it is hard to imagine a mode by which one member of a community could *insist* upon his rights vis-à-vis any other community member.

The inability to make demands is similarly key to understanding Paul's second metaphor for the organization of community: slavery. In two key texts, Paul describes the members of Christ communities as slaves. In the first case, he speaks to the community of believers in Rome "in human terms, because of the weakness of your flesh." Here Paul explains that, just as the community in Rome had previously been slaves to "impurity" (*akatharsia*) and "greater and greater illegality (*anomia*)," now the community, having accepted Christ, are constituted as "slaves to righteousness (*dikaiosynēi*) for the purpose of sanctification (*hagiasmon*)."[88] Similarly, when writing to the Galatians, in a rather convoluted passage, he urges (simultaneously) that the

87 A vast literature exists that seeks to draw parallels between early Christian communities and other, voluntary organizations throughout the Hellenistic and Greco-Roman world. See, for example, Harland 2003; Kloppenborg 2020.

88 Rom. 6:19.

Galatians should not submit to the yoke of slavery (by circumcising themselves), but should instead be free; in their freedom, however, they should not use their freedom to indulge their flesh (*sarki*), but instead should "be slaves to one another (*douleuete allēlois*) through love."[89] Theologically, the language of slavery is part of a broader set of Pauline binaries that animate complex theological ideas (like spirit/flesh): acceptance of Christ is both freedom and a form of slavery, and in this regard a path to eventual salvation. The power of the image lies in its harnessing of contradictory statuses. Similarly, the metaphor of slavery to Christ, at least among people who considered themselves in positions of authority, also suggested that, by way of their total devotion to their master, these leaders were themselves in some sense exalted.[90]

But as a way of imagining the nature of legal or political community, it evokes a further set of images that are equally important. Whatever else slaves were in the Roman-era Mediterranean, they were people who were bereft of legal rights. They were under no circumstances permitted to *insist* on their rights against others.[91] They were permitted to attempt to persuade, to impress, or to move to pity; they had, however, no legal recourse against their masters or their fellow slaves. In this regard, then, and whatever its broader theological connotations, the language of slavery comes to be a potent way of imagining a form of community that sits apart from communities of fellow *citizens* – that is, people who were fundamentally *free*, with the consequence that they tended to selfishly insistent on their individual rights against others. In that sense, slavery operates as a parallel mode of political imagining to the language of love but stresses the importance of abjection in preventing (rather than settling) conflict. It is also, pointedly, a rejection of the sort of reasoning characteristic of Aesop (see Chapter 5), whose legalism was essential for preserving whatever shred of autonomy he might have had as a slave (to say nothing of protecting his own body). Once again, even in rejecting imperial institutions like courts, another imperial legal institution (slavery) reveals its imprint on his thinking.

89 Gal. 5:19. 90 Martin 1990: 56–58.

91 With the important exception of those slaves who sought to dispute their status *as* slaves – a common exception in slave societies with developed legal traditions, and something that would be unacceptable to Paul. I thank Michael Peachin for pointing this out.

There is a final, if only tentative, mode of imagining political community. In his letter to the Roman colony of Philippi, Paul evokes a much more "civic" category of political organization. In thinking through the broader matter of "how you should conduct yourselves politically" (*politeuesthe*),[92] and in response to a variety of threats to the community, Paul argues the following:[93]

> Brothers, join in imitating me, and observe those who live according to the example you have in us. For many live as enemies of the cross of Christ; I have often told you of them, and now I tell you even with tears. Their end is destruction; their god is the belly; and their glory is in their shame (*aischynēi*); their minds are set on earthly things. But our *politeuma* is in the heavens, and it is from there that we are expecting a savior, the lord Jesus Christ. He will transform the body of our humiliation (*to sōma tēs tapeinōseōs hēmōn*) that it may be conformed to the body of his glory (*summorphon tōi sōmati tēs doxēs autou*), by the power that also enables him to make all things subject to himself.

The language here is vexing, not least since this is the only time it emerges in the Pauline letters. Lexically and historically, *politeuma* is a problematic category. It is not the same as a *politeia* – a community of citizens – but it is obviously related. *Politeumata* existed in various places throughout the Hellenistic world (though, it seems, exclusively in former Ptolemaic territories): these were communities of (notionally) ethnically similar people, such as the *politeuma* of Jews at Herakleopolis. They appear to have been polis-*like* institutions, with some degree of internal autonomy, that operated within and at the sufferance of a larger kingdom.[94] If we make the dubious assumption that Paul was striving for terminological precision, we might then conclude that he sought to evoke a civic metaphor that urged members of the community to self-govern, but only to the extent acceptable to a superior power.[95] But problematically, Paul also locates this ideal form of community "in the heavens" (*en ouranois*), rather than in the presently existing world. For the present world, it seems, all one

[92] Phil. 1:27. [93] Phil. 3:17–21.

[94] Some of the documents of this community have been preserved: see the collection *P.Polit.Iud.* A vast bibliography has sought to decipher the precise political status of this community: for a guide, see Patrick Sänger, "Herakleopolis, Jewish *politeuma*," *OCD* (2016). There is also a strong possibility that the term had little fixed meaning at all.

[95] For one attempt at terminological precision, see Oakes 2019 with further bibliography.

can do is to seek to become "fellow imitators" (*symmimētai*) of the behavior of the apostle himself. Again, we are left with comparatively little that might explain how to constitute a community, much less how to govern one.

***

It might be worth just a few words on the sorts of arguments advanced by the antinomians at Corinth. "All things are permitted to me!" is not a terribly complex argument, it must be admitted. (For present purposes we might take Paul at his word that this *was* their argument.) But the possibility of being liberated from law *tout court* was evidently profound. Equally profound was what they perceived as a radical disjuncture between the promise of transcending legality and the imposition of a hugely traditional moral code upon them at the same moment, as if the two were logically interrelated.

A few of these dissident voices are preserved, mostly as an example, by later Christians, of impermissible conclusions to draw from the promise of Jesus' mission and crucifixion. Of these, one holds out particular interest, for it seems to elaborate the instincts of the antinomians at Corinth. (Though there is no reason to think that they sit in any sort of genealogical relationship, either as a community or as intellectual descendants.[96]) The text, from an otherwise poorly known Epiphanes, was entitled *On Justice* (*Peri dikaiosynēs*).

Only a few paragraphs of the text survive, but it begins from radical premises: "The justice of God is a certain communality (*koinonia*) joined with equality (*isotētos*)."[97] Justice is not linked to particular institutions, not even particular *human* institutions. Mere empirical observation of all living beings suffices to show that radical equality and living in common are the rule, rather than the exception:

> Then, on the basis of communality, all are sown according to species. Common food rises from the soil for all cattle who graze, and for all equally. It is not controlled by any law. Rather, it is harmoniously present to all through the abundance of the Giver and Commander by means of justice. Nor is there

[96] I similarly take no position on the question of whether these views ought to be categorized as somehow "Gnostic" – the question is wholly uninteresting to me, and bears no import for what follows.

[97] Clem. *Strom.* 3.2, text and translation from Litwa 2022.

a law written (*nomon...gegrammenon*) for matters of reproduction, for it would be copied out. Animals sow their seed and reproduce with equality, having communality inborn at the hands of Justice. Upon all in common, the creator and father of all equally bestowed the eye for seeing, legislating (*nomothetēsas*) with Justice beside him. He did not differentiate female from male, rational (*logikon*) from irrational (*alogou*) – in short, anything from anything else. Rather, with equality and communality, he distributed the ability to see. In the same manner, and with one command, he bestowed it on all.

We might note just a few features of this line of reasoning. To begin with, it starts from empiricist premises to insist that humans are in no sense primary. Justice is evident just as much from the practice of animals as it is from any other source; in fact, the practice of animals, because it is uncorrupted by human institutions, is superior to seeking justice through history or anthropology. In so arguing, the text also insists that there is no necessary role for *logos* in deciding what justice is. Since justice is equally present in animal societies, peculiarly human forms of reasoning are irrelevant if not actively misleading. In this respect, the text might even be said to be anti-rational.

Epiphanes takes Paul very seriously: when Paul claims, in the Letter to the Galatians, that social status is obliterated in Christ, Epiphanes agrees wholeheartedly. Similarly, Epiphanes endorses Paul's claim, in the Letter to the Romans, that law enabled the knowledge of sin. In fact, he argues that these categories – mine and yours – crept in through law, perverting what was naturally the case: radical sharing and communalism.[98] Private property, accordingly, is an institution that cannot be sustained. Neither can prohibitions against the violation of private property, like theft. Finally, and perhaps most scandalously to Clement of Alexandria (who preserves these fragments of Epiphanes in order to rebuke them), marriage itself is defined as a subset of an otherwise unacceptable regime of private property:[99]

Therefore one must understand the legislator speaking this phrase as something laughable (*geloion*): "Do not desire." It is even more laughable to say, "your neighbor's property." For the very one (God) who gave desire to sustain reproduction commands that it be removed, though he has not removed it from any animal. And by his phrase, "your neighbor's wife," he forces what is common to become private, and speaks what is still more laughable.

[98] 3.2.7.2. [99] 3.2.9.2.

Here we can see the radical departure from Paul, and the ways that it must have grated to have Paul's deeply conservative regime of morality foist upon oneself, when the central Pauline claims seemed to point in a different direction. As Epiphanes protests, "But though people are born in this way, they nonetheless have denied the commonality that leads to birth, and they say (instead), 'Let the man who marries her, have her,' (1 Cor 7:2) even though all people can join together, just as God declared for the rest of the animals."[100] In order to ensure community harmony in a world where the law was abrogated, Paul sought to constrain desire: by limiting desire, he would limit conflict, and thus disharmony. He was forced to concede, however, to the community in Corinth that desire was real, and that it could be contained within the structures of marriage. Epiphanes rejects this concession totally: desire, he insists, is simply natural. God placed it in people and animals alike; it leads to procreation, which is both natural and good. To legislate against it is a human, rather than a divine trait. Far from a base yearning, desire is simply an empirical fact. It may differ between men and women – men have greater desires "for the persistence of human families, a desire which no law, custom, or anything else can destroy" – but they share the tendency to wish to reproduce.[101]

Epiphanes is not fully antinomian: he accepts that God (alongside Justice) has legislated fundamental facts about the human world. But nearly the entirety of human law, he insists, is not worth following. If the promise of Christ is real, then his followers have overcome legality as a whole: whatever remains is to live, as best as possible, in accordance with a natural regime that can be inferred from animal behavior. It was a path that was detestable to mainstream, educated Christian elites, both because it might enable non-Christians to impugn Christians more generally and because such ideas of radical equality threatened their positions as community leaders (for they denied the benefits of hierarchy).[102] But one can understand how, in this imperial world, such a set of conclusions might have enticed.

* * *

100 3.2.8.2. I have significantly modified Litwa's translation.

101 On desires and yearnings in the Rabbinic and early Christian traditions, see Rosen-Zvi 2011.

102 Cf. Pagels 1979.

To return, briefly, to Paul. Because he felt keenly the coming of God's judgment, Paul ultimately devoted little systematic thinking about how specifically to handle moments in a community where there might be good faith disputes over rights, honors, or other sorts of resources. This was, for him, a banal question as compared to the urgent necessity of bringing Gentiles into the community of Christ followers and exhorting them to comport their behavior to moral standards, so as to prepare the world for an imminent new age. But for writers of the generation following Paul, the urgency had abated somewhat. Christ was coming, but not, it appeared, immediately. The challenge of how to manage disputes within a community persisted. Writing under Paul's name, a pair of thinkers were left to articulate how such a community might act virtuously, and also as a sanctified community – that is, as a community set apart from, or a community that sought to transcend, the structures of quotidian administration.

To preserve community sanctity, these writers insisted, hierarchy – and its cousin, deference – were of the highest importance. Most importantly, the community had to be able to avoid the vexing scenarios that played out periodically but dramatically in the courts of the provinces, where children might sue parents, or wives husbands, and win. As I explained earlier (Chapter 3), the threat remained that, by harnessing the power of legalism, a notionally subordinate member of one of the new Christian "assemblies" might prevail over another member's desires and undermine his (or perhaps her) authority. The transcendent state of sanctity, then, would depend upon the creation of a community that occupied a space apart from the empire as a whole.

To get to this result would require some remarkable political thinking. The author of the Letter to the Ephesians gives perhaps the most well-elaborated account (parts of which he adapted from the earlier Letter to the Colossians). Surprisingly perhaps, he begins his argument by appealing, in large part, to Paul's least-developed category of communal organization, the language of citizenship. Similarly, he does it in a way that echoes the great transformations of the landscape over the first centuries BC/AD. The distinction between Jews and Gentiles, he insists, has been obliterated. Though the Gentiles were originally outside of the community (*politeias*) of Israel and were aliens (*xenoi*) from the promises of salvation, the blood (*haimati*) of Christ has now brought them near, and his flesh (*sarki*) has abolished enmity between the two groups.[103] What is more, Christ has made irrelevant (*katargēsas*) the law itself, with its commandments and ordinances. The effect of this, according to the author of Ephesians, is to have blended the two communities – Jews and Gentiles – into one new human being, a single body (*heni sōmati*) governed by peace.[104] The end result, the author contends, is the formation of a novel political community: whereas the Gentiles were once "foreigners and subject peoples" (*xenoi kai paroikoi*), now they exist as "fellow citizens" (*sympolitai*) with the holy ones and members of the same family (*oikeioi*) within the household of God.[105]

The promise of moving from "foreigners and subject peoples" to citizenship must have been counted as a highly desirable transition in the landscapes of the Greek cities of the first century AD. This was no mere metaphor: as a result of the changes of the political landscape in the first centuries BC/AD, real groups of people had been excluded from citizenship. For such people, the consequences of that exclusion were both material (in the sense that it rendered them prone to exploitation) and hostile to their dignity.[106] It is not irrelevant that, within such a world, people were constantly concerned to find ways to acquire citizenship and to improve their political status; it is upon these desires for inclusion in a new polity that the author of Ephesians plays.[107] The novelty, in his account, comes from the fact that this new political community is one in which the various commandments and requirements of the law (*nomon*) have been made irrelevant by the blood and flesh of Christ. The result is a new community, which can in turn be expressed as a new physical person (*kainon anthrōpon*), a single body in harmony with itself.

The metaphor of the community as a "body" had, of course, a lengthy pedigree in the Greco-Roman world more broadly.[108] Most importantly, it was used to explain social hierarchy: how distinct members of the community were made for specific tasks, and as such, should be content with their role and not seek to overturn the broader

[103] Eph. 2:11–14. [104] 2:15–16. See further Ophir and Rosen-Zvi 2018: 147.
[105] 2:19.
[106] E.g., Dio *Or.* 34, documenting the ways in which the city of Tarsus managed to enrage both its own population and those of its neighbors by lording its authority over the disenfranchised.
[107] E.g., Plin. *Ep.* 10.6.
[108] For a useful overview, Martin 1995: 38–55. See now Mebane 2024.

social order. That is, workers were hands, nobles heads and bellies, and so forth, each content with the position to which he or she was assigned because such a position contributed to a greater goal. The author of Ephesians follows in this tradition as well: as he explains, just as some were designated to be apostles, others to be evangelists, others to be shepherds and teachers, nonetheless all participate in the construction (*oikodomēn*) of the body (*sōmatos*) of Christ.[109] Unlike in broader Greco-Roman thinking, however, this bodily "construction" of society was not simply necessary for maintaining social harmony. It was also a thoroughly moral affair: building the body of Christ meant, first and foremost, abstaining from old practices, now coded as "Gentile" in nature.[110]

It is in this context that the author introduces the so-called *Haustafel*, the code of moral behavior that involves abstaining from drunkenness, fornication, idolatry, et cetera. These codes of behavior would structure a great deal of subsequent Christian thinking, being subject to elaboration in the subsequent "pastoral epistles" as well as in other texts. The codes are interesting of themselves: attempts to reduce political ordering to the prescription of moral behavior, and to frame the most urgent social questions as being those that concern the household. But to such codes of behavior the author elaborates a concept that had originally been experimented with by Paul, and which was a marked feature of the Mediterranean world writ large: the sanctification of hierarchy. Just as Christ is the head (*kephalē*) of the assembly, he argues, so too is the husband the head of his wife.[111] So similarly are children and slaves to conform to the dictates of the head of the household. It should immediately be added that these analogies – as Christ to community so husband to wife – compete with the metaphor of the body, where individual parts have distinct and complementary roles, rather than fractal relationships of domination. This seems not to bother the author. The language of domination is more than simply sanctified – it is also coded aesthetically and erotically. The domination of wives, children, and slaves is analogized to the love of one's own body: "for no one hates his flesh (*sarka*), but he nourishes it and cares for it, just as Christ does for the church."[112] When hierarchy is done correctly, the result is

[109] 4:11–12. [110] 4:17. [111] 5:22–24. Cf. 1 Cor. 11:2–16. [112] 5:29.

aesthetically pleasing: in a world where a husband loves his wife, the church as a whole can be presented as "not having a blemish (*spilon*) or a wrinkle (*rytida*), but being sacred and blameless."[113]

With this we are a long way from Paul. Flesh, in the letter to the Ephesians, is coded not as defective or problematic, a questionable thing that must be overcome to enjoy the kingdom of God. Instead, it exists in analogy to the flesh of Christ: just as Christ's flesh creates a new political community, so too can that community be described as an aesthetically pleasing body. The result is a moral community based on hierarchy, with no need to create separate spheres of contest, conflict, and adjudication. Disputes, on such a theory, are presumptively unnecessary, even immoral; their mere existence is only proof that the desirable hierarchy within the community has broken down.[114]

Within such a community, to insist on one's rights is, *a fortiori*, to operate without love, to despise one's own body, and to cause a collective "wrinkle" or "blemish." We might see here an echo of Dio's parable of rulership (below, Chapter 7): for the author of Ephesians, only the pathological or the disruptive would prefer to gaze upon something other than an unblemished body (perhaps ironic, given the importance of the upsetting aesthetic spectacle of the crucifixion in the thinking of Christ's followers just a generation earlier). Communities must seek to patrol the behavior of such disruptive people, or to eliminate their disruptions entirely. Such would be the price of transcendence.

Finally, we might draw attention to one other aspect of this second generation of Christian thinkers. I have dealt at length with the Letter to the Ephesians, because I think it the more fully elaborated attempt to think through the structure of an ideal political community. But the author of the earlier Letter to the Colossians makes a further contribution to the question of how one is to organize community. As in the Letter to the Ephesians, the author stresses that Christ is to be conceived as "the head of the body of the assembly" (*kephalē tou sōmatos tēs ekklēsias*), and that his crucifixion has, through the "body of his flesh" (*en tōi sōmati tēs sarkos autou*), allowed those who had previously been estranged to enter the new community and to live in peace.[115] This author too reminds his audience not to be

[113] 5:27. [114] The later 1 Tim. 6:3–6 draws this conclusion explicitly.
[115] 1:18–22.

concerned with legal minutiae, such as "Do not handle, do not taste, do not touch."[116] He too presents a household code of conduct as the basis for moral organization of community. But he adds an important detail:[117]

> Let the *logos* of Christ dwell in you richly. Teach and admonish one another in wisdom; and with gratitude in your hearts sing psalms, hymns, and odes to God. And whatever you do, in word or deed (*en logōi ē en ergōi*), do everything in the name of the Lord Jesus, giving thanks to the Father through him.

It is hard, in the broader political context, to see this as anything but a redefinition of, if not a rejection of, broader provincial claims about the importance of *logos*. That purpose of *that logos* was to contest, to articulate a vision of one's place in the world, and to advocate for the things that one needed to live in security and dignity. It manifested itself as a mode of speaking to those in power, demanding of them that their behavior conform to standards that were based in a shared rationality. It was, in that sense, a powerful political tool. For the author of the Letter to the Colossians, however, the *logos* of Christ is different: it is to be used not to articulate claims about how the world ought to operate, but instead to correct and teach one another, and to sing psalms, hymns, and songs to God himself. That is, the purpose of *logos*, in such a system, is not to contest, but to *amplify* the transcendent glories of a pre-established hierarchy. Once again, it seems, the quotidian politics of the Roman Empire have left their imprint even on the discourses that sought to reject such politics and to deny their value for subjects.

***

The earliest Christian texts cannot be separated from their provincial context, much less their provincial *legal* context. They speak not only to the presence of legal institutions in the broader landscape, but to the importance of those institutions in structuring people's self-understanding; even when that self-understanding is based on the very rejection of those institutions, their presence as mental and moral building blocks is nonetheless readily identified. What I have sought to show, in this chapter, is that these discourses deserve to be taken

[116] 2:21. [117] 3:16.

seriously, as both legal and political theory. They attest provincial realia, but they are also a sign of how deeply committed provincial populations were to thinking in legal categories, even as they wished to transcend them.

If the Pauline strain of Christianity rejected legalism as a path for creating an ideal community, groups of Rabbis came to embrace it. Though Jewish leaders had for generations made legal rulings on a variety of matters, rabbis of the late second and early third centuries came to fundamentally redefine Judaism as a religion of legality – even of legalism. They brought together a range of legal rulings and subjected them to a systematic restructuring as a code of law, the Mishnah. It was perhaps the first document in the Roman world that might reasonably be spoken of *as a code* – that is, as a project that sought to regulate aspects of life that ranged from criminal law to damages, from idol worship to quotidian obligations of prayer, and to marriage, divorce, wisdom, and everything in between, including rituals that seem to have been fully imaginary.[118]

Breathtaking in its ambitions, the Mishnah might in ways be understood as a project both quotidian and utopian.[119] For present purposes, we might note only three things. First, for a text produced in a Roman provincial context, though scholars have labored mightily to find specific legal rulings that echo the pluralistic context of the Roman world, they have turned up very little. That is, at the level of the individual ruling, there is almost no trace of the sorts of Roman or even broadly Hellenistic rules that, from other contexts, we can be certain Jews were following.[120] It seems less likely that this is an effect of Jews maintaining a single, persistent, authentically Jewish tradition of legal practices, rather than a deliberate attempt to recreate or regulate such practices through a medium that was interpreted as – or claimed to be – authentically Jewish *at that particular moment.*

[118] The bibliography is obviously enormous. Useful as an overview is Cohen 2022. Imaginary rituals: Rosen-Zvi 2012. I have benefited much from reading preliminary chapters of a forthcoming book on Mishnah and Midrash by Ishay Rosen-Zvi.

[119] Cohn 2022.

[120] This is obviously a controversial claim. Recently scholars have attempted to find such borrowings (e.g., Malka 2019; Malka and Paz 2019), but such claims run into severe difficulties (see, e.g., the response of du Plessis 2019 to Malka 2019). On Jewish practices in other contexts, see, inter alia, Cotton 1993; Oudshoorn 2007; Czajkowski 2017.

Put differently, the idea of creating – or recreating – a body of law specifically *as* Jewish law seems to be an effect of the very imperial world that these Jewish subjects inhabited. To regulate all aspects of daily life – down to the level of the thoughts that might lead to premature ejaculation – was to claim a huge territory of personal space *as* Jewish, and therefore presumptively off limits to other forms of regulation.[121]

Second, and relatedly, to the extent that this code rejected Roman or Hellenistic practices at the level of individual rules, the framing of these rules as a comprehensive code was deeply indebted to imperial practices. That is, to break one's law into fields such as damages, agriculture, purity, and so on was to define the body of Jewish law as comparable to *other* bodies of law within the Empire. Such a claim should be read in the context of other, introductory texts that claimed to break Roman law into discrete bodies. Most famously, in the *Institutes*, Gaius defined Roman law as being composed of persons, things, and actions; this was already an important improvement on legal organization from other periods, which simply sought to list rules as part of a running commentary on the praetorian edict.[122] But in the ways that the redactors of the Mishnah named these categories we can see something of a comment on these other practices: for Rabbis, law was just vastly *more* than for other peoples of the empire. And to the extent that a claim of *having* particular laws also entailed a claim that such law ought normally to be respected by imperial rulers, the Rabbis endeavored to place a huge if not exhaustive list of normatively Jewish things outside of the regulatory authorities of the Roman state. As such, we might see the Mishnah as a document that emerges in conversation with, but also in *competition* with, other imperial structures – even if such structures leave little to no imprint at the level of actual rulings.

Third, and related to the question of competition, the code that the Rabbis created (or redacted, as the case may be) was imagined to be fully oral. Again, the importance of this can be understood as both a reaction to, and a comment upon, the institutions of the empire more

[121] Premature ejaculation (as opposed to irregular seminal flow): *M.Zavim* 2:2.

[122] 1.8. Other forms of legal commentary are discussed below, Chapters 8 and 9, and in Schulz 1946.

broadly. To begin with, as scholars have long noted, the written word suffused the Roman Mediterranean.[123] To refuse (at least in theory) to *write* one's law was, at a very basic level, obviously counter-hegemonic. It also meant that law could only be accessed through immersion in the community, through face-to-face interactions with those who knew law, and with the bonds of sociability and affect that such relationships normally entailed. Another Rabbinic source, the *Sifre*, of roughly the same period dramatizes precisely this issue:[124]

> The government (i.e., Rome) once sent out two officials, ordering them, "Go and disguise yourselves as Jews, and find out what is the nature of their Torah." They went to Rabban Gamaliel at Usha (Yavneh?), where they studied Scripture, Mishnah, Midrash, halakhah and aggadah. As the officers were taking their leave, they said to the Sages, "All of the Torah is fine and praiseworthy, except one thing, and that is your saying that 'That which is stolen from a non-Jew is permitted, while that which is stolen from a Jew is forbidden.' But we will not report this exception to the government."

But orality was not just a commentary on writing; it was also a commentary on Roman jurisprudence itself, which retained traces of its oral composition well into periods in which writing was an essential part of what jurists did. Here, the comparison is both implicit and unmistakably competitive: if individual responsa are best given orally, then the Mishnah counts as a daring boast about what the role of orality ought, ideally, to be.[125]

The vision of Jews as a fully legalized community, with nearly nothing off-limits to the gaze of Rabbinic regulation, is understandable along the same lines as the Pauline rejection of legality. It would be hard to imagine that it did not develop, in some sense at least, in dialogue both with nearby Christian communities, as well as with more broadly Roman ideas about legality.[126] But it also embraced a form of legality that was, in theory, generated on the back of biblical texts, not through the work of daily practice; a legality that was, by

[123] Starting points: Woolf 1996; Ando 2000: esp. 87.

[124] *Sifre* 344, trans. Hammer 1986. Cf. *YT Bava Kamma* 4.3, *BT Bava Kamma* 38a.

[125] A great volume of literature is devoted to questions of orality in Jewish law. A consensus seems to be emerging that the fixation on memorization that developed in Babylonian contexts is at best an imperfect fit with earlier, Palestinian contexts. See, e.g., Vidas 2021; Furstenberg 2022.

[126] See esp. Boyarin 2004.

definition, inaccessible to the broader community whose voices might otherwise have constituted it. It was a vision of legalism as utopian in the sense that the same sort of pure community that Paul envisioned might be constituted *through* law and emerge *from* law, all without having to rely upon the institutions of the Empire or even constitute one's community as a polis – that is, as a form recognizable to the Empire. According to the logic of the *Sifre*, it could only be understood by immersion, and such immersion could be counted on to vitiate any attempts to co-opt it.

***

The fantasy of radical change in one's legal position – even the obliteration of law itself – ought to be taken seriously, not just as a mode of theology but as a mode of legal thought. It is of course most prominently on display in the texts discussed above, but these, it must be imagined, were themselves participants in larger bodies of discourse that took place across the provincial landscape more broadly. Some of the most radical voices were preserved only by accident – such as Epiphanes; others came, though only slowly, to serve as the normative sources of community. But none can be treated as separate from their political and institutional contexts. They were the imaginings of very imperial people, even when they sought to transcend the very institutions that constructed them.

7

The Politics of Amazement

For the men schooled in the practical realities of running cities within the administrative framework of the Roman Empire, the courtroom was a place to be avoided. The Greek elites who were in charge of the cities of the eastern empire had a flair for drama and for the public eye. They gave conspicuous gifts to their home communities and to others. They spoke in front of assembled masses and honored guests (including imperial administrators) at home and abroad. Some traveled to Rome to urge emperors to grace their cities with privileges or assistance in times of need. They competed with one another to preside over a host of sacrifices and rituals designed to show their loyalty to the gods and to the emperor himself. But they did not rush to court, nor did they imagine that they should.

There were obvious practical dangers. When prosecuting or defending a case, words might fail. The judge might be grumpy, sleepy, incompetent, distracted, or merely partial or venal. Trials were public events, and crowds might take the opportunity to raise embarrassing matters or just to heckle. A litigant's enemies might curse him, tying his tongue in court. One could of course take measures to anticipate such dangers; in fact, part of being a member of this elite class was having a robust toolkit for navigating tense situations in which one might have to talk one's way out of trouble. But the chance that one might fail was real.

The bigger problem that the courtroom posed for these elites was structural. Courtrooms operate through a peculiar logic. Within their confines, litigants pit rival accounts of the truth against one another and test the possibilities for making disparate and sometimes inconvenient facts conform to plausible stories. They do this to produce a verdict – an authoritative interpretation of facts that organizes the messy world of empirical reality into an apprehensible structure (even if it does so, in practice, only temporarily and contingently).[1]

As a matter of practical politics, framing problems as *legal* problems – that is, as justiciable questions that result in a verdict in which one party wins out over another – is not necessarily helpful. When a problem is pursued as a legal problem there can be no splitting the difference, no saving face.[2] The elites of the empire were masters of suasion, but to exist in their world meant that problems were ideally to be settled not by authoritative verdicts, but by forcing the large majority to show deference, while maintaining the bonhomie of those who were supposedly in charge.

As an ideological matter, Greek elites were supposed to emphasize their independence and thus avoid seeking the involvement of Roman authorities in their internal squabbles. Maintaining the peace and order of their cities was their primary duty. If Roman administrators had to get involved, this was an admission that local men had failed to govern effectively. Ideally, Roman governors were to play only three roles within cities. They might act as patrons, sponsoring cities they loved by beautifying them or improving their physical infrastructure. More ominously, they might be called in to handle dire cases, like famine, banditry, or civic unrest – efforts for which they would expect to be thanked profusely.[3] Finally, they might be brought in with the consent of the local elites themselves to make an example of lower-ranked subjects who stepped out of line – that is, to enact a

[1] Perhaps the best account of the work of the courtroom is Burns 1999. See also Burns 2009; Ferguson 2007.

[2] To be sure, an initial framing of a problem as a legal problem might force other sorts of negotiation in the background – the famous "bargaining in the shadow of the law" of Mnookin and Kornhauser 1979. Roman courts encouraged this sort of behavior and were happy for litigants to settle. None of this, however, has any great impact on my claims herein, where I am concerned primarily with ideologies rather than common practices. For an account of Roman litigation that takes into account the many ways that disputes might be settled outside of verdicts, see Kelly 2010; for late antiquity, Harries 1999, 2001.

[3] Erkelenz 2003: 177–88, 192–97.

dramatic tableau of imperial and local unity in punishing those who were the most deserving.[4] As a statement of this ideal we may take the praise of the third century scholar Philostratus for M. Antonius Polemo, one of the most important Greek elites of the century before. According to Philostratus, Polemo "benefited" the city of Smyrna in two main ways. First, because he brokered a series of important gifts from the emperor Hadrian, leading to the city's improvement in honor vis-à-vis her neighbors. Secondly, because he mediated disputes among citizens: "he did not allow the citizens of Smyrna to take their cases outside the city, but he settled them at home – the cases about money, I mean; those against adulterers or blasphemers or murders, which cause pollution if they are neglected, he ordered not just to be brought out but *thrown* out of Smyrna, for they required a judge with a sword in his hand."[5]

Such a model was easier to praise than to follow, and in point of fact the elites of the empire involved Roman governors, officials, and emperors in their problems with great frequency. They did in practice sue and get sued, and many were adept at negotiating a real courtroom.[6] Still, Polemo's "benefit" to the city of Smyrna speaks volumes about the legal ideology that emerged among these elites. Only the basest malefactors were to be punished by Roman governors (the "judge with a sword in his hand" being a reference to the governor's right to use capital punishment, the *ius gladii*). More respectable problems (or the problems of more respectable men) were, ideally, to be settled at home, through processes of negotiation. In contrast to what I termed, in earlier chapters, the ideology of subalterns or subjects (who put the courtroom front and center in their legal imaginary), the urban elites sought to avoid the courtroom or to sideline it. But there was more to their collective thinking than what we might call a "law avoidance" ideology. The idea that the courtroom was a

[4] That local elites in most cities, as a rule, had no authority to administer substantial punishments matters not – by supporting a governor's acts of punishment they made a virtue of necessity. For the exceptional cases, see Guerber 2009: 33–77, who details the privileges, including criminal jurisdiction, granted (rarely) to individual cities. For the more typical situation, see Fournier 2010.

[5] Philostr. *VS* 532. All translations of the *VS* are adapted from Wright, LCL.

[6] It is only in this context that the choice of forum granted to the admirals Seleucus of Rhosos or Asklepiades of Clazomenai makes sense: see Raggi 2006: 157–64.

problematic space for addressing problems implies that there were superior modes of dealing with problems, legal or otherwise. These modes, in turn, were anchored in competing beliefs about the nature of *logos* and its relationship to legality and social order.

These elites developed a competing set of modes for imagining law's ideal role in their world. For them, law was more than a system of rules or procedures, or even a set of practices that allowed for rational communication between unequal parties over the rules that must be observed. Rather, it was a system of speaking, seeing, self-fashioning, and knowing that allowed for easy communication and the solving of problems between men of rank and substance. Or perhaps more accurately, it was *two* systems: a system of rules and punishments for those of low rank, and an *affective* and ultimately *aesthetic* system of sociability and problem-solving for those of the privileged orders.

The courtroom might have been acceptable for efficiently processing peons who stepped out of line. It was not of course strictly necessary, for such offenders could be punished summarily. But it could be useful. Real social order, on the other hand, meant transcending such a grubby and unfortunate institution as the courtroom. It involved ascending Platonically, as it were, into a realm of "real" law. One could achieve such transcendence by cultivating political and aesthetic judgment, and, more importantly, by training one's mind, one's voice, and one's body. Like the communities that Paul addressed, these elites imagined that their educational training – *paideia* – allowed them to transform themselves both morally and physically, emplacing themselves within a new set of relations to power. They did this by using their *paideia* to move quotidian social relations into a space of *thauma*: the wonderous, the transcendent, and the ecstatic.

***

We might pause here before tackling the main thread of the argument to give some background as to who, precisely, these elites were, what their position in the empire was, and how that position came to be entangled with questions of body, aesthetics, and affect. To do this, we have to start with their institutional context (cities in an empire), before turning to their intellectual and ideological context (education/*paideia*). The educational system and its values, I will suggest, provided the framework for understanding how legal questions might be turned into aesthetic and affective questions. My account is necessarily schematic.[7] But the basic framework is important for understanding why this particular legal ideology emerged as it did.

It is perhaps a cliché to insist that the Roman Empire was a world of cities. But this phrase captures something essential about the nature of the political arrangements through which power flowed, especially in the eastern part of the Mediterranean. In particular, it captures why, in a world marked by an incredible diversity of actual political and institutional arrangements, Greek-speaking elite men from a relatively small number of urban areas bulk so large in our evidence, dominating the literary and epigraphic records. This is perhaps not unexpected: these men were committed to self-aggrandizement and self-commemoration, and evolved an epigraphic discourse of self-praise that they coupled with idealized images of themselves in the form of statues, which were in turn widely scattered through the urban landscape.[8] But the prominence of these men is nonetheless surprising when considering that there were in fact many other powerful people spread throughout this landscape: powerful Roman citizens, slaves and agents of emperors and senators, large landholders based both locally and in Rome, and, of course, Roman governors and their entourages. Yet the elites of Greek cities stand out.

The cultivation of groups of Greek-speaking local elites emerged long before Roman rule. In the wake of Alexander's conquests and the regimes of his successors a new wave of urbanism began to restructure the landscape of the formerly Achaemenid world. Cities sprung up (or were established by fiat) in new places, featuring typically Greek political institutions like councils and assemblies as well as a culture of conspicuous gift-giving by wealthy citizens to the

[7] In what follows I am heavily influenced by Gleason 1995. For an important study of sophists in the context of Roman administration, see Bowersock 1969, with the important corrective of Bowie 1982.

[8] For the Hellenistic period, see Ma 2013; for the Roman east, Smith 1998; Smith and Ward-Perkins 2016. See also Weisweiler 2015: 73–75 on the presentation of governors and their statues in the provinces. The link between the language of commemoration and the physical manifestation of the person commemorated supports the point that I make below about reducing political questions to aesthetic concerns. For some thoughtful but preliminary reflections on the problems posed by sculpture and the aestheticization of the political, see Ewald 2014; Ma 2024: 493–95.

community as a whole (known by modern scholars as "euergetism"). Cities were essential nodes in systems of monarchic control, for they were notionally self-governing and in charge of their surrounding territories – essential in a world in which monarchs themselves had relatively little ability to invest in extensive bureaucracies to bend far-flung regions to their wishes. Rome inherited and perpetuated this pattern. The Roman Empire governed through cities, and cities were governed, ideally, by local elites. Elites were offered respect and privileges (sometimes including Roman citizenship and subsequent promotion to high-status positions in imperial government), while cities themselves sent both tangible resources and expressions of loyalty, gratitude, and docility back to Rome.

Governing through cities was easier for Rome than governing directly – at least, if the cities were themselves well-governed. Democracy – and a number of Greek cities were still democracies – was an irritant to Roman governors, for it left responsibility for bad decisions problematically diffuse. In a process still poorly understood, it became sharply constrained.[9] Cities were to be run, ideally, by oligarchies, where a sufficiently small number of men might be held accountable for poor governance and praised for keeping order.[10] Failing that, cities might be run by individual tyrants (such, it seems, was the case in Sparta throughout the first century).[11] The urban pattern was pushed into areas in which it had been traditionally absent as well: a number of areas that featured low levels of urbanization were handed over to native or neighboring royalty, who were often granted Roman citizenship (such as Herod in Judaea) and encouraged to urbanize their territories.[12] These so-called "client kings" developed

[9] On the disappearance of democracy, see de Ste. Croix 1981: 518–37; Rhodes and Lewis 1997: 542–49. For more optimistic perspectives about the continuing importance of the people, see Fernoux 2011 (with the perceptive comments of Brélaz 2013); Lewin 1995; Ma 2024: 348–53.

[10] Cf. the Lycian dedication to the emperor Claudius on the occasion of Lycia's provincialization, discussed above, Chapter 2 (*SEG* LI 1832).

[11] On G. Julius Eurycles and his dynasty, see Bowersock 1961; Spawforth 1989: 97–104; Steinhauer 2010. On a possibly similar situation in Athens, see Jones 2011.

[12] Herod's building program at Caesarea and elsewhere: Holum 1988. Temple states: Jerusalem, Tcherikover 1964; temples of Asia Minor, Jones 2017: 352–53, though the territory of some temple states in Anatolia was broken up (e.g., Men Askaenos, Strab. 12.8.14; on others in the region see Mitchell 1993: I: 81–82). On Palmyra, Smith 2013.

close ties to the elites of the city of Rome and intermarried into one another's families. When their dynasties ended, they often remained elites in their home territories and beyond. Such, for example, was the background of the sophist Polemo, who was descended from a Pontic royal family that had been given Roman citizenship.[13]

The world of the East was wildly diverse, and there were dramatic variations within and between regions. But the basic pattern is clear enough: cities were increasingly run by councils composed of local elites, and council membership was normally life-long and based at minimum on a wealth qualification. The preference for oligarchy extended, in some contexts, even into the most "democratic" of city institutions, the popular assemblies: in some cases, the right to vote in the assembly was accompanied by a property qualification. Even Athens, with its proud democratic tradition, seems eventually to have adopted such a system. The larger public was not, of course, happy to be excluded. Thus, Dio Chrysostom might lament that the city of Tarsus would gladly sell its citizenship to outsiders for the sum of 500 drachmas but would not deign to allow the city's linen-weavers – who were part of an important export industry – to vote in the assembly (that is, without them paying up). This policy created a toxic dynamic, and Dio urged the Tarsians to include the weavers in the polity.[14] It is not clear that they listened. The Tarsians' exclusion of the linen weavers made sense within this institutional and cultural matrix. Tarsus was competing with its neighbors to show that it was the best of cities; to have the best citizens, Tarsus would only accept the best men *as* citizens. If this came at the cost of disenfranchising those lower-class individuals who, in another town or in the past, might have expected citizenship as their birthright, then so be it.

The Roman encouragement of oligarchies was more than just an instinctive attempt to implant metropolitan values on an alien landscape (though it was that too). It was also a practical mode of governing. When working with an oligarchy it was relatively easy, in a world with limited information and communication infrastructures, to know who to punish if something went awry in a particular locality,

[13] Thonemann 2004. On the eastern kings as "provincial monarchs," see now Ish-Shalom 2021. See also Jones 2017, on Strabo and his terminology for local rulers.

[14] Tarsus: Dio *Or.* 34, esp. 21–23. Athens: Rhodes and Lewis 1997: 59–60. Brélaz 2013: 372.

or to keep track of who was getting too big for his britches. And the elites were vulnerable. Though emperors starting in the second century in particular took especial care to exempt these local elites from the most degrading sorts of quotidian punishments, execution, exile, and confiscation of property were always on the table and, it seems, not uncommonly resorted to.[15] The oft-cited advice of Plutarch, to an elite young man getting ready to begin a political career, must surely refer to such dangers:[16]

> You should arrange your cloak more neatly and shift your gaze away from the general's tent and towards the governor's tribunal, neither taking pride in your crown nor trusting in it, since you see Roman boots above your head. Instead you should imitate actors, who put their own pathos and ethos and judgment into the show, but obey the prompter and do not transgress the rhythms and meters prescribed by those in charge. The result, in your case, is not hissing or mockery or booing, but rather, in many cases, "That terrible punishment, the axe that cleaves the neck," like in the case of your countryman, Pardalas, and his followers who overstepped their boundaries.

Though we know less than we would like about Pardalas, the basic message was clear enough: elite status was a great thing to have, but it was no protection against Roman rule. Quiescence was smart policy.

This, then, is the institutional matrix in which the Greek elites operated: accountable to emperors and governors (and periodically to one another), they were also expected to govern their cities. Successful governance meant beautifying the cities, keeping them quiet, and giving the ruling power no reason to prod into the cities' internal affairs. This would mean managing the public order, providing for the orderly payment of taxes and dues to the metropole, and building networks through which reciprocal aid might flow in times of necessity. The elites were rewarded for their hard work, often with conspicuous gifts from emperors, but just as often with Roman citizenship itself. The possibility of earning Roman citizenship also incentivized local elites to be favorably disposed to the imperial government. The provinces served as a recruiting ground for talent, and over the course of the second century a number of provincials came even to be adlected into

[15] I hope to return to the question of property confiscation in a future article. See, for now, Rivière 2016.

[16] Plut. *Praec. ger. Reip.* 813e–f, trans. Fowler, LCL.

the Roman equestrian order and senate. A number would make their careers at the bar, serving as *advocati fisci* (barristers specializing in imperial property); of these, some might eventually become jurists or serve in imperial bureaux. Of these, some, like Philo's nephew, Tiberius Julius Alexander, would rise to the highest of equestrian commands, such as the governorship of Egypt.[17] Others, like the Severus who tangled with Aelius Aristides (see further below), would serve not only as senators but also as consuls, and eventually as governors close to their ancestral homes. But they remained, as a group, mistrusted by the governors in charge of them.

Still, the Greek elites took pride in their role as leaders, conceiving of themselves as an aristocracy of virtue – the best citizens. This collective self-understanding was underwritten by the system of education in which they were socialized. In their schools they learned that they were an elite that *deserved* to rule on account of their excellence, gentility, grace, and learning – a package of attributes captured by the concept of *paideia*. Their wealth, combined with their training, ensured that they could provide the best services to their fellow citizens. And when they moved in elite circles at the provincial or regional level, they encountered other educated men, the best citizens of *their* cities. All alike both competed and collaborated with one another to negotiate the benefits and pitfalls of trying to craft for themselves a tolerable space in an empire.

***

The ideas of legality that emerged among this class took their origins from the system of education. Here, however, we ought to be alert to the dangers of anachronism. The elites of Greek cities were not *philosophes* joined to one another in some sort of republic of letters that linked them in a shared program of exercising and refining their rational capacities in the service of the broader improvement of knowledge. Though there certainly were technical branches of learning in this world (medicine, architecture, etc.), overzealous mastery of technical detail was considered ungentlemanly. The point of education was to train elite men to rule over others.[18] To do this, these men had to cultivate their bodies, their voices, their tastes, and their deportment.

[17] Halfmann 1979. [18] Lendon 2022.

To cultivate such citizens and instill in them the capacity to rule, education emphasized tradition. Students learned the ability to speak well – and extemporaneously – in public.[19] Speaking well was defined traditionally: an educated man would be expected to speak in a literary dialect of Greek, using a vocabulary derived from a relatively narrow canon of "classical" authors which remained largely stable over time. This meant that young elites in far-flung places would have emerged from their formative years knowing approximately the same things – or at the very least, the same texts.[20] The expected product of this miming and memorizing was moral development. As the rhetorician Aelius Aristides imagines the emperors Marcus and Lucius saying, it is "an attribute of the same man to be morally good and a good speaker" and "words follow character".[21]

An educated man, however, was not simply someone who spoke well and had memorized a certain number of classical texts but also someone who spoke with the right accent, who had good manners, who gestured in the right way, who trained his body in the gymnasium and who competed in athletic contests. It was training in both speech *and* body, and most of all in deportment.[22] The body was as important as the mind.[23] An elite young man thus would have been expected to serve as an ephebe, a mock recruit who underwent a period of militaristic training – a practice that originated in the days of citizen

[19] Much has been written about the content of the educational curriculum that prevailed in the eastern Roman world and on its socializing functions, and need not be reviewed in detail here. See, in general, Brown 1992; Schmitz 1997; Cribiore 2001, 2007; Borg 2004; Lendon 2022.

[20] Even in the distant Dakhla oasis in Egypt's western desert archaeologists have discovered a schoolhouse adorned with dipinti featuring bromides such as "[M]ay god grant my wishes that [you all] learn the Muses' honeyed works, with all the Graces and with Hermes son of Maia reaching the full summit of rhetorical knowledge. Be bold, my boys: the great god will grant you to have a beautiful crown of manifold virtue." Quotations from Homer and Euripides similarly adorned the walls. See the discussion in Cribiore 2015: 320, who also provides the translation.

[21] *Or.* 47.49. All translations of Aristides come from Behr 1981.

[22] Gleason 1995. See also Sidebottom 2009: 75–79.

[23] Note Peachin 2011a: 18 (citing a mass of further literature): "there existed for the Roman a copious and powerful semantic world that involved the body – its innate appearance, how it was clothed, how it was positioned and moved, and so forth. The point is that a Roman, by effecting a presence with (say) a particular hairstyle, outfit, stance, movements, or non-verbal exclamations, could establish many things about his or her relationship to those with whom he or she was interacting."

armies, but developed into a practice where young elite men cultivated their physical prowess at public expense in the city's gymnasium.[24] He would compete with others in horsemanship and other athletic pursuits, but also in demonstrating *euexia* ("bodily vigor"), *eutaxia* ("discipline"), and *philoponia* ("patience" or "diligence" – literally, "a love of work").[25] The body and the mind were thus expected to act in tandem: thus, the biographer Philostratus might compose biographies of great rhetoricians, but also a treatise on physical training, the *Gymnasticus*. Here he defended the proposition that athletic training, like rhetorical training, was a form of wisdom (*sophia*) that could be taught according to rational principles.[26]

But the links between body and mind went yet deeper. Proper intellectual training might inculcate ways not just of speaking, but of seeing and knowing. "With regard to perception," Lucian of Samosata wrote, in his essay *de Domo* ("On the House"), "the same law (*nomos*) does not hold for educated men (*pepaideumenois*) as for ordinary men (*idiōtais*)."[27] When confronted with something of beauty (that is, when making a judgment of taste), the ordinary man, on Lucian's telling, would only feel amazement (*thaumasas*), then slink silently away. An educated man, by contrast, would not only know that he was being presented with an image of beauty; he would rise to the occasion by using his linguistic abilities to praise it justly. Education, on this logic, served as both a means of knowing what to say, but also a mode of training that habituated educated viewers in a system of aesthetic values. Aesthetic knowledge could be powerful. Just as he could know to praise a thing of beauty, so too could an educated man be able to "read" the bodies of the men with whom he interacted, using their physical attributes as data to understand the contents of their souls – sorting noble from base, innocent from criminal.[28]

[24] On athletics, see in general van Nijf 2004; on the *ephebeia*, Kennell 2009, and on the example of Sparta, Kennell 1995. On the manifestation of these ideals in visual culture (with a focus especially on sarcophagi), see Ewald 2004: esp. 244: "To show oneself in well-trained nudity thus also signified belonging to a certain social class ... The male bodies we see are social constructs: they are the perfect results of Greek *paideia*, including rigid training in the gymnasium under qualified instructors, as well as bathing and diet."

[25] Hin 2007: 161–62. [26] On Philostratus' *Gymnasticus* see König 2005: esp. 333.

[27] Luc. *Dom*. 2. See the important discussion of Goldhill 2001b.

[28] See further Bryen 2014b.

The net result was the production of a relatively homogeneous class of "cultured" men who shared a common body of knowledge, manners, and mannerisms, much like a contemporary diplomatic corps. Not by accident did this elite similarly include the children of Italian elites as well. As far as the Greeks went, they developed into a group that, despite its formally subordinated position in the empire, nonetheless took exceptional pride in its manners, grace, and civilized discourse – and also in its close relationships with the ruling classes of Italy.[29] Collective pride in gentility and discernment did not, of course, mean that in practice this class abstained from immoderate drinking or loutishness. Certainly the generalized praise of their collective excellence belied more complicated realities, and we may assume that any given group of aristocrats will produce a fair harvest of brutish offspring incapable of internalizing, much less rising to, such standards of decorum. But the ideology of education and culture (*paideia*) is important nonetheless for understanding the legal ideology of the elites of the cities of the empire. For this system produced not only men of culture, but also a hagiography of learning and gentility – a tradition of biography and comment on learned life that is revealing of expectations about legal institutions. It stands in marked contrast to the stories of courts and litigants produced by the relatively more subaltern classes that featured prominently in earlier chapters.

Finally, and this cannot be overemphasized, in a world where even the leaders of cities were subjects, *paideia* was intimately connected to the physical body. It protected the body: the bodies of elite males became increasingly immune from certain degrading physical penalties, like condemnation to the mines, being forced to fight with beasts in the arena, or being burned alive.[30] Bodies also provided models of conduct: images of elite and excellent bodies – of politicians, leaders, and athletes alike – lined the cityscape, providing a reminder – indeed, a whole visual language – of aesthetically coded excellence. As Onno van Nijf has explained, there was, in the cities of the high Roman empire,

[29] Evidence of funerary commemoration from Schmitz 1997. On the politics and poetics of subordination, see Swain 1996; Goldhill 2001a; Whitmarsh 2001.

[30] See the remarkable framing of Gleason 2020: 160–61. Congdon 2021 argues for the idea that the moral status of the person is constantly performed and aesthetically perceived – as he puts it, "on normative display". Congdon focuses on those at the low end of the social spectrum, but such moral or institutional claiming can exist at the high end, too.

"a strong tendency to merge athletic and political representations."[31] Put differently, political status and physical presentation were tightly linked; these links had ramifications for how legal systems ought to recognize and process – or avoid – the targets of their regulatory ambitions.

***

How, then, did it work? That is, how did this system of education allow learned men to transcend the law, and what connects this transcendence to the training of bodies? Briefly put, rhetoric. This will seem puzzling at first. As a general term, all stories about legality – those of both subalterns and elites – might fall within the category of rhetoric. But the rhetoric in question is more than just speech, or even persuasive speech anchored in reason (*logos*). It is, rather, that subset of persuasive speech that can only be spoken by educated elites. These men can speak in that genre because they mastered a set of intellectual and physical skills that enable them to bewitch or amaze their audiences. The key term here is *thauma* – "amazement" – but a number of other words were used as well to convey the ways that language might operate to induce wonder or ecstasy.

Like the subalterns, Greek elites called this sort of speaking *logos*, but their use of the term operated within a divergent network of values. If the "subaltern" theory of law was that legality was constituted in acts of dialogue between ruler and ruled that were based on mutually accessible reason, the elite theory of law emerged in opposition to it. For elites, true legality was monologic; it was based not in reason but in affect; and it was knowable on the basis of physical clues. Its opposite was administration and litigation. Administration and litigation operated on the plane of the quotidian, in the here-and-now of paper pushing, at the level of grubby fact. Rhetoric, by contrast, could bring men into a different mode of being – a space of amazement, where reason might be suspended or transcended in favor of the contemplation of sublimity produced through language. Though produced in a world of particular institutions (empire, city, courtroom) and accepting of the reality, if not also the desirability of those institutions, Greek elites nonetheless offered a theory of legality that claimed to operate on a plane above.

31 van Nijf 2012: 54.

Perhaps the sharpest vision of the nexus between rhetoric, the body, and transcendence comes from a satire, Lucian's *Professor of Rhetoric*. Though not concerned explicitly with legality, it might serve as a model for understanding what assumptions the Greek elites attached to their idea of "rhetoric." The text is framed as advice to a young student: Do you want, the speaker asks, to be a rhetorician? Do you want people to be enthralled by you (*thaumazesthai*), and to have them fix their gazes upon you? Do you wish them to think you well-born, rich, and famous because of the way you speak (*apo tōn logōn*)? This is possible, promises the professor.[32] The professor then outlines for his student two paths forward. The first path is rocky and difficult. At the start of the path the student will be met by "a vigorous man with hard muscles and a manly (*andrōdēs*) walk, who shows a heavy tan on his body, with a manly countenance (*arrhēnopos*), and totally alert."[33] This parody of a manly man, the professor explains, is in charge of – literally the governor (*hegemōn*) of – the difficult path. But, the professor warns, the student wastes his energy on this path, for the manly man will tell the aspiring student to study hard, spend time on the classics, and abstain from pleasures. He is to be avoided at all costs.

The student should instead take the easy road, where he will meet a very different sort of bodily instantiation of his craft. "You will find many others along that other road, but among them will be a wholly clever (*pansophon*) and wholly pretty (*pagkalon*) man, one who walks daintily, with a thin neck, an effeminate (*gunaikeion*) glance, a honeyed voice, smelling of perfume, scratching his head with one finger, and carefully dressing his hair – what little he has now – which is curly and jet black."[34] If the student follows this man's advice, he will immediately become not just a rhetorician but an admired one – indeed, a king of speaking (*basileus en tois logois*).

As all good parody does, Lucian works from the same deep assumptions as the practice he satirizes. Rhetoric is indeed something vested in the body, although the two rhetorical bodies are coded as opposites. One can have manly rhetoric, which takes a long time, much learning, and many sleepless nights; or effeminate rhetoric, which works mostly

[32] *Rh. Pr.* 1–2. [33] *Rh. Pr.* 9. Translations adapted from Harmon, LCL.
[34] *Rh. Pr.* 11.

by bamboozling its audience. The former may be useful, but the latter will cause a man to be beheld by the masses with total astonishment (*hyperekpeplēgmemōn*); the same people will sing his praises but will also be dumbstruck (*tethēpotōn*) by him; they will cringe in his presence and hold him to be a sort of transcendent (*daimonios*) fellow.[35] The young man should accordingly follow the advice of the effeminate. First, he should begin his rhetorical training by forgetting everything he knows about morality. From there, he can work on his voice and his walk. Then finally he should dress himself up: fine clothes, a well-arranged cloak, and fancy shoes. The formally "rhetorical" part of the training is easy enough: just use odd Attic words like "sundry" (*atta*) and prattle on at great length, no matter what the context, "so that they may marvel" (*thaumazōsin*) at the performance.[36]

If one was shameless enough, it might just work. Thus, in his satirical treatment of the pseudo-philosopher Peregrinus Proteus, Lucian recounts that Peregrinus weaseled his way out of an accusation of parricide in his hometown by appearing in the assembly (not the courtroom) and offering to give away his property. The local people were not terribly clever, it seems, and they were slackjawed (*kekhēnotes*) by the offer. They accordingly acclaimed Peregrinus "the one and only philosopher." His enemies were dumbfounded and could find no one willing to hear their charges of parricide. It was a bravura performance. Alas, poor Peregrinus eventually ran out of material. Plumbing new depths to find a way to astonish (*ekplēxei*) and surprise (*thaumazein*), he devised a new spectacle (*thaumatopoiei*), and a distinctly corporeal one: he set himself on fire at the Olympic games.[37]

Lucian's satire might serve as a convenient model of the sort of rhetoric that was prized by elite men in the Greek cities. Short on content and long on performance, rhetoric works by inducing a state of astonishment. It is, moreover, not the property of all men; it is the property of an elite who can, in Lucian's telling, afford the leisure to learn the secrets of persuasive astonishment in the first place. What is more, as Lucian explains, the "secret" comes not primarily from study, but from a particular crafting of one's voice, stance, and body. From there, all one has to do is spout content-free platitudes and pleasurable nonsense – the ancient equivalent of the TED Talk.

[35] *Rh. Pr.* 13. [36] *Rh. Pr.* 17. [37] Luc. *Per.* 15, 20–21.

Logos, in this context, is far from "reason" or "reasoned argument" – that is, how the subaltern populations of the empire might have defined it. It is not a property vested in the minds of all men that enables communication, but the property of a learned few who craft their performances in particular ways. In this sense, it comes close to the definition of rhetoric advanced many centuries earlier by rhetoric's first teacher, Gorgias of Leontini: rhetoric is a drug that operates by colonizing the minds of others. Gorgias proposed his definition in a fragmented world composed of small, independent city-states struggling to maintain their autonomy. For Gorgias, rhetoric was a tool that enabled noble men to lead assemblies and to defend themselves in court within small, independent, ethnically homogeneous communities. The Greek elites of the Roman period resuscitated this idea of rhetoric within a wholly new imperial context: *their* rhetoric, and *their* performances, were to help them achieve autonomy in a complex, multi-ethnic empire – not by speaking in the courtroom, but by evading it and its forms of accountability.

***

We may take as an example the case of Aelius Aristides. An elite rhetorician and citizen of Smyrna, Aristides composed (in addition to a large number of preserved speeches) a lengthy text called the *Hieroi Logoi*, conventionally rendered as "Sacred Tales." The *Logoi* are most unusual: a diary-like narrative of Aristides' health and of his rhetorical career, they oscillate violently between the fleshy and the divine, between Aristides' sick body and his profoundly personal relationship to the god Asclepius, who appears to him in dreams. They interweave dreams and reality, rhetoric and travel, sickness and divinity in ways that are frequently baffling if not disgusting to modern readers – a seeming litany in which practices of healing (bathing, vomiting, enemas, fasting) are juxtaposed with religious devotion and rhetorical performance. We might think of the *Logoi* as a sort of auto-hagiography: a paean to the god Asclepius, and a self-congratulatory account of his most famous patient and the best rhetorician of his age.[38]

[38] Recent work has done much to explain this work in its proper context: Harris and Holmes 2008; Petsalis-Diomidis 2010; Downie 2013. Translations of Aristides come from Behr 1981.

The title itself, surely no accident, might serve as a pointed rejection of other, competing forms of *logos* in the world Aristides inhabited.

Yet while most of the *Logoi* recount Aristides' relationship to his body, an odd interlude intrudes at the end of the fourth *Logos*: an extensive narrative of Aristides' attempts to prevail over his enemies in court. This narrative about his battles over his property and his exemption from public services was in his mind a unit: something not to be dispersed throughout the chronological sections of the text, but rather hived off and made to serve as the culmination of the fourth *Logos* – a set of stories that demonstrated the power of Asclepius in supporting Aristides and his career. At the core of this narrative about litigation sits an important case study in the transformative power of elite male affect, on the one hand, and the transcendent amazement (*thauma*) or astonishment (*ekplēxis*) produced by learned rhetoric, on the other.

Aristides tells us about four distinct lawsuits.[39] Aristides' first time in court (or at least, the first time about which he informs us) began with a property dispute. He had purchased an estate called Laneion in rural Mysia. The terms of its acquisition were, it seems, dubious, and his neighbors contested his ownership. Aristides gives little credence to their arguments; he will not, he insists, deign to repeat their "slander." We should not be surprised to hear that Aristides' neighbors resented the intrusion of a new estate owner into their midst, nor should we doubt that powerful men might often acquire choice properties under dubious color: such appears to have been happening in the nearby city of Ephesus, for instance.[40] That Aristides refers to his neighbors only as "certain Mysians" also hints that they were an epichoric population without citizenship in a particular polity – and hence they had no city to protect them, or even to sue him in.[41] So while they initially tried to reason with him, they soon gave up and made their property claim using the oldest and most venerable

[39] On the "immunities narrative," see Bowersock 1969: 36–40; Swain 1996: 266–74; Lendon 1997: 201–14; Pernot 2008: 182–84; and especially Downie 2013: 155–82 (from whose work I adopt the term).

[40] *MARE* 78 = Oliver 1989: no. 71. Cf. Apul. *Met.* 9.35. A similar case of powerful men acquiring estates in the countryside might be found in *SEG* XXX 568, with Bryen 2021a.

[41] In general, Rizakis 1998.

method around. They gathered together a group of "slaves and hired men," approached his estate, pelted his staff with stones and clods of dirt, beat them thoroughly, and took over the house.[42]

Aristides panicked. Or at least he claims to have panicked. The remainder of the narrative is filled with implausibilities, and we may be certain that it fails to give an accurate portrayal of what happened next. Still, his *Tendenz* is informative. Aristides knew that the governor was in nearby Pergamum holding his annual assizes, but he did not know how precisely to gain access to him. A dream finally intervened: "And the last of my dreams was the Emperor Hadrian in the court of the Temple, honoring me, who had just now become acquainted with him, and offering me great hopes."[43] His communion with the divine guided the affairs that followed: it so happened that at the assizes the governor was seen chatting with the rhetorician Claudius Rufinus, an old friend, so Aristides went and told his troubles to Rufinus. Rufinus, in turn, brought Aristides into the presence of the governor, Julianus. It so happened that Aristides' dream was prescient, as the place he met Julianus was precisely the place in which Hadrian had appeared to him:[44]

> But the governor became so possessed by the god (*entheos*) that he immediately embraced me, as if he were an old, close friend. And taking me by the hand, he told me to have courage and attend to the god, but that these things would be his concern. And finally, he declared, "They will not scorn us (*ou mēn hēmōn kataphronēsōsi*)!" He arrived at court, and when he had called the suit and not many words had been spoken, he grew angry at what had happened and even threw into jail one of those who had participated in the attack. And he adjudged the estate to us, and we entered it under court order. Armed men, slingers, all those things yielded to the god.

The story is wildly implausible: something clearly happened to get Aristides' case on the docket in the first place and to bring his opponents to court at just the right time. Since they were in possession of the land – essentially daring Aristides to sue them – surely they did not initiate the lawsuit. If they didn't, Aristides did. Aristides minimizes this legal wrangling, emphasizing instead that the governor was "inspired by the god," with the result that he embraced Aristides as a friend. As two elite men, they used the power of affect to simply

[42] *Or.* 50.105. [43] *Or.* 50.106. [44] *Or.* 50.107–8.

come to a conclusion about the case itself. But the governor's love for Aristides was coupled with his righteous anger: the Mysians, he insisted, wouldn't be permitted to disrespect two venerable men (note that, in such a formulation, the governor and Aristides are construed as being equals). Accordingly, the governor unleashed his rage upon the social inferiors who dared to clog his docket and irritate his peers. Aristides got not only official sanction to hold on to his estate (something that would forestall any future litigation on the matter), but also the joy of watching his opponents suffer official violence.

The story Aristides tells about his Mysian estate recasts a story of litigation (and corruption!) as a story about the affective relationship between elite men (Aristides, Rufinus, and Julianus), on the one hand, and about the punishment of unnamed, low caste villagers, on the other. The system is two-tiered: because he is a friend, Aristides does not have to appear in court himself. It is sufficient that the relevant people are angry on his behalf. It is the job of such people to operate the wheels of justice, the quotidian system of legality – a system with which a man Aristides need not sully himself. He instead is free to devote himself to the work of transcendence, addressing himself to the worship of Asclepius, to his rhetorical career, and to the treatment of his body.

The battle over his estate, however, was easy compared to the protracted fight that Aristides soon engaged in with his fellow citizens. Just a year later, Aristides was engaged in a sort of fight that is well documented in papyri and juristic sources: an argument over his liability to perform compulsory services for his home city. This system of mandatory "gifts" from the wealthy to their hometowns backstopped local economies and substituted, in many respects, for public bureaucracies. Simultaneously a source of great pride (for to be asked to give meant that one was agreed to be wealthy and respectable) and a source of great cost and irritation, litigation over these services must have consumed a great deal of any given governor's docket. We shall see further examples when we turn, in the chapters that follow, to the Roman jurists (Chapters 8 and 9). In this case, Aristides' account allows us to see to what degree men of his class were willing to engage in complex procedural wrangling, even while denying that they were engaged in typical legal behavior.

Aristides was chosen by Smyrna to serve as the high priest of the provincial assembly of Asia – an expensive and burdensome public obligation. They summoned him to an assembly on a pretext and invited him, in the midst of great cheering, to accept the burden. He demurred, and they substituted their demand: that instead of the high priesthood, Aristides should take on the priesthood of his patron deity, Asclepius. (Asclepius' temple in Smyrna, it seems, was in the midst of construction, and the people needed someone to see it through – that is, to finance it.) Aristides' reply to their new request was a breathtaking act of chutzpah: "I said it was impossible for me to do anything, either important or trifling, without the god, and therefore it was not even possible to think of serving as a priest, until I had inquired about this from the god himself."[45]

Such a refusal to contribute was deeply un-civic behavior, and the Smyrnaeans were not impressed by his conspicuous claim of religiosity.[46] They ceased to "honor" Aristides with requests and instead simply appointed him to the priesthood. He managed to broker a delay, while also appealing to the governor for an exemption, which he finally won. This only served to infuriate the Smyrnaeans. As revenge, the Council, rather than the people, nominated Aristides to serve as tax collector – an unenviable position. Not only would he be liable for any shortfall in the expected revenues, he would have to figure out how to squeeze whatever revenues he could collect out of groups of hostile and mendacious peasants.[47] It was grueling work to determine who owed what, where they were, and whether they were entitled to a bewildering variety of exceptions. In many cases he would have to beat the money out of the peasants and then deal with whichever local bigwig was protecting them. It was dirty work, and certainly less glamorous than serving as a high priest.

Aristides again protested his appointment. This time, though, the governor's legate, a subordinate officer, handled the claim. The legate, unimpressed by his protests, merely confirmed the decision of the Council. The only hope was to appeal both to Rome and to the

[45] *Or.* 50.102.

[46] For a good summary of the ideology of benefaction, see Zuiderhoek 2009.

[47] The challenge of wringing goods from villagers is amply documented in papyri. Note, e.g., the challenges that faced Flavius Abinnaeus: *P.Abinn.* 5, 15, 18 (AD IV). The processes described by Libanius (*Or.* 47) must have only been different in degree, rather than in kind, from those that came to be in the second and third centuries.

governor – which Aristides did – and hope for a clear statement of exemption. Luckily, the god again intervened: Aristides had a dream in which he foresaw the intervention of his friends, as well as oracles predicting that the matter would come to an end and "you will make friends with your enemies." The god was indeed propitious: before the case itself was heard, the governor, "recognizing the simplicity (*apheleian*) of the legate, ordered him to come immediately, hold court, and correct his judgment." In other words, the result of the protest was to have the governor force his subordinate to conduct a *de novo* hearing, the conclusion to which was foreordained. Once the anticipated decision was reached, the ruling was forwarded to the (surely now disappointed) President of the Smyrnaean Council:[48]

> When this was dispatched, the President, who had opposed me with the utmost vigor ... becoming disturbed (*thoryboumenos*) and frightened sent to the governor's staff to inquire about the letter. But they gave no answer. He came to me and begged my pardon (*syggnōmēn*). And I went to the Council, was exempted from the service, and obtained immunity. First then, and afterwards, the President became a very dear friend, and the legate himself a very dear friend.

Such a reversal of fortune must have left a bitter taste in the mouths of the Councilors: they moved from exercising their autonomy and nominating, for the public good, a wealthy man who surely owed them, to having their prerogatives restricted, their favorable verdicts reversed, and their protests ignored. They were left having to beg a degrading pardon from a wealthy citizen who contributed nothing to the common good. For Aristides, however, the governor had simply righted a wrong. Without the need for a real hearing (the miming of a hearing would do), the god, through his agent, the governor, turned a legal battle into a relationship of friendship – and, one presumes, of deference.

Aristides could evade accountability for only so long. Eventually a new governor of Asia was appointed, a certain Severus, who was "proud in his ways" and loath to ever change his decisions.[49] Rumors of Aristides' attempts to weasel out of his obligations at Smyrna must have circulated widely, and Severus wanted to make an example of him.

[48] *Or.* 50.99. [49] *Or.* 50.71.

He found an opportunity when the city of Hadriani submitted a list of candidates for the position of eirenarch, a high official in charge of public security – a position that included dangerous tasks like hunting down groups of violent bandits. Aristides had a complicated relationship to Hadriani: he had been born in the territory that eventually became part of the city, but before it had been granted city status – and thus before it took a census of its new citizens to determine which among them would be liable for public services. For official purposes, Aristides considered himself a citizen of Smyrna, and liable only to the Smyrnaeans. Nonetheless, when the list of proposed candidates for eirenarch reached Severus, he ignored it and appointed Aristides instead, informing the citizens of Hadriani in a letter that he had chosen their new eirenarch.[50] It was hardly the sort of task at which a sickly man would excel, and one must give Severus some credit for having a dark sense of humor. The citizens of Hadriani, in turn, were surely less than pleased that a man like Aristides was to be in charge of their public safety.[51]

Severus' move was cunning. Since he had appointed Aristides, and since his decisions in such matters could not be appealed, it was unclear how Aristides might go about protesting his appointment. He certainly could not sue Severus. Aristides resorted to a dodge: he sued the officials of Hadriani who had brought him Severus' letter informing him of his appointment. This was at best a weak legal strategy. Again, however, an oracle intervened: the gods recalled an earlier oracle from Delphi, that Aristides would be helped by "white maidens." The "white maidens," it seems, were letters from the emperor's court – the very letters he had earlier requested when protesting his appointment as tax collector.[52] The letters conferred immunity upon him permanently, if it was the case that he was a rhetorician in the city of Smyrna. (Cities were allowed to appoint a fixed number of rhetoricians to public chairs, which conferred immunity from public services upon those who held them.) Once again the gods had smiled on him. He quickly wrote to Severus, informing him of his new(ly reconfirmed) status.

Severus was not one to be intimidated by letters conferring immunity. He commanded Aristides to show up at the upcoming assizes and explain himself. Aristides balked. This sort of courtroom wrangling was

[50] On the procedure, see Brélaz 2011. [51] As shrewdly noted by Behr 1968: 82.
[52] See Swain 1996: 271, on the learned reference that Aristides is here making.

not for him. He sent representatives instead, which only managed to irritate the governor. But the governor was not out of tricks. He could not very well ignore the exemptions given to Aristides by emperors. But he could give Aristides a taste of his own medicine. Before Aristides' representatives even had a chance to speak, Severus proclaimed:[53]

> "I have long known of Aristides, and I *marvel* at his reputation (*tēs doxēs agamai*) and I agree that he holds the first place in oratory, and these things have also been written to me by my friends in Rome. I *ask* him," he said, "to *share* in my administration (*synarxai moi*). But I also confirm to him the rights of immunity, and they remain in force." He said these things publicly. He inscribed them in the minutes.

This was a clever trick. The governor could smirk sarcastically that he was, indeed, amazed by Aristides. Still, he made a request, not a command. Aristides' immunity was confirmed and made part of the official record. He could, in the future, use the governor's confirmation to avoid future services. It was in that sense a triumph. But the result was nonetheless the same: he would have to serve as eirenarch, but on the grounds that he was doing the governor a favor, rather than because he was required to. Missing the irony, Aristides lamented that it was as if the governor was trying to start a friendship with him, rather than giving an order.[54] An order could at least be appealed. To reject the friendship of such a powerful man would have been both foolish and unspeakably rude.[55] He had not expected this outcome.

Predictably, the god intervened again. This time the divinity counseled mere bribery: five hundred drachmas.[56] Even Aristides knew that this was a bad strategy, and that there was no chance of buying off the decision of such a powerful man for so little. He wisely chose to avoid what seemed to be the god's advice. Instead, he rallied his friends and had them accompany him to the governor's assizes. Aristides and Severus would finally meet face-to-face, in the courtroom.

Severus was not out of tricks. Perhaps the emperors had given him immunity on the grounds that he was a rhetorician in the city of Smyrna,

[53] *Or.* 50.78.

[54] *Or.* 50.79: μὴ κρίσεως νόμῳ…ἀλλ' ὡσπερεὶ χάριν αἰτοῦντος καὶ φιλίας ἀρχήν τινα ταύτην ἀνατιθέντος.

[55] See esp. Lendon 1997. Cf. *I.Aph.2007* 8.103 (letter of Gordian III to Aphrodisias).

[56] *Or.* 50.81.

Severus conceded. But the Smyrnaeans had not appointed him to this position. "So go to the council then," Severus said, "and persuade your fellow citizens" – persuade them, that is, to appoint Aristides as a professor of rhetoric, so that he could enjoy his immunity.[57] Severus knew that Aristides had previously offended the Smyrnaeans; now he was to beg them for a professorship. It was essentially the same trick that another governor had used on Polycarp, asking him to beg a group of angry (Smyrnaean) citizens for his rights.[58] And the result was similar: the Smyrnaeans would do no such thing. They took Severus' hint and added insult to injury by appointing Aristides to a further office, that of *prytanis*. The stakes were now higher: Aristides had to wriggle out of two appointments, rather than one. And he would have to go to court and argue his case to do so.

Finally, he appeared in court, with the hopes of saving himself. But a divine force intervened. He arrived in court, though late because of his poor physical condition. It did not matter; the governor was not upset. As Aristides came into view, Severus sent his lictors but not to use violence against him – to help him along the path, so that his journey to court would be easy. The interaction that followed "took the form of a rhetorical display (*epideixeōs*) rather than a trial (*dikēs*)."[59] Aristides spoke freely (*parrhēsiai*) and at great length, using five full measures of the water clock. The audience was enraptured and listened with "astonishing goodwill" (*eunoia thaumastē*) like students at a lecture. The opposing counsel for the city of Smyrna made only a pro forma attempt to press his case. The result was finally good: Severus agreed to write to the Smyrnaean council, urging them to confirm his immunity. As for the task of serving as eirenarch for Hadriani, Severus conveniently forgot about it. Aristides could breathe a sigh of relief. It was only at this point that he came to understand the god's prophecy: for all of the travel he had done back and forth to courts and councils, the total cost came to five hundred drachmas.

For Aristides, legal problems – be they the possession of land or the obligation to serve one's home community – are routinely reframed as affective problems, that is, problems of the relations of mutual feeling

[57] *Or.* 50.87: πορεύθητι, ἔφη, πρὸς τὴν βουλήν, πεῖσον τοὺς πολίτας. On immunities for rhetoricians, see *Dig.* 27.1.6.1–12.

[58] Above, Chapter 4. [59] *Or.* 50.91.

and goodwill between men of rank and discernment. The courtroom is to be avoided. When at long last it can no longer be avoided, it must even then be treated not as a venue for dispute processing through making compelling legal arguments based in a mutually accessible *logos*. Rather, it should be turned into a venue for a different sort of *logos*, the aesthetically pleasing *logos* of the rhetorical school – a sort of *logos* that works not by *convincing* one's audience of the righteousness of one's position, but rather by *bewitching* them with the linguistic fireworks that one can display.[60] It is no accident, then, that Aristides emphasizes the degree to which language can operate to place an audience into a state of wonder – of *thauma*. For Aristides, this could only be achieved by rhetoric – which took the form of attending first to the transcendent power of the god, Asclepius, and secondly to his body.

***

Though unusual, Aristides was not exceptional. We might consider alongside his narrative a series of cases described by Philostratus, an early third-century hagiographer of learning and the sort of thinker who had to struggle to explain the politics of rhetoric, affect, and astonishment. We might begin with a story that he tells of another Smyrnaean rhetor, Niketes. Though excellent at both sophistic oratory and pleading cases, Niketes managed to offend the *corrector* Rufinus, a man of consular rank. Rufinus sat on his anger, but when Rufinus received from the emperor a further high-ranking command, he decided to prosecute Niketes for the insult he received. Accordingly, he wrote to the emperor Nerva, who, shockingly, allowed Rufinus to sit as both judge and accuser. Philostratus takes great pains to explain away this irregularity – how, Philostratus asks, could Rufinus learn to forgive him, if he was not in a position to hear him out? – but it is clear that, if the story is accurate, Rufinus had prepared a trap for Niketes. Niketes was accordingly summoned to Rufinus' court in Gaul. But rather than be presented with his guilt (and punishment) as a fait accompli, he nonetheless managed to defend himself effectively.

60 Goldhill 2007: esp. 6. For another example, cf. Jos. *Ant.* 14.171, on Herod's appearance before the synedrion, where he "astonishes" (*kateplēxen*) the court to the extent that they refuse to judge him.

He did so not by mustering legal arguments, but by so "astonishing" (*kateplēxe*) Rufinus with his defense speech that the governor himself began to cry – buckets of tears, at that, "more than the water in the water-clock." The two made up, and Rufinus sent Niketes back to Smyrna with honors.[61]

When read alongside the wranglings of Aristides, the story of Niketes reveals what will prove to be a pattern. The everyday world of governance and administration causes tensions and frictions, the sorts of problems that eventually lead to litigation. But in each case, litigation – and verdicts in particular – are avoided because of rhetorical skills. Rhetoric does not help one *succeed* in court, but to *avoid* having to partake in processes of legal accountability. It does this by altering the affective state of another elite man: by producing astonishment, transcendence, and ecstasy.

These stories similarly work to reinforce the roles of certain high-ranking imperial power brokers like emperors and governors: like rhetoricians, they are also the kinds of men who, because of *their own* learning and cultivation, are capable of suasion by such performances. That is, these are not stories about resistance to empire by Greek elites. They are, instead, stories about political order. They emphasize that the proper channels through which power flows are those of affect and amazement, not those of administration and rule-following. Like the competing stories told by subalterns, these dramas of learning, rhetoric, and *thauma* are the building blocks of political theory.

Still, rhetoric could not always achieve the ends to which it aspired. Plenty of men of learning and grace were dragged before governors and emperors. They tried their best to evade obligations or even criminal sanction, and they failed miserably.[62] So what determined success? And how ought one to diagnose the causes of failure? This was an urgent problem in the world of the Greek elites. Philostratus theorized this problem through concrete examples, rather than by recourse to analytical abstractions.

[61] *VS* 512.

[62] Indeed, Philostratus' star protagonists are uniquely bad at dealing with normal court cases: cf. *VS* 517–18 (Scopelianus loses a will contest – and all his property – with his dead father's slave), 525 (Polemo defends a man from Lydia at the governor's court; the sophist in the audience admits that he has talent, but not for litigation); 614 (Heracleides has his property confiscated).

We might take the case of Favorinus of Arles. Philostratus begins his brief narrative of Favorinus by focusing on his physical appearance, which was unusual: "He was born double-sexed, a hermaphrodite, and this was plainly shown in his appearance; for even when he grew old he had no beard; it was evident too from his voice which sounded thin, shrill, and high-pitched, with the modulations that nature bestows on eunuchs also."[63] None of these things kept Favorinus from the highest echelons of power, or from popularity. He was a favorite of the Ephesians, though he too had a complex relationship with the communities in which he lived. The Corinthians voted him a statue, but they eventually became angry with him and took it down.[64] He was accused of adultery in Rome, but somehow managed to avoid conviction. He was, at the least, an evasive fellow.

As with Aristides, Favorinus' birthplace tried to capture some of his wealth, and so nominated him for a compulsory public service. Like Aristides, Favorinus attempted to get out of it by making an appeal to the emperor Hadrian on the grounds that he was a philosopher (and hence should receive immunity from burdensome public services). However, his case did not go as well:[65]

> But when he saw that the emperor intended to vote against him on the ground that he was not a philosopher, he forestalled him in the following way. "O Emperor," he cried, "I have had a dream of which you ought to be informed. My teacher Dio appeared to me, and with respect to this suit admonished and reminded me that we come into the world not for ourselves alone, but also for the country of our birth. Therefore, O Emperor, I obey my teacher, and I undertake this public service."

Hadrian and Favorinus had quarreled in the past, and surely this weighed heavily on the emperor, who took pleasure in watching Favorinus squirm before his court. Doing so was an enjoyable diversion from the requirements of governance. So if he was robbed of the opportunity to deny Favorinus a favorable verdict, this was a

[63] *VS* 489. On Favorinus and his body more generally, Gleason 1995. Physical descriptions that begin accounts of sophists in the *VS*: 512–13 (Isaeus, who then gave up his poor behavior to become a worthwhile orator); 565 (Aristocles dresses squalidly as a philosopher before he cleans up to become a sophist); 570–71 (the beauty of Alexander, which gets him in trouble with the emperor). Note also *VS* 528–29 (a description of the countenance of Marcus of Byzantium).

[64] [Dio] *Or.* 37. [65] *VS* 490.

small enough loss. The communities in which Favorinus lived, however, were highly distressed: upon hearing that Favorinus did not lose his appeal but rather volunteered to do the service, a group of powerful Athenians gathered together and smashed a bronze statue of Favorinus. According to Philostratus, the Athenians did this on the grounds that Favorinus "was most hostile to the emperor."[66] We might also propose a different explanation: like Polemo in Smyrna, the Athenians were deprived of the opportunity to see Hadrian rule against Favorinus – that is, they objected to men of rank colluding to avoid being held accountable within the same institutions – courts – to which they themselves were subject.

So why did Favorinus fail? The key was deportment, long training that instilled in the body, the appearance, and the voice and diction the *habitus* of the right sort of man. Some men had it, others did not.[67] Thus the emperor Caracalla, Philostratus reports, withdrew the immunities from public services from the rhetorician Philiscus because, when Philiscus appeared in court, "he gave offense by his gait, he gave offense by the way he stood, his attire seemed far from suitable to the occasion, his voice effeminate, his voice tedious and directed to any subject rather than to the matter at hand." The emperor found such a spectacle so distasteful that he began to cut Philiscus off (*epestomizen*), exclaiming that "his hair shows what sort of man he is! his voice what sort of orator!" Stunned that the emperor would fail to understand the nature of the performance, Philiscus made a last-ditch attempt to argue legalistically: "But you granted me immunity from public services by giving me the chair of rhetoric at Athens!" Not one to be one-upped by a last-ditch attempt at legalism, Caracalla proclaimed the end of *all* immunities for teachers of rhetoric.[68]

The story of Philiscus does more than just show the effects of a performance that failed. It reminds the audience of the dangers of the courtroom: not all emperors were agreeably disposed towards bravura rhetorical performance, and this was a standing threat. Some, like Caracalla, might be brutish, more interested in foolish consistency than in producing the "right" answer to the question

[66] On Hadrian and Favorinus, see Swain 1989. [67] Gleason 1995.
[68] *VS* 622–23. Cf. *VS* 572–73 (Alexander before Antoninus Pius in Rome).

of how to handle learned subjects. More importantly, through this story Philostratus reminds his audience that the performance of the words is as important as their composition: Philiscus, he is at pains to emphasize, composed well enough; what he could not do was to align his body to his words. The result was first dissonance, then disgust: categories of primarily aesthetic perception and evaluation.

Logos, on this account, is not an inherent property of the propositional content of the things spoken; rather, the force of speech is contingent upon external factors such as deportment, which are in turn proxies for social rank. Who speaks, and how he speaks, are just as important as what is said – or even more, for what is said might only be worth hearing when delivered in the proper manner, by the right kind of person. We might consider, in this context, a story told by Aulus Gellius about a conversation he had with the philosopher Lucius Calvenus Taurus. Asked whether a wise man should get angry, Taurus replied by telling a story about Plutarch, the intellectual godfather of Greek men of high learning:[69]

Plutarch once gave orders that one of his slaves, a worthless and insolent fellow (*nequam homini et contumaci*), but one whose ears had been filled with the teachings and arguments of philosophy, should be stripped of his tunic for some offence or other and flogged. They had begun to beat him, and the slave kept protesting that he did not deserve the flogging: that he was guilty of no wrong, no crime. Finally, while the lashing still went on, he began to shout, no longer uttering complaints or shrieks and groans but serious reproaches (*verba seria et obiurgatoria*). Plutarch's conduct, he said, was unworthy of a philosopher; to be angry was shameful: he (Plutarch) had often discussed the evil of anger and had even written an excellent treatise *On Avoiding Anger*; it was in no way consistent with all that was written in that book that its author should fall into a fit of violent rage and punish his slave with many stripes. Then Plutarch calmly and mildly made answer: "What makes you think, scoundrel, that I am now angry with you? Is it from my expression, my voice, my color, or even my words (*ex vultune meo an ex voce an ex colore an etiam ex verbis*), that you believe me to be in the grasp of anger? In my opinion my eyes are not fierce, my expression is not disturbed, I am neither shouting madly nor foaming at the mouth nor getting red in the face; I am saying nothing to cause me shame or regret; I am not trembling at all from anger or making violent gestures. For all these actions, if you did but know it,

[69] *NA* 1.26.4–9, trans. Rolfe, LCL.

are the usual signs of angry passions." And with these words, turning to the man who was plying the lash, he said: "In the meantime, while this fellow and I are arguing (*dum … disputamus*), keep at it."

The anecdote is remarkable as a meditation on the relationship between language, deportment, and violence. The poor slave, denigrated as a man of no account, is faced with a philosopher like Plutarch; but the slave has had – or thinks he has had – an education in philosophy. Accordingly, he tries multiple registers of argument: first, he makes a legal argument: he is innocent and does not deserve to be beaten. To no avail: Gellius dismisses this as mere noise; well-founded complaints, it seems, are just mere "shrieks and groans," inchoate rumblings. But the slave tries again to speak in the register of reason. Plutarch's conduct, he alleges, fails on several counts: it does not befit his role as a philosopher; anyway it is in itself wrong. It is further contrary to the traditions he espoused, and finally contradictory of things he had written.

Plutarch, by contrast, uses bodily proofs: he cannot be angry because there is no trace of change in his bodily expressions or his voice, he has not gone red or trembled or gestured incorrectly. His bodily conduct – and his ability to control it – not only authorizes his use of violence against a social inferior but allows him to ignore or even transcend claims of reason. What is more, Plutarch bases this claim on learned tradition: "For all these actions [sc., of the body], if you did but know it, are the usual signs of angry passions." The reference here is to texts in the physiognomic tradition; had the slave but read these (rather than dabbling in things he considered philosophical), he would know that he had made an error in accusing Plutarch of being angry. Such an amateurish error – to say nothing of the poor slave's trespass on the rhetoric of learned men – authorizes the continuation of violence. (It seems to be lost on Gellius that the slave is complaining about *unfairly being beaten*, rather than about Plutarch being angry.)

Gellius' anecdote is not a mediation on legality per se (although, as I have argued in Chapter 5, the punishment of a slave might serve as a way of thinking through the limits of legal concepts), but it nonetheless goes some way in helping us to unpack the network of concepts that animates Philostratus' account of Philiscus' failure. In Philostratus, and in the hagiography of learning more generally, *logos* is not available to anyone. The ability to speak well comes from the fact of training. *Logos* is anchored in bodily practices, and the outward appearance of bodies determines who ought to speak and who ought to listen. In Plutarch's world, there would be no Aesop, no Gevi'a worth listening to. This is a radically different account of the relationship between speech, reason, and physical body than the one found in the more subaltern registers of discourse.

***

Deportment would not always save the day, nor would a lack of deportment always result in defeat. It is in this vein that Philostratus offers us one of his most remarkable court narratives, that of Herodes Atticus before Marcus Aurelius.[70] The richest man of his time, Herodes features extensively in Philostratus' account of the learned men of his era. The scion of a wealthy Athenian family with Roman citizenship, he made an advantageous marriage in Rome and climbed to the top of the *cursus honorum*, serving as consul and *corrector* of the free cities of Asia. He spent lavishly on benefactions, both in Athens and beyond. And like other learned men – but to a far greater extent – he came into conflict with his fellow citizens, with Roman aristocrats, and with others.

A few of these conflicts saw Herodes haled into court. Philostratus does his best to minimize these. He makes reference to a trial in Rome, but is vague about the specifics. He merely suggests that the accusations laid against him by the Athenian Ti. Claudius Demostratus were serious, and that Demostratus pursued them viciously. It is from a different source, the letters of Fronto, that we learn how nasty the trial was. The issue was the legality of a scheme through which Herodes defrauded the Athenians of the monetary gifts given to each Athenian citizen in the will of Herodes' father, Atticus: rather than giving the citizens their money, Herodes totted up what he thought each citizen owed *his* family, and offset their debts against the bequests. Some received a mere pittance; others, he claimed, owed more than the

70 The conflict, its background, and its dynamics have now been richly treated by Kuhn 2013; see also Kennell 1997. For an overview of the Quintilli, see Esch 2018. On Herodes more generally, there is a vast bibliography; useful guides are Ameling 1983 and Tobin 1997. For a recent attempt at reinterpreting Philostratus' portrayal of Herodes, see Stradzins 2019.

amount promised to them by Atticus; Herodes had them chained up in the marketplace as debtors.[71] Fronto, who helped Demostratus argue the case, makes clear how violent this was: "I have to talk about free persons cruelly beaten and stripped, one even killed, truly; I have to talk about a disloyal son and one who forgot his own father's prayers; barbarity and greed must be exposed; a certain person must be identified as an executioner."[72] The emperor, Marcus Aurelius, had to step in to make certain that things did not get overly heated. The result of the trial is unknown – presumably Herodes was acquitted, but Philostratus gives no specifics.

Herodes was brought to court another time on the grounds that he murdered his wife, Regilla. The accuser was Regilla's brother, Bradua, "a very illustrious man of consular rank."[73] At a trial in Rome, Herodes was acquitted. Yet Philostratus' account of the trial, though brief, is revealing of his ideology and of the role of law in his hagiography of learning more generally. "When Bradua appeared before the Senate in Rome he brought no convincing evidence of the charge that he was making, but delivered a long panegyric on himself dealing with his own family." Herodes defended himself by discrediting his accuser: pointing to Bradua's footwear, which featured consular insignia, he quipped, "You have your pedigree on your toe-joints." The quip translates poorly, but the point is clear enough: Herodes did not engage Bradua on his own terms, or in legal terms. Instead, his defense was a *bon mot* – precisely the sort of pointedly delivered, cutting wit that elite men specialized in, and a style of courtroom repartee that harkened back to the golden age of Republican litigation. Its function was to determine or reinscribe hierarchy, and to put pretentious people in their place. And this, rather than normal, provincial modes of engaging in litigation through reason, argument, and evidence, is what, according to Philostratus, won the day in court.

Philostratus might have been able to minimize the importance of Herodes' earlier interactions in court in order to paint him as an ideal rhetorician and someone totally in control of himself. But he could not minimize the importance of his most famous trial, one that took place before Marcus Aurelius. The origins of the conflict are unclear,

[71] *VS* 549. [72] *Ep.* 3.3, trans. Richlin 2007: letter 9.
[73] *VS* 555–56. For an attempt at reconstructing the trial, see Pomeroy 2007: 123–27.

but seem to fit well within the broader pattern of avoidance of legal judgment. In this midst of his conspicuous mourning for his wife, Regilla, Herodes escalated a quarrel that he had with the Quintillii brothers. This had been a long-simmering feud, and its details, involving the internal politics of honor in Athens and beyond, need not concern us here. At the time, however, the Quintilii were the *correctores* of the free cities of Achaea (a position functionally equivalent to governors). They accepted an invitation to the Assembly from the citizens of Athens (who hated Herodes after the nasty trick he played on them with his father's inheritance); there the Athenians complained to the brothers about Herodes' tyranny.[74] The Quintilii forwarded the Athenians' complaint to Marcus Aurelius. Herodes, in turn, accused them of conspiring against him, and when, in the wake of the Athenian complaints about Herodes, a number of leaders appeared in Athens who were openly opposed to Herodes, Herodes indicted them on the grounds that they were "conspiring to set the people against him." He laid his charges in the court of the proconsul, but fearing Herodes' influence (and we should not forget that he had a reputation for using violence) the accused men escaped and took shelter at the court of Marcus Aurelius himself, who was off with his armies in Pannonia.

There things came to a head. Herodes' opponents lodged near the emperor, who welcomed them graciously. Philostratus claims that this was because he was benevolent towards the Athenians (he had been a student in Athens – a student, in fact, of Herodes), but also because his young daughter took the side of the Athenians in the quarrel, and Marcus wished to indulge her. Herodes, by contrast, lodged in a suburb nearby. He brought along his own family, and in particular the two young daughters of his freedman Alcimedon, who he loved as his own children.

The night before the trial, tragedy struck: a lightning bolt hit the tower in which the girls were staying, and they were killed. Their deaths drove Herodes into a crazed state. He appeared the next day before the emperor's tribunal "out of his mind and longing for death" (*oute ennous kai thanatou erōn*). He spoke bluntly: "When he came forward to speak he launched into insults against the emperor, and

[74] *VS* 559–60 with Kuhn 2013: 447–48.

he did not even dress up his language, though it might be expected that a man who had been trained in this type of oratory would have been able to manage his anger." Instead, "with an aggressive and unguarded tongue" he said the unspeakable. "This is what I get for showing hospitality to [your brother] Lucius, even though it was you who sent him to me? This is how you judge me – sacrificing me to the whim of your wife and a three year old child?" Bystanders, shocked, tried to intervene to put the performance back on the rails. The praetorian Bassaeus, jolted, asked if Herodes was *trying* to die; "an old man fears little," Herodes replied. And with this, he stormed out of the courtroom.

Were this a Christian text, this would have been a bravura performance: Herodes would have died and been subsequently venerated. That it is not gives us some insight into how remarkable and offensive the performances of the Christians (or of other provincials who dared to insist on their rights to speak) were to the learned elites of the Greek-speaking world. Philostratus' Herodes is an inversion of the values of the subaltern legal discourse – a sort of dark parody of a Christian martyr. Christians were expected to deliver their confessions bluntly: Vettius Epagathus, in the *Martyrs of Lyons*, gave his confession *lamprotatēi phonei* – with the clearest voice he could.[75] Christians like Pionius were accused of having lost their minds and rushing towards death.[76] Herodes, however, refused to "dress up his language" – *oude schēmastisas ton logon*. He spoke with "an aggressive and unguarded tongue" – one that was literally *naked* (*gymnēi*) and *bare-elbowed* (*apēgkōnismenēi*). Gone was the Herodes who was poised; who delivered well-timed, witty barbs at his enemies; and who spoke with a diction that "was pleasing (*hēdys*) and abounded in figures (*euschēmōn*) and had grace and beauty."[77] The spectacle he presented was harsh, unpolished, raw – naked and unadorned. And it was, for Philostratus, scandalous and aesthetically offensive.

[75] *Mart. Lyon* = Euseb. *HE* 5.4, text from Rebillard 2017. This is of course a play on words: Vettius' voice is both exceptionally clear, and exceptionally high class.

[76] *Mart.Pion.* 20.2: διὰ τί ἀπονενόησαι; 20.5: διὰ τί σπεύδεις ἐπὶ τὸν θάνατον; The character of the judge's attendant who speaks up is similarly common: note the surprise of Lucius in Justin *Second Apology* (above, Chapter 4), and *Sifre Deuteronomy* 307.

[77] *VS* 564.

There was yet a lesson to be learned from this miserable performance:[78]

But among the eminently philosophical actions of Marcus we must include his behavior in this trial. For he never furrowed his brow or turned aside his eyes, as might have happened to a judge, but he turned to the Athenians and said: "Make your defense (*apologeisthe*), Athenians, even if Herodes does not give you leave." As he listened to the speeches in defense he was pained (but without showing it) by the many things he heard. But when the decree of the Athenian assembly was recited to him, in which they openly attacked Herodes for trying to corrupt the magistrates of Greece with the honeyed strains of his eloquence, and when they exclaimed "Oh, what bitter honey!" and "Happy were those who perished in the plague!" his heart was so gripped by what he heard that he began to weep openly.

The direct, uncultured performance of Herodes was in the end saved by the bodily perfection of the emperor Marcus, who, like the Rufinus who sought to destroy Niketes, began by holding together his composure and ended by weeping. Marcus' performance was affectively correct. Like Plutarch beating his slave, the emperor was able, through his education in philosophy, to control his body and his emotions, such that he could harmonize it with the requirements of jurisdiction. And perhaps more importantly, his emotional state served to channel his violence. "Since the Athenian defense contained an indictment not only of Herodes but also of his freedmen, Marcus turned his anger against the freedmen, employing a punishment which was 'as mild as possible.'"[79] As in the case of Aristides and his Mysian enemies, the force of law was turned against the socially inferior. Herodes and Marcus eventually made up. The affective relationships of elite men were restored.

***

We might read the story of Herodes and Marcus as a sort of folktale of justice, in Robert Cover's sense: a story about the limits of law, especially as it regards historical characters who are in some way exceptional. But we might also note that, in telling this story,

[78] *VS* 561.

[79] In fact, the judgment was far more complicated, as a contemporary inscription from Athens attests: Oliver, *Greek Constitutions* no. 184. See further Ameling 1983: 145–51; Kennell 1997; Karambelas 2020.

Philostratus makes a key move: he converts what might, under other circumstances, be considered a legal and a political problem into an aesthetic and affective one. Aesthetics and affect are not of course the same things, but in the ideology of the Greek elites they came together in a sort of a horizon. Reframing political and legal questions as aesthetic ones, moreover, provided elites a valuable tool for reimagining their world: this reimagined world was no longer a set of jurisdictions governed by rules, staffed by administrators, and accountable to systems of justice and appeal. It was not a world governed by mutually intelligible claims made in the register of rational discourse.

In the imagination of the Greek elites, there was little need to discuss questions of legitimate authority, its boundaries, and its consequences. It was instead sufficient to reimagine them as questions of beauty and ugliness – categories that aspired to be immediately, pre-rationally apprehensible to men of culture and respectability. (And if men lacking culture and respectability failed to appreciate that a particular thing was beautiful or repugnant, it would be construed as those men's failure.) The result was to place "true" knowledge of guilt and innocence, virtue and vice, outside of the procedures of the courtroom.

In the world of the courts, guilt was discernable through evidence, arguments, and proofs. In the world of the learned virtuoso, it was something vested in the body, immediately apprehensible to a man of discernment. Thus, in his biography of the sage and philosopher Apollonius of Tyana, Philostratus emphasizes that the truly learned man knew how to discern the guilty from the innocent:[80]

Now twelve men were being led to execution as bandits, and looking at them Apollonius said, "Not all, for one of them has been falsely accused and will go free." To the executioners who were conducting them he said, "I order you to slow your pace, to go more slowly to the pit, and to kill this one last, since he has nothing to do with the charge. It would be an act of piety if you spared these men for a small part of the day; it would be better if you did not kill them at all." At the same time he lingered over his speech, drawing it out to a length unusual for him, and his purpose in doing so quickly became apparent. When eight of the men had had their heads cut off, a horseman rode up to the pit shouting, "Spare Pharion!" He was not a bandit, it seemed, but had falsely

80 *VA* 5.24. Translations of the *VA* are adapted from Jones, LCL. For a similar capacity being attributed to Plotinus, see Porph. *Plot.* 11.

accused himself for fear of being tortured, and the interrogation of others had proved him a good man (*chrēston … andra*).

Apollonius could see more than one's immediate innocence. As he travelled up the Nile to visit the "Naked Philosophers" of Ethiopia, he came upon another example of wrongful guilt: a man wandering around, dressed as a citizen of Memphis. Wondering about why he was wandering so far from home, Apollonius' companion, Damis, asked their local guide, Timasion, for the reason. Timasion explained that the wanderer had killed another Memphite, though accidentally, and was now condemned "by the laws of Memphis" to wander in exile until the Naked Philosophers chose to pardon and purify him. Thus far, they had showed no signs of interest in relieving the poor man of his suffering. The Naked Philosophers, proclaimed Apollonius, "are not wise if they do not absolve him, or realize that Philiscus, whom this man killed, was descended from Thamus the Egyptian who once ravaged the Naked Philosophers' land." At the revelation, Timasion was amazed (*thaumasas*). Apollonius explained further: Thamus had, thirteen generations prior, plotted a revolution, and the Naked Philosophers had exposed him. In revenge, Thamus became a bandit, and began to pillage the Philosophers' lands. The poor man wandering about awaiting purification, Apollonius explained, should have killed Philiscus *even on purpose*, had he had the opportunity. (We need not detain ourselves over the fact that no society contemporary to Apollonius made exceptions for revenge killing, much less thirteen generations later.) Hearing this reversal of a verdict, Timasion was dumbstruck (*ekplagen*) – and Apollonius purified the man himself.[81]

One might note two things about these cognate stories. First, such stories only make sense in a world where miscarriages of justice were both real and common. Given the nature of the evidence, we know of fewer of these than we might like.[82] But it is in any context true that official justice is prone to error, and that the errors it does make tend to fall hardest upon the least sophisticated. In the Roman world, this would have meant first the poor, rural population – a population often imagined as either rubes or bandits. It did not help that bandits

81 *VA* 6.5.

82 But note, e.g., Suet. *Gai.* 30; Lucian, *Alexander* 44; Tert. *Spect.* 19; or *P.Oxy.* XXXI 2560 (AD 258), a case of mistaken identity in an arrest.

were also often subject to summary justice.[83] But such justice would likely have been as often as not misdirected. Only the truly learned man – a man like Apollonius – could have used his senses to know a real malefactor from an innocent man or even a benefactor. Thus, and second, these stories work both to denigrate particular imperial institutions – the system of everyday justice – and to mark the wise man as an alternative, or even an improved, source of power and authority.[84] Third, as with the performances of other learned men, Apollonius' performance results in astonishment – a state where the normal functioning of reason is transcended.

Just as he could tell a guilty man from a worthy one, so too could Apollonius use his aesthetic sense to discern sources of social dysfunction more broadly. Thus, when summoned to relieve the city of Ephesus from a plague, he led the Ephesians to the theater, where they found an old beggar. Apollonius was able to see that he was "craftily blinking his eyes," and urged the Ephesians to gather round the old man and stone him. The Ephesians were shocked (*thaumazontōn*) but overcame their natural instincts and began to stone the man, in spite of his pleas for mercy. It turned out that the sage was correct: as they began to stone him, the beggar blinked, then glared, then revealed fire in his eyes. The Ephesians, now convinced of the justice of their actions, stoned him to death; when they later removed the stones, it turned out the poor beggar was in fact a massive dog, frothing at the mouth. By killing the beggar/dog/spirit, the city was cleansed of the plague, and the Ephesians raised a statue of Heracles the Averter over the spot where he was killed.[85]

We might imagine that, if this story has any relation to a real event, what Apollonius suggested would have constituted an act of mob justice of the most reprehensible sort. The collective ire of the citizens was turned on one of their social inferiors, an old beggar – a character who must have been a common sight in the cities of the

[83] Summary justice for bandits, e.g., *Dig.* 49.1.16 = Mod., 6 *Diff.*, Frg. 28 Lenel; *I.Boubon*[2] 5; In general, Shaw 1984; Keenan 1985; McGing 1998; Riess 2001. On the over-zealousness of local officials, see now Brélaz 2020.

[84] Similar points could be made about the *VA*'s denouement, the trial of Apollonius before Domitian, or about the civil suit that Apollonius helps the Indian king judge (2.39). On the latter text, cf. Aul. Gell. *NA* 14.2.

[85] *VA* 4.10.

Roman Empire. And here we would do well to remember that text had a pedagogical purpose: the lesson is to defer to the authority of the sage, and to overcome even the normal sense of moral propriety that stands in the way of venting one's collective rage on a pitiful spectacle such as a beggar. Indeed, the Ephesians almost resist the order of Apollonius – they're astonished by it. But the sage's aesthetic and physiognomic knowledge allows him to know the truth about others from their bodies – in the case of the beggar, from his glance alone. The assembled crowd, in turn, has to transcend their everyday morality (to say nothing of the sort of legal procedures that ought to have protected even the abject from mob rage). Like Plutarch beating his slave, a source of real wisdom allows them to transcend the space of everyday reason to direct their violence at a social inferior. And when they do, the result is good: the plague is lifted, and a city purged of the most offensive sort of character. Had they clung to their instincts, refrained from mob justice, listened to his pleas for mercy, and afforded the man the normal sorts of procedures designed to prove innocence, they would only have suffered more.

***

Just as aesthetic sense allowed legal categories to be placed outside of the normal methods of evaluation (that is, evaluation by what others claimed to be *logos*), so too could it cause political categories to be placed in a space apart. In the subaltern discourse, legal and political power were supposed to be subject to dialogue and discussion, contest and negotiation. Thus as we have seen, Pionius tormented his local interlocutors by insisting that they did not have the right to punish him, while Justin Martyr could insist that high officials had to conform to rules of law that were, at the very least, not inconsistent with reason. These kinds of arguments were, I suggested, a mode of political theory.

The elites of the Greek world developed a competing mode of political theory, one crafted in opposition to this more subaltern mode. Political authority, they insisted, was not located in rules, procedures, and rational dialogue, but rather in an innate sense of beauty and disgust. These senses could not be explained or learned; they had to be developed by habituation – by the long training of one's mind and body. In this vein of political theory, justice *just was* beauty, and injustice ugliness.[86] On such a reading, an Aesop or a Geviʿa were exactly what they appeared to be.

Perhaps the most important text in this tradition is Dio Chrysostom's *First Oration on Kingship*.[87] Delivered probably before Trajan, the *Oration* is not particularly original: like Dio's work more generally, it recapitulates a great number of philosophical tropes that floated throughout the world of learned men more generally.[88] This is precisely its advantage for the study of elite attitudes towards legality.

Like his contemporaries, both elite and subaltern, Dio was concerned about the relationship between the monarch and justice, and between the monarch and law.[89] But whereas the more subaltern discourse focused on the practical act of jurisdiction as the moment that best reflected the attitude of the monarch to justice, Dio's starts with the character of the king more generally. The problem with such a line of reasoning is that the real character of a king is necessarily hidden. Thus the character of a king – a *true* king, rather than a mere tyrant – has to be inferred from the relations that he has with others. His enemies must fear him, but his subjects must seek to associate with him. Those who approach him must feel neither terror nor fear, but rather courage. Perhaps more importantly, they ought to feel "amazed" (*thaumazein*) in his presence.[90] It is hard not to hear a note of elite projection in such a formulation.

86 On the givenness of aesthetic sensation and the communities it creates, see Bourdieu 1984, with the perceptive discussion of Neer 2005.

87 For other examples, note Aristid. *Or.* 24.44 (*ekphrasis* of concord and discord), Aul. Gell. *NA* 14.4 (defending Chrysippus' portrayal of justice). More generally, see Goldhill 2007. Ekphrasis as *political* art, note Blanshard 2004: 7–8 on the depiction of *demos* in Plin. *NH* 35.69: "Pliny is not describing a work of art. He is doing precisely what one must inevitably do on encountering a depiction of the Demos: take a political position. Any attempt at critical engagement with the representation inevitably results in political expression."

88 Although see Sidebottom 2006 for Dio's originality with respect to genre.

89 For an overview of the opinions of contemporaries, see Noreña 2012.

90 *Or.* 1.25. Cf. 1.18. Close readers will note that, in the same passage, Dio stresses that subjects should not feel either *phobos* or *ekplēxis* in the presence of the monarch. This seems to be an innovation on his part. On the king as a source of *thauma*, there is a similar tradition in the text of Diotogenes and other Pythagorean philosophers. The inability of scholars to converge on a date for these texts' composition, however, makes them of limited use for present purposes. The importance of *thauma* to accounts of royalty in these Pythagorean sources has been noted by Wallace-Hadrill 1982: 34.

This rhetoric of praise does not dwell on the evaluation of individual acts, but rather on impressions. In actual fact the administration of the empire consisted in a management challenge on a colossal scale: the management of many thousands of discrete requests from subjects; of a volatile and often violent aristocracy; of frontiers and armies; and of the care and feeding (and hence the public opinion) of the populace of the city of Rome.[91] It is not surprising that, for ideological reasons, Dio should prefer to minimize these tasks and their attendant challenges. But it is nonetheless important that he locates the power of the ruler not only in his ability to make the correct affective impression upon his subjects: the true emperor, on Dio's account, is not just a virtuous man, but also a man who succeeds by changing or managing the emotional state of those subject to him. Such a king, Dio asserts elsewhere, "is more lawful than a jury chosen by lot."[92] Focusing on the effects that the king has on others entails a further consequence: on such logic, it is not for subjects to evaluate the performance of an emperor at any individual task, or even his menu of tasks taken collectively. By locating imperial legitimacy at the level of affect, Dio takes off the table the normal mode by which subjects make evaluations of rulers. And the logic is dangerously circular: to the extent that the affective states of individual subjects *fail* to align with what they should be, this is presumably the fault of the individual subject, not the fault of the ruler.

So then to what degree is the ruler responsible for how he actually governs – that is, for individual decisions? The government (*dioikēseōs*) of the entire universe, Dio explains, operates according to a set of natural rhythms, which are in turn structured by divine providence. The forces of the universe craft humans in turn, with the result that we live under a single judgment (*thesmōi*), a single law (*nomōi*), and in effect, inhabit a single polity (*politeias*). The king who respects and supports this rhythm is therefore the king who is lawful (*nomimos*).[93] He derives his particular powers from Zeus. This is the standard stuff of Hellenistic political theory. But Dio also knows that by following this logic to its natural conclusion he will eventually back himself into a corner. It is fine to say that rulers rule in accordance

[91] The classic account of this workload is Millar 1992. [92] *Or.* 3.4–5.
[93] *Or.* 1.42.

with natural law, but this leaves open the obvious question of the content of that law.[94] Filling in this picture with substantive answers to this question would necessarily relate those answers back to discrete acts of governance – that is, it would allow rulers to be judged by subaltern members of the polity who evaluate the ruler on the basis of his particular acts. This is precisely what Dio would prefer to avoid.

Accordingly, he quickly shifts gears: to speak of Zeus would go on too long, he insists (scarcely credibly); rather, he should like to explain the problem of governance through a myth – or rather, a "sacred and edifying *logos* that takes the *form* of a myth."[95] It is a *logos* that he claims he heard while he was wandering around as an exile, from an old peasant woman tending to a shrine of Heracles.[96] Heracles, she explained, was a king – a great king, in fact, who ruled over all the Greeks. As preparation for his rule, his father summoned Hermes to guide the young man. Hermes brought the young Heracles to a clearing where he showed the future monarch two mountains: the first, sacred to Zeus, was called Mount Royalty; the second, Mount Tyranny. Mount Royalty was blessed with a clear and straightforward path, Mount Tyranny with a crooked and dangerous one. But, as if the point was not clear enough, Hermes urged Heracles to look more closely. The two ascended the path of Mount Royalty. Upon the peak, Heracles saw a further image: a woman seated upon a throne, clothed in white, bearing an otherworldly scepter. "Her face was bright and august, such that worthy men would take courage when seeing it, but a wicked man could not bear to look on it, just as when one with weak eyes tries to stare at the transit of the sun. Her form was steadfast and fixed, and she did not turn her gaze."[97] She was, moreover, surrounded by a group of women, and a man:[98]

> "Who are these people?" he asked, "how noble and magnificent and manly!" Replied Hermes: "This one, who is seated at her right, the one whose gaze is both terrible and gentle, is Justice (*dikē*) – she is illuminated by the greatest and most apparent beauty. Next to her is Political Order (*eunomia*) – she is

[94] On divine and natural law, see Hayes 2015. [95] *Or.* 1.49.

[96] On the importance of the countryside in Dio more generally, see Desideri 2000. Peasants are the heroes of Dio's world, existing in a space without politics: see Bryen 2019a.

[97] *Or.* 1.71. [98] *Or.* 1.73.

quite similar and only differs slightly in her appearance. On the other side is a woman who is most graceful, sitting delicately and smiling gladly – they call her Peace (*eirēnē*). Standing right beside Royalty, in fact just in front of her scepter, is a man – he is mature and high-minded. They call him Law (*nomos*), but he is also called Right Reason (*orthos logos*), Councillor (*sumboulos*), and Attendant (*paredros*). Without him, it is not lawful (*themis*) for these women either to do anything, or even to plan it.

From Royalty, Hermes and Heracles move on to the other mountain to view Tyranny. She sits on a grander and more expensive throne, but she is ugly and sallow; though she tries but fails to compose herself as Royalty does, she nonetheless shifts uncomfortably in her throne.[99] Like the beggar that Apollonius of Tyana encounters, her eyes shift repeatedly, and her mood oscillates violently. She too is surrounded by a council: Cruelty (*ōmotēs*), Degrading Violence (*hybris*), Lawlessness (*anomia*), and Civil War (*stasis*).[100] Asked which of the women he preferred, Heracles responded: "The other one! For I am amazed by her (*thaumazō*), and I love her (*agapō*)."

Heracles' conclusion is inescapable: when faced with such a choice, only the pathological would choose differently. This is the point: by explaining good rule in this way, Dio has turned a political question – a question of the rationale by which one person exercises power over another – into a primarily aesthetic one. When describing the problem of legitimacy and its boundaries as a problem of style, there can only be one right answer: there is only one image that is sublime and provokes ecstatic astonishment. To desire anything else would be to expose oneself as a rube or a pervert – or both.

Finally, the mere *ability* to describe something like Royalty, Tyranny, or Justice was located in networks of learning and therefore also of power. It is not the case, for Dio and his ilk, that the capacity to give such descriptions is evenly spread across the community as a whole. The ability to describe – also the ability to decide *which* questions were really aesthetic – was to be located firmly in the hands of the educated classes. To return to Lucian, whom I quoted earlier: "Concerning images, there is not the same law for the educated as there is for regular people."[101] The regular person might gaze upon an image, but the best he could do would be to merely

99 Cf. Aristides, *Or.* 24.44. 100 *Or.* 1.82. 101 *Dom.* 2, Goldhill 2001b.

admire it (*thaumasas*) – and then he would go off mute (*kōphon*), leaving its aesthetic qualities unarticulated (*alogon*). But such behavior was unacceptable for a learned man: it would show him to be a rube (*agroikia*), to be vulgar (*apeirokalia*) and uneducated (*amousia*). The educated were to speak and describe, and to govern through their aesthetic sense; their inferiors were to gape in amazement.

***

With this in mind, we might return, finally, to the role of law in the world of the Greek elites. It is not surprising, given their interest in transcendence and their disinterest in normal procedures for seeking justice, that law *as a category* comes to be rejected as something unphilosophical, as something that one might eventually outgrow in a world that functions according to divine plan. This belief transcended individual philosophical schools.[102] Thus the Epicurean Diogenes of Oinoanda might agree that not all humans might have the capacity for wisdom, "But if we assume it to be possible, then truly the life of the gods will pass to men. For everything will be full of justice and mutual love, and there will come to be no need of fortifications or laws and all the things which we contrive on account of one another."[103] It would not be erroneous to hear, in such a description, an echo of the form of ideal, affective community that Paul had argued for some years before.

But one might theorize the law in a more extreme way as well – not as something that would eventually become vestigial as human society improved, but as a necessary evil for those who might fail to rise to the level of philosophical transcendence. Thus, in the *Corpus Hermeticum*, Thrice-Great Hermes proclaims to his interlocutor, Tat, that:[104]

> [T]hose human souls that do not have Mind as a guide are affected in the same way as souls of animals without reason (*alogōn zōiōn*). When Mind connives with them and gives way to longings, the rush of appetite drives such souls to the longings that lead to unreason and, like animals without reason, they never cease their irrational anger and irrational longing, and they have never had enough of evil. For angers and longings are irrational vices that

[102] O'Meara 2003: 34. [103] Fr. 56, trans. and ed. Smith 1992.
[104] 12.4, trans. Copenhaver 1992.

exceed all limits. God has imposed the law (*nomon*) upon these souls as a torment (*timōron*) and a reproof (*elegchon*).

Hermes explains further: god has given to humans alone two things, mind and rational speech (*logos*). To the extent that they use these things "as they should," they can await an afterlife in which they shed their mortal bodies and commune with the gods. But what then, Tat reasonably inquires, of those "animals without reason" – and, presumably, the humans without mind who resemble them? Do they not have *logos* as well? They do not, Hermes explains: they make sounds, but they have only *voice* (*phonē*), not *logos*. They make noises, but those noises need not be respected as rational discourse.[105] We are not far here from Plutarch and his unfortunate slave.

Though written in Egypt, in a religious and civic context far removed from the sophisticated world of the cities of Asia Minor, Hermetic texts nonetheless circulated throughout the empire.[106] They both partook of and helped to create ideologies of law that were in broader circulation, as competing claims about the nature and location of justice in an empire pressed against one another. We might close this harvest of dismal verdicts about the nature of law with a final source, this one from an unknown early Christian author in a text now known as 1 Timothy:[107]

Now we know that the law is good, if any one uses it lawfully, understanding this, that the law is not laid down for the just but for the lawless and disobedient, for the ungodly and sinners, for the unholy and profane, for murderers of fathers and murderers of mothers, for manslayers, immoral persons, sodomites, kidnappers, liars, perjurers, and whatever else is contrary to sound doctrine, in accordance with the glorious gospel of the blessed God with which I have been entrusted.

On the account of the author of 1 Timothy, the courtroom was not a space for the exchange of ideas and information. It was rather a meat

105 The distinction goes back to Aristotle, but it here repurposed as part of a set of claims about law more generally. Cf. Dio, *Or*. 36.38.

106 Copenhaver 1992: xxxi.

107 1.8–11, trans. RSV. Cf. Gal. 3:19, but in a narrower sense (historical/chronological, rather than structural). Cf. also Tatian, *Or*. 26, making a different case for the invalidity of legislation, based instead on its observed tendency towards contradiction – although also arguing that it would be desirable for all to share in a common *politeia*.

grinder, an unfortunate institution that was good only to the extent that it inflicted pain on the miserable and the wicked. The wise could transcend this, through their capacity with language, through their training of the flesh, through their commitment to sociability with their equals and their commitment to transcendence. The rest were either to defer, or to be punished.

PART IV

LAW AS BOOKS

8

Writing about Governance, from Cicero to Ulpian

The populations of the eastern provinces were a cacophonous bunch. Committed to particular ideas of justice, they were happy to assail the tribunals of governors; to write interminable petitions detailing their supposed rights and the supposed wrongs of their neighbors; to complain to friends and neighbors about legal processes; and to weave dramas about justice into their folktales, their entertainment, and their theology. Their supposed betters, the elites of the cities – in reality prolific litigators – copied their inferiors if only by way of inversion, creating elaborate and ideological accounts of their own being as supra-legal: they prattled on about the beauty of their bodies and their voices, the way their language provoked *thauma*, and their impressive performances before the emperors, all carefully calculated to avoid admitting publicly that they were enmeshed in the same systems as the less privileged classes. In some sense, their behavior was an explainable (if also, to modern tastes, repellent) reaction to a world in which many of their social inferiors thought themselves lawyers. We can thus understand, though not sympathize, with a man like Dio Chrysostom, who, when proposing a set of moral reforms of the Greek cities, might insist that the poor must ideally be expelled to the countryside, but failing that, they not become "scriveners (*syngrapheis*) who draw up contracts and summonses or, in general, documents that have to do with trials and complaints, and claim knowledge of legal forms; nor must they be learned and clever shysters (*dikorrhaphous*) and pleaders (*synēgorous*) who pledge their services for a fee, even to the greatest scoundrels, and even undertake to defend unblushingly other men's crimes, and to rage and rant and beg for mercy for men who are neither their friends or kinsmen."[1]

Surveying this morass of opposing commitments and understandings in the late second century, the jurist and imperial administrator Ulpian must have felt a sense of unease, if not alarm. Ulpian was a keen observer of provincial culture and politics, not least because he grew up in a provincial context himself. From the city of Tyre in Phoenicia (which in his lifetime had received the status of a Roman colony), Ulpian grew up in precisely the milieu which generated such powerful and opposing commitments to ideals of legality.[2] But his path was different. He became educated in Roman civil law (precisely how we do not know) and chose to express himself in Latin. He served in the courts of the emperors, including as a secretary *a libellis* – that is, in charge of the management of the flood of petitions and requests that came from all corners of the empire – during a time of uncertainty and violence.[3] He rose eventually to the highest of equestrian commands, serving as manager of the grain supply and soon thereafter as the praetorian prefect, the chief judicial and administrative officer of the empire, before being murdered in AD 223.

Ulpian was talented, but not unique. Some other provincials made their careers as jurists, and among them, a few exceptional talents rose to high levels of government.[4] These people will be at the center of this chapter and the next. Among them, Ulpian serves as a pivotal figure. Earlier jurists, at least in Rome, had largely ignored broader questions of government in favor of exploring and shaping a Roman

1 *Or.* 7.123, trans. LCL with modifications. See further Bryen 2019a.

2 Useful surveys of Ulpian's life and work can be found in Kunkel 1967; Kunkel 2001; Crifò 1976 tends to be credulous with respect to sources; Honoré 2002 (original ed. 1982) has proven controversial (see not least Frier 1984; Millar 2004 [1986]), but contains some important insights; Marotta 2000–2004 is especially useful for placing Ulpian in his broader context; while Marotta 2024 is helpful on the various vexed chronological questions posed by Ulpian's career. Schiavone 2012: 391–460 makes interesting interventions, but also in my judgment pays too little attention to specific historical context (see my discussion in Bryen 2012b); and Harries 2014, who is strong on the importance of cultural context.

3 On the ramifications of this disorder for jurists, see Herz 2018; Brutti 2020: 9–24.

4 On jurists from provincial contexts, see Jones 2007 for a survey from the east; Millar 2004 [1999] for a case study; Dolganov 2020b for the elites of North Africa, and Furstenberg 2023 for rabbis. Honoré 1994 for the central chancery.

law that was, primarily, a citizens' law, designed primarily for the city of Rome. They also largely ignored the fact of a massive empire that stretched across the Mediterranean, with all of its attendant legal challenges.

Ulpian could not do this. One of his abiding concerns was to attempt to explain provincial governance as a law-governed activity. By this I mean not an activity that involved lots of complex and competing commitments to different accounts of legality, but as a set of practices, offices, and institutions that might be explained according to rational and legalistic principles. Looking out over the eastern world in which he grew up, one might reasonably speculate that Ulpian was acutely aware that no such account existed, nor was there any common consensus as to the nature, content, obligations, or boundaries of imperial power.

Ulpian's approach to the question of provincial governance stands out as an important marker of a broader shift that stands at the center of this chapter and the next: a move by the central state (or by people who perceived themselves as closely connected to the central state) to bring to heel this vibrant but discordant set of provincial arguments about the nature of law, the importance of rhetoric, and the source and location of rights. In this respect, it was very much a reaction to – and therefore a result of – the culture of legalism that developed in the east. In some key respects this move honored the wishes of the most subaltern of legal voices – voices like those of Aesop or Geviʿa (above, Chapter 5) – but with an important difference. Ulpian and his contemporaries took up the challenge of thinking of the provinces as law-governed or even law-suffused spaces, but they had no patience for the politics of *logos* or *thauma* – no patience, that is, for an account of law that was porous or open to provincial language. Instead, they began a process of rethinking Roman provincial *governance* by reference to the language of Roman *jurisprudence*. The juridification of governance – and the juridification of the provincial landscape more generally – was to be their most consequential achievement. It would not be completed in the age of Ulpian, but he and his fellow jurists planted the seeds of a larger, more radical transformation.

This move might be interpreted – along with analogous developments in the early third century AD – as the first and most consequential step towards the great closing off of provincial legal culture. Though this revolution started among jurists from the eastern world, like Ulpian, it would eventually encompass the entirety of the Mediterranean basin as their ideas and assumptions came to be encoded within imperial statutes. But the works through which they elaborated these new ideas were targeted at a world that was imagined, normatively, to be Greek, with all the attendant politics of the Greek cities that we have outlined thus far.

The consequences of this transformation would take time to be felt, but they would eventually be substantial: the replacement of complex and open-textured provincial commitments to legality with a vision of law as something ideally written by jurists, contained normatively in books, and accessible primarily in specialized libraries – or tucked into the pack of a governor. In contrast to dominant provincial understandings of law (where law *emerged* through dialogic engagement with men in power), the jurists' and eventually the emperors' vision of law was as something ideally bounded and contained – a set of internally consistent rules and ideas *to be applied* to imperfect and contentious people. Such knowledge was to be embodied in books – physical artifacts which could be handed to men in charge and kept in a central location to determine the contours of their practice. These books were imagined to be superior to the *disiecta membra* of stone and papyrus, scattered throughout the landscape, that had previously set the rhythms of provincial practice. The juridification of governance was to be a quiet revolution, but a consequential one, for it determined not only the authoritative location and form of legal knowledge, but also, in turn, *who* was authorized to be a legal interpreter more generally.

***

It is best to start, however, not with the jurists themselves, but with the people who were trusted to run the empire in the first place. Aside from a capacity to handle a great number of practical challenges at once, was there some broader theoretical commitment that emperors and governors brought to bear on governance more generally?

It is of course tempting to think of the Romans as a uniquely untheoretical people. Among imperial peoples more generally, Romans do stand out as being especially reluctant to articulate the legal basis of their rule over others. Unlike medieval Islamic societies, with their rich tradition of *adab* manuals for all sorts of officials, or the South Asian societies contemporary with Rome whose elites produced texts like the *Arthaśāstra*, Romans, for the most part, wrote only incidentally about governance.[5] They were, of course, happy to tell their subjects what rules they expected them to follow, and to evaluate both particular subjects and governing elites as being either defective or worthy of emulation in carrying out their duties. But although the vast bulk of the Roman elite was somehow involved in the practice of governance, the governance of provinces was not a seemly topic of extended written reflection – either among jurists or, for that matter, anyone else. The primary reason for this seems to be that the governing elite understood the running of an empire not, primarily, as a package of legal duties, but instead as a largely moral exercise.[6] Yet even while Roman elites were prone to write extensively about morality, there are almost no extended discussions of provincial governance in such a register.

There is one exception, which comes not from the Principate, but from the Republic: the letter of Cicero to his brother, Quintus, on the occasion of the extension of Quintus' term as the governor of the province of Asia. Cicero's "letter" reads like a short treatise, and was no doubt intended for public consumption.[7] As such, it is worth looking more closely at this remarkable document to understand both how Roman elites might have imagined their relationship to provincial governance, as well as why thinking about governance as a law-based activity might have lacked appeal.

The legal frameworks through which Quintus was to govern Asia are conspicuously absent in Cicero's letter. Cicero would certainly have known about them. Early in Cicero's career, in his prosecution of the former governor Gaius Verres, Cicero had complained extensively about Verres' edict for the province of Sicily. Neither was Cicero a stranger to jurisprudence. He bragged, in a different

5 Islamic societies: Heck 2002; Allehbi 2021; South Asia: Olivelle 2013; McClish 2019. Compare the wealth of legal, historical, and philological reflections that the empires of the new world posed for Mediterranean intellectuals, richly detailed by Lupher 2003. On Roman genres of legal writing, still unsurpassed as a survey is Schulz 1946; for a more theoretically sophisticated treatment of genre see now Mantovani 2018.

6 Lendon 1997.

7 *Q. Fr.* 1 S-B (I.1). Public consumption: Shackleton Bailey 1980: 147.

letter, that his own private library contained works of the great jurists. Yet he nowhere raises the question of what sort of juridical framework ought to prevail in Quintus' province.[8] One might have expected something to that effect, not least since, at the start of his "letter," Cicero acknowledges that the main challenge that Quintus will encounter in governing Asia is the crush of legal business. The Greek inhabitants tended to fight amongst themselves; Asia was also filled with Roman citizens, mostly tax-farmers or wealthy business-people, who tended, in turn, to fight with the various communities of Greeks. In other words, one might think the governorship of Asia a prime candidate for reflections on conflict-of-laws – or even more basic questions of the sources of rights of individuals and communities – that might need to be addressed with some explicit attention to legal frameworks.

Cicero's strategy was different. Good governance, on Cicero's account, involved not legal expectations, but the control of personal desires. In governing, avarice is presumed; and while Cicero is quite sure that Quintus can avoid being bribed, he instructs Quintus nonetheless to keep a close eye on his staff, who may become overwhelmed by temptations to greed. Similarly, he urges Quintus to manage the desires of those he governs, for they too are avaricious and will try to befriend him to line their own pockets. What is more, interacting overly much with such morally incontinent subjects might jeopardize the character of the administrator himself. In Quintus' case, there is a danger that, having observed horrid behavior on the part of his charges, Quintus in turn will lose his self-control and indulge in his tendency towards violent outrage – another instance of failing to manage his composure.[9] To survive this minefield of desire and opportunity, *integritas*, *continentia*, and *pudor* are necessary – all virtues by which one regulates one's own desires, and hence the desires of others.[10] When these virtues are practiced, the result is good governance: banditry and rioting subside, cities are well managed and well financed, worthy local elites manage local problems, and tax payments flow smoothly.[11]

[8] Verres' edict: e.g., *Verr.* 2.1.44–46 (113–21); Cicero's legal library: *ad Fam.* 331 S-B (VII.22). Cicero's (slowly) developing relationship with jurisprudence more generally: Harries 2006.

[9] 40. [10] 18. See esp. Kaster 2005. [11] 25.

Of course, any problems that do exist will eventually find themselves before Quintus' tribunal. But Cicero insists that this crush of judicial business raises no serious concerns:[12]

As it seems to me, the administration of Asia presents no great variety of business; it all rests in the main on the dispensation of justice. The actual knowledge involved in that, especially in a province, is no problem (*in qua scientiae, praesertim provincialis, ratio ipsa expedita est*), but there is a need of constancy and firmness (*constantia est adhibenda et gravitas*) to resist even the suspicion of partiality.

The assumption here is a critical one: correct answers to legal problems emerge only from morally upright rulers who do not give in to their baser impulses towards favoritism. Legality, while admittedly a branch of knowledge (*scientia*) – though, it seems, an easy one to get the gist of – produces good governance if and only if it is the precipitate of good character.

This line of reasoning transfers over to the management of one of the central, structural conflicts of provincial governance: the endemic conflicts between Roman tax farmers (*publicani*) and provincial subjects. One might reasonably suspect that such conflicts would also produce thorny legal conflicts – disputes over sureties, inheritance, requirements of good faith, and so forth. The *publicani* themselves were most certainly no practitioners of *integritas* or *continentia*. Yet Cicero avoids thinking of them as a primarily legal problem. They should be appeased, he counsels Quintus, by reminding them that "we" (presumably Cicero and Quintus themselves) owe them a great deal, and by flattering them that tax collectors command great amounts of honor and respect (*dignitas*). No matter what, conflicts with them ought to be solved on the basis of Quintus' authority (*auctoritas*) without bringing to bear his legal prerogatives as a proconsul, much less the capacity for coercion that accompanies these prerogatives (*remoto imperio ac vi potestatis et fascium*).[13]

One can spare some sympathy for Cicero on this point. A legalistic approach to the *publicani* was likely a foolish strategy. They were a powerful interest group, protected by senators in Rome. They were quite capable of having laws changed to give validity to dubious contracts. Girding for legal combat with them was unwise, as Cicero no

[12] 20, trans. Shackleton-Bailey, LCL. [13] 35.

doubt knew (and would later get to experience personally).[14] None of this, however, should detract from the broader point: that in dealing with powerful constituencies, moral suasion was the most effective policy. In fact, legal regulation – the patient creation of boundaries and the fair assignment and protection of rights – is not even imagined as an option for Quintus. The only option besides relying on authority and moral suasion, and not a desirable one, was to rely on one's coercive powers: the *imperium* (power to issue commands) vested in a governor, or the *vis* (force, violence) that came from his powerful office.

At the heart of Cicero's account of provincial government is an account of morality and desire, rather than an account of legality or institutions. Morality – in the sense of cultured self-restraint, the management of the appetites of oneself and one's charges – is what makes governance possible, even effective.[15] This was a broad and longstanding assumption among Roman elites.[16] It was not original to Cicero and would persist well beyond his time, even though subsequent writers declined to imitate Cicero in his short treatise on provincial governance.[17] On such an account the Roman state, such as it

[14] *Att.* 114 S-B (V.21). [15] Cf. his later account in *RP* 1.2, with Valvo 2010.

[16] On the politics of controlling desire, see Kaster 2005; and with attention to a broader linguistic and chronological spectrum, Harris 2001.

[17] There were of course many treatises containing moral exhortation – Seneca's for instance. But though they urged moral behavior (the avoidance of anger, etc.) they were not specifically concerned with administration. Likewise, there were plenty of examples of attempts at suasion towards good governance by provincial subjects directed at their imperial rulers (i.e., Dio's *Orations on Kingship*). But, with the exception of Frontinus' work on water management (on the polemical ambitions of which see Peachin 2004) and the technical treatises of the Gromatici (see Campbell 2000), in no case does a Roman administrator write about administration, much less of a province. There is, remarkably, a Ptolemaic guide to administration: *P.Tebt.* III 703 = *Sel.Pap.* II 204 (III BC), as well as another Hellenistic administrative guide, likely based on Aristotle (see Saba 2013, with the discussion of Thonemann 2013b). I bracket here the question of how to read book 10 of Pliny's *Letters*. While certainly shedding tremendous amounts of light on the day-to-day activities of governor, and while in some sense (but obviously at one remove) painting Pliny as an excellent specimen of a governor and leaving open the possibility (at yet a further remove) that the optimal governor would be like Pliny, this is not a treatise on governance, and adduces no attempts at abstraction. For a strong argument that the book 10 should be read as treatise-like, see Woolf 2006. For a rather less convincing one, see Stadter 2006. Coleman 2012 provides a thorough overview of the bureaucratic idioms present in the *Letters*. Pliny took imperial ideals seriously, but I agree with Coleman that reading bureaucratic correspondence as an *account* of governance rather than as an *effect* of ideals of governance is a problematic exercise.

was, was constructed primarily out of *networks* of elite men (bound together by strategic choices in marrying elite women) whose bonds of loyalty and reciprocal commitments to elite morality permitted government to operate.[18] Violence too was always an option, but in practice it had to be deployed selectively – at the right sort of social inferior, and with the right audience in mind. Governance, on such an account, was the art of knowing whom to flatter, whom to persuade, and whom to harm – and when. On such an account, it is no surprise that control of one's emotions occupied center stage.

***

So much for governance as a primarily moral undertaking. We have already seen (Chapters 2 and 3) that such an account of governance provoked a series of problems on the ground. Not least among them was that thinking of government as a series of networks provided an incentive structure for people loosely aligned to official sources of power to take advantage of provincial populations, a problem I there called the "laundering of state power." It also offered minimal decision-making traction for an administrator who had to sort through complex and competing rights-claims made by subjects. These might be imagined to be precisely the sorts of problem amenable to rationalization by juristic thinking. Yet such questions leave no traces in the vast output of Roman juristic writing over the bulk of the first two centuries AD. Why, then, were jurists so reluctant to discuss provincial governance?

When jurisprudence emerged in the Republic, it had radical potential for rethinking and rationalizing social and political relations. In

[18] E.g., Brown 1984: 26: "It [an account of *paideia* as a lubricant to government] is insufficient because it assumes that, throughout, there was a 'machine of government' whose actions were camouflaged or facilitated by a *décor* of literary culture, a common *paideia* to which all the educated governing class paid lip service. In fact, what this view overlooks is that, in late antiquity – and, indeed, in most of the ancient and medieval world – there was no such thing as a 'machine of government'; there was only a network of interpersonal relations that *was* government. Plainly, in such a situation, the 'creation of a kind of person' by means of a traditional culture was a serious matter." The bibliography on networks of elites is extensive: Lendon 1997 is fundamental; Peachin 2011b collects a wide variety of perspectives on relationality. Fergus Millar offers the fundamental account of the bureaucratic thinness of the Roman endeavor. See in particular the essays collected in Millar 2004. See also Garnsey and Saller 1987.

the register of jurisprudence, senatorial elites wrote treatises on public, private, and religious law, incorporating historical events, statutory commentary, and linguistic analysis within their broader discussions. These elites were not "jurists" in the modern sense of the term, for "jurist" was not a profession; they were, rather, elites who claimed specialized knowledge of law, or *ius*.[19] Such elites sought to explicate law precisely so that the populace could not simply solve its problems in whatever way it wished.[20]

Ius, a category which encompassed both substantive law itself and discussions *about* substantive law (like Torah in Rabbinic traditions), was thus a fundamentally anti-democratic concept. *Ius* existed beyond the realm of everyday practice, providing an account of the "right" way to conceptualize, structure, and solve problems between citizens. Even as many of the main conclusions of *ius* came to be written down, it existed ideally as a body of oral rulings, backed by the authority of powerful and respectable men. Through the elaboration of the obligations of citizens, it sought to craft a normative vision of what a citizen of Rome should be. In the elegant formulation of Aldo Schiavone, *ius* was designed around the "social disciplining of the city."[21] The development of the idea of – and the elaboration of the category of – *ius* made sense in particular in the violent and unstable world of the Late Republic, for *ius* was something ideally stable and slow to change in a political world that oscillated violently between competing positions.

It was not to be. Despite its potential as a way of reckoning with language, tradition, and the obligations of citizens (that is, politics and civil society), jurisprudence was proving inadequate to its aspirations even in the late Republic. In the age of emperors, jurisprudence retreated decisively from questions that might be imagined as politically sensitive.[22] Even fundamental questions – like what, legally, was

[19] For an overview, see recently Lehne-Gstreinthaler 2019.
[20] Cf. Pomponius, *Ench.*, Frg. 178 Lenel = *Dig.* 1.2.2.6: *quas actiones ne populus prout vellet institueret certas solemnesque esse voluerunt.*
[21] Schiavone 2012: 133. See also esp. Frier 1985. A sense of the diversity of the concerns of Republican "jurists" can be gleaned from the pages of the first volume of Huschke et al. 1909: history, calendars, religion, magistracy, and language all feature prominently. On the intellectual ferment of the late republic, including in jurisprudence, see esp. Moatti 2015.
[22] Schiavone 2012. On its contraction, starting in the age of Augustus, see also Bryen 2018, on M. Antistius Labeo.

the emperor and from where did he derive his power – only seem to have been openly discussed starting well into the second century AD. Even then, these discussions are marked not only by inconsistency but also by a certain squeamishness.[23] Jurisprudence, it seemed, was not fit to be political theory, nor a guide to good governance. It was barely adequate as a metalanguage for describing the entirety of a citizen's duties and obligations, even when, in the age of emperors, these came to be radically contracted.

Jurisprudence came, instead, to be a technical, problem-solving enterprise: determining the best answers to the questions of who could sue whom, for what, under which circumstances, and under which chapter of the edict of the Urban Praetor at Rome.[24] The Praetor's Edict – the fundamental text upon which jurists commented – was the crucial document, occupying the great bulk of the interpretive bandwidth of the jurists in the first and second centuries AD. From the tradition of discussing it – and as many imaginative permutations and fact patterns as could conceivably be applied to it – a subtle and clever language game emerged. Could X count as Y for the purposes of falling under the rubric of a particular legal enactment? In what order should we place competing claims A and B? What should be done in the case of vagueness or error with respect to some transaction C? The hazards of the game tended to be statutory. Had the assemblies, senate, or emperor ever intervened to make a potentially easy question harder?

The men who specialized in this particular sort of expertise cultivated, like their Republican predecessors, a basically conservative habitus, guarding the boundaries of their endeavor as specialized territory.[25] This was perhaps understandable, since a number came not, like their earliest predecessors, from senatorial families, but from families of slightly lower social rank. Unusual opinions would have impressed no one and made impossible competition for imperial favor – in particular, the right to give authoritative rulings (*responsa*) on behalf of the emperors. For such men, conservatism and caution were prudent (to pun just slightly); periodic threats from deranged

[23] Gai. *Inst.* 1.5; Pomponius, *Ench.*, Frg. 178 Lenel = *Dig.* 1.2.2.11. In general, Tuori 2016.

[24] I thank Ted Lendon for help with this formulation.

[25] See further Bryen 2016b.

emperors like Caligula would have reinforced these tendencies substantially.[26] By contrast, mandarin attention to the praetor's edict (and a few other edicts, such as that of the aediles, or market regulators) or to the elaboration of discussions of previous jurists gave the imperial jurists cover. Since the Urban Praetor was fundamentally in charge of civil or private law, by commenting on his edict the jurists would not have to say much about potentially sensitive matters like criminal law – and certainly not criminal law as it was actually practiced, in Rome or elsewhere (i.e., badly, and under the force of great political pressure).[27] Similarly, though jurists might in practice advise an emperor or a governor on particular aspects of his job, they certainly would not have to go on at length about how a governor ought to run his province. Such a topic was unseemly – beyond the bounds of literary decorum – and potentially dangerous.

***

None of this should be taken to mean that there was not a great deal of "provincial" law, or even provincial cases that made their way to Rome. The epigraphic and papyrological records are suffused with legislation by emperors and governors that related to matters pertaining to particular provinces. Jurists might also remark on such things periodically, if only in passing, or because provincial practices might shed light on other questions (like the nature of imperial jurisdiction).[28] But the very difference of the provinces meant that jurists could easily ignore provincial problems. Insofar as *ius* was, at its

[26] On the vexed question of the *ius respondendi*, see Tuori 2007: 71–134; on the social background of the jurists of the early empire, Syme 1958: II: 760–62; Bauman 1989; and in general Kunkel 2001; as counselors of emperors, see Crook 1955, and of governors, Weaver 2002; Kantor 2017b. Caligula threatening to abolish jurisprudence as a profession: Suet. *Gai.* 34.

[27] Such is the verdict of lawyers going back at least to Mommsen 1899: 340; cf. "very unsatisfactory" (de Ste Croix 1963: 11); Harries 2007: 28–42 attempts a partial rehabilitation. On juristic neglect of criminal law, see Fanizza 1982, who gathers the meager pre-Antonine sources on pages 4–11. On the ways in which courts tended to replicate social relations, see Meyer 2006; Meyer 2016. The "processes" that came to light with the publication of the *SC de Pisone Patre* in the 1990s did little to reassure the lawyers.

[28] E.g., Jul. 1 *Dig.*, Frg. 5 Lenel = *Dig.* 1.18.8. Note also a rare moment of candor from a first century jurist: Proculus, 4 *Ep.*, Frg. 9 Lenel = *Dig.* 1.18.12: a governor should do what *ought* to be done at Rome, rather than how things actually are done at Rome.

core, an account of the obligations that attached *to citizens*, things in the provinces were necessarily different – each community would of course have its own sets of rules, which pertained to its own citizen body.[29] Those communities were free to discipline their citizens in whatever way they liked, provided they did nothing that was overly repugnant to Romans.

Yet the very press of provincial claims made this position untenable over the longer term. To begin with, despite the formal or theoretical difference between province and metropole, there was a remarkable amount of convergence in the substantive laws of particular communities. Provincial communities were also often governed by edicts, generated in Rome, and these seem to have converged over time. What is more, the provinces were filled with Roman citizens. Some were Italians permanently settled in provincial contexts (like colonists); others were mere sojourners there for commercial opportunity, travel, or war. Yet others were themselves also citizens of provincial communities who for one reason or another had received Roman citizenship, or the freed slaves of Roman citizens who had returned to their hometowns.[30] Finally, provincial subjects themselves had, over the course of the first two centuries, become especially adept at a rhetoric of complaint that was carefully calibrated to engage the sympathies of Roman administrators, regardless of the precise personal status of these provincial subjects. The provinces, in other words, were rife with opportunities to think, at great length, about the operation of government, the conflict of laws, or the responsibilities of a citizen or subject to his or her community or communities.

This process of legal accretion had been going on since the first century BC. It lived in archives, diffused across various points of the provincial landscape, or was memorialized in stone inscriptions that local communities chose to put on display. It may have provided an important set of resources to provincial communities, but its very local nature and its uneven character meant that the central state was essentially at a disadvantage with relation to all of these various sources of law. This must have frustrated jurists as well, who would have known – had they taken an interest in such things – that they worked with a highly incomplete record.

[29] Gai. *Inst.* 1.1. [30] On the relative numbers of such Romans, see Lavan 2016.

One solution might have been to craft a broader framework for provincial law, if only as a default. Even then, it is not until the second century AD that we finally see a juristic work attempting to comment on the pretorian edict as it applied in the provinces. This work, Gaius' *ad Edictum Provinciale*, is worth some attention. It is the earliest work of Roman jurisprudence to take a specifically province-centered perspective. We might ask what, if anything, would have been at stake in that choice.

As with all works of Roman jurisprudence, Gaius' commentary comes to us incomplete. It is preserved as a series of fragments, excerpted or edited by the compilers of Justinian's *Digest*. And though the number of fragments is comparatively large, the bulk of the work is lost. Still, the Justinianic compilers worked quickly and frequently preserved material that was not formally relevant. The compilers were told to bring all the works of jurisprudence up to date to function in the empire of the sixth century AD – thus in theory any headings that dealt specifically with law as practiced in the provinces would have been removed. This poses a substantial challenge to modern scholarship, for at least in theory anything capturing provincial difference would have been made formally irrelevant by the extension of Roman citizenship to the free portion of the population in AD 212. Of course, the matter was never so simple in practice. More important, for present purposes, is that the compilers were notoriously incomplete, and in at least some cases we can often see shadows of what was left behind. As with all fragmentary literatures, caution is important but ought not to block attempts at interpretation.

Even taking these later edits into account, Gaius' commentary *On the Provincial Edict* is remarkable primarily because it is disappointing. The great bulk that remains addresses questions relevant only to Roman citizens or communities of Latin citizens in the provinces. It manages to avoid nearly all specific references to governance. One would be hard pressed to use it to understand what made the work of a Roman governor unique or difficult, or even what sorts of problems a man in such a position would be likely to find, much less what sorts of matters were of concern to his subjects. It is hard to avoid the conclusion that, in attempting to think through a "provincial edict" (whatever such an edict may actually have consisted of, a question on which scholars disagree sharply) Gaius found himself at something of a dead end, and chose to focus instead on the sorts of cases that he was most comfortable with as a jurist who wrote primarily about the laws of the city of Rome.[31]

There are, however, a few hints that the provinces were a place of difference. Insofar as this text is about law operating in the provinces, Gaius periodically takes pains to remind his readers that what "they" do "there" is different, in important ways, than what might be expected at Rome. We might take as an example the law of sale. Sale, Gaius insists, does not operate according to models whereby earnest money (*arrha*) seals the transaction; instead, it is completed at the moment where there is intersubjective agreement about a thing and a price.[32] Buried behind this seemingly picayune distinction might be something deeper. Discussions of *arrha* marked some sensitivity to difference: *arrha* was indeed a feature of Greek and Near Eastern law (though Gaius does not specifically say that *arrha* was a Greek practice, nor that agreement about a thing and a price was a particularly Roman practice). So we might take this discussion as evidence of Gaius' awareness that things in the provinces might be done differently – and an attempt to remind Roman citizens that such different practices did not apply to them.

We should not be surprised by a warning about difference. Indeed, we have already met the claim, in Gaius' *Institutes*, that "all peoples who are governed by laws and traditions use partly their own laws, and partly the law common to all peoples; that which each people makes for itself is distinct to it, and is called its civil law (*ius civile*)."[33] Difference, on such an account, is not surprising or problematic. But such observations are deeply inadequate, especially compared to what we might expect of a Roman jurist who may well have spent long sections of his career in the provinces.[34] They are inadequate because they are essentially pre-ethnographic: they note difference, but they are not connected to a broader understanding of how difference

31 On the broader problem of the "provincial edict," see Buckland 1934; Guarino 1994 [1969]. On Gaius' *Ed. Prov.* specifically, Honoré 1962: 70–96 thinks the work was intended as an aide to working governors; Diósdi 1976, largely unconvinced, finds the work puzzling.

32 10 *Ed. Prov.*, Frg. 238 Lenel = *Dig.* 18.1.35.pr-4. Cf. Gai. *Inst.* 3.139.

33 1.1. Compare also Gaius' remarks on bilingual stipulations: *Inst.* 3.93.

34 Honoré 1962 makes much of this; it is not impossible.

works within a larger system, or why it occurs in the first place. That is to say, they fail to explain it.[35]

There is only one small hint in Gaius' *Provincial Edict* that "provincial" is a category that does more than mark geographic distance, but refers rather to a world that operates with different assumptions about power and privilege. Gaius contemplates a scenario where a middling or unremarkable plaintiff might desire to get back a disputed object from an opponent, only to find that his opponent connived to transfer the object to a person who might be harder to sue – someone who was simply more powerful (*potentiorem*) or someone in a different province. Here we finally have some sense that we are in a world in which standard Roman assumptions about private law work less than optimally. Because provinces were bounded units, a plaintiff might be at an especial disadvantage in getting back an object which had left his province. To get his object back, he would have to travel to the court of a different governor to initiate a lawsuit, which would prove costly. Hence the analogy with trying to get an object back from a more powerful person: both would involve more than normal effort and expense.

But this particular analogy is telling in another way as well. Roman jurists did not, as a general matter, build into their hypotheticals characters like "more powerful" opponents. In the normal language game of Roman jurisprudence, a category like "more powerful" was simply outside of the rules: it was vague and unmeasurable, utterly unworkable as a driver of analysis.[36] For a jurist, thinking through the categories of Roman citizens' law where parties were only unequal according to a carefully defined schema, "more powerful" was as relevant to the analysis as "taller" or "more attractive." Yet "more

[35] This observation has nonetheless not stopped modern scholars from treating *arrha* at great, if not peculiar length. See, with further bibliography, Jakab 2005. Failure to meet the challenge of explaining difference in law might well have begun with Gaius; it continues to bedevil the field of comparative law today. See the remarkable discussion of Ewald 1995. For a provocative exploration of how encounters with legal difference might serve as provocations to richer imaginings of law, see Constable 1994. On the category of "provincial," and the sort of work it did for Roman thinking more generally, see Ando 2011.

[36] Cf. Callistratus, 2 *Ed. Mon.*, Frg. 63 Lenel = *Dig.* 4.6.9. Precious few references to *potentiores* exist prior to the age of Gaius: there are two possible exceptions: Paulus quoting (probably) Ateius Capito (manuscripts have Antaeus, otherwise unknown): *Dig.* 39.3.14 = 49 *Ed.*, Frg. 635 Lenel; possibly an opinion of Labeo: *Dig.* 2.9.1.1 = Ulp. 4 *Op.* = Lab. 11 *Ed.*, Frg. 24 Lenel. See further Wacke 1980.

powerful" did have particular salience in the provinces. Provincial complaints are filled with claims about the remarkable power of particular opponents, and their abilities to block attempts at litigation.[37] This was more than mere rhetoric. There were, in fact, people in the provinces who, because of the ways that Roman governance devolved governance onto local communities, were simply "more powerful." Here it is tempting to think that Gaius is actually reflecting a real circumstance that would be characteristic of a provincial context, rather than a mere hypothetical.[38] Tellingly, he slips into the first person to complain about the potential unfairness of an object being transferred to a more powerful man: "we cannot be equal (*pares*) with a more powerful man," he complains, especially in his own province.[39]

There is a glimmer, in this discussion, of a recognition that the provincial world is different in a way that matters: that it is characterized by an extractive empire where the powerful do not always or often engage in fair play but operate by intimidation. According to Gaius, such dirty tricks required the intervention of the governor. The governor, in such circumstances, should allow the plaintiff to sue the original defendant for the amount that it is worth to him "to not have a different adversary." One cringes imagining the procedures by which such a sum might be calculated, but the central insight is important, if again underdeveloped: how, more generally, might a governor operate to ensure that actual differences in power are mediated through legal forms? Was that, in fact, his job? And what sorts of intellectual adjustments had to be made to take account of a world in which certain people were structurally "more powerful" than others?

***

Jurists had largely failed to take up this challenge. The attention to the city of Rome, to a context where jurists could hypothesize a world of citizens who fit into a small number of categories, had long served to

37 E.g., *P.Mich.* III 174 (AD 146–47); *PSI* XIII 1323 (AD 147–48); *P.Wisc.* I 33 (AD 147); *P.Lond.* II 358 (= *M.Chr.* 52, AD 150–54); *P.Fouad.* I 26 (AD 158–59); *SB* XVI 12678 (AD 179); *P.Sakaon* 36 (= *Sel.Pap.* II 293, AD c.280). Cf. the rhetoric of the epigraphic petitions found in Hauken 1998.

38 Cf. Wacke 1980: 577.

39 4 *Ed. Prov.*, Frg. 112 Lenel = *Dig.* 4.7.1–3. Cf. a similar usage in Gaius' monograph on the XII Tables: 6 *XII Tab.* Frg. 441 Lenel = *Dig.* 44.6.3.

make the work of jurisprudence possible. To the extent that empirical noisiness intruded upon such a system, recourse could always be had to legal fictions that papered over it.[40] To take account of actual differences, where certain actors might, in fact, be marked by substantial differences in their capacities, was a harder challenge. The language of private law offered few resources for this sort of undertaking, and we might imagine that a governor would have preferred to see himself as operating in a Ciceronian world where moral suasion and the threat of violence might more often win the day. But the question of how to account for the world of the provinces in the language of law was not going away. In fact, it had started to take on a greater sense of urgency in the second half of the second century AD. The sources of concern were, in fact, the same sources that seem to have concerned Gaius, and those who were of concern to provincial subjects more generally: the "more powerful."

To redescribe the world of Cicero and Quintus in the language of jurisprudence would prove a remarkable challenge, and one with lasting consequences. The first such attempt is evident in a small number of fragments by the Antonine jurist Venuleius Saturninus, who produced, among other works, a book *de Officio Proconsulis* (*On the Duties of the Governor*). Our knowledge of Saturninus is limited – nearly nothing reliable about his biography can be reconstructed.[41] Worse yet, only a few meager fragments of his book on the proconsul are preserved. Still, the preserved fragments are interesting. They deal with the holding of trials, the position of the *legatus* (the assistant magistrate to the governor, whose job was to handle cases in the governor's stead), the role of municipal magistrates, and the role of soldiers. Obliquely, they begin to construct answers to the questions posed by Gaius.

With Saturninus' fragments we are already in a different world from that of Gaius. The first insight seems basic and is contained in the title: to discuss the provinces meant to write about governors. Whereas Gaius had stuck to a well-trodden path (a running

40 Ando 2015.

41 There is only agreement that he is different from (though possibly related to) the jurist Claudius Saturninus, who composed a treatise *On the Punishment of Civilians*. See Liebs, apud Sallmann 1997: 133–35.

commentary on an edict), Saturninus innovated by recuperating an old genre to describe a new question. To write about an office was to resuscitate a Republican-era tradition in which jurists wrote treatises on officials (though at Rome, not in the provinces). Thus, a contemporary of Cicero, L. Cincius, seems to have written a book *On the Power of Consuls* (*de consulum potestate*); a generation later, G. Ateius Capito wrote a treatise *On the Duties of Senators* (*de officio senatorio*). Only the meagerest fragments of either are preserved, and the genre, such as it was, seems to have gone into hibernation thereafter.[42] Saturninus reanimated it to deal with the question of governance, not of Roman citizens, but of others. To write *de officio proconsulis* was new and would have given Saturninus a freedom that would have been absent if he had chosen to write, like Gaius, on the "provincial edict" more generally.

So far as content goes, though admittedly exiguous, the fragments of Saturninus' work share two leitmotifs: a heavy reliance on the texts of imperial statutes and an interest in punishment. The interest in discrete statutes is not surprising. Starting in the late second century, attempts were being made at least to gather, if not to rationalize, the great bulk of legislation that had emanated constantly from emperors and governors over the first centuries AD.[43] Other jurists started to read and to quote texts like imperial *mandata* (the instructions issued to governors by emperors). In the provinces themselves, the permanent staff of imperial offices can occasionally be found making digests of rules that had previously existed in scattered places.[44] Although such a thing cannot be proven, it is tempting to see in these attempts at gathering and digesting some response to provincial demands that governance – and the use of violence in particular – operate in

42 Fragments in Huschke et al. 1909: 26, 67. Recently the study of the genre *de officio proconsulis* has been reviewed and put on a solid footing by the dissertation of Crews 2016. The fragments are also edited, with discussion, in Dell'Oro 1960.

43 One might take as an example the *Libri XX de constitutionibus* by Papirius Justus, depending on how one chooses to date this work. See the new edition by Licandro and Palazzolo 2021.

44 On other official or semi-official digests of legislation, note the two copies of the *Gnomon* of the *Idios Logos*, now both dated to the Antonine period: Dolganov 2020a. For another attempt at digesting relevant rules, note the Customs Law of Asia (ed. Cottier et al. 2008), dating from the Neronian period. The *Gnomon* strikes me as a vastly more sophisticated effort than the cut-and-paste job of the first century. On *mandata*, see Marotta 1991.

accordance with *logos*. It was also a move designed to craft authoritative interpretations of local rules and by so doing, to put blocks in the path of provincial legal creativity. In this respect, we might imagine Saturninus as writing to solve what he perceived as a pressing political and administrative problem.

More interesting, however, is the attention to punishment. Here Saturninus seems to have made great efforts to begin to delineate the relative powers of provincial and local officials. But Saturninus also found himself wrapped up in a basic problem of writing about administration as a law-governed activity. The problem, for Saturninus, was not with governors, but with other agents acting under state authority: more powerful than normal provincial subjects, but at best semi-sovereign by comparison to the governor. So, for instance, Saturninus puzzled over the power of the governor's subordinate, the *legatus*, to administer punishments.[45] Municipal magistrates – and presumably, the elites of the Greek cities – similarly created a world of messy headaches. They were supposed to be in charge of the members of their own communities, and to ensure that the cities that they controlled were peaceable and orderly. They kept custody of subjects who awaited subsequent judgment, but were also potentially capable of making decisions about arresting and releasing subjects. At that level, we might imagine that they were sovereigns. So, to what degree might they be allowed to punish, and what might be the difference between a punitive act and a merely administrative one?[46] More generally, to what degree ought they to be trusted by the governor himself? Did they deserve deference, and, if so, then under what circumstances? Even during his days as a governor, the emperor Antoninus Pius had wrestled with precisely this problem.[47] These magistrates were also famously malfeasant, engaging in a variety of corrupt shenanigans that would provoke yet further complaints from provincial subjects.[48] Yet to describe them in the language of jurisprudence raised challenges.

In Saturninus' fragments we see the beginning of a theory of provincial difference, even if the contours of that difference resist specific

45 2 *Off. Proc.*, Frg. 48 Lenel = *Dig.* 49.3.2.

46 On the problems posed by this distinction in contemporary law, see Dubber 2005, 2018.

47 *Dig.* 48.3.6.1 = Marc. 2 *Iud. Pub.*, Frg. 204 Lenel.

48 2 *Off. Proc.*, Frg. 50 Lenel = *Dig.* 48.3.10.

articulation. In comparison to the city of Rome, at least as hypothesized by the jurists, the provinces were a site of potentially overlapping centers of power. (The comparison to Rome surely weighed upon Saturninus: he had also written a treatise on Roman criminal courts.) With the various constituencies present in Saturninus' work, a bureaucratic flowchart would do little to explain the proper role of each party. Each was, in a sense, partially sovereign. What becomes apparent on the basis of these fragments is that, if there is no single theory of provincial difference, there is at least the sense that the nature of difference is something that deserves interrogation.

***

It would not be until the Severan period that an answer to the question, "how should a province be governed" would start to be developed through the language of law, along with a set of theoretical presumptions that would allow government and law to be rethought together. Ulpian sits at the center of this story, combining in his work a remarkable attention to actual provincial administration, an almost comprehensive understanding of imperial legislation, and a set of presumptions about how provincial governance actually operated. Ulpian was, as a general matter, deeply sympathetic to the sorts of exploitation that provincial subjects faced. Throughout his works he attempted to align jurisprudence to moral concerns to avoid the production of unnecessary suffering. He also took special pains to think through the legal complexities created by the sorts of semi-sovereign and "more powerful" actors that caused such problems for the thinking of Gaius and Saturninus. But at the same time, Ulpian quietly but decisively rejected the very thing that provincial subjects had been insisting on: that law operate according to fundamentally *local* understandings of reasonableness and consistency. In his remarkable success in adapting metropolitan *Roman* jurisprudential categories to the provincial context, Ulpian ended up crafting an account of provincial governance that had, at the end of the day, very little need to listen to provincial subjects themselves.

Both of these strains of thinking jostle with one another in Ulpian's attempt to understand provincial government, *de Officio Proconsulis* ("On the Duties of the Governor," henceforth just *Proconsul*). It is on the one hand a text that seeks, through a set of benevolent instincts, to bring provincial communities within a system of law that is equitable.

But to achieve this, Ulpian has to postulate a world where governance is in important ways reducible to punishment, and where law is evacuated of its potential to serve as a language of political theory. Despite its success as a legal text, the *Proconsul* must have been read, from a provincial perspective, as at best a deeply flawed work; at worst, one that, because it emerged from a very provincial context, produced a "solution" to the problem of governance that sat uncomfortably with provincial demands that law conform to *logos*. But the text, and its place in Ulpian's thinking more broadly, nonetheless mark a milestone in the history of Roman thinking about provincial government. Ulpian's comprehensive attempt to define governance as *both* moral and juridical (or to insist that the two are identical) represents an important response to provincial demands. We shall turn, in the next chapter, to the effects of this sort of thinking on provincial legal and political landscapes more generally.

***

In Ulpian's ideal world, the responsibilities of governors would henceforth be laid out in books, rather than derived from archives. Instead of dialogue mediating face-to-face encounters between governor and subject where legality *emerged*, law would originate in an ontologically distinct sphere of idealized practices, as something to be *applied*. And instead of rhetorical fireworks that dazzled audiences and inspired awe, the governor would operate as a quiet functionary, correctly slotting problematic acts into categories and punishing accordingly. In each aspect of his account of ideal governance, we can see a deep engagement with, and a rejection of, the core ideas of legal politics that had been developing in the provincial world.

To get to the heart of Ulpian's thinking, though, involves a series of risks. To begin with, there is the issue of surfeit: Ulpian's writings are extensive, ranging across a wide variety of topics. He is the best preserved of the Roman jurists, occupying almost a third of the entire *Digest*. His preserved writings touch on a huge variety of topics, summarize generations of earlier juristic thinking, and attempt to integrate and explain acts of legislation. They range generically as well: commentaries on the praetorian edict and on earlier authors take their place alongside the treatise *On the Duties of the Proconsul* and other monographic works on things like adulteries or trusts – to say nothing of the volume of rescripts that Ulpian likely drafted.[49] The volume of work is genuinely staggering, even if we can say little about the chronological relationship between the works or their revision history.[50] But they leave the impression that Ulpian sought to produce something like a comprehensive restatement of the Roman legal tradition, reconciling divergences where possible, but also serving as an umpire between competing positions when necessary.

Equally important is Ulpian's context. It would not be extreme to speak of the Severan period as an age of legal revolutions. These came in multiple forms: attempts at promoting legal consistency in patterns of urbanization (such as the normalization of Egyptian towns as proper *poleis*, complete with councils); extensive legislation and the preservation of a steady stream of communications with provincial subjects and governors, which resulted in something like the acknowledgment of a precedential and increasingly bureaucratized vision of legality; and of course, the massive transformation of personal status across the empire that came as a result of the universalization of Roman citizenship in AD 212.[51] To what extent Ulpian might be taken as a cause or an effect of these developments is highly uncertain. In some measure, this is because we cannot confidently know the date of many of his individual works. But it is also because the Severan monarchs – coming themselves from the milieux of the provinces and with close connections to the multicultural and multiethnic world of the military – similarly were prone to take a great

49 Honoré 1994.

50 Honoré 2002 (orig. 1982) thinks the individual items in the corpus datable; I find his claims thoroughly unpersuasive. Many arguments might be offered against such an exercise (e.g., Frier 1984), but the most straightforward is the implausibility of the writing schedule that Honoré is forced to hypothesize. But even if this were plausible (and it is not), one might simply reflect on the ideological underpinnings of stylistic choice. Perhaps Ulpian composed quickly and orally. Such a thing is far from proven on stylistic grounds, but more to the point, an oral *effect* in writing might also be an ideological position that *ius* is not bound to texts but to people. Such a position, for instance, characterized the late antique Rabbis as well as the Roman jurists. On Honoré's claims about the authorship of constitutions, see Riedlberger 2020: 116–18 with further bibliography.

51 There is a massive literature on all of these matters. On the status of Egyptian towns/cities, see Bowman 1971. On Severan legislation, Coriat 1997; Herz 2018. On citizenship and the *Constitutio Antoniniana*, see recently Pferdehirt and Scholz 2012; Lavan 2016; Lavan and Ando 2021. For an overview of the period, see Ando 2012a. See now Herz 2025.

deal of interest in provincial management and governance. In other words, while context is obviously of great importance in assessing this body of evidence, it is precisely this context that remains elusive in the most important details. With that said, there are important affinities between Ulpian's ideas and Severan tendencies more generally; and I shall turn, in due course, to the relationship between Ulpian's jurisprudential project and the most important Severan innovation – the universal grant of Roman citizenship.

We might begin with Ulpian's benevolent side, noting some important features of Ulpian's work more generally. First and foremost, he was a careful student of provincial realia. He knows, for instance, that the praetorian interdicts that applied to certain types of water ("cold waters" or *aquae frigidae*) would not by easily applied in other places: thus, at Hierapolis in Asia "hot waters" (*aquae calidae*) were used for irrigation, just like cold waters in Italy.[52] Similarly, whereas in other provinces governors might relegate a convicted criminal to an island, in Egypt such a criminal could be exiled to one of the oases; and whereas in most provinces a governor could bar a convict only from his province, certain governors (those of Syria and Dacia) could bar a convict from several provinces at once.[53] Even the definitions of crimes might differ from place to place. Thus, he reports that in Egypt destroying water infrastructure like dykes was punished with condemnation to the mines, whereas in Arabia,[54]

> skopelismos is called a crime. Its nature is this: a number of enemies *skopelizein* the land of the person to whom they are hostile, that is, they place stones as a sign that if anyone cultivate the land, he will die horribly by reason of the plot of those who place the stones; this creates such fear that no one dares to approach this land, fearing the maleficence of those who place the stones. Such conduct the governor should punish severely, even with the capital penalty; for the very act threatens death.

For Ulpian, the provinces are not a world of potential or theoretical difference. They are a world of actual difference, where local peculiarities need to be taken into account in order to govern effectively.

[52] 70 *Ed.*, Frg. 1569 Lenel = *Dig.* 43.20.1.13.
[53] 10 *Off. Proc.*, Frg. 2243 Lenel = *Dig.* 48.22.7.5, 14.
[54] 9 *Off. Proc.*, Frg. 2234–35 Lenel = *Dig.* 47.11.9–10.

What is more, the provinces are different because they are the site of material extraction. Ulpian in general has a skeptical attitude towards practices of taxation and resource extraction. We have already noted how the extraction of resources – in the provinces in particular – was characterized by collusion and the laundering of state power (Chapters 2 and 3). Remarkably, even compared to other provincial authors, Ulpian seems fully aware that Roman government is a system that operates on the basis of taxation and, when necessary, compulsion and violence. He is, in fact, unusually if not refreshingly frank about such matters. Perhaps more importantly, however, when dealing with the topic of resource extraction Ulpian crafts his jurisprudence to mitigate the consequences of the structural inequality that characterizes these transactions.

We might consider two examples to better understand how Ulpian deals with the problem of inequality and resource extraction. First, the case of tax farmers (*publicani*). We have already had occasion to encounter Ulpian's lament that "Nobody is unaware of the extent of the audacity and insolence (*quantae audaciae, quantae temeritatis*) of cliques of tax farmers." In Ulpian's case, however, this was more than just generalized moaning about the necessary evils of empire; it was connected to a series of shrewd observations about the legal frameworks that ought to regulate practices of extraction. The starting point was a chapter of the praetorian edict that provided relief for anything wrongfully taken by a tax farmer (*publicanus*) or by one of his slaves (*familia*). This chapter of the edict was designed in the Republic, to deal with the predations of large companies of *publicani*; however, it was broadly interpreted in the first three centuries AD to cover tax collection more generally – and indeed, *publicani* were still responsible at the very least for the collection of indirect taxes (like taxes at ports or provincial checkpoints), but likely more taxes as well.[55] Though operating on nothing near the scale of their Republican predecessors, they were despised nonetheless, and known for shaking down whatever sorts of unlucky souls passed through their various checkpoints.[56] The provisions in the praetorian edict could thus be construed comparatively broadly.[57]

[55] Brunt 1990.
[56] van Nijf 2008. [57] Ulp. 55 *Ed.* Frg. 1304 Lenel = *Dig.* 39.4.1.1.

What is novel in Ulpian's analysis is that he operates from the presumption that, in the case of taxation, these imperial actors were prone to cheat not only with respect to the amounts that they extracted, but in terms of the personnel by which such amounts were extracted:[58]

It should be understood that in this context the title *familia* covers the tax farmer's slaves. However, if somebody else's slave is serving as a slave of a tax farmer in good faith, he is included as well. Perhaps, this is also so if he is serving as his slave in bad faith, since wandering and fugitive slaves are often (*plerumque*) even knowingly (*scientibus*) employed in this kind of work.

Through the haze of dispassionate juristic interpretation, we see close attention to the realia of governance. Knowing that the praetorian edict gave recourse to those who might blame the slave of a tax farmer for an illegal shakedown, tax farmers schemed to elude responsibility by employing an inscrutable mix of hangers-on as hired muscle. It takes no great act of imagination to understand why: should someone complain about excessive or illegal exactions, the tax farmer in charge would simply deny that *his* slave was responsible, pushing responsibility for proving the ownership of the slave in question back onto the unlucky defendant. Ulpian's solution is an elegant act of juristic expansion: even those who are not technically the owner's slaves would simply be counted as his slaves for the purpose of these transactions. *Publicani* were similarly constrained from hiding the identities of their slaves: the praetorian rule was that the wronged party had to state the identity of the slave who committed a wrong. But Ulpian also would permit the injured party to state in court, "Bring all of them so that I can pick out which one it is." As with slaves, so too with their owners: just as anyone who helped a tax farmer was deemed to be his slave, so too would anyone who was in charge of these slaves deemed to be their "owner." Though the praetor specifically said that liability for the slaves of tax farmers rested "against their owners" (*in dominos*), Ulpian construed this to mean, "against their partners in tax collection" (*in socios vectigalis*).[59]

All of these cases attest to the jaundiced eye of the experienced imperial administrator, impatient with sneaky defenses that rested

[58] 38 *Ed.*, Frg. 1072 Lenel = *Dig.* 39.4.12.2.
[59] 55 *Ed.*, Frg. 1306 Lenel = *Dig.* 39.4.1.6.

on debatable and fungible claims about the internal administration of a tax-extraction organization. Knowing that such defenses would produce interminable delays in a lawsuit and piles of worthless paperwork, the problem was avoided by deeming the relationships close enough and moving on. The point of the edict was, after all, to ensure accountability. But the ultimate justification for it, in Ulpian's eyes, was based in morality: "The reason for imposing a condition of this severity is that tax farmers ought to select good slaves for this type of work."[60] We might take this as a partial answer to the question raised by Gaius, above: on such a theory, the duty of government is to promote fairness in transactions that pit the weak against the strong by placing extra burdens on those in a position of advantage.

A second example will bring the picture into better focus. As we have already had occasion to note, municipal magistrates raised a seemingly impossible set of questions about the relationship between the weak and the strong with respect to property. Their case is interesting as a comparison to the *publicani*, since they were in a similar position. Responsible for the collection of direct taxes, the elites of the subject cities of the provinces were, as we have noted, a source of concern for Roman administrators. Governors were required to trust them and needed their cooperation, but they were well aware that they were also fundamentally an exploitative class who would take advantage of their positions when possible. The question remained, however, to what extent such magistrates could dispossess their own subjects of their property. These sorts of questions about the extent of semi-sovereign powers were especially bedeviling for attempts to theorize the practice of government.[61]

In the case of municipal magistrates, the solution that Ulpian found was essentially *opposite* to the solution he proposed for dealing with the depredations of tax farmers: whereas tax farmers had to be treated in a special way, distinct from private citizens, to check their tendency to unfairness, municipal magistrates should be treated almost exactly as private citizens. If, in the course of their normal

60 *Ibid.*

61 18 *Ed.*, Frg. 627 Lenel = *Dig.* 2.1.12; 42 *Sab.* Frg. 2896 Lenel = *Dig.* 47.10.32. Cf. 11 *Ed.*, Frg. 371 Lenel = *Dig.* 4.2.3.1.

duties of extracting resources, they caused damage inappropriately, they were to be held liable under the terms of the basic Roman statute on damages, the *lex Aquilia*:[62]

> Municipal magistrates may also be liable under the *lex Aquilia* if they do any damage unlawfully. So if one of them seizes your cattle by way of security (*pignori cepisset*) and kills them by starvation because he would not allow you to take them food, you must be allowed an action on the facts of the case. Again, if he thinks he is taking security under the provisions of a statute but he does not take it in accordance with the law and he returns your things worn and spoiled, it is said that the *lex Aquilia* applies. And, indeed, the same must be said even if he did make the seizure properly under the statute; but, on the other hand, if a magistrate does some injury by violence (*violentius*) against someone who resists lawful process, he will not be liable under the *lex Aquilia.*

The discussion here focuses on the taking of security (*pignus*). Behind the technical questions, we might imagine a transaction of the following sort: in each of these cases, the magistrate is extracting taxes, and has a claim on the property of one of his subjects because the subject owes a payment in cash or kind. Because of the nature of agricultural cycles, the subject might not have, or might not yet have, the requisite payment near to hand. In lieu of payment, the magistrate would have two choices: (a) to extend to the subject a loan, on terms very favorable to the magistrate (thus eventually ensuring a cycle of indebtedness to local bigwigs that would operate to the benefit or aggrandizement of the latter); or (b) to seize other property as security, presumably to be returned upon discharging the original debt (the taxes owed in cash or kind). The former was obviously the preferable option for the municipal magistrate; the latter more of a threat to get the subject to agree to the former. It also makes clear why, when seizing goods like animals as a pledge, the magistrate might be prone to treat them badly or with indifference.

Still, at a theoretical level, this sort of transaction should be straightforward: Roman praetorian law placed obligations on the holder of a security or pledge to keep the secured object in good condition and to return it upon discharge of the debt. But as anyone who has had the misfortune of working with a pawnbroker knows, the formalities

[62] 18 *Ed.*, Frg. 627 Lenel = *Dig.* 9.2.29.7.

of such transactions often belie a nastier reality.[63] As Ulpian hints towards the end of the passage, such seizures might at times be resisted (illegitimately) by violence, and if violence was returned it created no liability. But Ulpian also understood the darker side of these transactions, and he tried to interpret the law so as to correct them. Even though the parties might be unequal, both parties were to be treated, at law, as formally equal: a magistrate would be liable, just as any other ordinary subject, for any damages to the seized property, and liable, under the terms of the *lex Aquilia*, to pay double damages in cases where he did not ensure a high standard of care for the seized property. Similarly, he would be liable even if, thinking he was acting lawfully, he was nonetheless mistaken in taking the property in the first place. In contrast to the tax farmers, whose inequality necessitates putting them in a legal space distinct from normal people, the municipal magistrates are brought to a point of fairness by treating them as if they were simply other subjects, with duties to their fellows. It might be added that this is, in important ways, also a way of gently reminding such men that what they felt was their natural superiority over their fellow citizens was, in fact, no such thing.

In both cases – *publicani* and municipal magistrates – the law can be interpreted to operate to the advantage of the weaker parties, thus placing them into a relation of greater equality with respect to their legal adversaries. But to come to the correct legal conclusion in such acts of legal interpretation, one must keep one's attention on the fact of inequality. Thus, in a different work, Ulpian wonders about the question of extortion: to what degree should a claim for illegal compulsion or extortion (*metus*) be entertained? Which cases of compulsion might be rectified by the governor's ability to offer the remedy of "restoration" of the status quo ante (*restitutio in integrum*)? This was an unusual and somewhat extreme remedy, normally restricted to minors and wards. People who were neither minors nor wards nonetheless complained with great frequency, both in court and likely to anyone else who would listen, about exactions that they had paid but

[63] For comparison, see Woloson 2009; Smail 2016. For a case of animal seizure from the Byzantine world, *P.Cair.Masp.* I 67002 (AD 567). There is little reason to think that structural features of the earlier Roman period would have prevented identical behavior. See Lepelley 1983.

later regretted paying. They might easily declare that they only paid them under duress. Evidence would necessarily be hard to come by. Were such claims, then, deserving of a remedy designed for children?

As in the cases just enumerated, Ulpian's solution is to look to the relative rank of the parties. In the case of a man of rank, such a claim ought not to be heard unless the man of rank can present "the most manifest proofs of violence" (*apertissimas probationes violentiae*). But in the case of a weaker man, a different standard applies: "If, terrified by a reasonable fear of an inquiry to which a powerful opponent (*potens adversarius*) has threatened to bring him in chains, a person sold under compulsion what it was lawful for him to keep," the governor will give that person the remedy of restoration (*restitutio*).[64] The distinction between weak and strong was founded in the experience of governance: a wealthy man, Ulpian argues, need not ask for the unusual remedy of restoration – he can simply go to court and sue. A weak man could, in theory, do the same. But he wouldn't, and Ulpian knows this.

We might take this attention to inequality as the putting into practice of Celsus' definition of law and jurisprudence itself, a definition that Ulpian himself praised as particularly "elegant": that law (*ius*) is "the art of the good and the fair" (*ars boni et aequi*).[65] Such a claim can obviously be brushed aside as mere puffery, or even as a myth that a lawyer might tell himself. It seems to have been just this for Celsus – that is, it was at best a highly abstract or aspirational principle. But for Ulpian, schooled in the realia of provincial government, this sort of claim had deeply practical ramifications: it meant that, in cases where under color of law a stronger person might take from a weaker, the jurist was under a responsibility to construe the law in such a fashion as to mitigate the effects of inequality on the transaction – and always with an eye towards the likelihood that a powerful party, especially in a situation of semi-sovereign privilege, would

[64] 4/5 *Op.*, Frg. 2333 Lenel = *Dig.* 4.2.23.1–2; this fragment should be read in conversation with 12 *Ed.*, Frg. 428 Lenel = *Dig.* 4.6.10, on *restitutio* in cases where officials in a municipality (among others) bind people in chains such that they cannot look after their own business. On the importance of the category "child" in thinking through imperial governance, a provocative comparative study can be found in Premo 2005.

[65] 1 *Inst.* Frg. 1908 Lenel = *Dig.* 1.1.1.pr.

be prone to cheat. This is more than an abstract belief in "human rights" or some other such category;[66] it is instead an agenda for legal interpretation's role in guiding government by constructing checks on all of its subjects and especially the most powerful among them. Ensuring fairness might be taken as the foundation of a hugely ambitious interpretive and administrative project.

***

It was no doubt a major horizon in thinking about provincial government for a jurist to become concerned about exploitation. This concern allowed imperial rhetoric about benevolent government to echo in the register of jurisprudence in ways that it had not thus far. It was perhaps even more remarkable to acknowledge that the problem of the "more powerful" meant making adjustments to one's interpretive moves. But there was a darker side to Ulpian's thinking as well. To speak more extensively, even systematically, about provincial governance required a different tactic. To adequately explain the duties of the governor meant, for Ulpian, to speak about violence and punishment.

The *Proconsul*, written sometime in the early 200s, finds itself in precisely this quandary.[67] It tries to hold in equipoise the demand for equity and the requirement for violence, skepticism towards the powerful and the need to keep order. It was similarly an attempt to bring together the two strands of thinking on provincial government that had begun to diverge in the first century BC. That is, it is simultaneously a work of jurisprudence *and* an attempt to align the actions of the proconsul with a thoroughly moral vision of government. Implicitly, it makes the claim that these are in fact parts of a whole. That is, it asserts that the practice of government can be described in the language of jurisprudence, and that jurisprudential language can be made to align sufficiently with moral concerns to provide an exhaustive or at least adequate description of the duties of the governor. It is, in this sense, an attempt to juridify provincial governance *as a whole*. The *Proconsul* is thus a hugely ambitious text. It is also a deeply flawed one.

We might begin at the level of form. Unique among works of jurisprudence, the *Proconsul* begins with a book on the journey of the

66 "Human rights": Honoré 2002. 67 In general, Mantovani 1993–1994.

governor to his province and closes with a book about his departure. The unique form was no doubt consciously chosen to suit Ulpian's broader goal of presenting the governor as a fundamentally moral agent. This section of the text is hortatory, thick with verbs that describe customary and acceptable action: what the governor "ought" to do (*debet*, *oportet*), or what is customarily done (*solet*).[68] An unusual amount of attention is paid to the expectations that provincial subjects have of the governor himself. An example might suffice to illustrate the general tone of the first and last books:[69]

> While it is indeed better (*melius quidem est*) that a proconsul go out to his province without his wife, he can also do so with her, provided he is aware that during the consulship of Cotta and Messala the Senate decided that for the future if any delinquency were committed by the wives of those who had gone off to take up office, they themselves would be held to account for it and to make satisfaction therefor. The proconsul, before crossing the bounds into the province assigned to him, ought (*debet*) to send on an edict announcing his own arrival; this should contain some commendation of himself, such as perhaps that he is on friendly terms with citizens of the province or is related to them, and, most important, it should excuse the inhabitants from coming to meet him either publicly or privately, on the ground that it is right and proper for everyone to receive him in their own country. He will be doing the right and mannerly thing (*recte autem et ordine faciet*) if he sends the edict to his predecessor and gives him notice on which day he will arrive over the boundary. For uncertainties and unexpected events are especially upsetting to provincials (*provinciales turbant*), and they interfere with business. He must observe this point (*observare opertet*) in making his entry, that he enters by that part of the province where such entries are customarily made (*moris est*), and that he pays attention to what the Greeks call *epidēmiae* (stopping-off places) or *kataplous* (ports of entry), whatever be the city to which he first comes or at which he first lands. The provincials set a high value on fidelity to that custom and to prerogatives of this kind (*magni enim facient provinciales servari sibi consuetudinem istam et huiusmodi praerogativas*).

Ulpian thus bookends the *Proconsul* with a lengthy discourse on how to operate not just lawfully or morally, but also according to the expectations of subjects. Patience and the impression of pliability sit at the heart of this account. The governor must at all costs avoid offending his subjects. This is an important move in the argument.

[68] Mantovani 1993–1994: esp. 205.
[69] 1 *Off. Proc.* Frg. 2142 Lenel = *Dig.* 1.16.4.1–5.

First, it makes a claim that there is no conflict between acting according to the expectations of subjects and acting lawfully and morally. The governor is supposed to listen carefully to speeches prepared by provincial subjects, to put up with being forced to take interminable tours of local monuments, and to pretend not to be irritated by this. He is expected to receive gifts – though of course not all of them – thus putting on a show of binding himself within reciprocal relationships to local elites and their cities.[70] Provincial customs are to be respected – and such customs are *presumed* to be respectable. Not a word is said about provincial customs that might be considered offensive or primitive, like child sacrifice at Carthage, or merely gauche, like jabbering on in Greek about one's city's connection to the Trojan War.[71] Though marked by difference (in language, customs, and status), provincial subjects are to be construed as *partners* in the broader transaction of governance. The governor, in turn, is expected to behave as if governance were purely consensual – as a favor one does for one's subjects. It was of course no such thing.

This ethical discussion of the work of the governor is therefore also, *mutatis mutandis*, a discussion about the conduct and structure of provincial politics. "Political" claims are to be articulated, ideally, by representatives of particular communities. Others are to stay in their own territories and await the governor's subsequent arrival. The remainder of those present for these political affairs are, ideally, to be onlookers, and perhaps to cheer at the appropriate moment. Politics, on such a reading, consists of a realm of space for communication and reciprocity. The governor is supposed to listen and receive gifts, and to praise local attractions. To do so is to respect local customs and to salve local egos. Surprises are to be avoided.

In defining his terms in this way, Ulpian makes a subtle but critical move. In the *Proconsul*, politics happens in a space largely apart from jurisdiction. Politics is what one does when arriving and departing – what one does when establishing the consensus required for governance. Governance, by contrast, becomes a matter of organizing courts, managing local officials, and applying laws – criminal

70 2 *Off. Proc.* Frg. 2147 Lenel = *Dig.* 1.16.7.pr; 1 *Off. Proc.* Frg. 2145 Lenel = *Dig.* 1.16.6.3.

71 If, indeed, it was still occurring. See further Shaw 2016.

laws, in particular. We shall turn to the laws presently, but it is worth noting, at the outset, that this move to separate politics from jurisdiction ought to be read in the broader context of provincial claims about the centrality of the courtroom. For these subjects, the court of the governor was a privileged place to interrogate imperial power and to articulate claims about community, fairness, and reason. Ulpian, himself from a provincial context, would have grown up in a world suffused with the sorts of stories about jurisdiction that made up such an important part of "provincial" legal ideology, be it elite or subaltern. Yet he refuses to accept their premises. Courts, for him, are not a space for negotiating the conditions of fair governance, nor a place for elaborate and bewitching rhetorical fireworks. They are, and ought to be, a space apart from politics. They are a place to produce order. To follow the logic of the *Proconsul*, to do this might be divided into two broad headings. First, was to figure out how best to assign public burdens and distribute public honors. Second, to produce order meant to punish. In both cases, the goal was to preserve jurisdiction as a space apart from political contest. The structure of *de officio proconsulis* as reconstructed by Lenel (1889).

Book I
- On arrival
- On delegated jurisdiction
- On gifts

Book II
- On touring the province
- On jurisdiction

Book III
- On tutors and curators
- On municipal magistrates

Book IV
- On municipal law (Part 1)

Book V
- On municipal law (Part 2)
- On the assizes

Book VI

On guilds
On rights to inheritances
On manumissions

Book VII

On public order
On processing accusations
On custody of the accused
On failure to appear
On temple robbers [and Christians?]
On fortune tellers and prophesiers
On the Julian law concerning treason
On the Cornelian law concerning assassins and poisoners
On the Julian law concerning bribery

Liber VIII

On the Julian law concerning public and private violence
On the Pompeian law concerning parricides
On the penalties of the Cornelian testamentary law
On witnesses
On torture
On the cruelty of masters
On shipwrecks and arson
On speculators in grain
On rustlers
On thieves
On burglars and plunderers
On cheating

Book IX

On punishing freedpeople
On pickpockets
On prevaricators
On illegally possessing estates
On the movement of boundary stones
On the annona
On the Fabian law
On various delicts

On presenting the accused
On punishments (Part 1)

Book X
On punishments (Part 2)
On the goods of the condemned
On leaving the province

We might begin with the materials preserved in Books III–VI. Ulpian begins his discussion with questions of *tutela* and *cura*, two of the most burdensome public obligations that members of cities were asked to undertake (see further the discussion in the next chapter). In a society with extremely high rates of adult mortality, a disproportionate number of children might be deprived of their parents and left without a family member who might see to their affairs.[72] In some cases, a deceased parent might have provided by will for a particular person to serve as the child's guardian; but in the case of children with neither an appointed guardian nor a close relative, magistrates simply appointed private individuals as financial guardians. These guardians were responsible for the full property of their wards, under the obligation to manage their assets to a high standard of care, to represent their wards in any litigation, and to approve of any transactions that affected the ward.[73]

Undertaking such obligations was burdensome not only because the management of such estates was complicated on a day-to-day basis, but also because the tutor or curator would be held personally liable for any mismanagement. He could be – and, it seems, frequently was – sued by his ward and by others both during and after undertaking his obligation. If proven to have engaged in mismanagement, he would incur *infamia*, the degradation of one's civic rights. And as one can imagine in any situation that involved interfering in the politics of families, the management of personalities was a sometimes-Herculean task, and one at which even the most diplomatic guardian might fail. Thus, it is not at all surprising that few were eager to undertake the

[72] Saller 1994; Hübner and Ratzan 2009.

[73] Similar things were true in the case of tutors appointed to supervise the estates of adult women with neither parents nor husbands; however, by the period in question the authority of such tutors had become more of a formality.

obligation, and that one so burdened might try any reasonable strategy by which to excuse themselves.

It was, however, the job of the governor to make these assignments, not just in the cases of children and women, but also in delicate cases where a local person might have been deemed to be lacking in capacity. These cases called for discretion and respect. Though few fragments are preserved from this section, they seem to point in this direction: giving the governor maximum deference.

Similar things go for the materials preserved concerning municipal administration. Ulpian is concerned with finding ways to rank the members of the municipal council such that they might not fight amongst themselves on questions of honor or priority, but also so that burdens fall upon those most suitable for taking them on. This is the normal stuff of provincial oversight, and likely consumed a great deal of the governor's workload. As we saw in the case of Aelius Aristides (Chapter 7), those unwilling to take on their fair share might create bucketloads of work. This Ulpian is keen to avoid. Thus, in the case of assigning priorities in honors when listing a city's magistrates, Ulpian urges that, if the local law is unclear, the governor should come up with some rational – and presumably uncontroversial – principle for assigning priority, like seniority, former officeholding, etc.[74]

The governor should also avoid getting involved in any cases where people might appeal to some unusual local custom to avoid undertaking their burdens: if such a custom has not previously been tested in contentious litigation, Ulpian insists that it cannot be appealed to in a case of assigning public burdens.[75] (Cleverly, this doctrine seems to be a one-way ratchet: it is hard to see how any new "customs" could ever, under such a test, subsequently be introduced in court.) Finally, Ulpian puts forth rules that try to keep cases out of court. If anyone who dares to summon others to court for anything but a good reason – thus clogging the governor's docket – he shall be made to pay his opponent's expenses.[76] The leitmotif of these rules was to find ways to minimize local wrangling in court and maximize the chances that people would simply take on the burdens assigned them. In other

[74] 3 *Off. Proc.*, Frg. 2162 Lenel = *Dig.* 50.3.1.
[75] 4 *Off. Proc.*, Frg. 2170 Lenel = *Dig.* 1.3.34.
[76] 5 *Off. Proc.*, Frg. 2175 Lenel = *Dig.* 5.1.79.pr.

words, an effective governor would be one who would manage to best prevent political wrangling over questions of honors and burdens to occur in his court. Jurisdiction, on such an account, is essentially about getting local bigwigs to follow rules.

A similar pattern prevails when Ulpian turns to the broader question of punishment, which occupies the second major section of the *Proconsul* (Books VII–IX).[77] The *Proconsul* deals extensively with criminal law and punishment. It is likely that the sections on criminal law and punishment (which occupied most of the second half of the treatise) were preserved by the Justinianic compilers primarily because they each began with pithy definitions of what particular laws prohibited. Here the hand of the compilers seems especially evident: the material on crimes is largely definitional, explaining the crime itself, as well as whatever other offenses were, over time, folded into the original category (e.g., that people who participated in illegal organizations were now treated as those who had used armed gangs to occupy temples of public spaces – that is, those who used to be punished under *leges de vi*).[78] The late antique compilers were not especially interested in the intricacies of these discussions, and so excised most of the material that we might think of as traditionally "jurisprudential" – the patient exploration of the boundaries of these categories, and the complexities that they might pose in practice. These were surely there in the original text, but were removed (often in favor of the analysis of other contemporaries of and successors to Ulpian).[79] But even with the evident intrusion of the late antique editors (who also removed a large section of Book 7, which dealt with imperial legislation against Christians), the outline of the text is clear enough: the job of the governor was to enforce the laws and to punish those who transgressed them.[80]

And there were a great many transgressions that a governor had to watch out for. There were, of course, the occasional local prohibitions

[77] The contents of Book VI are something of a grab bag. Only four short fragments are preserved: one on illegal guilds, two on inheritance, and one on manumissions.

[78] 6 *Off. Proc.*, Frg. 2177 Lenel = *Dig.* 47.22.2.

[79] For an overview of the relationship between the texts found in the *Collatio* and those of the *Digest*, see Wieacker 1959: 390–408; Marotta 2000–2004: II: 100–18.

[80] For an overview and more detailed commentary on the individual provisions, see Nogrady 2006.

that he had to enforce: we have already seen, for instance, the unusual prohibitions on damaging dykes in Egypt or placing stones in Arabia. But the great bulk of the law that the proconsul had to enforce came from the traditional criminal statutes of the city of Rome. Thus, the text contains discussions of important Republican criminal statutes, like Julian laws concerning treason (*maiestas*), public violence (*vis*), and bribery (*peculatus* – a statute that had developed, under the Empire, to extend to counterfeiting); Sullan laws on assassins and poisoners (*sicariis et veneficiis*) as well as forgers of wills; and possibly also a Pompeian law on parricide.[81]

In addition to what we might consider these statutory crimes, the *Proconsul* also covers a series of what we might term "common law" crimes, many of which had been subsequently more carefully defined by imperial statutes: pillaging shipwrecks, driving off cattle, theft, and the rather more recently named and open-ended offense of "swindling" (*stellionatus*, literally, acting like a lizard).[82] In brief, the *Proconsul* shows that a great percentage of the work of the governor will actually consist not of the performance of consensual governance with his subjects (listening to speeches, receiving gifts, or visiting local monuments), but instead by holding those subjects accountable within a grid of offenses defined, historically, at Rome.

So, the text highlights both morality *and* punishment, consensual behavior *and* violence. To a modern audience these might seem like contrasts; yet we must work from the assumption that, to Ulpian, they are parts of a broader whole. The relationship seems to be causal. Punishment produces morality, violence consensus. Those not actively being punished are construed not as potential partners in the misdeed (who need to be warned of the governor's terrible power), but as a thankful audience, pleased that injustice has been ferreted out:[83]

> It befits a good and responsible governor to see that the province he rules is peaceful and orderly (*pacata atque quieta*). This he will achieve without

[81] The headings are mostly conjectured by Lenel 1889, but normally on the basis of sound reasoning and with reference to similar titles preserved in the *Collatio*; for a more robust justification for considering Frg. 2204 Lenel = *Dig.* 48.9.6 under the heading of a Pompeian law, see Nogrady 2006: 213–14.

[82] See now Lendon 2022: 107–9, with further literature.

[83] 7 *Off. Proc.*, Frg. 2181 Lenel = *Dig.* 1.18.13.pr.

difficulty, if he works conscientiously at ridding the province of wicked men (*malis hominibus*) and at seeking them out to that end. For he is duty-bound to search out temple robbers, bandits, hijackers, and thieves and to punish them each according to the evil he has done, and to punish (*coercere*) those who harbor them (*receptores*) – for without their help a bandit cannot lie hidden for too long.

So how does one square this commitment to punishment with the broader commitment towards protecting the weak from the predations of the strong? To begin with, it is worth noting that these punishments are directed, at least in part, towards powerful parties in the provinces. That is, whereas criminal justice in the contemporary world is largely directed towards the control and coercion of the poorest elements of society, Ulpian's working assumption is that, even if it is the case that poorer members of society are involved in the commission of crimes, they are also connected to more powerful men who operate to protect them. In this respect, there is a commonality between the first part of the treatise (dealing with bringing order to the affairs of the local aristocracy) and the second. Here, for each bandit or thief, there is also a *receptor*, and such a person is no less deserving of the governor's attention.[84]

This should not be taken to mean that governors were not to punish the poor. They were expected to do just that. But Ulpian uses punishment to reflect on a broader problem that accompanies governance. Governors, he argues, have an unfortunate tendency to punish the weakest, since the weakest are naturally far less capable of wheedling their way out of charges (much less were they protected by any of the provisions that had developed, since the second century AD, to protect the uppermost classes from degrading physical punishments).[85] But punishing the weak might not have the broader, socially desirable effects of actually keeping the province pacified. We might take the case of the robbers of temples as exemplary:[86]

The proconsul ought to impose the penalty for sacrilege more or less severely, depending on the status, age, and sex of the person, the nature of the property, and the time. I know indeed (*et scio*) that many have been condemned

[84] Shaw 1984: 15–16. Cf. Marcian, 2 *Pub. Iud.*, Frg. 199 Lenel = *Dig.* 47.16.1.
[85] Protection from degradation: Garnsey 1970; Rilinger 1988.
[86] 7 *Off. Proc.*, Frg. 2190 Lenel = *Dig.* 48.13.7(6).

to the wild beasts for sacrilege, some even burned alive, and others hanged on the gallows. But the penalty should be tempered to restrict condemnation to the beasts to those who have formed a band, broken into a temple, and carried off from there the god's offerings by night. But he who in the daytime takes an article of moderate value from a temple should be punished by sentence to the mines, or, if he was born to a higher position, he should be deported to an island.

Ulpian was not, of course, squeamish about the use of violence per se: he writes approvingly of personally having seen cattle rustlers in Rome having been thrown to the beasts, for instance.[87] What he seems to object to, in the case of the provincial governor, is the rush to punish the weak or the hapless in the harshest and most public way possible. The sorts of terrifying public punishments that operated to educate provincial audiences should be aligned to the most terrifying offenders. The weakest still need to be punished, of course, just not in such a dreadful and public way.

We might also note that there is an assumption about the power of punishment as a visible display: it does the most work for governance, it seems, when the person so displayed is actually terrifying or powerful (or both). This is in keeping with longstanding assumptions about the excitement provincial communities felt when truly problematic individuals got their just deserts: thus Cicero reports upon the deep disappointment, even anger, of the people of Sicily when Verres refused to display a captured pirate leader in public;[88] we have already met (Chapter 4) the anger of crowds in provincial cities when disruptive but influential Christians were brought out for public punishment. Ulpian's claim, however, has a further entailment. Because actually punishing powerful people in public is difficult and politically dangerous, governors may be tempted instead to present a simulacrum: they might claim that a weak person or a modest offender is actually a dangerous and powerful offender, merely to placate a

[87] 8 *Off. Proc.*, Frg. 2220 Lenel = *Coll.* 11.8.4: *Romae tamen etiam bestiis obici abigeos videmus: et sane qui cum gladio abigunt, non inique hac poena adficiuntur.* Parts of the text (without the first-person discussion) are also preserved as *Dig.* 47.14.1.3. The Severan jurists in general tend to be concerned about rights to private violence. This, it seems, comes especially to the fore in their various monographs *de Adulteriis*. These deserve a broader treatment.

[88] Cic. *Verr.* 2.5.65–67. Cf. *Dig.* 48.19.28.16–16 = Callistratus, 6 *Cog.*, Frg. 47 Lenel.

bloodthirsty crowd. But, for Ulpian, the miming of justice and the doing of justice are not, in fact, the same thing.

To make such a claim, even obliquely, betrays an understanding of the problems inherent in the office of the governor more broadly. Many men who served as governors failed to measure up to the challenge before them. In keeping with his skepticism towards powerful parties, Ulpian is not above critiquing governors and their common practices. Some, he insists, tend too much towards violence, or at least negligence. Thus, Ulpian insists that governors are not supposed to leave people to rot in jails, or to bind them over the long term in heavy chains; despite this, many are accustomed (*solent*) to doing so anyway.[89] Others are afraid to punish when necessary. Thus, governors must not hesitate to punish their own slaves and subordinates, should they offend – "indeed," Ulpian insists, "they *must* do this, so that others, deterred by this example, might offend less."[90] Governors, in other words, need to find the interior fortitude to engage in acts that they may find personally difficult or distasteful, rather than taking the path of ignoring difficult questions. Yet they must also balance this tendency towards – or need for – using violence with a commitment treating the weak fairly and not engaging in knee-jerk cruelty.

Such a balance was difficult to achieve, and many failed. Provincial defendants were a clever bunch, long practiced in finding pressure points on the criminal justice system. We might take as an example the question of what to do in cases where a party who has recently been found guilty suddenly proclaims that he or she has "evidence" of a plot against the emperor – a familiar ploy to avoid or delay in the application of a criminal sentence.[91] Most governors, Ulpian insists,[92]

> are so timid that, even after sentence has been passed on the man, they suspend the punishment and do not dare to do anything; others have no patience at all with persons who make any such allegation; while some do not [make it

[89] 9 *Off. Proc.*, Frg. 2241 Lenel = *Dig.* 48.19.8.9.

[90] 9 *Off. Proc.*, Frg. 2238 Lenel = *Dig.* 48.19.6.1.

[91] Evidence for this sort of shenanigan starts in the earliest days of the reign of Augustus (see the second Cyrene edict). That it persisted for so long and with such evident success speaks to a broader Roman failure to think through criminal jurisdiction.

[92] 9 *Off. Proc.*, Frg. 2237 Lenel = *Dig.* 48.19.6.pr.

a habit] either always or never to send them up, but inquire what they wish to bring to the notice of the emperor and what they may have to say concerning his well-being, after which they either suspend the punishment or do not. This appears to be the rational middle way.

The same goes for judicial torture. "This is a delicate and dangerous thing, and one that may pervert the truth" (*res est fragilis et periculosa et quae veritatem fallat*). All subjects, Ulpian insists, are different: some will be able to resist even the harshest forms of torture; others will lie and falsely incriminate others to avoid it.[93] Whether or not to believe a confession should be based not on assumptions about the nature of the person, but on a full consideration of the facts of the case and the testimony.

***

Subtly, throughout the *Proconsul*, Ulpian builds a picture of the governor as a sort of literary ideal. At the heart of this account is an abstracted, model governor who manages to successfully control and balance his violence. He must avoid the temptation to overuse it – that is, to direct maximal violence at parties that are minimally deserving – as well as the temptation to under-use it by indulging his own slaves or subordinates or by letting the powerful off when they truly deserved it. But when used properly, however, the violence he wielded could be a productive force in governing.

How, then, would violence relate to jurisdiction, and to politics? As we have already noted, the *Proconsul* proposes a space of politics, where the governor communicates with his subjects to produce a vision of consensus and mutual respect, as well as a space of legality, which is devoted primarily to the creation of order through the application of violence to rule-breakers. What, then, if politics should threaten to invade the courtroom? Would there be a way to insulate legality from quotidian politics?

The invasion of politics into the courtroom was a live possibility. Courts were spaces in which unequal parties might meet with great frequency. Ulpian indicates, in the texts discussed above, that the threat of going against a powerful adversary would often compel weaker

93 8 *Off. Proc.*, Frg. 2211 Lenel = *Dig.* 48.18.1.23. On torture, cf. the inscription recently published by Reger 2020.

parties to make choices that did not reflect their desires. So how, then, could such interactions be managed? To begin with, Ulpian proposed a traditionally "legal" solution: equip the weaker subjects with better expertise by giving them lawyers. The governor must strive to be patient with these advocates, but not so patient that they take him for a chump. He should ensure that they stick to the rules of the court – otherwise he should ban them, prohibiting them from representing clients.[94] Most importantly, he insists that advocates must be given to litigants in any cases where they might appear necessary: thus the proconsul should supply an advocate to "women, wards, and anyone who is weak, as well as to those who are not of sound mind," should he be asked to do so. But even if he is not asked, he should consider supplying an advocate anyway. He should also give representation to anyone who says that, "because of the power of his adversary" (*per potentiam adversarii*) he cannot find anyone to represent him. "For it is not right for someone to be oppressed by the power of an adversary – and in fact it causes hatred (*invidiam*) for the person in charge of a province, if someone should conduct himself with such arrogance that everyone is afraid to engage in advocacy against him."[95]

It is worth lingering over this discussion, for it brings together the main strands of Ulpian's thinking. When the illusion of consent, produced outside the courtroom, is shattered by the intrusion of the very relations of power that the law is called upon to regulate, then the law can no longer stand *outside* of social relations. When that happens, the governor will be hated, and consent will be broken. Goodwill turns into *invidia*. We have already met *invidia* in the courtroom (*phthonos* in Greek): the choking hate that one feels for another because the other person has a thing that they do not deserve to have. In this case, the *invidia* is targeted at the governor's powers, his ability to compel his subjects by using the prerogatives of his office. When the governor enmeshes himself in local systems of power, his ability to use violence authoritatively loses its moral anchor. It becomes merely the arbitrary power of the strong.

Ulpian's mistrust of the powerful is thus not only a problem in absolute terms (i.e., because it's bad for the strong to take advantage of the weak). It is a problem because abuse by the powerful might call

94 2 *Off. Proc.*, Frg. 2150 Lenel = *Dig.* 1.16.9.2; 10 *Off. Proc.*, Frg. 2246 Lenel = *Dig.* 48.19.9.pr-8.

95 2 *Off. Proc.*, Frg. 2152 Lenel = *Dig.* 1.16.9.5.

the entire project of governance into question. Subjects will see that the governor is unwilling to stand up to local bullies, conclude that he must be on the bullies' side, and seethe with rage. The result will be that the careful performance of consensual governance that Ulpian otherwise outlines in the introductory and concluding books will be just that – a performance, and not a particularly convincing one. The governor must therefore demonstrate that he is not merely replicating local power structures, arming with lawyers those people willing to challenge local authorities, no matter how dangerous they might be.

For Ulpian, ever the consummate lawyer, law must stand outside of social relations. This is the only way that the tensions in Ulpian's visions can be reconciled. The governor must play a dual role (precisely how is not explained): he has to be both *inside* a zone of social relations, enough that he can fraternize with and reassure provincial subjects; but simultaneously outside of it, the embodiment of a law that is, ultimately, transcendent of social interactions. Such a law must exist in a different ontological space.

We can see, in this reasoning, how the *Proconsul* might be conceived as a response to provincial demands: Ulpian is strongly committed to the proposition that provincial governance, to be effective, must be fair and equitable. A governor must not disavow his powers; he must instead channel them and be careful to hit the right targets. But he can only do this as a *law-applying* figure, presiding over a courtroom that is a space apart from normal political relations, or where normal social and political relationships are put into a state of suspension or equipoise for long enough that the governor can apply a law that is fundamentally free of quotidian concerns. He is to apply a law that was originally articulated in Latin, in the metropole, or by emperors. It is emphatically *not* a law to which provincial voices themselves contribute. Provincial populations, even though formally now citizens by the application of the *Constitutio Antoniniana*, are conceived of as being, in an important way, even more fully *subjects*. If there is *logos* here, it is the *logos* of lawyers, who could boast that,[96]

> [W]e cultivate the virtue of justice and claim awareness of what is good and fair, discriminating between fair and unfair, distinguishing lawful from

[96] 1 *Inst.* Frg. 1908 Lenel = *Dig.* 1.1.1.1. Cf. 1 *Reg.*, Frg. 2362 Lenel = *Dig.* 1.1.1.10: *iuris prudentia est divinarum atque humanarum rerum notitia, iusti atque iniusti scientia.*

unlawful, aiming to make men good not only through fear of penalties but also indeed under allurement of rewards.

To do this, according to Ulpian, was to practice "real philosophy, not sham philosophy."[97]

It must have deeply stung a careful provincial reader to hear such words: to hear a jurist insist that politics was fundamentally consensual rather than contentious; that the courtroom was to be a space in which punishments were determined and applied rather than a space for struggling over the terms by which someone was to be governed; that law was to come, unproblematically, from statutes and the decrees of emperors, rather than to be co-constructed by subjects in dialogue with the governor himself. Such were the basic postulates of provincial legal politics. Yet on Ulpian's theory, a governor would only need to hear minimal contents of certain sorts of provincial claims. Once a governor knew the parties, accounted for their status, and could find a pigeonhole into which to place their complaint, he would not have to put up with listening to them complain at great length, or even seeing them for more than a minimal amount of time. The governor becomes, on such a reading, ideally a processor of complaints into categories, rather than an active interlocutor with his subjects.[98] Discussion, such as it is, is relegated to his arrival and his departure. Broader provincial contests over the nature of documentation, the status of *logos*, the relationship between rules and *thauma* – all of these things now become incidental to the operation of provincial government, even distracting.

Creating a boundary between the application of law (the governor's jurisdiction) and the sorts of customary performances of respect to provincials (the traditions of the governor's arrival, the need to listen to provincials praise their hometowns) had other effects as well. When law is secured in an ontological space apart from social relations, practice comes to be something that could be measured against an abstracted ideal – nearly always to be found deficient in some aspect or another. Hence it becomes easy enough for Ulpian to criticize the acts of individual governors (keeping

[97] On the various contexts for this passage, see Nörr 2003 [1973].

[98] He also becomes subject to law himself, a point that I take up more fully in the following chapter.

people in chains or in prison, etc.) not on the basis of particular judgments about whether an act constituted cruelty or betrayed defective moral character, or even on the basis of whether an act was in keeping with the acts of historic governors before him, but instead on the basis of what a theoretical, ideal governor ought to do. Like the elusive "reasonable man" of the common law, such a governor was unconstrained by the misfortune of having to act in the moment to make best guesses and manage political outcomes. Such a governor was unconstrained even by the misfortune of being a material, living being.[99]

***

The *Proconsul* did not succeed in totally juridifying governance. We shall turn, in the next chapter, to other jurists and to their application of the language of Roman jurisprudence to provincial government. They painted on a much more ambitious canvas than Ulpian, desiring to describe not only the duties of the governor, but provincial bureaucracy more generally. Their collective contribution to the larger rethinking of the late ancient state would be to stretch the language of jurisprudence past the point of breaking to conceive of government more generally as an abstracted and radically decontextualized practice that might be approached not as an ethical endeavor, but as an exercise in rule-following. Ulpian would not go so far. For him, governance was undoubtedly a moral and ethical practice. He would insist, if obliquely, that there was to be no contradiction between ethical governance and legality. He would be fighting a losing battle.

Governance was henceforth to be discussed in the language of the metropole, anchored in a metropolitan framework, reducible to just another chapter in a long series of works on Roman private law. It was to be explained, ideally, by experts – not by subjects. And it was to be explained in an idiom, jurisprudence, that had long since lost its ability to speak convincingly about political engagement.

[99] Cf. Herbert 1927: 11–20.

9

Radical Bureaucracy

This chapter will serve as something of a coda. It seeks to describe the process by which the Roman government transformed itself, from a large, loose, and baggy monster of complexity, overlap, and political argument into something resembling a bureaucracy, defined by a rule of law.[1] At the center of this story sit two main actors: jurists and emperors. Their relationship was often fraught. Jurists hoped (sometimes against all odds) that emperors would take their counsel; and while emperors often promoted jurists to high office, they were also free to ignore them. Often they did. Their relationship was also chronologically discontinuous: the jurists of the early third century were responsible for outlining a vision of lawful governance; but it was the emperors of the fourth century and later who were to attempt, most energetically, to put this vision into practice.[2] Earlier emperors could and did collaborate, but the intervening chaos of the third century forestalled the transformation of juristic fantasy into actual fact.

The main target of the jurists' concerns was the provincial experience of legalism writ large: the bombastic politics, the endless claim-making, the demanding rhetoric, the perplexing kaleidoscope of jurisdictions over which governance was to be enacted. Ulpian had already taken the first step, imagining a political space based on affect

[1] Loose and baggy monsters: the phrase is an adaptation of Henry James' description of Tolstoy's *War and Peace*.

[2] See now Herz 2025.

and reciprocity that was radically discontinuous with the world of governance and jurisdiction, which in turn were reducible mostly the assigning of burdens and the enactment of punishment (Chapter 8). The jurists of the Severan period, both contemporaries and intellectual descendants of Ulpian, took the project yet further: they stretched the language of traditional Roman jurisprudence past the point of rupture to redescribe provincial government as fundamentally rule-bound. The result is a body of works that have been described, normally pejoratively, as fading into a period of "post-classical" or "epi-classical" jurisprudence.[3] This is, to be sure, the aesthetic judgment of lawyers, and should be discounted accordingly. But I should like to suggest that this aesthetic judgment is not entirely wrong. It is, at least, on to something. The sort of jurisprudential energy and imagination that characterized works that focused primarily on old controversies within private law are reduced, when they turn to questions of governance, into lists of rules and regulations. Their authors give the impression of being irritated with the constant din of provincial complaining. Gone, in much of this literature, are the old nods to dispute; gone are the gestures, even in writing, made to orality and dialogue.[4] The works that capture this attempt to redefine governance can be called "jurisprudential" primarily at the level of form: they are written in Latin (mostly), by men who were jurists. Yet unlike the works of private law (which these same jurists also wrote), the texts on governance do not sparkle with controversies and arguments. They simply define what ought to be done in particular situations. They are, in a sense, not jurisprudence but legislation.[5] It is in this respect that these texts represent the "radical" break with the traditions that preceded them.

Jurists trained their interests on provincial institutions that were previously taken for granted, and in so doing, these jurists took a

[3] Kunkel 1966: 114–15; Liebs, *apud* Sallmann 1997: 216–17. For a more balanced judgment, Ibbetson 2005. On the question of the continuation of jurisprudence in the so-called post-classical period, see e.g., Liebs 1993. On *ius controversum* as a feature of "classical" law, see Bretone 2008.

[4] Orality as a feature of juristic literature: Bretone 2008. From a different perspective, Bryen 2019b. For a provocative comparative study, see Rubenstein 2003.

[5] I take inspiration here from Schiavone 2012, though my chronological and causal explanations differ substantially from his. For an interesting comparative study, see Fishman 2011.

remarkable intellectual risk in essentially inventing a new body of law: the law of government.[6] Jurists' law, in this respect, was no longer just the law that prevailed to mediate relationships between Roman citizens; its language could also be adapted to mediate relationships between citizens and the state, and between the various constituent units of the state. And once the state was defined as a fully law-bound entity, it could no longer be imagined, even for ideological purposes, as primarily a network of elite men, bound together by a common culture and by an interlocking set of affective bonds. On the theory of the law of government, it would be impossible to maintain the ideological stance that society was ordered as a pyramid of reciprocity that linked Roman elites to local elites, and local elites to their populations – the very thing that Ulpian had sought to preserve, as a space apart from law, in his *Proconsul*. Instead, the state would emerge, in the law of government, as a counterpart to "society" more broadly.

This had two effects. First, in crafting the state, governed by law, as an entity that was essentially discontinuous from a broader "society," jurists had to rethink the place of affect in this system more broadly. Affect was a problem: as an ideological matter, affect was supposed to be distributed through society, linking people to their rulers.[7] But this came with the problem that affect was also imagined to make governors amenable to local politics (for they were required to *feel for* their subjects). Affect also gave discretion to elites and governors to do what they needed to produce a "just" solution on the ground and in real time. But this also meant, from the perspective of these later jurists (with their impatience for the politics of the governed), that officials ran the risk of becoming enmeshed in local systems of value – it was just politics all the way down. Affect, accordingly, was reimagined as normatively vested primarily if not exclusively in an emperor who was uniquely capable of sensing injustice and transcending the hidebound bureaucracy whose apex he represented. One might say, hearkening back to an earlier chapter (7),

[6] A designation I prefer to "public law," which both over- and under-describes the phenomena in which I am interested, or "administrative law," which strikes me as anachronistic for this period.

[7] Ando 2000.

that the emperor came to usurp the aesthetic and emotional role of imperial elites, and in so doing, reimagined the elites of the empire as the merest functionaries.

Second, in construing "government" as radically discontinuous from "society," and in imagining it as amenable to juristic rationalization, the jurists build a foundation for a fundamentally distinct idea of the role and nature of law. In the law of government, the writings of a jurist could always suffice to provide the framework for how government ought, ideally, to operate. Practice would by definition not have any effects on the ideal; it was always to one degree or another a defective cousin to writing. The ideal form of legality was thus to be found not in the courts of Rome or of the provinces, but rather in books, written by jurists. The only person permitted to make changes in this system was the emperor himself, and he would be required to do so through a series of exceptions, or through legislation – itself a textual practice, ideally stripped of the give-and-take of politics more generally. To put it differently, one could say that law was transformed, over the course of late antiquity, from a register of *speaking* about certain types of problems, to a mode of *writing*. It was a register, moreover, that was thoroughly monologic in character.

***

We might begin by noting what the law of government was *not*. The "law of government" never sought to define the entire government. Describing certain parts of government was straightforward and uncontroversial. Offices related to the governance of the city of Rome had long histories, and were amenable to juristic discussion: Ulpian, for instance, could write treatises not just on the duties of the Proconsul, but also on the duties of the Urban Prefect, the Prefect of the Night Watch, or the office of the Quaestor, among others; his contemporaries, such as Paulus and others, would write about similar offices, describing the various responsibilities of the office-holder, and in some cases, the origins of the office and its boundaries.[8] As I noted

[8] Note the historical analysis of Arcadius Charisius, 1 *Off. Praef. Pr.*, Frg. 2 Lenel = *Dig.* 1.11.1.pr.-1, writing in the age of Diocletian. On jurists' approach to history more generally, see Mantovani 2018.

in the previous chapter (8), the late second century brought a decreasing squeamishness about turning juristic attention away from the traditional categories of private law and towards the job of officials.

But there were nonetheless still important aspects of government that resisted explicit articulation. Only the politically inept would have dared to write a juristic treatise on the emperor himself, or on his household. (Though I shall return, towards the end of this chapter, to treatises *de iure fisco* – on the law concerning representatives of properties owned by the emperor himself.) Discussions about the functioning of the imperial family and household were better articulated through the idiom of panegyric – a language of stylized praise for the current occupant of the throne, wherein any critique took the form of references to historical practice. In any case, such fawning orators never dared to arrogate to themselves the ambition to define the state as in the language of law. Morality and tradition were their primary registers for speaking about the nature of imperial government. To the extent that they engaged in questions of law, it was to remark, always at a high level of abstraction, that good emperors followed or respected it – despite their acknowledgment that they were, in fact, superior to it.

In this the panegyrists were no doubt prudent. It would be fine for jurists to generalize about the position of the emperor: for instance, that he was not bound by the laws that he himself had made (this claim alone released the jurors from having to engage in certain types of analysis, for which they were surely grateful).[9] But pushing any farther than this could lead to awkwardness. Thus, if the emperor was released from the laws, was the empress similarly released? What about other members of the imperial family? What about imperial slaves – what recourse might a victim of their malfeasance have against their master? Jurists would balk at analyzing such awkward questions that constituted some of the deepest *arcana imperii*. Ulpian would come the closest, but his sense of anxiety was palpable: the emperor was formally released from the laws, Ulpian insisted, but the empress ought not to be understood as formally released; nonetheless, the emperors somehow gave empresses the same privileges as

[9] Marotta 2000–2004.

themselves.[10] Better to ask no more. It was hard enough to live within the contradiction – or in Ulpian's case, to die within it. To untangle it would make nothing easier.

The law of government was thus not political theory – or at least not comprehensive or normative political theory. Rather, it was a jurisprudential project that emerged to give description to those governmental institutions that were either uncontroversial (traditional magistracies at Rome) or, more importantly for present purposes, those institutions that caused political problems in the management of provincial government. The government of cities other than Rome loomed large in the law of government, as did criminal law and the law of procedure. The law of government, then, was very much a law concerning subordinate units of government, rather than the central features of the imperial system itself. It emerged, in the late second and early third centuries, as a way of trying to get a handle on all of the conflicts that these subordinate units of government posed by attempting to reinscribe them in an orderly and rationally apprehensible structure. Were it not for the awkwardness of the term, one might term the law of government apolitical theory, or even antipolitical theory.

***

We might start at the level of city government. One can hardly fault jurists for wishing to get a handle on the problems posed by city government and its attendant politics. The great bulk of any given city's acts of self-government in the first three centuries involved elaborate arguments over how to share and shift the financial burdens posed first by the necessity of the day-to-day upkeep of city facilities, and second by the requirement that individual urban units collect taxes on behalf of the imperial government. Despite the so-called "beneficial" ideology, in which the city's wealthy normatively were required to make contributions for the greater good (and in exchange, were rewarded with honors and praise), to participate in city governance was generally an expensive and low-reward endeavor.[11] Thus in

[10] Ulp. 13 *L. Iul. et Pap.*, Frg. 2027 Lenel = *Dig.* 1.3.31. Cf. the awkwardness of the Roman Senate in explaining the role of Livia in the punishment of Plancina: *SC de Pisone Patre*, ll. 115–20.

[11] The phrase comes from Nutton 1978. On the ideology of civic euergetism, see Veyne 1976; Zuiderhoek 2009.

practice, assignment to everyday duties was met with various forms of evasion, argumentation, and attempts to shift the burden onto one's local enemies – or just anyone stupid or weak enough to have to take it on himself.[12] We might here just recall the case of Aelius Aristides (in Chapter 7), determined not to meet his burdens to Smyrna (or elsewhere) on the grounds that he was simply too talented a rhetorician. His case was perhaps unusual, but similar things might be said about the otherwise unremarkable Achilles, nominated by the council of Hermopolis to the office of *kosmētēs*. Wishing to avoid such a nuisance assignment, Achilles volunteered, instead, to take the office of *exēgētēs* – notionally of higher rank – but only on the condition that he would pay a limited sum and be released from overseeing lands under lease. Yet his colleagues smelled obfuscation and sensed that Achilles had no intention of ever paying the proper amount of money for the office of *exēgētēs* in the first place. Thus, his colleague on the council, Olympiodorus, issued what was, in fact, a dare, cloaked in the form of imperial praises: "The fortune of our lord the Emperor ungrudgingly provides offices and increases the means of the city – how else could it be under the blessed governorship of Larcius Memor? So then – if Achilles wishes to be crowned *exēgētēs*, let him pay his entrance fee *immediately*; otherwise, he should be considered to have nominated himself to the office of *kosmētēs*!" Other members of the council piled on: "Throughout the day Achilles beat me, and, as I attest in these minutes, I am going to indict him before the governor for violence!" The *strategos*, presiding over the meeting, can be forgiven for having then called an intermission.[13] To find competent people to handle normal public service assignments was nothing if not a headache.

The division of city burdens was complex enough under the best of circumstances. It was yet more complicated because the duty to share burdens was undercut by an intricate system of excuses and immunities. By a process of accretion that took place over centuries, an increasing number of people procured for themselves the right to avoid sharing in common burdens. Sometimes this was on the grounds

12 In general, see Abbott and Johnson 1926; Quass 1993; Lewis 1997; Dmitriev 2005.

13 *P.Ryl.* II 77 = *Sel.Pap.* II 241 (AD 192). In general, see Bowman 1971. On the politics of civic burdens in Egypt prior to Septimius Severus, see Bowman and Rathbone 1992.

of citizenship and personal status (the citizens of a particular city were only responsible for civic burdens in their hometown, for instance), sometimes on the grounds of previous military service, or participation in public affairs or the provision of food supply, or on the grounds of disability or poverty.[14] A nontrivial proportion of papyrological evidence from the province of Egypt focuses on precisely these attempts to obtain immunity from various sorts of civic duties.[15] But immunity was not only important for material reasons. It was also expressive of the notional hierarchies of status that marked members of the elite as distinct from one another – it was, in essence, a mode of defining personal status, and thus fiercely contested on any and all grounds that might be found.[16]

Accordingly, the task of making distinctions between competing claims of immunity and finding resolutions to the distribution of civic burdens might occupy a huge tranche of any particular governor's time and energy. Governors, in turn, produced reams of regulations relating to public services, and provincial courts dealt with such cases on a regular basis. The result must have been a confusing mess, and properly placing a civic burden on someone capable of successfully paying for it seems to have been a recurring challenge.[17]

Framed in such terms, it makes sense that such a chaotic system might come to seem unacceptable to a jurist. Perhaps what is most surprising is that it did not seem so earlier. In fact, all attempts at rationalizing it come from the late second and early third centuries. We might rule out some reasons why this complex but urgent matter

[14] For a general overview, Millar 2004 [1983].

[15] Useful samples of which can be found in Abbott and Johnson 1926: 507–71; Johnson 1936: 609–20; for general surveys, Oertel 1917; Lewis 1997.

[16] Note, e.g., *P.Mich.* VI 426 (AD 199–200), where nomination to a liturgy is equated to a grave insult. For a case from the other end of the empire, cf. Eckhardt 2020.

[17] E.g., the Edict of Ti. Julius Alexander (*OGIS* 669). I bracket here a larger question of whether, and if so precisely when, there was a decline of the "curial class." A lengthy historiography has attempted to reconstruct these processes. See, e.g., Rostovtzeff 1957: I: 481–92; Jones 1940: esp. 182–83 (arguing for problems beginning in the third century); Lepelley 1983 (arguing for continuity into the fourth); Lepelley 1979–1981: esp. I: 197–242 (focusing on the case of Africa); Carrié 2005 (arguing for continuity of key features through at least the Severan period, and in many respects into the fourth century); Millar 2004 [1983]; Liebeschuetz 2001 (locating causation in the third century, but a lengthy process extending into the age of Justinian). See more recently Magalhães de Oliveira 2020 (failures of leadership); Pont 2020.

escaped notice for so long. First, there is no reason to think that the complex system of immunities and attempts to dodge responsibility was a new development in the Severan period. There were indeed Severan innovations in the broader landscape, but these tended to operate by homogenizing the statuses of various cities in the Empire, rather than by creating rules regarding city structure and finance anew.[18] Neither, similarly, did the *Constitutio Antoniniana* appear to change much with respect to the ways that civic burdens and immunities were distributed: indeed, Roman government had, since at least the time of the Antonines, built a legal framework through which grants of citizenship could be made without fundamentally altering a person's relationship to the requirements of his home city.[19] In other words, there was no evident external stimulus that raised new questions for jurists, and there seems to be nothing especially interesting about the early third century that would have necessitated some sort of large-scale juristic redescription of the problem of city governance. Even if there were, we ought not to assume that legal writing is a reflex of broader administrative changes, much less a lagging one.

We might do better by reversing the problem. The jurists were not trying to flesh out a set of Severan or even Antonine legal developments with respect to civic burdens, akin to the way lawyers at a modern administrative agency might try to write regulations to fill in the details of a vague statute. The relationship between juristic text and material or even legal reality is nowhere ever so simple.[20] The better answer seems to be that, as the jurists began to take interest in government more generally, they similarly took interest in municipal government. They attempted to create order in a body of practices – assignments to public service obligations – that was often disruptive to the smooth functioning of government. And the order that they sought to create endeavored to minimize political dispute on the ground.

[18] Carrié 2005.

[19] As evidenced by the *Tabula Banasitana*, which gives its grant of citizenship *salvo iure gentis*: Seston and Euzennat 1961.

[20] Otherwise we might expect, inter alia, that our juristic treatises on the Julian law on adultery might cluster closer to the time of the law's passage in the early first century AD, rather than in the late second and third centuries AD. For a remarkable set of meditations on this problem, see recently Bubb and Peachin 2023.

We might turn, with this in mind, to some of the early attempts to bring order to the question of city government. It is striking that, in at least two juristic treatments of city government, jurists prefer to write in Greek, rather than in Latin. These were texts that were meant to be used – or at the very least, they were composed in a form that itself made a rhetorical claim by an act of deixis: *this* is how one ought to run a city. The point is driven home clearly in the tone of Papinian's *astynomikos monobiblios* (*Single Book on City Management*). Unfortunately only a single fragment survives, but it is remarkable in its format: a series of commands, given in the imperative, directing how local officials are to maintain local roads. "Let them (the *astynomoi*) take care that no one dig up the streets or pile anything up in them or build anything in them; and if someone does, if that person is a slave let him be whipped by whoever discovers it, and if he is free, let him be denounced to the *astynomoi*, who shall fine him according to the law and clear the streets accordingly."[21] These are not juristic hypotheticals or complex fact patterns, but mere instructions. It is striking, moreover, that Papinian seems to have put relatively little work into this treatise: the existing passage seems to be a comparatively light rewrite of a Hellenistic law on city governance, a version of which was reinscribed in Pergamon in the second century AD.[22] What remains of Papinian's pamphlet, it will be admitted, does not address the questions of the distribution of local obligations. Perhaps it raised these questions in another section, perhaps one dealing with the appointment of such local officials – one cannot be sure on the basis of such an exiguous fragment. But the departure that this text marks from the rest of Papinian's *oeuvre* is no less remarkable: a quick pamphlet (just a single book), dashed off with the expectation

[21] Frg. 28 Lenel = *Dig.* 43.10.1.2.

[22] *OGIS* 483, ll.72–90. On the Pergamene law, see Saba 2013; Thonemann 2013b. The text has proven something of an embarrassment to admirers of Papinian: note the judgment of Honoré: "Leaving aside some perhaps early writings on Greek road officials (*astynomikoi*) and adultery, Papinianus is best known for 37 books of *Quaestiones*" (*OCD*[4], s.v. Aemilianus (RE 105) Papinianus). Others have rejected its authenticity: e.g., Schulz 1946: 247 ("One can hardly believe that that 'true Roman' Papinian would have written on law in Greek, still less that he would have written on the *astynomoi* of Greek cities, a subject of not the slightest importance to a man in his position"). See Liebs, *apud* Sallmann 1997: 119 ("eine Frühschrift"), with further bibliography.

that Greek-speaking subjects would obey, seems to be the work of the tired and harried administrator, impatient with local incompetence and the many arguments that it would have produced in court as local litigants sought to shift burdens and blame.

We may reasonably suspect that Papinian was ignored. At the very least, there seems to be no corresponding decrease in the demands for immunity. But it is striking that issues of local government, and immunity in particular, were revisited, in Greek, a mere generation later, by another jurist, Herennius Modestinus, in a work "On Excusal from *Tutela* and *Cura*" (henceforth just *Excuses*) in six books. Most importantly, and nearly unique among juristic works, the editors of the *Digest* preserved the dedication of the work:[23]

> Herennius Modestinus to Egnatius Dexter. Having composed what strikes me as a most useful treatise, which I have entitled "On Excusal from *Tutela* and *Cura*," I have sent it to you. I seek to make my elucidation of these matters as clear as I am able, explaining the rules in the Greek language, even as I recognize that these ideas are hard to render in translation. I also include in my explanations the actual words of the laws, if in some cases I find it necessary, so that, having both right things to say and to read out we might provide a comprehensive and useful account to those in need of one.

Large extracts of the *Excuses* were eventually preserved by the Justinianic compilers. In a sense, it matches their tastes: the preserved sections are mostly running lists of who can be excused from particular responsibilities, with occasional extracts from imperial legislation that supports these claims.[24] But while not necessarily especially edifying to read (a point which Modestinus himself seems to concede in his dedication), the *Excuses* seems to mark an intellectual watershed. As we have seen (Chapter 8), *tutela* and *cura* (or, more generally, "guardianship") were extremely burdensome responsibilities

[23] Frg. 54 Lenel = *Dig.* 27.1.1.pr-2. For an important new edition of this text with extensive commentary, see now Maffi et al. 2021.

[24] Crucially, the compilers of the *Digest* preferred Modestinus' work over comparable works of Paulus and Ulpian. Fragments of those works were preserved almost exclusively in the *Fragmenta Vaticana*. The preserved fragments of Ulpian's *de Excusationibus* (in a single book) are very similar to the work of Modestinus, albeit in Latin (perhaps unsurprisingly, since Modestinus was Ulpian's student). The fragments of Paulus' book *de Officio Praetoris Tutelaris* are exiguous but seem to participate in a similar tradition. On the relation between the three works, see Maffi et al. 2021: 14–22, 38–39.

that weighed heavily on the governing classes, or even on the stratum of people who might, like guildspeople, make up the modestly prosperous middle classes.[25] Exemption from these obligations might stand as exemplary of the sorts of hierarchies that cities (and governors) wished to promote or sustain. From a close treatment of them, a world of city politics might be revealed, from which could be derived analogous modes of balancing the internal political problems of cities themselves. Modestinus' work, then, might be imagined as a practical guide to the rules of mandatory guardianship, but also as an exercise in finding some tool to cut through the bluster of those who did not wish to take on burdensome obligations.

In the generation before Modestinus wrote, the din of protests against mandatory guardianships had reached the courts of emperors, who had, in turn, produced a volume of ad hoc legislation trying to gain control over the question of exemptions. Modestinus sought to bring order to this tangle of rulings. Over the course of the six books, he covered excuses based on age, number of children, and number of others under guardianship; excuses related to profession, magistracy, and origin; excuses on the basis of military service or ill health; procedures for securing an exemption; and a grab-bag of various other excuses that might be proffered (mostly excuses that would *not* work). The tone of work, as a whole, shares similarities with that of Papinian's fragment on the *astynomoi*: in nearly all cases there is no interest in equitable balancing; there is just the insistence that a particular excuse would or would not work – that is, each excuse is reduced to a simple binary. In such a world, the application for an excusal would be akin to filling out a particular form, where one checked a box and added the necessary documents.[26]

We can take as an example of this binarism a case which Modestinus handles perfunctorily. Could one be excused from being appointed by will as a guardian because the proposed guardian and the decedent had fallen into deadly enmity? Perhaps, Modestinus explains: but only if the enmity was proven to have arisen *after* the will was made would such enmity allow for excuse. Neither, he continues, would a hatred conceived prior to the writing of the will *necessarily* let the proposed guardian off the hook: "[If,] although the hatred preceded

[25] See further Venticinque 2016. [26] I thank Barbara Welke for this formulation.

the will, it was considered a good move to appoint him to the tutelage so that he would be loaded with its burdens and administrative cares," then the enemy must nonetheless take on the guardianship.[27] One must wonder about such a father (and such a son). One must also shudder imagining the litigation that such a decision would inevitably produce. But despite the normal juristic concern for balancing equities and avoiding enmity in such a situation (to say nothing of the juristic solicitude for wards and children more generally),[28] the path forward for Modestinus was clear: the tutor was simply obligated, and he would be required to undertake the guardianship of his enemy's son unless the narrow exception to the rule was met. The treatment of appeals from appointment followed a similarly strict logic: tutors were required to protest their appointment within fifty days of the time of learning of the appointment, or the protest was invalid; one day's grace would be added on for each additional twenty miles that the proposed tutor had to travel to register his protest. Only the narrowest exceptions related to *force majeure* were sufficient to pause the clock.[29] The equitable judgment of a jurist or administrator was not permitted to enter the picture.

The tone of Modestinus' work thus shares, in important ways, the impatience of an Ulpian or a Papinian. Excuses were to be construed as narrowly as possible, and whenever possible in favor of taking on the guardianship. But among the vast catalogue of "Nos," Modestinus' text reveals a world of people attempting to avoid their obligations. A mere excerpt will have to suffice:[30]

> The sacred constitutions provide that neither secretaries (*librarious*) nor accountants (*kalkoulatouras*), who are called counters, have an exemption. Jews are to be guardians to non-Jews just as they undertake all other public duties; for *constitutiones* provide only that they are not to be troubled with matters that appear to be defiling to their religion. Being in charge of a city's accounts does not even count as one guardianship. The freedmen of women of senatorial rank, even if they manage their affairs, are not exempted from the obligation of guardianship; for this is only conceded to the freedmen of

[27] 2 *Exc.*, Frg. 60 Lenel = *Dig.* 27.1.6.17.
[28] In general, McGinn 2013. On the jurists' attitudes towards *restitutio* for children, see further below.
[29] 4 *Exc.*, Frg. 63 Lenel = *Dig.* 27.1.13.7.
[30] 6 *Exc.*, Frg. 67 Lenel = *Dig.* 27.1.15.5–10.

male senatorials. If a city magistrate, that is the *archon*, becomes liable for a guardianship because it lies with him to make appointments, [sc., and he has not appointed a suitable candidate], he cannot count this as an ordinary guardianship [and thus towards an exemption from additional guardianships]; neither can a guarantor for guardianship nor those appointed honorary tutors. One who farms a city's taxes is not exempted from guardianship.

In reading this text we are not in the normal, staid, fully imaginary world of Roman jurisprudence.[31] In those other works – the typical works of Roman jurists – what might in reality be complex fact patterns are reduced to simply placeholders (Seius, Titius, Stichus the slave, etc.) for the purpose of legal analysis, to allow jurists to make elegant distinctions. With Modestinus' work we are, instead, in the thick of human affairs – at the desk of the administrator, as it were, looking at vivid examples of how people must have sought to protect themselves from a costly duty that would likely leave them in legal peril.

It is tempting to read this text only as an attempt to bring local political claim-making to heel. It is precisely that, of course. But it evinces not only a distrust of local political organs like the sort we met above (i.e., the boisterous meeting of the Hermopolis council), but also of provincial governors themselves. It is a pity that we know so little of the text's addressee, Egnatius Dexter, such that we could put a finer point on the text itself.[32] But given that the Egnatii were a relatively prosperous senatorial family, we ought to presume that Modestinus imagined his dedicatee as a governor of a province, or some other high-level senatorial administrator who might have need of a book in Greek, either for himself or for his staff. The goal of the text, in other words, might also have been to constrain the freedom of action for an imperial administrator – under the friendly guise of "helping" him to understand the rules.

It is worth wondering why this might be the case, and what sort of intellectual work might be accomplished by construing a governor or similar official as bound tightly to particular rules. It was well-known that governors might simply make mistakes of law, not realizing particular technicalities – for instance, that jurists teaching in the provinces

31 Cohen 1935.

32 Maffi et al. 2021: 41–42 summarize the possibilities mooted by scholars, but rightly conclude that no direct match is available on current evidence.

were not exempt from guardianship, whereas jurists teaching in Rome were.[33] Such mistakes of law were regrettable, productive of headaches and unnecessary paperwork, and might, when aggregated over many instances, end up squandering resources that could be put to better uses. But I suspect there is more to the matter. The fact that so many cases were trickling up to the emperors themselves seems to indicate that mistakes of law were not primarily the problem Modestinus had in mind: in each case, emperors simply clarified what the rules were and sent the case back. This might be a waste of their otherwise limited time, but something that could be handled by a well-trained staff.[34]

The problem, rather, seems to be that governors were overly ready to hear these cases in the first place, and overly ready to grant exemptions on the basis of purely affective criteria. That is, it might be hard for a governor to avoid feeling sympathy for particular persons who were stretched thin and anxious about embroiling themselves in complex and hate-filled family affairs. One can also understand how a governor might "find" an exemption for a particular individual he deemed especially pitiable, favorable, beautiful, or useful – leaving the person subsequently burdened with the obligation to have to sue to relieve himself of it. Alternatively, the governor might have played his gatekeeper role only half-heartedly: officially prohibiting such people from attaining their exemption, but quickly allowing an appeal to see if they might find a way around the problem (or if the problem might burn itself out in the interim). It would be under those circumstances that such cases would trickle up to the imperial court. Imagined as such, the problem, for Modestinus, was that the governor's ability to control his affect – his ability to stand firm against people crying and complaining – could not be trusted. The governor, on this reading, was not immune to the politics of his province and had to be understood as potentially enmeshed in them. His scope of action had to be constrained accordingly.

***

[33] Frg. 60 Lenel = *Dig.* 27.1.6.12.

[34] Note the numerous examples of jurists venting frustration by insisting that a point of law is well settled, too many to cite herein, but taking the form *saepe constitutum est*, *ut est saepissime constitutum/rescriptum*, *et ita multis constitutionibus cavetur*, etc., or the especially enjoyable *et hoc certo certius est et saepe constitutum*. The evidence is gathered in Gualandi 2012: I: 203–64.

The problem of the governor's scope for action – and its potential to be poisoned by misplaced affect – also emerges in another body of writing typical of the jurists of Modestinus' age, one typical of the law of government more generally. Specifically, there emerges, in this period, a new body of juristic writing on the conduct of trials, both at Rome and in the provinces. The material on trials at Rome – under the heading of books *de iudiciis publicis* – is mostly focused on the traditional categories of criminal law well known from other periods. It is the material on provincial courts that is the most revealing of the problem of how to control local politics, as well as the tendency of a governor to find himself ensnared in local systems of affect.

We might begin by noting that a number of jurists raise questions about the emotional disposition of governors. Governors were overburdened and prone to fly off the handle, both at litigants and at private individuals outside of the courtroom. A governor might choose to abuse such people verbally or even physically. What, then, was the legal status of those so abused? Might they have, in fact, suffered *infamia* – the state of civic degradation that accompanied a guilty verdict in certain socially problematic offenses? The jurists of the late second and early third centuries continually returned to this problem. Thus, the jurist Marcianus insisted that "a beating with cudgels does not carry *infamia*" – the issue, rather, was whether the individual was convicted of a particular wrong.[35] Similarly, the jurist and administrator Papinian had to explain to a litigant that, "The words, 'you appear to have instigated the suit by a clever lie' in the judgment of the provincial governor increase humiliation rather than, it seems, inflict disgrace (*ignominia*)."[36] Ulpian himself wrestled with a case in which a governor chose to give a far heavier sentence than was deserved: "It makes a good deal of difference," he explained, "whether something was delivered as a judgment on the case before the court at the end of the hearing or whether certain things were comments in passing; for *infamia* is not inflicted because of the latter."[37]

35 *Dig.* 3.2.22.pr. Printed editions of the *Digest* give the passage as coming from the Antonine jurist Ulpius Marcellus; on the basis of other manuscripts, Lenel thinks it a part of Marcianus' treatise *de Iudiciis Publicis*, giving the text as Frg. 209.

36 1 *Resp.*, Frg. 405 Lenel = *Dig.* 3.2.20.pr.

37 6 *Ed.*, Frg. 288 Lenel = *Dig.* 3.2.13.6. Emperors later picked up where the jurists left off. Cf. *CJ* 2.11.1 (Severus or Severus and Caracalla); 2.11.17 (Gordian); *CJ* 2.11.19 (Carinus and Numerianus).

The problem was not restricted to governors: taking the lead of governors, other, local magistrates might also beat people, and thus potentially jeopardize their status. Thus, the jurist Callistratus pondered a situation in which everyday people – sellers of daily provisions (*utensilia*) – might be beaten by the city aediles. In that case, he reasoned, the mere fact that they could be rightly beaten – or even the fact that they *had been* rightly beaten – would not prohibit them from serving on the city's council.[38] (He quickly added that it was in no way *desirable* to have such people on the council, and that their appointment should be avoided when possible.)

But the problem for jurists was not simply that people might get angry and punish out of line. Such an approach to governance was broadly tolerated and might even be imagined to be praiseworthy so long as it restrained itself somewhat. The problem was not severity, but leniency. We might, in this vein, consider a ruling by Aemilius Macer: "The provincial governor cannot bring it about that a convicted thief does not incur *infamia*."[39] Of course, it is hard to know, from such a fragment, what the precise context was. But two options seem especially plausible: that the governor, feeling pity for a particular person but otherwise faced with an incontrovertible case of theft, sought to mitigate his sentence by enforcing the penalties against thieves but declining to enforce the life-long status of civic degradation that accompanied it; or alternatively, that he sought to rehabilitate the reputation of a particular person by lightening an earlier sentence. In either case, Macer finds the idea intolerable: governors were not free to tinker with sentences and their consequences out of pity. Callistratus agreed. Even if the governor could be certain that he had made a mistake in sentencing, only the emperors themselves could lighten or change the sentence, no matter how unfair it was, how pitiable the litigant, or with whatever dire consequences for that person's heirs.[40]

It was bad enough when the governor's innate sense of pity or shame prevented him from delivering a sentence or urged him towards mitigating one. It was worse if he felt compelled to bend to the pressure of his subjects. Thus Modestinus insisted that governors were

38 6 *Cogn.*, Frg. 44 Lenel = *Dig.* 50.2.12.

39 2 *Pub. Iud.*, Frg. 30 Lenel = *Dig.* 47.2.63.

40 5 *Cogn.*, Frg. 33 Lenel = *Dig.* 48.19.27.pr.

not free to remit sentences as a favor to the people (*favore populi*): if a criminal was sentenced to the beasts, he must go. But, he added, almost tauntingly, "if the people to be punished are *so* strong or *so* clever that they're worth being exhibited at Rome, then the governor should consult the emperor."[41] Otherwise the governor ought to stiffen his spine and get on with punishing.

The goal behind all of these rulings was to curtail the governor's freedom of action. Jurists worried in particular that the governor would not be able to restrain his demeanor, and that this failure of self-control would produce a criminal law that was tainted by the wrong sorts of feelings. It is in this vein that we might understand the flurry of writing concerning trials and punishments. Modestinus wrote such a treatise in four books. Paulus wrote three separate treatises, each in a single book: "Concerning the Punishment of Soldiers" (*de Poenis Militum*), "Concerning the Punishment of Villagers" (*de Poenis Paganorum*), and "Concerning the Punishments of All the Laws" (*de Poenis Omnium Legum*), as well as a treatise on the property of those who had been sentenced (*de Portionibus Quae Liberis Damnatorum Conceduntur*).

Among these, perhaps the most interesting (not least because the best preserved) is Callistratus' treatise *On Trials* (*de Cognitionibus*). As his name seems to indicate, Callistratus was likely himself of Greek-speaking, provincial descent.[42] Unfortunately further biographical detail is elusive. But it is telling, nonetheless, that he chose to take on the *cognitio* as a topic of inquiry, whereas jurists of his period preferred to start with crimes arranged under the broad heading of Roman statutory offenses. The *cognitio* was the normal form of trial in the provinces (at least by this period), and one that tended to offer the governor maximum latitude to construe the particular offense and punishment – so much so that it has been continually criticized by modern lawyers as offering little in the way of procedural protections or even formal structure.[43] Thus it was an

[41] 3 *Poen.*, Frg. 163 Lenel = *Dig.* 48.19.31. Cf. 3 *Poen.*, Frg. 164 Lenel = *Dig.* 48.8.16, urging that emperors must be written to before punishing *decuriones*, unless the anger of a crowd makes this impossible (*nisi forte tumultus aliter sedari non posse*).

[42] For a new edition, with comprehensive bibliography and contextualization, see Puliatti 2020.

[43] E.g., de Ste Croix 1963: 11–12 ("arbitrary and irresponsible"). The nature of the *cognitio* has produced a massive bibliography, very little of it pertinent to what follows. See, e.g., Garnsey 1970.

act of intellectual daring and creativity to seek to organize a treatise around what, on first principles, was notionally "outside of" the normal order of statutory offenses (*extra ordinem*). It would probably also have been regarded by a previous generation of lawyers as somehow beneath them.

Callistratus' concern to constrain the affective disposition of the governor is evident from the earliest sections of the treatise:[44]

> The administrator of justice ought to see that he makes himself easily approachable, but should not tolerate being looked down upon (*contemni*). Hence, it is added to warrants of appointment that provincial governors shall not admit provincials into too close familiarity; for conversation on terms of equality breeds contempt for his office. But also when trying cases he must not go off like a firework (*excandescere*) at those whom he thinks wicked, nor be moved to tears (*inlacrimari*) by the entreaties of the miserable. For it is not in the character of a firm and right-minded judge that his expression gives a clue to his emotions (*cuius animi motum vultus detegit*).

By raising the problem of the governor's affect at the start of the treatise, Callistratus offers a clue as to how we should understand the project as a whole. The ideal governor, on Callistratus' reading, is something of a sphinx: inscrutable to defendants and prosecutors alike and in complete control of his emotions.

Emotional control, however, was to be ultimately secured not by personal discipline (which Callistratus knew would vary wildly from person to person), but by developing a rational structure by which individual trials could be taxonomized. Accordingly, the bulk of the treatise is devoted to laying out a typology of trials and a hierarchy of punishments over which a governor will preside. Despite the fact that, by his own admission, the world of trials "is not easily broken down into types," Callistratus argues for a four-part distinction: trials, he argues, deal either with honors or civic obligations, personal status and rank, property, or capital crimes.[45] Of these, the discussion of capital crimes and punishments – the site where official anger was most likely to be expressed – occupies a disproportionate amount of the text, beginning in book three and continuing through the sixth

44 1 *Cog.*, Frg. 2 Lenel = *Dig.* 1.18.19.

45 1 *Cog.*, Frg. 5 Lenel = *Dig.* 50.13.5.pr. See also Harries 2007: 32–33.

and final book. Yet criminal punishment seems to feature prominently throughout.[46]

The creation of rational order might be imagined as a strategy by which overwhelming workloads might be approached with purpose and equanimity. But even Callistratus must admit that actually existing criminal law sometimes fails to make rational sense:[47]

Capital punishments are basically these: the most severe form of punishment (*summum supplicium*) seems to be crucifixion; there is also burning alive. This is rightly counted as part of the "most severe" forms of punishment, but to the extent that this form of punishment was invented later, it comes in second place. Next there is beheading. Then, nearest to this is being confined to the mines, and after this deportation to an island.

Yet even if such an ordering fails to make intuitive or even historical sense (was it really the case that burning alive came later than crucifixion?), by creating a hierarchical arrangement of punishments a broader goal is achieved. Once the hierarchy is laid out, different types of offenders can be matched to it on the basis of a series of definitions and basic calculations. Thus, poisoners get capital punishment, unless their station prohibits it, in which case they get deportation; highwaymen (*grassatores*) are considered similar to robbers (*latronibus*): if they are armed and use the roads, they are sentenced to capital punishment, and otherwise to the mines or deported to an island, and so on. Hierarchy in punishment is insisted upon even when obviously inapposite. Thus being burned alive is said to be for slaves who endanger their masters' lives, though Callistratus concedes it also sometimes happens that free plebeians and people of lower class are burned alive too. Arsonists suffer capital punishment, if they burn things in the city out of enmity or for the sake of gain, but they're also often burned alive. Even when the "system" breaks down, Callistratus believes that a hierarchy of punishments will enable the rational application of sentences.

Callistratus was committed to the ideological position that punishment ought ultimately to be rational and rule-governed, rather than discretionary and based on the anger or the pity of the governor. Thus,

[46] For instance, in the small amount of preserved text on personal status and rank, the question is raised about the effect of criminal punishments on personal status, and on the transmissibility of criminal liability to children: 1 *Cog.*, Frgs. 10–11 Lenel = *Dig.* 50.12.5.1–3, 48.19.26.

[47] 6 *Cog.*, Frg. 39 Lenel = *Dig.* 48.19.28.pr.

the hierarchy can be used not just for matching a malefactor with his deserved punishment (mostly), but also for aggravating sentences with cause. Accordingly, if the relegated (banned for time) return early, they are to be sent to an island; should they escape the island, they can be sentenced to capital punishment. Likewise, if a guilty person escapes temporary custody, he can be permanently exiled; if he returns, he can be sent to the mines; should he escape the mines, he can be lawfully executed.[48] This commitment to the idea that punishment can be reduced to a basic calculus leads Callistratus to develop typologies that might strike us as remarkably picayune. Thus, in dealing with cattle rustlers (*abigei*), Callistratus argues that what distinguishes a thief from a rustler is the theft of a "herd" (*gregem*): ten sheep make a herd, but only four or five pigs. A single horse or cow also qualifies as a herd. And if the thief is a habitual offender, he becomes a rustler even by the theft of a single animal.[49]

The typologies work until they don't, however. Callistratus concedes that "infamous bandits" have to be crucified on the spot where they practiced their banditry, "so that others, by seeing them, may be deterred from similar crimes, and so that there can be some comfort for the families of those whom they killed by having the punishment carried out in the same places in which they committed their murders" – though he also concedes that plenty of bandits were also sent to fight with beasts.[50] The tension between the reality of punishment (with its emphasis on the emotional responses of anger, disgust, and revenge) and the ideal of punishment (a calculable, rationalized structure) is constantly made present, but never achieves resolution.

What then are we to make of this, as an intellectual artifact or as the articulation of an ideology of punishment? At the most basic level, the proposition that criminal law – or even trials in general – can be reduced to a hierarchical, rationalized structure is designed primarily to limit judicial choice. Punishments, on such a reading, should be applied with minimal discretion: all one needed to know was what sort of offender was dealt with (was he a slave or free, of protected or unprotected status?) and what sort of crime he had committed. Even

[48] 6 *Cog.*, Frg. 45 Lenel = *Dig.* 48.19.28, drawing on a rescript of Hadrian.
[49] 6 *Cog.*, Frg. 48 Lenel = *Dig.* 47.14.3.
[50] 6 *Cog.*, Frg. 47 Lenel = *Dig.* 48.19.28.15.

proving this could, in theory, be reduced to something of a formal process, if not a science: thus, Callistratus lays out procedures for determining whether a witness is or is not credible, and, in contrast to the tendency of Roman jurists more broadly, tends to think of credibility as something of a binary.[51] Criminal justice, on such a vision, could be reduced to something like criminal *processing*.

But reducing the scope for the governor's independent action is only, I would argue, part of a broader problem that motivates this text. Two passages in particular suggest that the problem went deeper. First, Callistratus asks about the case of a judge presented with imperial constitutions: what if he deems them not relevant to the case at hand? Has he given judgment illegally – *contra constitutiones*? No, Callistratus argues: though the issue is subject to appeal, the ruling will stand until then.[52] Second, what about the case in which someone has fled to a statue of the emperor – that is, attempted to cling to the imperial image as a way of seeking asylum? This, Callistratus, insists, is almost totally forbidden. In general, he explains, it is prohibited to flee to a statue "for the injury of another" (*in iniuriam alterius*) – a long-established legal principle. "And since the laws provide security for *all* men equally," Callistratus thunders, "for good reason it seems that to flee to a statue or image of the emperors is more 'for the injury of another' rather than in one's own defense." The only reason, he insists, for which someone might validly flee to the statues of the emperor would be "if one is being kept in chains or imprisoned by powerful people (*potentioribus*)."[53] This is a shocking decision: not only is it fully impractical to imagine that a person being detained by "the powerful" could actually exercise such an option, the insistence that an equal law "for all people" obviates the need to flee to the statues simply begs the question. It is like saying that those protesting police brutality should stop protesting because police brutality is illegal.[54]

At the heart of Callistratus' concerns, I would argue, is that the proffering of constitutions and the invocation of the moral power of the emperors were both part of the normal array of tactics by which

[51] 3 *Cog.*, Frg. 28 Lenel = *Dig.* 22.5.3.pr. [52] 3 *Cog.*, Frg. 18 Lenel = *Dig.* 42.1.32.
[53] 6 *Cog.*, Frg. 45 Lenel = *Dig.* 48.19.28.7.
[54] On the emperor's statue, Hopkins 1978.

provincial subjects would attempt to put pressure on their governors. One could imagine a case where, faced with a pile of precedents that may have been tangentially related to the case, a governor might simply have conceded that the litigant should have whatever he or she wanted – lest otherwise the governor himself be charged with disrespecting previous rulings. (Indeed, a similar question was put before Pliny – see Chapter 3.) One could similarly imagine a litigant gesturing to, or even clasping, an imperial statue, evoking the moral order that the emperor ensured. Governors, on Callistratus' imagining, might not have been able to withstand this pressure. Yet to govern effectively, they must.

The combination of the typologies and hierarchies of punishments and wrongdoers is thus the answer to Callistratus' larger worry: that the men in charge of this system needed those hierarchies in order to be able to withstand moral pressure from subjects. The typologies and hierarchies operated to backstop "the system" as it ought, ideally, to operate, and to insulate it from the sort of everyday discretion and equity that might otherwise make punishment palatable – or even explainable – to subjects. It is in this context that we might further reflect on a problem with a long historiography: did the Roman state become "harsher" over the long course of late antiquity? The answer is, to some extent, absolutely yes: there was a substantial increase in the number of crimes that were deserving of the death penalty, to say the least.[55] This was mostly the work of emperors, and mostly emperors of the fourth century and beyond. But the jurists are also imagined to have had a role in this process. And to the extent that the "law of government" features texts like Callistratus', it would make sense to claim that jurists too were participants in the process of making the legal world harsher. But, I think, the emphasis on "harshness" occludes an important part of what motivated authors like Callistratus. His interest was not per se in being punitive, although he had no objection to it. His interest was in being *consistent*, and in making provincial practices formally rational. At the heart of his endeavors, however,

[55] Garnsey 1968; Callu 1984; MacMullen 1990 [1986]; Pölönen 2004. Harries 2007: 41–42 hews to a more middle path. Krause 2014: 254–72 has recently revisited the question, insisting, I think reasonably, on a distinction between criminal law and criminal practice.

was the desire to constrain the judgment of men in charge, and to insulate them, if not isolate them, from their broader political milieu – at least when they were in court. In that respect, his project is not dissimilar to Ulpian's, even if Callistratus lacks Ulpian's broader political and ethical commitments to fairness. In both cases, the desire came from a broader juristic impatience with, if not a distaste for, the politics of legality that characterized life in the provinces more generally.

***

So where ought affect, and its cousin, discretion, ideally sit in such a system? If not with a governor, then with whom?

The question is raised, most sharply, in two works by the jurist Paulus: his *Decrees* in three books (*Decretorum*) and his *Sentences* in six books (*Imperialium Sententiarum in Cognitionibus Prolatarum*). The two works relate cases heard by Septimius Severus (and sometimes also Caracalla) in whose court Paulus was present as a dispenser of judicial advice. Unlike other texts in the *Digest* that might report "real" cases (but where the parties have been anonymized through the use of fictitious, placeholder names), here the jurist mostly seems to use the actual names of litigants, and sometimes even those of the judges in their cases.[56] The texts are thus, in a sense, semi-autobiographical – they report cases that Paulus was personally a witness to.

If these case reports were well preserved, they would constitute a remarkable aperçu into the workings of the emperors' court. Unfortunately, they are not. To begin with, the relationship between the two works is elusive.[57] A very small number of fragments of the *Sentences* remain extant; at least some of this material appears in the rather fuller remains of the extant *Decrees*. The two may represent different subsequent traditions through which Paulus' texts passed, or the two works may represent different stages of the same work (an earlier *Decrees* later reedited and expanded by Paulus into the *Sentences*, or vice-versa). What is more, if the cases that Paulus reported followed a standard pattern (description of the litigants, the

[56] Although Titius is used in *1 Dec.*, Frg. 57 Lenel = *Dig.* 50.2.9.pr. In some sections the matters over which the litigants appear to be disputing seem to have been changed into more generic categories: e.g., *2 Dec.*, Frg. 68 Lenel = *Dig.* 32.27.pr.

[57] The most comprehensive treatment is the new edition of Brutti 2020. On the history of the texts, Brutti 2020: 43–45. See also the important study of Daalder 2022.

issue at hand, the disputes of the jurists on the emperor's *consilium*, and the emperor's eventual verdict), then a number of the cases have unquestionably been shortened considerably by Justinianic compilers or by others – sometimes to the extent that they simply record a single position on an issue. The rub, however, will become clear presently: in these highly shortened cases, it is impossible to always say whether the position recorded is that of Paulus, that of the emperor, or that of another interlocutor – and since Paulus and the emperor often disagree, this leaves us in a state of radical uncertainty as to what position prevailed in a particular trial. Similarly, even among the cases that are preserved at greater length, there is the possibility that these have also been shortened; it is, however, far from clear where or in what respect this shortening has taken place. There is, moreover, considerable debate as to whether sections of the text have been interpolated. The contemporary tendency is to accept that texts were shortened but to reject the hypothesis of full-scale rewriting or adding by subsequent editors.[58] In either case, however, we would do well to approach the work as a whole with due caution.

Even with such extensive caveats, the cases Paulus presents are remarkable as artifacts of the interactions and dialogues that took place between a jurist and an emperor and between an emperor and his subjects. On display is the variety of personal commitments towards the law more generally. And unlike in the world of panegyric, emperor, jurists, and litigants do not necessarily agree. Similarly on display is the fact that one party holds vastly more power than the others: it is ultimately the verdict of the emperor that matters. This is an important enough lesson. Though all would have admitted its truth (and jurists conceded it repeatedly – every time they cited an imperial constitution in their work), to frame the issue so starkly as to show a jurist being overruled was a forceful reminder that the world of law – the creation of the jurists – sat within a world of political power.

What is novel, however, about the political world evoked by the *Decrees* and *Sentences* is that they evoke not a world of standard

[58] This is the approach of Brutti 2020. Note, though, the concerns of Cascione 2021. For an in-depth testing of the theory of interpolations as applied to one case, see Peachin 1994 (rejecting interpolations in favor of deeper historical contextualization).

cases, chosen for their straightforward application of legal principles, but a world of strained intimate relationships and pitiable individuals. Intimate, family affairs are at the forefront of concern: inheritances, *fideicommissa* (trusts), the division of family property, the affairs of children and slaves. A number of cases involve Roman aristocrats known from other contexts. Interestingly, in at least two of these cases, we may reasonably suspect that the family affairs that are subject to the emperor's judgment are complicated because they were tangled up in confiscations dating back to before the Severan dynasty.[59] In the background, in many of the cases, sits the imperial fiscus, the great confiscatory force that loomed large over many transactions. If the world portrayed by Modestinus is the world of the grumpy administrator, hurriedly applying the rules even to people who beg for relief in the most abject terms, the world of the imperial court portrayed by Paulus is a world in which the vulnerable and those who have been stripped of status beg justice from an emperor who is always willing to hear their case, to find complexity and nuance, and to let pity suffuse his judgment. Through the emperor's ability to feel for his subjects, he achieves literal *consensus* or *homonoia*: oneness of feeling with his subjects.

We might reflect on just two relatively well-preserved cases from the *Decrees* to get a sense of the role that affect plays within this system. We might begin with a case that is typical of the problems that continually arise in this text, one that brings into focus a world of complex planning for family and for one's own legacy. The facts of the case were as follows. Fabius Antoninus had two children, Honorata and Antoninus, the latter still a child. In his will, he disinherited both children, and made their mother, Junia Valeriana, his heir. He gave a sum of money and some items to his daughter as a legacy, and then asked the mother to restore the whole inheritance to Antoninus when he reached or completed his twentieth year (*cum ad annum vicensimum aetatis pervenisset*). If Antoninus died before that, she should give everything to Honorata. We might note, in this arrangement, a desire, common among certain tiers of elite families,

[59] 1 *Dec.*, Frg. 59 Lenel = *Dig.* 10.2.41, with a doublet as 1 *Imp.Sent.*, Frg. 877 Lenel = *Dig.* 37.14.24 (the estate of Camilia Pia, on which see Peachin 1994); 2 *Dec.*, Frg. 67 Lenel = *Dig.* 28.5.93 (the will of Pactumeius Androsthenes).

to avoid breaking an estate into fragments (as well as the sort of sexism that should not surprise us in a patriarchal world). The ultimate desire of Fabius Antoninus, it seems, was to ensure that his son inherited the bulk of his estate, but failing that, to make certain that his daughter would.

Yet despite Fabius Antoninus' best plans, the arrangement did not work. Fabius died, leaving the estate to his wife, the mother of the two children, charged with the legally enforceable duty (*fideicommissum*) to hand over the entire estate to Antoninus if he lived until twenty. Yet before this could happen, the mother died intestate, leaving both children her heirs. Antoninus died shortly afterwards, entering, but not completing, his twentieth year. Antoninus also left a young daughter, Fabia Valeriana, as his heir. Honorata then sued, demanding the initial legacy (which had never been paid out) as well as a share of her father's inheritance – presumably the entirety of the portion bequeathed to Antoninus, as expressed in the *fideicommissum* to her deceased mother. The provincial governor decided in favor of Honorata.

We might note two types of problems here, both social and legal. Socially, such an all-or-nothing arrangement, designed to prevent the fragmentation of the estate, was bound, under these circumstances, to operate to the impoverishment of one of the litigants. The choice of whom to favor, in such a case, was far from straightforward: Honorata surely evoked a pitiable spectacle, but Fabius Antoninus should have anticipated the fact that his son might have had a child before his twentieth year. Leaving a granddaughter impoverished was surely no part of his intention, but his planning strategy was in that respect defective. Legally, the case poses additional complications. How ought one to construe the requirements of the initial *fideicommissum*? When would the estate have vested in Antoninus? The text offered *cum ad annum vicensimum aetatis pervenisset* – but did that mean upon "entering" his twentieth year, or upon completing it? The Latin is fundamentally ambiguous.

When the case went to appeal, both of these issues were raised. The tutors who represented young Valeriana made clear that the decision would be ruinous to their ward (and possibly to them, as well). But they had a legal argument as well: in cases of responsibilities for public services (*munera*), the emperor Hadrian once decreed that age was to be reckoned as complete when someone entered, rather than completed, their appointed year. But should a single constitution, presented as an analogy, settle the matter? Paulus was adamant that it did not. That particular imperial enactment may have sufficed for *munera*, but the controlling interpretation ought to have been based in a much earlier, and more comprehensive, act of legislation, the *lex Aelia Sentia*. That law specified that, in the case of being eligible to manumit slaves, a person had to have *completed* their twenty-fifth year. The rule of the *lex* was well established, and should trump the decree of Hadrian, since the latter might be construed as narrowly tailored to the problem of *munera*. Hence, by strict law, the inheritance should be given to Honorata.

The emperor, however, disagreed with the jurist. "The emperor was moved (*motus est*) by equity (*aequitas*) and by the words of the testament itself." It is worth lingering over this detail. It might easily be read as two separate reasons for ruling in favor of Valeriana: that both equity and the actual words of the testament both militated in favor of not impoverishing the poor young woman.[60] But this fails to answer a fundamental question: if the text of the *fideicommissum* was not so ambiguous, why then was the case not fundamentally an easy one – that is, why did it need to be appealed to the emperor?

The text was not in fact self-interpreting. Instead, the disposition of the emperor towards pity is what gives him the hermeneutic keys to decipher the will. "Being moved by equity" puts the emperor in a privileged affective state that determines, or at least informs, the way in which he construes something fundamentally ambiguous: by *feeling for* his subjects in a particular sort of way, he can see things that are concealed. This sort of interpretive capacity is in important ways analogous to that of a sage like Apollonius of Tyana, who could use his privileged status to gaze into the soul of a person and determine whether he was, in fact, a criminal (above, Chapter 7). In the case of Apollonius, the privileged form of knowledge came from mastery of philosophy and Greek *paideia*; in the case of the emperor, it came from having the proper sort of affective disposition to know how best to construe the desires of the original testator, how to interpret

60 This is the conclusion of Brutti 2020: 143–44 and Daalder 2022: 168. Cf. the language of the emperor in *P.Harr.* I 67 (c.150).

his ambiguous language, and how to know which party to optimally impoverish. What is more, the emperor does this *in spite of* the judgment of Paulus, his trusted advisor, and in spite of the fact that when the emperor made his judgment, he made it in favor of Valeriana "even though he knew that, in a different case, Marcus ruled someone was *not* excused from a guardianship even though he had entered his seventieth year." In other words, the power of the emperor, and of his affect, was that he could also construe the law as necessary to show that he was solicitous of the most vulnerable.[61]

The second case deals with the circumstances under which a minor is capable of receiving "restoration to one's previous status" (*restitutio in integrum*), a remedy given to people under twenty-five who had improperly been duped (because of youth), pressured, or otherwise inappropriately lured into entering into a transaction that caused them loss. In this case, a man named Aemilius Laurianus bought a tract of land from a man named Ovinius, but he bought it subject to a *lex commissoria*, namely, a provision in the contract under which the seller, Ovinius, could rescind the purchase under certain circumstances: in this case, if half of the total price was not paid in the first two months after the sale or if the balance of the price was not paid within two months after that. Laurianus, however, died within the first two months, leaving his underage daughter (*pupilla*) as heiress. Because she was a minor, she was subject to *tutores*, or guardians. These *tutores*, however, neglected to hand over the requisite money to Ovinius, despite his frequent reminders that they pay up. Ovinius eventually sold the land to another man. At some point – we do not know how long thereafter – the daughter challenged this sale in court, asking for *restitutio in integrum*. Paulus continues:[62]

> Having lost the proceedings both before the praetor and the urban prefect, she appealed. I thought the judgment was correct because the contract had been made by her father and not by the *pupilla* herself. However, the emperor was moved (*motus est*) by the fact that the day on which the sale might be rescinded fell in the time of the *pupilla* (that is, after her father's death), and therefore *she* had brought it about that the conditions of the sale were not observed. I said that a better reason for granting *restitutio* would be that the seller, by giving a warning after the day on which it had been agreed that the

[61] 2 *Dec.*, Frg. 70 Lenel = *Dig.* 36.1.76.1. [62] 1 *Decr.*, Frg. 58 Lenel = *Dig.* 4.4.38.

sale might be rescinded and by seeking the price, is held to have departed from his own condition. I also said that I was not concerned by the fact that the time had run out after the death of the father, any more than if a creditor had sold a pledge when the day for payment had passed after the death of the debtor. Nevertheless, because the *lex commissoria* displeased (*displicebat*) him, the emperor awarded *restitutio in integrum*. The fact that the former tutors who had not sought *restitutio* had been declared suspect also moved the emperor (*movit…imperatorem*).

Here, we have both a case on *restitutio*, as well as a story about law's limits. In this mini-drama, the *pupilla* and her property serve as a litmus test for evoking imperial *pathos*. Paulus, the dispassionate attorney, thinks that the case was rightly decided (*putabam bene iudicatam*): restitution only being available for cases in which the minor him- or herself engaged in the transaction. In taking this position, Paulus stands as the guardian of law as a system. Juxtaposed to him is the emperor, whose affective state was "moved" (*motus est*) such that he wished to intervene in the case. As in the previous case, we have a conflict between emperor and jurist and their respective normative and affective orientations.

Yet unlike in the previous case, where Paulus is simply overruled, in this case there is a further level of drama. It begins when the emperor tries to play jurist, claiming that the *pupilla* herself engaged in the transaction, because some part of it happened on her watch (*dies committendi in tempus pupillae incidisset*), and that because she (or her tutors) had kept it from being carried out, that this was more or less the same as her having entered into it in the first place (*eaque effecisset, ne pareretur legi venditionis*). The reasoning is faulty; it is a parody of jurisprudence, for to do nothing is not to have done something, much less to enter into a transaction in the conventional sense. But it is a parody that is matched by Paulus' response. Realizing that the emperor wishes to prevail regardless of circumstances, Paulus quickly proffers a reason to conform to Severus' understanding of law: because the seller begged the tutors to conform to the terms of the agreement, the seller had in fact violated his *own* terms of the agreement. He would have done better, on this logic, to have simply sold the land off right away. In other words, any time a seller seeks to work with a buyer who owes part of a bill, the seller relinquishes his rights under the original arrangement. Paulus' conclusion is a travesty of equitable reasoning, and a threat, in its absurdity, to overturn basic notions of fair dealing. It is similar to saying that, when I ask a mugger to take the money but spare my life, that I've consented to giving away my money.[63] Paulus' solution promises that, in the future, the law will punish the basic inclinations to sociability that keep us from a state of nature. In its own way, it is a tit-for-tat with the emperor himself: it is a claim that imperial intervention, when it engages in faulty attempts at masquerading as juristic reason, will cause the jurists to shake the very foundations of good sense itself. It is a trump card that, due to their specialized knowledge, the jurists always hold, but due to their self-appointed role as "priests" of the law, they refuse to play. The result is a standoff between juristic reason and imperial power.[64]

Yet the drama quickly finds closure. The emperor merely is displeased by the *lex commissoria* (*lex commissoria displicebat ei*); the girl's *tutores* have been declared "suspect," as well, for not carefully overseeing the *pupilla*'s interests. This too influences the emperor (*movit...imperatorem*). (It will be added that the declaration that a tutor is "suspect" is no small issue, and could in cases rise to the level of an offense that carried *infamia*.) Notice that here the standoff has ended: the emperor no longer engages in jurisprudence, but is instead reinstated in his proper role as a primarily *affective* actor who polices community morality and protects the weak. This is not to say, of course, that he cannot contribute to the body of law as shaped by jurisprudence, but only that he cannot contribute *unreasonably*. He cannot make a contribution that a jurist himself would not be able to naturalize within the system. He can, however, operate outside of the system as a source of pity – or, in the case of the tutors, as a source of anger.

***

More might be said about Paulus's *Decrees*. The few fragments that remain are remarkable as evidence of a jurist – and an exceedingly thoughtful and practical one – meditating on the problem of imperial pity, anger, and affect, and their relationship to a legal system more broadly construed. But I should just wish to make two further points.

63 Those who doubt that such reasoning poses a threat to legal systems because it could be held to be formally valid would do well to look at the case of Joel Rene Valdez.

64 Compare Cuomo 2007: 226.

First, aside from Paulus and the emperor, throughout the text there is also a further character who lurks in the background: the imperial fiscus. Throughout the extant fragments of the *Decrees*, the fiscus stands ready to confiscate things from those who fail to follow the rules; in some cases, the fiscus itself has *already* confiscated things, and now the challenge is for the litigants to force it to disgorge its ill-acquired gains.[65] The fiscus is both a representative of the interests of the emperor and an actor in itself: potentially rapacious, constantly threatening to upend the careful plans that families make to transmit their wealth from generation to generation. This looming threat of confiscation seems, in important respects, to reflect broader imperial realities. The emperor was the largest landholder in the empire, and therefore a large number of his subjects were engaged in transactions with respect to imperial properties (especially the leasing of lands or *vectigalia*). What is more, because confiscation was a consequence of errors, arrears, and misdeeds, the odds that an imperial subject would himself have, or have a family member who had ended up in a legal contest with the fiscus were high.[66] The extent of the fiscus's reach was such that it was also the training ground for those who sought a career in the legal profession as an *advocatus fisci* – a lawyer who argued on the fiscus' behalf.[67] In brief, the fiscus would have been a constant presence in people's lives – much more so than the emperor himself.

Yet the fiscus was also a part of the emperor's household – it was, in a sense, the emperor's menacing shadow. It could raise families up

[65] As, perhaps, in the case of Camilia Pia (Peachin 1994). Other cases from the *Decreta* in which the *fiscus* features: 1 *Dec.*, Frg. 63 Lenel = *Dig.* 22.1.16.1 (no litigants named); 1 *Dec.*, Frg. 64 Lenel = *Dig.* 49.14.47 (two cases, one of Moschis, and one concerning Aemilius Ptolemaeus); 2 *Dec.*, Frg. 68 Lenel = *Dig.* 32.27.1 (estate of Pompeius Hermippus); 2 *Dec.*, Frg. 72 = *Dig.* 49.14.48.pr-1 (tacit *fideicommissum* to Pompeius claimed by *fiscus*; and another case where a son sues to get contents of a *fideicommissum* from a confiscated estate); 3 *Dec.*, Frg. 74 Lenel = *Dig.* 46.1.68.1 (responsibilities of sureties in a case where the *fiscus* had confiscated a property); 3 *Dec.*, Frg. 75 Lenel = *Dig.* 49.14.50 (a dispute between the *fiscus* and a tenant as to fruits from a piece of imperial land); 3 *Dec.*, Frg. 77 Lenel = *Dig.* 16.2.24.

[66] In general, Lo Cascio 2015; on large-scale confiscations by emperors, see Maiuro 2012: 82–88. Mackil 2023 has recently developed a model assessing the frequency of confiscation in Classical Greece, arguing that it would have been far more frequent than normally surmised. A similar pattern may have prevailed in the Roman world as well, though for very different reasons. See, in the interim, Rizakis 2015 (focused more on large-scale political shifts).

[67] Dolganov 2020b.

but also ruin them. As such, it served as something of a litmus test for judging the affective disposition of the emperor himself. Was he disciplined with regards to his own self-enrichment? Did he display *verecundia* (moderation, restraint)?[68] How well, or to what extent, was he capable of disciplining those who operated on his behalf? It will be clear enough that these questions were highly sensitive. But it was a major revolution in the law of government that the jurists began taking them on squarely. Both Paulus and Callistratus wrote treatises *de iure fisci*, seeking to bring the actions of the fiscus into line with normal principles of legalistic or bureaucratic government.[69] As such, the presence of the fiscus in Paulus' text is not incidental: if one goal of the *Decrees* was to show the proper role of affect in a system of legality, then it was a choice of some consequence to put the emperor on display managing his emotions with respect not just to pitiable litigants, but with respect to his *own* interests as well. It linked the ability to feel for his subjects to his ability to control his appetites.

It would have been obvious to any reader of the *Decrees* that the generation of emperors prior to Severus had been put to the identical test and had failed it badly: Commodus had famously confiscated massive quantities of goods; Severus' enemies, in the civil wars that ensued in the wake of Commodus' reign, were hardly known for their financial probity.[70] (Severus himself, of course, also confiscated the properties of his rivals in the civil wars which brought him to power, but this fact goes politely unmentioned.) Severus' ability to maintain equanimity with respect to his own coffers works as a sort of quasi-ascetic exercise that enables him to feel the right amount of pity and solicitude for his subjects. In this regard, the emperor's relationship to his fiscus is not radically dissimilar to the relationship between the Christian ascetic and his body: his capacity for self-denial is what enables him to act on behalf of his community.[71] Yet precisely because those coffers are *his*, this sort of balancing act is off limits to his subordinates, the provincial governors.

[68] Brutti 2020: 51.
[69] Fragments of an additional, anonymous treatise *de iure fisci* are also preserved: *FIRA* II 627–30.
[70] Brutti 2020: 16. [71] See, classically, Brown 1971.

Therefore, and secondly: a text like the *Decrees* has to be read alongside the broader endeavors of the law of government to reduce government to something optimally defined in juristic texts. The *Decrees* represents the *uniqueness* of the role of emperor within a broader legal system, not the norm to which governors ought to aspire.[72] A good governor was *not* one who would disagree with a jurist; he was *not* someone who would go beyond the clearly written rules of the law, as expressed primarily in the voice of the emperor himself, through rescripts and legislation.[73] The governor was, on this logic, unable to feel for his subjects in the same way as the emperor. He was, instead, a functionary: his role was ideally to enact the things that the jurists laid out in their well-crafted treatises on imperial government.[74] To the extent that he was encouraged to let his feelings guide his practice, it was to take umbrage with subjects who refused to play their roles: those who refused to take on the daily work of running cities, to take on the obligations of guardianship, or to follow the rules that the state imposed upon them. It was a much narrower role than the governors had previously been allowed.

The law of government, then, was radical in the extent to which it sought to make state practices legible to emperors and central administrators, if not to subjects. It might be considered alongside the other, fundamental Severan legal development, the universal grant of citizenship in AD 212. Both share key features. Both can be explained, at least in part, as stemming from a discomfort with the provincial tendency to raise political questions through the language of law. And both respond to this discomfort by redefining legal practice not as something that emerges historically from the relationship between individual governors and local people, but rather as ideally derived from imperial regulations and abstract juristic reason. To the extent that law is historically derived, the relevant history is ultimately the *internal* history of the metropole. In this respect, both the universal grant of citizenship and the law of government operate not as the great opening of provincial culture to the benefits of Roman citizenship, but rather as the first stages of its great closing – the closing of law as a language for exploring political possibilities, and the (notional, never

72 Noreña 2011, 2012. 73 See Cover 1992a. 74 Cf. Noreña 2011.

actual) end of law as a practice that emerges through face-to-face interactions with specific historical individuals.[75]

Defining governance in juridical terms, even with great skepticism towards processes of abstraction (as in Ulpian's case), may have emerged from an essentially benevolent impulse to articulate a set of basic standards that might cut through the tangle of local relationships and forestall acts of unjustified exploitation. But the ultimate effect of such an intellectual project – and its rapid emergence as a canonical guide to the work of a governor – was to remove law from the world of face-to-face transactions, claims, and documents, and to locate it, instead, in treatises and abstractions from which practice could only ever deviate.[76] It was to render law no longer living – to place it, through writing, into an ontological space upon which quotidian practice and provincial argumentation could not impinge.

***

So did it work? That is, were the efforts of jurists to redescribe governance through the language of jurisprudence ultimately effective? And, if they were, where and when should we look for such effects? Such questions can scarcely begin to be answered here. It would take another volume, perhaps of equivalent size, to trace the development of this process through the course of Late Antiquity. Such a volume would have to account not only for the transformation of cultures of litigation and legal understanding, but also their relationships to new forms of theological and ecclesiastical politics that developed between the fourth and seventh centuries, and to explain how these politics seem to have supplanted the provincial politics of legality.[77] I should like here only to point to a set of features that I think indicate that, over the long term, this radical vision of law and government did indeed seek to reshape the legal world, often with success. It should go without saying that what follows is highly schematic.

75 The extension of citizenship as a liberatory narrative: Sherwin-White 1973.

76 *de officio* as a canonical text: *I.Eph.* 217.

77 For important steps in this direction, see Harries 1999; Humfress 2007. Ecclesiastical and theological politics: Lim 1995; Drake 2000; Letteney 2023. On the case of the ecclesiastical (though not theological) politics of North Africa, see Shaw 2011. I have not yet been able to obtain a copy of Smolin 2024, which seems to promise much on this set of questions.

The juristic vision of government was attractive to emperors. Though nearly seventy-five years separate the jurists of the Severan period from the restoration of political order in the wake of the so-called "crisis of the third century," what seems to emerge as the goals of the imperial state in the end of the third and beginning of the fourth century is different in both ambition and tone and relies, at its core, on a vision of government that would have made sense to a jurist. We might take as a significant moment in this process an edict of Constantine, published "to all of the provincials" shortly after his elevation to sole rulership:[78]

> If there is any man of any position, station, or rank who believes that he can truthfully and manifestly prove against any one of my governors (*iudices*), *comites*, friends, or *palatini* something that appears not to have been done honestly and justly, let him fearlessly and confidently approach and address Me: I Myself will hear, I Myself will judge everything, and if the allegation is proven, I Myself will avenge Myself. Let him speak – let him speak with confidence and good conscience: if he proves (what he says), I, as I have said, will avenge Myself upon him who has deceived Me up to that time with feigned integrity, but I will increase the rank and wealth of the man who makes known and proves this (crime). May the supreme deity thus always be propitious and preserve Me, and, so I desire, may the state be most blessed and prosperous.

Such a policy need only to be stated for its basic absurdity to be revealed: the very officials named by Constantine had, as their purpose, the regulation of access to the emperor himself. There would be no possibility that the emperor himself could hear complaints, directly from the mouths of those injured, against those closest to him. But the emperor's disdain for his agents fits comfortably with a new vision of governance in which the emperors do not announce themselves, even for ideological purposes, as collaborators with men of elite status and great influence in the running of the affairs of state. There will be no gentle interplay between Constantine and his officials along the lines of that between Trajan and Pliny. There is, instead, only the suspicion that the agents of government act ultra vires and that they need to be

[78] *C.Th.* 9.1.4, trans. with valuable discussion in Dillon 2012: 97–107. Drake 2000: 325–36 makes a persuasive case that Constantine was also motivated by "Ulpianic" concerns (namely for *miseri homines*) in crafting his reforms to the jurisdiction of bishops in *Const.Sirm.* 1.

restrained, lest they harm their charges. That is, the vision of governance underpins this declaration is far removed from the world of the first or second centuries AD.[79] Yet it is also basically coherent with the vision of Paulus insofar as it poses the emperor and his subjects as the two actors in this system whose feelings ultimately *matter* to make the legal system work.

At the same time, Constantine's vision is overlaid over a radically changed institutional world: a world of smaller provinces, governed by equestrian functionaries, supervised by a dramatically increased hierarchy of mid-tier officials. In such a world, the endless staff of court officials whose job it was to process complaints into categories and ensure the smooth functioning of the legal machinery are construed normatively as automata, and at worst as self-interested. Like an expensive piece of machinery, they are in need of imperial supervision; should they malfunction, however, they are the object of imperial wrath and revenge.[80] It would make sense, on such a vision, to narrow the ideal scope of the work of any given official, and to place him within a more densely populated hierarchy of supervision.[81]

Such a vision of governance is dismally Weberian. At its best, such a bureaucracy can only operate efficiently – never virtuously. To be sure, Constantine himself seems unaware of what a bleak vision of governance inheres in his words, such that the "prayer" at the end of the edict strikes one as being as absurd as the policy itself. But underlying it, I think, is something that is fundamentally recognizable as the vision of the third century jurists. Their isolation of "government" as something to be regulated by abstract rules would enable a flurry of late antique legislation seeking to bring its powers to heel.

What is more, the insistence that law ought normatively to be contained in books enabled another set of important transformations of late antique government. We might imagine this as a two-part process, with an initial degree of provincial creativity rapidly evoking a harsh

79 There is of course a large literature documenting changes in presumptions about governance. Note, importantly, MacCormack 1981, whose chronological parameters broadly echo my own. For a recent reconsideration of the issue of change in the office of the emperor, see Hekster 2023.

80 Harries 1999: 153–71. Cf. *CJ* 10.17.2 (Constantine "to the people," AD 320 = *C.Th.* 11.7.3, 8.34.3).

81 In general, see Kelly 2004.

and indignant imperial reaction. Thus, one can see the attempt by provincial litigants, as the texts of Roman jurists begin to be treated as normative, to adapt the texts of jurisprudence to their own particular needs. Thus we see, in an exchange between a governor and the city of Ephesus, that the text of Ulpian's *de Officio Proconsulis* seems to be accepted, or at least presented, as a valid guide to Ephesian privileges, alongside other imperial grants to the city.[82] The papyrological record seems to evince a similar move: thus a fragment of Ulpian's commentaries similarly appear in the late third century, though for whose purposes we cannot say.[83] Provincial litigants had, after all, many generations of practice in adapting "rules" to their own desires.

Yet the reaction was swift. These early preserved sections of jurisprudence in private hands quickly come, over the course of the fourth century, to be subject to a set of central hermeneutic controls.[84] These controls take the form of marginal annotations or paratexts directing their readers to construe the text in a particular way – to ensure that readers derive, from the text, only a *single*, authorized meaning.[85] There is every reason to suspect that these were "authorized versions" of texts, complete with a paratextual apparatus that operated, by a new form of deixis, to point to the most significant features of a text: "mark this!" (*sēmeiōsai*) (Figure 9.1). *This*, the annotators insisted, was the thing to be committed to memory; *this* the thing to be applied in *that* context. It has not been lost on modern commentators that, in urging this particular form of reading, the commentaries on jurists show similarities to the emerging genre of commentaries on biblical scripture.[86]

This is in keeping with other developments. Over the course of Late Antiquity, we begin to see institutional elaboration of – and hence agreement with – the most central claim of jurists, dating back to their origins in the late Republic: that law was not simply *one*

[82] *I.Eph.*II 217. Kantor 2009; Filippini 2019. [83] *LDAB* 4130.

[84] An initial collection of the evidence can be found in the appendix to Lenel 1889, collected by L. Sierl. An up-to-date catalogue is currently being made by the project REDHIS (*Rediscovering the hidden structure: A New Appreciation of Juristic Texts and Patterns of Thought in Late Antiquity*), led by Dario Mantovani. Their results to date can be accessed at http://redhis.unipv.it/index.php/texts-static. The annotations are also collected in McNamee 2007: 493–512.

[85] McNamee 1998: 276.

[86] McNamee 1998: 285–86. It might be interesting to broadly compare the style of reading advocated by such paratexts to the styles of reading discussed by Chin 2007.

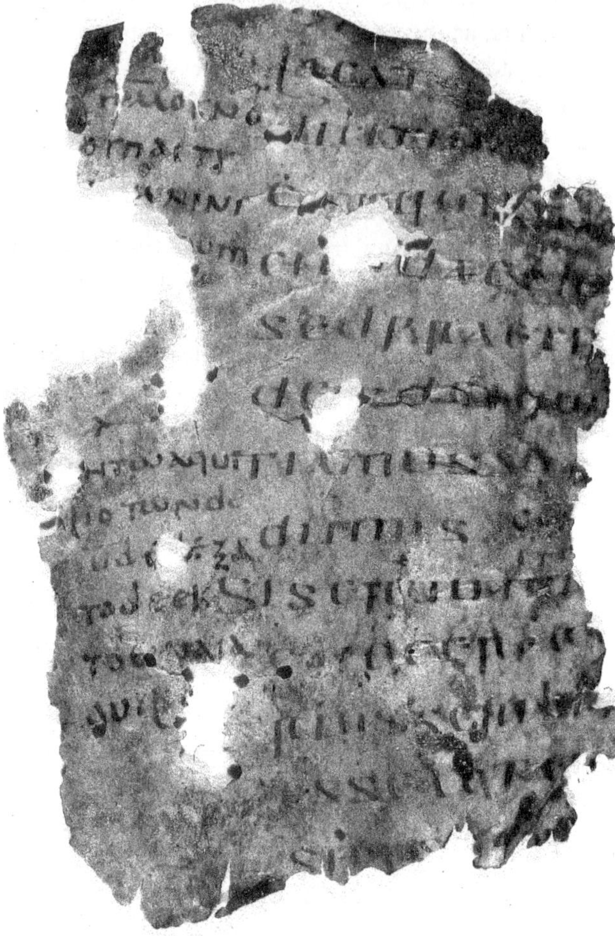

FIGURE 9.1 *PSI* XIV 1449 = *LDAB* 62939: Papyrus containing paratextual features. Latin text (Ulpian, *ad Edictum* 32) with lawyerly Greco-Latin on the left margin. The note at the top instructs the reader "mark this!" = $\overline{\text{σημ}}$ = *sēm(eiōsai)*. Florence, Biblioteca Medicea Laurenziana, by concession of the MiC.

register through which someone might speak of a problem, but a self-contained learned discipline that one must endeavor to master – and to master in Latin. Thus, sometime in the third century a law school, the first that we know of, was opened in the city of Berytus.[87]

[87] Collinet 1925; Hall 2004: 192–217.

The sources on the early structure and content of legal training at Berytus are scarce and uninformative. But it seems clear enough that, following the mastery of Latin, legal training became, in the words of Gregory Thaumaturgus, a "passport" (*ephodion*) to a successful career in the imperial service.[88] Even if the early insistence on the primacy of Latin began to fade in Berytus over the fourth and fifth centuries, and even in light of competing institutions devoted to the study of law (in Alexandria or Constantinople), the idea that legal study emerged from the formal study of legal *texts* – rather than the experience of governing – came to be firmly rooted across the imperial landscape. Rival modes of argument were increasingly drowned out. Emperors even attempted to winnow considerably the corpus of acceptable juristic texts themselves, such that, in AD 426, the emperors could insist that only a small number of jurists were to be taken as canonical:[89]

> We confirm all the writings of Papinian, Paulus, Gaius, Ulpian, and Modestinus, so that the same authority shall attend Gaius as Paulus, Ulpian, and the others, and passages from the whole body of his writings may be cited. We also decree to be valid the learning of those persons whose treatises and opinions all the aforesaid jurisconsults have incorporated in their own work, such as Scaevola, Sabinus, Julianus, and Marcellus, and all others whom they cite, provided that, on account of the uncertainty of antiquity, their books shall be confirmed by a collation of the codices. Moreover, when conflicting opinions are cited, the greater number of the authors shall prevail, or if the numbers should be equal, the authority of that group shall take precedence in which the man of superior genius, Papinian, shall tower above the rest, and as he defeats a single opponent, so he yields to two.

Such an attempt to reduce legal correctness first to jurisprudence, and then second to jurists arranged by mere mathematical weight, was, evidently, an attempt to yet further curtail the sorts of political and rational arguments that would normally have characterized legal interpretation. It was the end result – unimaginative, to be sure – of a process whereby the state committed itself to not listening to the voices that had previously constituted the law.

What, then, of the culture of petition, of provincial politics, and of the insistence upon the legal rights of subjects, now citizens? We

[88] *Panegyric on Origen*, 60. [89] *C.Th.* 1.4.3.pr.–2, trans. Pharr 1952.

should start from the assumption that cultures change slowly – legal cultures in particular. The fact that a model of juristic government had been sketched out by the start of the third century did not mean that we immediately begin to see changes "on the ground." Quite the opposite: there remains a remarkable degree of continuity in the epigraphic and papyrological records attesting to the continued efforts of provincials to use the language of law to try to achieve their goals.[90] It is not until the fourth century AD that one begins to see a marked shift in tone in the language of complaint: rather than the assertion of rights through the language of law, complaints become exceedingly florid, and marked by a language of abjection and self-abasement that would have been surprising in an earlier period.[91] What is perhaps surprising is that this language of abasement starts not at the level of the normal provincial subject, but at comparatively elite levels.

We might take the case of a provincial lawyer, the *scholasticus* Ammon of Panopolis. Notionally trained in the law, Ammon came from the place in the social hierarchy that should, theoretically, have gotten him access and rewards. His brother, Harpokration, was a rhetor attached to the imperial court. Yet when Harpokration went on a tour with the imperial entourage, he left three slaves with Ammon, who in turn entrusted them to another friend. Delayed by travels, Harpokration failed to return in a timely fashion. In the meantime, another imperial official, Eugeneios, claimed that Harpokration had died, and that the slaves were unowned property (*bona vacantia*). He therefore grabbed the slaves and denounced the property as vacant to the *catholicus* of Egypt (who would have been in charge of vacant property). Eugeneios also anticipated Ammon's claims on his fraternal property by getting a fast-tracked rescript from the emperor Constantius II declaring the slaves his if no one claimed them in the meantime. Ammon himself tried heroically to get the slaves back, only to find that he ended up having to concede to the powerful Eugeneios a half share of them. Having been bested by a stronger party, Ammon

[90] Herrmann 1990 argues for an intensification in the third century; I find his broader conclusions unlikely (that the intensification in petitioning reflects systemwide instability), but it is striking in the petitions he collects that the language of law has reached so far down the social scale. Similar things might be said for the petitions of Egyptian Great Oasis collected in *P.Kell.*

[91] In general, Kovelman 1991; Feissel and Gascou 2004; Fournet 2004, 2019.

steadied himself to compose a petition, asking for the return of his rightful property. Pieces of no fewer than nine drafts exist. From these fragments, the florid and verbose introduction can be reconstructed:[92]

> [The Thebaid remembers your magistracy there,] my lord, and throughout that time I was filled with true happiness [--] while the goodwill of the gods together with Agathos Daimon was guiding the land of the Upper Egyptians, and among the Lower Egyptians and all the rest of mankind [we] were considered to be blessed and enviable because of such good fortune like unto which [neither] before did that province [have] nor hereafter may it expect to behold another (such) kindly guardian. Now the inhabitants of the most splendid city are successors to that prosperity of ours; but I myself too reckon that at present I have again come into a share of good fortune since it has been allotted to me too that I appear in court pleading my case before so great a magistrate and judge, whose unmatched judgment among diverse peoples both hitherto and now experience has shown. While I myself, to be sure, know that a quiet life free from business befits those educated in philosophy and rhetoric, I have come, my lord, constrained by those who have caused me to be investigated in this affair, and provoked to this present protestation. For if it were possible for those who have chosen [seclusion?] according to the dictates of their nature to enjoy to the end [---]. But envy threatens the honorable [--].

It is almost certain that Ammon lost – certainly in this round of litigation, and probably again later. Even if he had not won, one can hardly take confidence in the legal system from the spectacle of a man of high renown, from a distinguished family, having to concede a half-share of ownership in his brother's slaves to a man whom the brother had likely never met. To the extent, then, that Ammon was a lawyer, it must be admitted that he was not a very good one. But the florid rhetoric, packed with self-abasement of the petitioner, and the endless aggrandizement of the recipient, spread through the landscape nonetheless, culminating in the interminable, endlessly self-abasing, and nearly unreadable petitions of the sixth century notary Dioscorus of Aphrodito.[93]

This is more than the mere "rhetoricization" of law. It bespeaks a fundamental shift in the things that the state itself was willing to hear. The redefinition of law as a textual, mandarin practice meant the

92 *P.Ammon* 7–15.1–13 (AD 348), trans. eds. Cf. Shaw 2015, on the case of Augustine.
93 In general, MacCoull 1988; Fournet 2004.

exclusion of a great number of voices from the legal arena by defining their complaints as somehow not-law. To assert one's rights in the language of law thus came, in an important sense, to be unspeakable – at least when they took the comparatively strident tone of the high Empire. Stridency might be practiced by a bishop or a distinguished ascetic – even then cautiously – but never by a layperson.

But the effects of this transformation went still further: by removing "the law" to an ontological space radically divorced from the world of practice, the late Roman state, following the jurists, left to daily practice *only* the language of pity and abjection – only the language of affect. As Philo of Alexandria had once said, subjects are the slaves of rulers; but such a situation was tolerable insofar as the relationship of domination was guided by law, rather than the will of the ruler himself.[94] Following the lead of Philo, we might say that this form of domination was acceptable so long as it was a three-part relationship – ruler, subject, law. Over the long course of Late Antiquity, and as a consequence of the law of government, the relationship would become two-part. Without the ability to speak to a ruler in a language that promoted problem-solving and the mutual recognition of rights and duties, power was simply revealed for what it was: a form of naked domination that depended on the sufferance of rulers. Better, under such circumstances, to present oneself as a dutiful slave seeking the aid of a benevolent master. Aesop would have raised an eyebrow.

[94] *Legat.* 119, discussed above, Chapter 5.

Epilogue

Why Premodernity?

As the Roman world transitioned into what we now call Late Antiquity, the legal system transformed alongside it. Law became increasingly a specialized discourse, tucked away in books, and divorced from quotidian social interaction. Accordingly, it became less worth fighting over, and less worth fighting *through*. In a world of legal mandarinism, it no longer offered the inhabitants of empire a resource for thinking through their place in the social and political landscape, or for articulating the responsibilities of government towards its subjects.

Never having been especially fond of the legal politics of its subjects, in Late Antiquity the Roman state found its allergies only aggravated. The doing of justice, which had previously been the most important ritual through which important truths about the imperial state were negotiated with and displayed to the public, was increasingly done indoors, behind curtains, and in offices – *in secretario*.[1] It was only in the rarest of cases that justice would return to the public sphere. When it did, it would be carefully stage-managed, lest it invite comment, discussion, or negotiation.[2] Politics did not die in Late Antiquity, but legal politics did. And without legal politics, the universe of political discourse found itself dramatically curtailed if not impoverished. Politics happened first among bishops, meeting in

[1] Färber 2014.

[2] On the sixth century trial at the borders of empire described by Agathias, see Sizgorich 2006; Ando 2021.

councils, and secondly by the clergy preaching to the laity.[3] In neither case did it happen in the public spaces of the early imperial cities – unless one is so certain of the natural domination of Christianity that one wishes to count a church a public space. Even on that account, to the extent that the broad population was present, it was ultimately as an audience, and one that needed *instruction*, rather than a group that might have had a competing claim to make.[4]

Public spaces of course did not go away. The populace, assembled in the theater or the circus, remained a potent force. In such contexts, the collective shouts of subjects (guided by professional *claqueurs*) did come to operate as official judgments of the quality of the work of imperial servants, or as a way to make formal requests to visiting emperors and dignitaries.[5] But such politics were not legal in nature, and they were without hermeneutical value for subjects. They did not turn on negotiating the rules and principles by which the population agreed to live, nor did they provide a register by which subjects might think through the nature of their status in the world. No matter how much modern apologists might recognize agency in such collective behaviors, one must admit that, in contrast, for example, to the scenes Philo described in first century Alexandria, this was a deeply attenuated form of political communication. Small wonder, then, that attempts at political communication often resolved into riots, which were, just as often, bloodily suppressed by raw state power.[6]

***

This long episode of law's closing might seem the cousin of a better-known, modern European episode. As the Roman Empire melted away, it left behind a world of legal localism. Church law, city law,

[3] The bibliography on sermons is immense. As an especially productive and evocative starting point, see Shaw 2011.

[4] This did not, of course, relieve the emperors of the burden of governing, or the populace of the burden of trying to obtain rights: e.g., Schmidt-Hofner 2008. But the shift in ideology is important, and the corresponding decline in the importance of public contest meaningful.

[5] Liebeschuetz 1972: 208–19; Cameron 1976: esp. 230–49; Roueché 1984; MacMullen 2008: 12–23. Haas 1997: 67 takes the position that Alexandria lacked claques; it was sufficiently riotous, it seems, that no formal or informal leadership was necessary.

[6] On Alexandria, Haas 1997; Watts 2010. More generally, Magalhães de Oliveira 2020.

local law, merchant law, and more divided the European world into an infinite number of overlapping jurisdictions (if that is indeed the right word).[7] The forms of political power that remained in such a radically decentralized landscape either tolerated this legal cacophony or took it as a natural fact. Eventually, the rediscovery of Roman law added new rules to the mix, along with a vision of European unity and legal consistency. By a haltingly slow process – the details of which remain hotly debated by historians – political and legal powers restarted processes of centralization. The eventual goal of these leaders was the production of homogeneity: that jurisdictions should be regularized, that law should be predictable and rational, that local atavisms be eliminated from the system more generally. Haltingly – again – over the course of the long period that we now name Early Modernity (vague in the same ways as Late Antiquity), modern states eventually were made to develop. Legal precision and consistency marked a state as fundamentally "complete" in the Weberian sense: as being able to exercise the legitimate use of force, according to roughly predictable rules, across all of its particular territories. The last step, for most European polities (or, as one likes it, nations *in statu nascendi*), was the creation of complete codes of so-called "black letter" law: such codes were far more specialized products than their antique predecessors, but they represent, in an important sense, an analogous process of centralization.[8]

For better and for worse (though on balance perhaps for better), we live in this black-letter world today – or, at least, we live in a world in which law starts, and often finishes, in books: statutes, decisions, treatises, and texts. Our legal education systems are highly specialized institutions designed to train aspiring minds in construing and

[7] In a recent paper on medieval slavery, Hannah Skoda has recently presented a valuable critique of the "legal pluralism" of the medieval world, rejecting the term as offering too tempting an analogy to an ordered system of competing jurisdictions. She argues (to my mind persuasively) that the world was composed of overlapping legal *tendencies*, rhetorics, and repertoires of possible rules that could be applied. These all could be drawn on in varying combinations, by litigants and judges alike. I look forward to her paper's eventual publication.

[8] E.g., Berman 1983. The Anglophone world is the conspicuous outlier with respect to codification, but this seems to have had little net effect overall: common law systems still seem to produce no more – and possibly even fewer – legal surprises or inconsistencies than their continental peers. In both cases, expertise triumphs.

producing such texts. This sort of specialization seems well suited to a world of tremendous jurisdictional, transactional, and economic complexity. By choice and by necessity, law in the modern world is everywhere a mandarin practice, self-consciously distinguished from the everyday.

This necessarily makes law feel distant from and inaccessible to the contemporary citizen. And even though, as two generations of legal anthropologists have long since demonstrated, modern citizens have strong normative commitments to ideas of legality, "official" law rarely feels compelled to meet citizens where they stand, or even meet them half-way.[9] We live, that is, in an era where the divorce between "law" and "society" has been thoroughly finalized.[10] And despite the optimism of a small class of critics who seek to locate law-*making* capacities in the world of the everyday, this situation seems unlikely to change much if at all.[11] To live in this world is a gain, but also a loss – it is to lose the critiques of an Aesop, the protests of a Philo, and the cunning of a Dionysia.

In a sense, then, there are analogous processes of legal transformation between Late Antiquity and Early Modernity: they both might be said to map a change from diversity to homogeneity, from amateur to specialist, from inclusive of difference to exclusive of difference, and from diffuse and unpredictable modes of state power to concentrated and efficacious ones.[12] What, then, might be learned from the premodern case? Does premodern history only offer us a way of remembering that modernity is not nearly as unique as we might hope? That everything new is somehow old again?

***

I should like to argue a somewhat different point: that the study of the premodern legal transformation is not meaningful only by reference to some better-documented analogy. I should like to suggest that it

[9] Merry 1990; Yngvesson 1993; Markovits 2010.

[10] Sarat 1985. This is in spite of important *cries de cour* like that of Nonet 1978, who both insists on the blurriness of the boundaries between the two *and* imagines a world in which sociological inquiry serves to improve law's practice.

[11] Cover 1992b; Constable 2014. For a fascinating meditation on these problems in a pluralist/imperial context, see Richland 2008.

[12] On ancient state power, see Ando and Richardson 2017.

can teach us something positive, something that helps us to better understand aspects of the more contemporary world that have, perhaps, been hiding in plain sight.

I start from a perhaps unlikely source. In his classic reading of the late fourth century historian Ammianus Marcellinus, Erich Auerbach located a shift in perspective that emerged alongside the changes that I have mapped across the chapters of this book: the world of the Late Antiquity, he argued, had become more "magical and sensory" "at the expense of the human and objectively rational." Social relationships were reduced to "a physical relation based on magic and brute force." "Everywhere," he wrote, "human emotion and rationality yield to the magically and somberly sensory, to the graphic and the gestural."[13]

One does not have to argue for the "spread of irrationalism" to understand that Auerbach captured something important. We have since come to better understand the structure and content of imperial ceremonial, and the way it operated to link the emperor, as head of state, to his subjects through a set of deeply evocative rituals.[14] But, as Auerbach noticed, the entire attitude towards *logos* had shifted. To the extent that *logos* was an important part of a broader system, it was no longer the sort of *logos* that was presumed to be available to all subjects. It was instead the language of the panegyrist. It was the impeccably trained, exceedingly formal language of ceremony. Allusive, evasive, evocative – or, in Auerbach's words, somberly sensory, graphic, and gestural – such language was indeed magical, in the sense that it was designed to evoke a figure – the emperor – who transcended the normal constraints of human materiality. Through the language of panegyric, a consensus was enacted. It was a consensus that the state was held together by a figure who mediated between this world and another. The emperor was virtue and victory embodied, he was a bringer of light, his physical person brought peace, and so forth. He was not historically produced, but rather unitary and transcendent. Whether there was a common rationality that bound the state to its subjects was totally beside the point.[15]

[13] Auerbach 2003 [1953]: 52–54. [14] MacCormack 1981.

[15] Common rationality: Ando 2000. On the end of *civilitas* as a virtue, and the waning importance of the judgment of subjects, see MacCormack 1981: e.g., 59, 82–83, 110. The chronological occurrence of statuary in the late antique period seems to largely echo this transformation: Smith and Ward-Perkins 2016.

So how does this relate to the question of legality? The ways legality is conceived has effects on the aspirations of the state more generally. The presumption that the capacity to reason meaningfully about rules is spread across society means that law must be conceived as a mode of reasoning with one's subjects through a process of dialogue. By contrast, the presumption that law is a sort of specialized, technical discourse that is the property of the state means that law is conceived, first and foremost, not as a means to reason with subjects, but as a force to mold them. Armed with such a theory, one can engage in the process of trying to recreate one's subjects to one's liking – one can endeavor to create, through the language and force of law, a vision of utopia. In the Christian vision of this legal utopia that emerged over late antiquity (taking its most developed form from the late fourth century onwards), legality and state power could be fused together to stamp out heresies and create a populace marked by unanimity of thought and belief. Through the "brute force" of the state, and through legislation's magical power to change people's status through speech acts, embedded in texts, the fact of diversity and heterogeneity, with all of its vast shades of difference, could be immediately transformed and recast. A heterogeneous community could resolve, through the force of legal prohibition, into a world of *two* communities – one virtuous, and another worthy only of punishment, exclusion, and eventual eradication.[16] Within such a system, the ambitions of the state to use legality to achieve long-sought-after unanimity are more easily indulged. The fantasy of creating a virtuous – if necessarily subservient – populace that falls into line is more easily indulged. And the image of unanimity that undergirds such acts is fundamentally magical or transcendent: it seeks to arrange things,

[16] I owe a great deal here to the remarkable treatment of Sizgorich 2009: esp. 132, which focused on the role of the ascetic. Whether the state lagged other militant communities in the Empire remains an open question. As I suggested above (page 366), there is an important convergence between the particular understandings of the emperor and the particular features of the ascetic – and these relate to more than just the capacity of each to exercise actual power in society. There is also a question of its relation of each form of power to an increasingly militant neighbor. On interimperial competition and the crafting of state ideologies, see Canepa 2009. On toleration and its limits in the Sassanian context, Payne 2015 and now Gross 2024. It should also be noted that Rabbinic arguments are similarly both utopian and reductive: see, most importantly, Boyarin 2004. The transformation was broadly late antique.

even temporarily, into a tableau of perfect harmony that approaches the perfect or divine.

In other words, once law stops being a register of *shared* communication through which subjects can articulate their expectations of government (and vice versa) and begins to be a mode of ordering a broader "society," a whole range of transformations, no matter how violent, can be affected under the theory that one is doing the work of transcendence. This conclusion is, to be sure, not exclusively late antique: there were earlier, if more inchoate, attempts to use legislation to create moments of near-magical unity, such as the mandate for universal sacrifice in the middle of the third century. But with the benefit of hindsight this edict appears instead to be a harbinger of a longer and much more intensified process: the attempt to create, through acts of law, unity from diversity. The process might be traced from the Diocletianic edict of Maximum Prices through the edict of Constantine "To all the Provincials" (discussed in Chapter 9), coming to a point of completion in the reign of Theodosius I.

These would be fully magical moments: acts of political willpower that attempted to transcend the brute facts of everyday life. Put differently, this new theory of law would equate acts of legislation with acts of political theology, where, through an act of law, the state could sweep away the ugly mess of politics and material reality and aspire towards perfection and utopianism. Such a mode of legislating is deeply authoritarian and deeply illiberal. It is also tempting, because it offers the possibility of formally drawing lines through the complexity of actually existing communities, leaving in its wake just the virtuous and those who must suffer exclusion. Law, on such a reading, becomes Schmittian in the most grotesque sense: as simply the most efficacious tool for forcibly reducing the multifarious political world to *just* a question of friend and enemy. And as Schmitt himself would have been the first to point out, such a move was founded, in its first principles, on essentially theological (or, should we prefer, cosmic) presumptions.

The magical-utopian feature of late antique legislation is, I would argue, one of the outcomes of a state asserting total control over law itself. Such control was made possible by reimagining it as a book-based technology, rather than a mode of speaking about problems. I should like to suggest that these transformations are present in more contemporary contexts as well. We all too rarely admit that law in modern society has magical or transcendent properties. Our contemporary legal systems are, for the present, strongly committed to the idea that legality is, fundamentally, an enlightened and rational mode of thinking and reasoning. Our modern state, moreover, is a notionally disenchanted one: a Weberian bureaucracy, an iron cage. Yet clawing at the edges of our supposed commitment to the secular, the liberal, and the enlightened is the fantasy of law as *redemption*: of legislation as the final verdict upon our enemies, as capable of turning back time to a notional golden age by outlawing people or behaviors "we" find abhorrent; as the avenging sword of justice and punishment; or the agent of transcendent liberation through the conferral or withdrawal of rights. This is just as present in the attempt to define the modern nation state along totally ethnic lines as it is in the attempts to ban particular discourses from an educational or public sphere, or from the attempt to define certain groups as formally outside of a system that they had previously felt included them.[17] The list of similar projects proposed and desired, if not enacted, might be extended. It would be long indeed.

If the story of the premodern roots of law's capacity to engage in magical transformation can teach us anything, it is that our self-confidence about "our" secular technologies and technical expertise can be reduced, quite quickly in practice, to a sort of magical thinking, the same sort for which we might otherwise mock, say, a fifth- or sixth-century emperor. Yet we find ourselves, increasingly, just as often operating from identical assumptions regarding the possibility of law and legislation. We similarly endorse the role of the state and the person of the ruler as a totemic figure capable of producing emancipation and unanimity. And to our great discredit, we engage in utopian fantasies whereby we imagine achieving consensus without the hard work of reasoning – individually and, perhaps more uncomfortably, intimately – with those with whom we might disagree, or even with those we hate. This, perhaps, should alarm us.

[17] On the violence of defining states as nations, see the remarkable account of Judt 2005.

Bibliography

Abbott, Frank Frost, and Johnson, Allen Chester. 1926. *Municipal Administration in the Roman Empire*. Princeton: Princeton University Press.

Adams, J. N. 2003. *Bilingualism and the Latin Language*. Cambridge: Cambridge University Press.

Alcock, Susan E. 1993. *Graecia Capta: The Landscapes of Roman Greece*. Cambridge: Cambridge University Press.

Allehbi, Mohammed A. 2021. "Law and Sovereignty: Criminal Justice in Premodern Islam." PhD, Vanderbilt University.

Alonso, José-Luis. 2013. "The Status of Peregrine Law in Egypt: 'Customary Law' and Legal Pluralism in the Roman Empire." *Journal of Juristic Papyrology (Papyrology AD 2013: 27th International Congress of Papyrology)* 43: 351–404.

2020. "The Constitutio Antoniniana and Private Legal Practice in the Eastern Empire" in Kimberley Czajkowski and Benedikt Eckhardt, eds., *Law in the Roman Provinces*. 44–64. Oxford: Oxford University Press.

Alston, Richard. 1995. *Soldier and Society in Roman Egypt: A Social History*. London: Routledge.

1997. "Philo's 'In Flaccum': Ethnicity and Social Space in Roman Alexandria." *Greece & Rome* 44: 165–75.

2020. "Ethnic Violence in Roman Alexandria: A Comparative Approach." *Acta Classica* 63: 1–29.

Ameling, Walter. 1983. *Herodes Atticus*. 2 vols. Hildesheim: George Olms Verlag.

Amitay, Ory. 2006. "The Story of Gviha Ben-Psisa and Alexander the Great." *Journal for the Study of the Pseudepigrapha* 16: 61–74.

Anagnostou-Canas, Barbara. 2004. "La valeur des précédents judiciaires dans l'Égypte romaine: État de la question." *Droits et Cultures* 47: 47–65.

Anastasiades, V. I., and Souris, George A. 2000. *An Index to Roman Imperial Constitutions from Greek Inscriptions and Papyri: 27 BC to 284 AD.* Berlin: de Gruyter.

Ando, Clifford. 2000. *Imperial Ideology and Provincial Loyalty in the Roman Empire.* Berkeley: University of California Press.

2010a. "'A Dwelling Beyond Violence': On the Uses and Disadvantages of History for Contemporary Republicans." *History of Political Thought* 31: 183–220.

2010b. "Imperial Identities," in Tim Whitmarsh, ed., *Local Knowledge and Microidentities in the Imperial Greek World.* 17–45. Cambridge: Cambridge University Press.

2011. *Law, Language, and Empire in the Roman Tradition.* Philadelphia: University of Pennsylvania Press.

2012a. *Imperial Rome, AD 193–284: The Critical Century.* Edinburgh: Edinburgh University Press.

2012b. "The Roman City in the Roman Period," in S. Benoist, ed., *Rome, A City and Its Empire in Perspective: The Impact of the Roman World through Fergus Millar's Research.* 109–24. Leiden: Brill.

2015. "Fact, Fiction, and Social Reality in Roman Law," in M. Del Mar and W. Twinning, eds., *Legal Fictions in Theory and Practice.* 295–323. Boston: Springer.

2017. "The Ambitions of Government: Territoriality and Infrastructural Power in Ancient Rome," in Clifford Ando and Seth Richardson, eds., *Ancient States and Infrastructural Power.* 115–48. Philadelphia: University of Pennsylvania Press.

2019. "Hannibal's Legacy: Sovereignty and Territoriality in Republican Rome," in Karl-Joachim Hölkeskamp, Sema Karatas, and Roman Roth, eds., *Empire, Hegemony, or Anarchy? Rome and Italy, c. 201–31 B.C.E.* 55–81. Stuttgart: Franz Steiner.

2020. "The Certainty of Documents: Records of Proceedings as Guarantors of Memory in Political and Legal Argument," in Clifford Ando and William P. Sullivan, eds., *The Discovery of the Fact.* 155–74. Ann Arbor: University of Michigan Press.

2021. "Performing Justice in Republican Empire, 1–565 CE," in Katell Berthelot, Natalie B. Dohrman, and Capucine Nemo-Pekelman, eds., *Legal Engagement: The Reception of Roman Law and Tribunals by Jews and Other Inhabitants of the Empire.* 69–85. Rome: École française de Rome.

Ando, Clifford, and Richardson, Seth. eds. 2017. *Ancient States and Infrastructural Power: Europe, Asia, and America.* Philadelphia: University of Pennsylvania Press.

Arnaoutoglou, Ilias N. 2020. "An Outline of Legal Norms and Practices in Roman Macedonia (167 BCE–212 CE)," in Kimberley Czajkowski and Benedikt Eckhardt, eds., *Law in the Roman Provinces.* 284–312. Oxford: Oxford University Press.

Auerbach, Erich. 2003 [1953]. *Mimesis: The Representation of Reality in Western Literature*. Trans. by Willard R. Trask. Princeton: Princeton University Press.

Bagnall, Roger S. 1997. "A Kinder, Gentler Roman Army?" *Journal of Roman Archaeology* 10: 504–12.

Bagnall, Roger S., and Frier, Bruce W. 1994. *The Demography of Roman Egypt*. Cambridge: Cambridge University Press.

Barnes, T. D. 1968a. "Legislation against the Christians." *Journal of Roman Studies* 58: 32–50.

1968b. "Pre-Decian Acta Martyrum." *Journal of Theological Studies* 19: 509–31.

Bauman, Richard A. 1967. *The Crimen Maiestatis in the Roman Republic and Augustan Principate*. Johannesburg: Witwatersrand University Press.

1989. *Lawyers and Politics in the Early Roman Empire*. Munich: C. H. Beck.

Baumgarten, Albert I. 1997. *The Flourishing of Jewish Sects in the Maccabean Era: An Interpretation*. Leiden: Brill.

Bauschatz, John. 2013. *Law and Enforcement in Ptolemaic Egypt*. New York: Cambridge University Press.

Behr, Charles A. 1968. *Aelius Aristides and the Sacred Tales*. Amsterdam: A. M. Hakkert.

1981. *P. Aelius Aristides: The Complete Works*. 2 vols. Leiden: Brill.

Benton, Lauren A. 2010. *A Search for Sovereignty: Law and Geography in European Empires, 1400–1900*. Cambridge: Cambridge University Press.

Benton, Lauren, and Ross, Richard J. eds. 2013. *Legal Pluralism and Empires, 1500–1850*. New York: New York University Press.

Berkowitz, Beth A. 2011. *Defining Jewish Difference: From Antiquity to the Present*. Cambridge: Cambridge University Press.

Berman, Harold J. 1983. *Law and Revolution: The Formation of the Western Legal Tradition*. Cambridge, MA: Harvard University Press.

Berthelot, Katell. 2011. "Philo's Perception of the Roman Empire." *Journal for the Study of Judaism in the Persian, Hellenistic, and Roman Period* 42: 166–87.

2021. *Jews and Their Roman Rivals: Pagan Rome's Challenge to Israel*. Princeton: Princeton University Press.

Betz, Hans-Dieter. 1979. *Galatians: A Commentary on Paul's Letter to the Churches in Galatia*. Philadelphia: Fortress Press.

Bispham, Edward. 2007. *From Asculum to Antium: The Municipalization of Italy from the Social War to Augustus*. Oxford: Oxford University Press.

Blamire, A. ed. 1989. *Plutarch: Life of Kimon*. London: Institute of Classical Studies.

Blanco-Pérez, Aitor. 2015. "Apamea and the Integration of a Roman Colony in Western Asia Minor," in Saskia Roselaar, ed., *Processes of Change and Integration in the Roman World*. 136–53. Leiden: Brill.

Blanshard, A. J. L. 2004. "Depicting Democracy: An Exploration of Art and Text in the Law of Eukrates." *Journal of Hellenic Studies* 124: 1–15.

Blouin, Katherine. 2005. *Le conflit judéo-alexandrin de 38–41: L'identité juive à l'épreuve*. Paris: L'Harmattan.

2014. *Triangular Landscapes: Environment, Society, and the State in the Nile Delta under Roman Rule*. Oxford: Oxford University Press.

Bohak, Gideon. 1996. *Joseph and Aseneth and the Jewish Temple in Heliopolis*. Atlanta: Scholars Press.

Borg, Barbara. ed. 2004. *Padeia: The World of the Second Sophistic*. Berlin: de Gruyter.

Bourdieu, Pierre. 1984. *Distinction: A Social Critique of the Judgment of Taste*. Trans. by Richard Nice. Cambridge, MA: Harvard University Press.

Bowden, William. 2011. "'Alien Settlers Consisting of Romans': Identity and Built Environment in the Julio-Claudian Foundations of Epirus in the Century after Actium," in Rebecca Sweetman, ed., *Roman Colonies in the First Century of Their Foundation*. 101–16. Oxford: Oxbow Books.

Bowersock, Glen Warren. 1961. "Eurycles of Sparta." *Journal of Roman Studies* 51: 112–18.

1969. *Greek Sophists in the Roman Empire*. Oxford: Clarendon Press.

1995. *Martyrdom and Rome*. Cambridge: Cambridge University Press.

2003. "The Tel Shalem Arch and P.Nahal Hever/Seiyal 8," in P. Schaefer, ed., *The Bar Kokhba War Reconsidered: New Perspectives on the Second Jewish Revolt against Rome*. 171–80. Tübingen: Mohr Siebeck.

Bowes, Kim, and Grey, Cam. 2021. "Conclusions: The Roman Peasant Reframed," in Kim Bowes, ed., *The Roman Peasant Project, 2009–2014: Excavating the Roman Rural Poor*. 617–40. Philadelphia: University of Pennsylvania Press.

Bowie, E. L. 1970. "Greeks and Their Past in the Second Sophistic." *Past and Present* 46: 3–41.

1982. "The Importance of Sophists." *Yale Classical Studies* 27: 29–60.

Bowman, Alan K. 1971. *The Town Councils of Roman Egypt*. Amsterdam: A. M. Hakkert.

2017. "The State and the Economy: Fiscality and Taxation," in Andrew Wilson and Alan K. Bowman, eds., *Trade, Commerce, and the State in the Roman World*. 27–52. Oxford: Oxford University Press.

Bowman, Alan K., and Rathbone, Dominic. 1992. "Cities and Administration in Roman Egypt." *Journal of Roman Studies* 82: 107–127.

Boyarin, Daniel. 1994. *A Radical Jew: Paul and the Politics of Identity*. Berkeley: University of California Press.

1999. *Dying for God: Martyrdom and the Making of Christianity and Judaism*. Stanford: Stanford University Press.

2004. *Border Lines: The Partition of Judaeo-Christianity*. Philadelphia: University of Pennsylvania Press.

2009. *Socrates and the Fat Rabbis*. Chicago: University of Chicago Press.

Bradley, Keith. 1987. *Slaves and Masters in the Roman Empire: A Study in Social Control*. New York and Oxford: Oxford University Press.

2000. "Animalizing the Slave: The Truth of Fiction." *Journal of Roman Studies* 90: 110–25.

Branham, R. Bracht. 1989. *Unruly Eloquence: Lucian and the Comedy of Traditions*. Cambridge: Harvard University Press.

Brélaz, Cédric. 2005. *La sécurité publique en Asie Mineure sous le Principat (Ier – IIIeme s. ap. J.-C.)*. Basel: Schwabe.

2011. "Aelius Aristide (Or. 50.72–93) et le choix des irénarques par le gouverneur: à propos d'une inscription d'Acmonia," in N. Badoud, ed., *Philologos Dionysios: Mélanges offerts au professeur Denis Knoepfler*. 603–37. Geneva: Librarie Droz.

2013. "La vie démocratique dans les cités greques à l'époque impériale romaine: Notes de lectures et orientations de la recherche." *Topoi* 18: 367–99.

2016. "Des communautés de citoyens romains sur le territoire des cités grecques: statut politico-administratif et régime des terres," in François Lerouxel and Anne-Valérie Pont, eds., *Propriétaires et citoyens dans l'Orient romain*. 69–85. Berdeaux: Ausonius Éditions.

ed. 2017. *L'Heritage grec des colonies romaines d'orient: Interactions culturelles dans les provinces hellénophones de l'empire romain*. Paris: De Boccard.

2018. *Philippes, colonie romaine d'Orient: Recherches d'histoire institutionelle et sociale*. Athens: École Française d'Athènes.

2020. "Local Understandings of Roman Criminal Law and Procedure in Asia Minor," in Kimberley Czajkowski and Benedikt Eckhardt, eds., *Law in the Roman Provinces*. 157–84. Oxford: Oxford University Press.

2024. "Rural Communities and Early Christianity in Roman Philippi: A Tale of Missed Opportunities," in Alan Cadwallader, James R. Harrison, Angela Standhartiger, and L. L. Welborn, eds., *The Village in Antiquity and the Rise of Early Christianity*. 275–93. London: T&T Clark.

Bretone, Mario. 2008. *Ius controversum nella giurisprudenza classica*. Rome: Bari Editore.

Broughton, T. Robert S. 1935. "Some Non-colonial Coloni of Augustus." *Transactions of the American Philological Association* 66: 18–24.

Broux, Yanne. 2019. "Imperial vs. Non-imperial *ousiai* in Julio-Claudian Egypt." *Chronique d'Égypte* 94: 149–76.

Brown, Peter. 1971. "The Rise and Function of the Holy Man in Late Antiquity." *Journal of Roman Studies* 61: 80–101.

1984. "Late Antiquity and Islam: Parallels and Contrasts," in Barbara Daly Metcalf, ed., *Moral Conduct and Authority: The Place of Adab in South Asian Islam*. 23–37. Berkeley: University of California Press.

1992. *Power and Persuasion in Late Antiquity: Towards a Christian Empire*. Madison: University of Wisconsin Press.

Brunt, P. A. 1961. "Charges of Provincial Maladministration under the Early Principate." *Historia* 10: 189–227.

1975. "The Administrators of Roman Egypt." *Journal of Roman Studies* 65: 124–47.

1990. "Publicans in the Principate," in *Roman Imperial Themes*. 354–432. Oxford: Clarendon Press.

1990 [1966]. "Procuratorial Jurisdiction," in *Roman Imperial Themes*. 163–87. Oxford: Clarendon Press.

Brutti, Massimo. 2020. *Iulius Paulus Decretorum Libri Tres Imperialium Sententiarum in Cognitionibus Prolatarum Libri Sex*. Rome: L'Erma di Bretschneider.

Bryen, Ari Z. 2012a. "Judging Empire: Courts and Culture in Rome's Eastern Provinces." *Law and History Review* 30: 771–811.

2012b. "Review of Schiavone, *The Invention of Law in the West*." *Bryn Mawr Classical Review* 2012.06.16.

2013. *Violence in Roman Egypt: A Study in Legal Interpretation*. Philadelphia: University of Pennsylvania Press.

2014a. "Law in Many Pieces." *Classical Philology* 104: 346–65.

2014b. "Martyrdom, Rhetoric, and the Politics of Judicial Procedure." *Classical Antiquity* 33: 243–80.

2016a. "Reading the Citizenship Papyrus (P.Giss. 40)," in Clifford Ando, ed., *Citizenship and Empire in Europe, 200–1900*. 29–43. Stuttgart: Franz Steiner Verlag.

2016b. "When Law Goes off the Rails, or, *Aggadah* among the *iurisperiti*." *Critical Analysis of Law* 3: 9–29.

2018. "Labeo's *iniuria*: Violence and Politics in the Age of Augustus." *Chiron* 48: 17–52.

2019a. "Politics, Justice, and Reform in Dio's *Euboicus*." *TAPA* 149: 127–48.

2019b. "Responsa," in Simon Stern, Maksimillian Del Mar, and Bernadette Meyler, eds., *The Oxford Handbook of Law and the Humanities*. Oxford: Oxford University Press.

2021a. "Citizenship and Its Alternatives: A View from the East," in Clifford Ando and Myles Lavan, eds., *Roman and Local Citizenship in the Long Second Century AD*. 41–68. Oxford: Oxford University Press.

2021b. "A Frenzy of Sovereignty: Punishment in P.Aktenbuch," in Katell Berthelot, Natalie B. Dohrmann, and Capucine Nemo-Pekelman, eds., *Legal Engagement: The Reception of Roman Law and Tribunals by Jews and Other Inhabitants of the Empire*. 89–108. Rome: Ecole Française de Rome.

Bubb, Claire, and Peachin, Michael. 2023. "Setting Medicine and Law Apart, Together," in Claire Bubb and Michael Peachin, eds., *Medicine and the Law Under the Roman Empire*. Oxford: Oxford University Press.

Buckland, W. W. 1934. "L'edictum provinciale." *Revue historique de droit français et étranger* 13: 81–96.

Burbank, Jane, and Cooper, Frederick. 2010. *Empires in World History: Power and the Politics of Difference*. Princeton: Princeton University Press.

Burkhalter, Fabienne. 1990. "Archives locales et archives centrales in Egypte romaine." *Chiron* 20: 191–216.

Burns, Robert P. 1999. *A Theory of the Trial*. Princeton: Princeton University Press.

2009. *The Death of the American Trial*. Chicago: University of Chicago Press.

Burton, G. P. 1975. "Proconsuls, Assizes and the Administration of Justice under the Empire." *Journal of Roman Studies* 65: 92–106.

1998. "Was There a Long Term Trend to Centralisation of Authority in the Roman Empire?" *Revue de Philologie* 72: 7–24.

2000. "The Resolution of Territorial Disputes in the Provinces of the Roman Empire." *Chiron* 30: 195–215.

Caillemer, A., and Chevallier, R. 1954. "Les centuriations de l''Africa vetus'." *Annales ESC* 9: 433–60.

Callu, Jean-Pierre. 1984. "Le jardin des supplices au Bas-Empire," in *Du châtiment dans la cité. Supplices corporels et peine de mort dans le monde antique*. 314–59. Rome: École Française de Rome.

Cameron, Alan. 1976. *Circus Factions: Blues and Greens at Rome and Constantinople*. Oxford: Clarendon Press.

Cameron, Averil. 2014. *Dialoguing in Late Antiquity*. Washington DC: Center for Hellenic Studies.

Camia, Francesco. 2014. "Political Elite and Priestly Posts in Athens during the Roman Imperial Period: Some Considerations." *Zeitschrift für Papyrologie und Epigraphik* 188: 139–48.

Campbell, Brian. 2000. *The Writings of the Roman Land Surveyors: Introduction, Text, Translation, and Commentary*. London: Society for the Promotion of Roman Studies.

Canepa, Matthew P. 2009. *The Two Eyes of the Earth: Art and Ritual of Kingship between Rome and Sasanian Iran*. Berkeley: University of California Press.

Carrié, Jean-Michel. 2005. "Developments in Local and Provincial Administration," in Alan K. Bowman, Peter Garnsey, and Averil Cameron, eds., *The Cambridge Ancient History, Vol. XII: The Crisis of Empire, A.D. 197–337*. 269–312. Cambridge: Cambridge University Press.

Cascione, Cosimo. 2021. "A Roman Jurist in the Imperial Council (Rev. of Brutti 2020)." *Classical Review* 71: 578–80.

Chadwick, H. 1967. "The Beginning of Christian Philosophy: Justin – The Gnostics," in A. H. Armstrong, ed., *The Cambridge History of Later Greek and Early Medieval Philosophy*. 158–67. Cambridge: Cambridge University Press.

Chakrabarty, Dipesh. 2000. *Provincializing Europe: Postcolonial Thought and Historical Difference*. Princeton: Princeton University Press.

Champlin, Edward. 1991. *Final Judgments: Duty and Emotion in Roman Wills, 200 B.C.–A.D. 250*. Berkeley: University of California Press.

2003. *Nero*. Cambridge, MA: Belknap Press.

2005. "Phaedrus the Fabulous." *Journal of Roman Studies* 95: 97–123.

Chin, Catherine. 2007. *Grammar and Christianity in the Late Roman World*. Philadelphia: University of Pennsylvania Press.

Clarke, John R. 2006. "Three Uses of the Pygmy and the Aethiops at Pompeii: Decorating, 'Othering', and Warding off Demons," in Laurent Bricault, Miguel John Versluys, and Paul G. P. Meyboom, eds., *Nile into Tiber: Proceedings of the 3rd International Conference of Isis Studies, May 11–14, 2005*. 155–69. Leiden: Brill.

Claytor, W. Graham. 2018. "The Municipalization of Writing in Roman Egypt," in Anne Kolb, ed., *Literacy in Ancient Everyday Life*. 319–34. Berlin: de Gruyter.

Claytor, W. Graham, and Bagnall, Roger S. 2015. "The Beginnings of the Roman Provincial Census: A New Declaration from 3 BCE." *Greek, Roman, and Byzantine Studies* 55: 637–53.

Cline, Brandon Duane. 2016. "Petition and Performance in the Apologies of Justin Martyr." PhD, University of Chicago.

Cockle, W. E. H. 1984. "State Archives in Greco-Roman Egypt from 30 BC to the Reign of Septimius Severus." *Journal of Egyptian Archaeology* 70: 106–22.

Cohen, David. 1995. *Law, Violence, and Community in Classical Athens*. Cambridge: Cambridge University Press.

Cohen, F. S. 1935. "Transcendental Nonsense and the Functional Approach." *Columbia Law Review* 35: 809–49.

Cohen, Shaye J. D. 1984. "The Significance of Yavneh: Pharisees, Rabbis, and the End of Jewish Sectarianism." *Hebrew Union College Annual* 55: 27–53.

2014. *From the Maccabees to the Mishnah*. 3rd ed. Louisville: Westminster John Knox Press.

ed. 2022. *What Is the Mishnah? The State of the Question*. Cambridge, MA: Harvard University Press.

Cohn, Naftali S. 2022. "Mishnah as Utopia," in Shaye J. D. Cohen, ed., *What Is the Mishnah? The State of the Question*. 204–31. Cambridge, MA: Harvard University Press.

Coleman, K. M. 1990. "Fatal Charades: Roman Executions Staged as Mythological Enactments." *Journal of Roman Studies* 80: 44–73.

2012. "Bureaucratic Language in the Correspondence between Pliny and Trajan." *Transactions of the American Philological Association* 142: 189–238.

Collinet, Paul. 1925. *Histoire de l'école de droit de Beyrouth*. Paris: Société Anonyme du Recueil Sirey.

Congdon, Matthew. 2021. "The Aesthetics of Moral Address." *Philosophical Topics* 49: 123–44.

Connolly, Serena. 2010. *Lives Behind the Laws: The World of the Codex Hermogenianus*. Bloomington: Indiana University Press.

Constable, Marianne. 1994. *The Law of the Other: The Mixed Jury and Changing Conceptions of Citizenship, Law, and Knowledge*. Chicago: University of Chicago Press.

2014. *Our Word Is Our Bond: How Legal Speech Acts*. Stanford: Stanford University Press.

Conybeare, Catherine, and Goldhill, Simon. eds. 2021. *Classical Philology and Theology: Entanglement, Disavowal, and the Godlike Scholar*. Cambridge: Cambridge University Press.

Cooley, Alison. 2023. *The Senatus consultum de Cn. Pisone Patre: Text, Translation, and Commentary*. Cambridge: Cambridge University Press.

Copenhaver, Brian P. 1992. *Hermetica: The Greek Corpus Hermeticum and the Latin Asclepius in a New English Translation, with Notes and Introduction*. Cambridge: Cambridge University Press.

Corbier, Mireille. 1990. "City, Territory, and Taxation," in John Rich and Andrew Wallace-Hadrill, eds., *City and Country in the Ancient World*. 211–39. London: Routledge.

Coriat, Jean-Pierre. 1997. *Le prince législateur: la technique législative des Sévères et les méthodes de création du droit impérial à la fin du principat*. Rome: Ecole française de Rome.

Cornu Thénard, Nicolas. 2020. "The Legal Construction of the Fact, between Rhetoric and Roman Law," in Clifford Ando and William P. Sullivan, eds., *The Discovery of the Fact*. 39–71. Ann Arbor: University of Michigan Press.

Corsten, Thomas. 2005. "Estates in Roman Asia Minor: The Case of Kibyratis," in Stephen Mitchell and Constantina Katsari, eds., *Patterns in the Economy of Roman Asia Minor*. 1–51. Swansea: Classical Press of Wales.

Cortés-Copete, Juan Manuel. 2018. "Koinoi Nomoi: Hadrian and the Harmonization of Local Laws," in Olivier Hekster and Koenrad Verboeven, eds., *The Impact of Justice on the Roman Empire*. 105–21. Leiden: Brill.

Cottier, Michel, Corbier, Mireille, Crowther, C. V., Ferrary, Jean-Louis, Levick, Barbara, Salomies, Olli, and Wörrle, Michael. 2008. *The Customs Law of Asia*. Oxford: Oxford University Press.

Cotton, Hannah. 1993. "The Guardianship of Jesus Son of Babatha: Roman and Local Law in the Province of Arabia." *Journal of Roman Studies* 83: 94–108.

Cover, Robert M. 1992a. "The Folktales of Justice," in Martha Minow, Michael Ryan, and Austin Sarat, eds., *Narrative, Violence, and the Law*. 173–201. Ann Arbor: University of Michigan Press.

1992b. "Nomos and Narrative," in Martha Minow, Michael Ryan, and Austin Sarat, eds., *Narrative, Violence, and the Law: The Essays of Robert Cover*. 95–172. Ann Arbor: University of Michigan Press.

Crawford, Michael H. ed. 1996. *Roman Statutes*. London: Institute of Classical Studies.

Crews, Rex B. 2016. "The Handbooks *de Officio Proconsulis*: Authorship and Audience." PhD, University of North Carolina, Chapel Hill.

Cribiore, Raffaella. 2001. *Gymnastics of the Mind: Greek Education in Hellenistic and Roman Egypt*. Princeton: Princeton University Press.

2007. *The School of Libanius in Late Antique Antioch*. Princeton: Princeton University Press.

2015. "Literary Culture and Education in the Dakhla Oasis," in Roger S. Bagnall, Nicola Aravecchia, Rafaella Cribiore, Paola Davoli, Olaf E. Kaper, and Susanna McFadden, eds., *An Oasis City*. 309–32. New York: Institute for the Study of the Ancient World, NYU Press.

Crifò, Guiliano. 1976. "Ulpiano: Esperienze e responsibilità del giurista." *ANRW* II.15: 708–89.

Crook, John. 1955. *Consilium Principis: Imperial Councils and Counsellors from Augustus to Diocletian*. Cambridge: Cambridge University Press.

Cuomo, Serafina. 2007. "Measures for an Emperor: Volusius Maecianus' Monetary Pamphlet for Marcus Aurelius," in Jason König and Tim Whitmarsh, eds., *Ordering Knowledge in the Roman Empire*. 206–28. Cambridge: Cambridge University Press.

Czajkowski, Kimberley. 2017. *Localized Law: The Babatha and Salome Komaise Archives*. Oxford: Oxford University Press.

2019. "Jewish Associations in Alexandria?," in Benedikt Eckhardt, ed., *Private Associations and Jewish Communities in the Hellenistic and Roman Cities*. 76–96. Leiden: Brill.

2020. "Law and Administration at the Edges of Empire: The Case of Dura Europus," in Kimberley Czajkowski and Benedikt Eckhardt, eds., *Law in the Roman Provinces*. 115–33. Oxford: Oxford University Press.

Czajkowski, Kimberly, and Eckhardt, Benedikt. 2018. "Law, Status, and Agency in the Roman Provinces." *Past & Present* 241: 3–31.

eds. 2020. *Law in the Roman Provinces*. Oxford: Oxford University Press.

Daalder, Elsmieke. 2022. "*Aequum putavit imperator*: Imperial Representation and Juristic Self-fashioning in the *Decreta* and *Imperiales Sententiae* of Julius Paulus." *Zeitschrift der Savigny-Stiftung für Rechtsgeschichte, Romanistische Abteilung* 139: 123–91.

Dalla Rossa, Alberto. 2014. "Prolegomeni allo studio della proprietà imperiale in Asia Minore: La questione dell'imperatore come acquirente." *Studi Classici Orientali* 60: 329–48.

2020. "Les affranchis de citoyens romains dans les centres ruraux de la province d'Asie: considérations à partir de deux études de cas," in Gabrielle Frija, ed., *Être citoyen romain dans le monde grec au IIe siècle de notre ère*. 21–40. Bordeaux: Ausonius Editions.

Daniel-Hughes, Carly, and Kotrosits, Maia. 2020. "Tertullian of Carthage and the Fantasy Life of Power: On Martyrs, Christians, and Other Attachments to Juridical Scenes." *Journal of Early Christian Studies* 28: 1–31.

de Ste Croix, G. E. M. 1963. "Why Were the Early Christians Persecuted?" *Past & Present* 26: 6–38.

1981. *The Class Struggle in the Ancient Greek World from the Archaic Age to the Arab Conquests*. Ithaca: Cornell University Press.

Dehandschutter, Boudewijn. 1993. "The Martyrium Polycarpi: A Century of Research." *ANRW* 2.27.1: 485–522.

Dell'Oro, Aldo. 1960. *I libri de officio nella giurisprudenza romana*. Milan: Giuffré.

Desideri, Paolo. 2000. "City and Country in Dio," in Simon Swain, ed., *Dio Chrysostom: Politics, Letters, and Philosophy*. 93–107. Oxford: Oxford University Press.

Dietler, Michael. 2005. "The Archaeology of Colonization and the Colonization of Archaeology: Theoretical Challenges from an Ancient Mediterranean Encounter," in Gil J. Stein, ed., *The Archaeology of Colonial Encounters*. 33–68. Santa Fe: School of American Research.

Dillon, John Noël. 2012. *The Justice of Constantine: Law, Communication, and Control*. Ann Arbor: University of Michigan Press.

Diósdi, György. 1976. "Gaius, der Rechtsgelehrte." *ANRW* 2.15: 605–31.

Dmitriev, Sviatoslav. 2005. *City Government in Hellenistic and Roman Asia Minor*. Oxford: Oxford University Press.

Dohrmann, Natalie B. 2003. "The Boundaries of the Law and the Problem of Jurisdiction in an Early Palestinian Midrash," in Catherine Hezser, ed., *Rabbinic Law in Its Roman and Near Eastern Context*. 83–103. Tübingen: Mohr Siebeck.

2013. "Law and Imperial Idioms: Rabbinic Legalism in a Roman World," in Natalie B. Dohrmann and Annette Yoshiko Reed, eds., *Jews, Christians, and the Roman Empire: The Poetics of Power in Late Antiquity*. 62–78. Philadelphia: University of Pennsylvania Press.

Dolganov, Anna. 2019. "Reichsrecht and Volksrecht in Theory and Practice: Roman Justice in the Province of Egypt (P.Oxy. II 237, P.Oxy. IV 706, SB XII 10929)." *Tyche* 34: 27–60.

2020a. "A New Date for the Oxyrhynchite Epitome of the Gnomon of the Idios Logos (P. Oxy. XLII 3014)." *Chiron* 50: 167–88.

2020b. "*Nutricula causidicorum*: Legal Practitioners in Roman North Africa," in Kimberley Czajkowski and Benedikt Eckhardt, eds., *Law in the Roman Provinces*. 417–35. Oxford: Oxford University Press.

2021. "Documenting Roman Citizenship," in Clifford Ando and Myles Lavan, eds., *Roman and Local Citizenship in the Long Second Century AD*. 185–228. Oxford: Oxford University Press.

Downie, Janet. 2013. *At the Limits of Art: A Literary Study of Aelius Aristides' Hieroi Logoi*. Oxford: Oxford University Press.

Drake, H. A. 2000. *Constantine and the Bishops: The Politics of Intolerance*. Baltimore: Johns Hopkins University Press.

du Plessis, Paul J. 2019. "Disqualified Witnesses between Tannaitic Halakha and Roman Law: A Response to Orit Malka." *Law and History Review* 37: 947–54.

Dubber, Markus Dirk. 2005. *The Police Power: Patriarchy and the Foundations of American Government*. New York: Columbia University Press.

2018. *The Dual Penal State: The Crisis of Criminal Law in Comparative Historical Perspective*. Oxford: Oxford University Press.

Dunbabin, Katherine M. D., and Dickie, M. W. 1983. "*Invida rumpantur pectora*: The Iconography of Phthonos/Invidia in Greco-Roman Art." *Jahrbuch für Antike und Christentum* 26: 7–37.

Eberle, Lisa Pilar. 2014. "Law, Land, and Territories: The Roman Diaspora and the Making of Provincial Administration." PhD, University of California, Berkeley.

2016. "Law, Empire, and the Making of Roman Estates in the Provinces during the Late Republic." *Critical Analysis of Law* 3: 50–69.

Eberle, Lisa Pilar, and Le Queré, Enora. 2017. "Landed Traders, Trading Agriculturalists? Land in the Economy of the Italian Diaspora of the Greek East." *Journal of Roman Studies* 107: 27–59.

Eck, Werner. ed. 1999. *Lokale Autonomie und römische Ordnungsmacht in den kaiserzeitlichen Provinzen vom 1. bis 3. Jahrhundert*. Munich: R. Oldenbourg.

2014. "Das Leben römisch gestalten: Ein Stadtgesetz für das *municipium Troesmis* aus den Jahren 177–180 n. Chr.," in Gerda de Kleijn and Stéphane Benoist, eds., *Integration in Rome and in the Roman World*. 75–88. Leiden: Brill.

2014 [2011]. "Die römischen Repräsentanten in Judäa: Provokateure oder Vertreter der römischen Macht?," in Werner Eck, ed., *Judäa – Syria Palästina: Die Auseinandersetzung einer Provinz mit römischer Politik und Kultur*. 166–185. Tübingen: Mohr Siebeck.

2020. "The *leges municipales* as a Means of Legal and Social Romanization of the Provinces of the Roman Empire," in Kimberley Czajkowski and Benedikt Eckhardt, eds., *Law in the Roman Provinces*. 315–31. Oxford: Oxford University Press.

Eck, Werner, Caballos, Antonio, and Fernández, Fernando. 1996. *Das Senatus consultum de Cn. Pisone patre*. Munich: C. H. Beck.

Eckhardt, Benedikt. 2020. "Law, Empire, and Identity between West and East: The Danubian Provinces," in Kimberley Czajkowski and Benedikt Eckhardt, eds., *Law in the Roman Provinces*. 417–35. Oxford: Oxford University Press.

Eckstein, Arthur M. 2006. *Mediterranean Anarchy, Interstate War, and the Rise of Rome*. Berkeley: University of California Press.

Edmondson, Jonathan. 2008. "Public Dress and Social Control in Late Republican and Early Imperial Rome," in Jonathan Edmondson and Alison Keith, eds., *Roman Dress and the Fabrics of Roman Culture*. 21–46. Toronto: University of Toronto Press.

Edwards, Laura. 2011. "The Peace: The Meaning and Production of Law in the Post-revolutionary United States." *UC Irvine Law Review* 1: 565–85.

Edwards, M. J. 1995. "Justin's Logos and the Word of God." *Journal of Early Christian Studies* 3: 261–80.

Eich, Armin. 2009. "Diplomatische Genauigkeit oder inhaltliche Richtigkeit: Das Verhältnis von Original und Abschrift," in Rudolf Haensch, ed., *Selbstdarstellung und Kommunikation: Die Veröffentlichtung staatlicher Urkunden auf Stein und Bronze un der römischen Welt*. 267–99. Munich: C. H. Beck.

Elm, Susanna. 2012. *Sons of Hellenism, Fathers of the Church: Emperor Julian, Gregory of Nazianzus, and the Vision of Rome*. Berkeley: University of California Press.

Engberg-Pedersen, Troels. 2010. *Cosmology and the Self in the Apostle Paul: The Material Spirit*. Oxford: Oxford University Press.

Erkelenz, Dirk. 2003. *Optimo praesidi: Untersuchungen zu den Ehrenmonumenten für Amtsträger der römischen Provinzen in Republik und Kaiserzeit*. Bonn: R. Habelt.

Esch, Tobias. 2018. "Die Quintilii aus Alexandria Troas: Aufstieg und Niedergang einer Familie," in Elmar Schwertheim, ed., *Neuer Foschungen in Alexandria Troas*. 1–60. Bonn: Rudolf Habelt.

Ewald, Björn C. 2004. "Men, Muscle, and Myth: Attic Sarcophagi in the Cultural Context of the Second Sophistic," in Barbara Borg, ed., *Paideia: The World of the Second Sophistic*. 229–67. Berlin: de Gruyter.

2014. Review of R.R.R. Smith, *The Marble Reliefs from the Julio-Claudian Sebasteion. Aphrodidias. Bryn Mawr Classical Review* 2014.09.40 (https://bmcr.brynmawr.edu/2014/2014.09.40/).

Ewald, William. 1995. "Comparative Jurisprudence (I): What Was It Like to Try a Rat?" *University of Pennsylvania Law Review* 143: 1889–2149.

Fanizza, Lucia. 1982. *Giuristi crimini leggi nell'età degli Antonini*. Naples: Editore Iovene.

Färber, Roland. 2014. *Römische Gerichtsorte: Raumlichen Dynamiken von Jurisdiktion im Imperium Romanum*. Munich: C. H. Beck.

Feissel, D., and Gascou, J. 2004. *La Pétition à Byzance*. Paris: Association des Amis du Centre d'Histoire et Civilisation de Byzance.

Ferguson, R. A. 2007. *The Trial in American Life*. Chicago: University of Chicago Press.

Fernoux, Henri. 2011. *Le Demos et la Cité: Communautés et assemblées populaires en Asie Mineure à l'époque impériale*. Rennes: Presse Universitaire de Rennes.

Filippini, Alister. 2019. *Efeso, Ulpiano e il Senato: la contesa per il primato nella provincia "Asia" nel III sec. d.C.* Stuttgart: Franz Steiner.

Fishman, Talya. 2011. *Becoming the People of the Talmud: Oral Torah as Written Tradition in Medieval Jewish Cultures*. Philadelphia: University of Pennsylvania Press.

Fögen, Marie-Theres. 2002. *Römische Rechtsgeschichten: über Ursprung und Evolution eines sozialen Systems*. Göttingen: Vandenhoeck and Rupprecht.

Foti-Talamanca, Guiliana. 1979. *Ricerche sul processo nell'Egitto Greco-Romano 2.1: L'introduzione del Giudizio*. Milan: A. Giuffrè.

Fournet, Jean-Luc. 2004. "Entre document et littérature: la pétition dans l'Antiquité tardive," in Denis Feissel and Jean Gascou, eds., *La pétition à Byzance*. 61–74. Paris: Association des Amis du Centre d'Histoire et Civilisation de Byzance.

2019. "Anatomie d'un genre en mutation: la pétition de l'Antiquité tardive," in A. Nodar and Sofía Torallas Tovar, eds., *Proceedings of the 28th*

International Congress of Papyrology, Barcelona 2016. 571–90. Barcelona: Publicacions de l'Abadia de Montserrat, Universitat Pompeu Fabra.

2020. *The Rise of Coptic: Egyptian versus Greek in Late Antiquity*. Princeton: Princeton University Press.

Fournier, Julien. 2010. *Entre tutelle romaine et autonomie civique: l'administration judiciaire dans les provinces hellénophones de l'empire romain, 129 av. J.-C-235 apr. J.-C.* Athens: Ecole française d'Athènes.

Frank, Tenney. 1933. *An Economic Survey of Ancient Rome, Volume 1: Rome and Italy of the Republic*. Baltimore: Johns Hopkins Press.

Frede, Michael. 1999. "Origen's Treatise *Against Celsus*," in Mark J. Edwards, Martin Goodman, Simon Price, and Christopher Rowland, eds., *Apologetics in the Roman Empire: Pagans, Jews, and Christians*. 131–55. Oxford: Oxford University Press.

Fredriksen, Paula. 2017. *Paul: The Pagans' Apostle*. New Haven: Yale University Press.

2021. "Paul, the Perfectly Righteous Pharisee," in Joseph Sievers and Amy-Jill Levine, eds., *The Pharisees*. 112–35. Grand Rapids: William B. Eerdmans Publishing Company.

Freedman, H., and Simon, Maurice. eds. 1983. *Midrash Rabbah*. 10 vols. London: Soncino Press.

Frier, Bruce W. 1984. "Law on the Installment Plan (rev. of Honoré, *Ulpian*)." *Michigan Law Review* 82: 856–68.

1985. *The Rise of the Roman Jurists: Studies in Cicero's Pro Caecina*. Princeton: Princeton University Press.

2021. *A Casebook on the Roman Law of Contracts*. Oxford: Oxford University Press.

Fuhrmann, Christopher J. 2011. *Policing the Roman Empire: Soldiers, Administration, and Public Order*: Oxford: Oxford University Press.

Furstenberg, Yair. 2022. "The Invention of the Ban Against Writing Oral Torah in the Babylonian Talmud." *AJS Review* 46: 131–50.

2023. "The Rabbinic Movement from Pharisees to Provincial Jurists." *Journal for the Study of Judaism* 54: 1–43.

Gadamer, Hans-Georg. 1989. *Truth and Method*. Trans. by Joel Weinsheimer and Donald G. Marshall. 2nd ed. London: Continuum.

Gagliardi, Lorenzo. 2015. "Fondazione di colonie romane ed espropriazioni di terre a danno degli indigeni." *Mélanges de l'Ecole Française de Rome – Antiquité* 127: 353–70.

Gallo, Italo. 1996. "Biografie di consumo in Grecia: Il *Romanzo di Alessandro* e la *Vita del Filosofo Secondo*," in Oronzo Pecere and Antonio Stramaglia, eds., *La Letteratura di Consumo nel Mondo Greco-Latino*. 237–49. Cassino: Università degli Studi di Cassino.

Galsterer, Hartmut. 2000. "Local and Provincial Institutions and Government," in Alan K. Bowman, Peter Garnsey, and Dominic Rathbone, eds., *The Cambridge Ancient History, Vol. XI: The High Empire, A.D. 70–192*, 344–60. Cambridge: Cambridge University Press.

Gambetti, Sandra. 2008. "In Defense of a Historical Reading of 'P. Yale' II 107 (= 'P. Giss. Lit.' 4.7)." *Zeitschrift für Papyrologie und Epigraphik* 165: 191–208.

2009. *The Alexandrian Riots of 38 C.E. and the Persecution of the Jews: A Historical Reconstruction*. Leiden: Brill.

Garnsey, Peter. 1966. "The Lex Iulia and Appeal under the Empire." *Journal of Roman Studies* 56: 167–89.

1968. "Why Penalties Become Harsher: The Roman Case, Late Republic to Fourth Century Empire." *Natural Law Forum* 13: 141–62.

1970. *Social Status and Legal Privilege in the Roman Empire*. Oxford: Clarendon Press.

1988. *Famine and Food Supply in the Graeco-Roman World: Responses to Risk and Crisis*. Cambridge: Cambridge University Press.

Garnsey, Peter, and Saller, Richard P. 1987. *The Roman Empire: Economy, Society, and Culture*. Berkeley: University of California Press.

Genovese, Eugene D. 1965. *The Political Economy of Slavery: Studies in the Economy and Society of the Slave South*. New York: Pantheon Books.

Gessen, Masha. 2017. *The Future is History: How Totalitarianism Reclaimed Russia*. New York: Riverhead Books.

Girardin, Michaël. 2022. *L'offrande et le tribut: Histoire politique de la fiscalité en Judée hellénistique et romaine (200 a.c. – 135 p.c.)*. Bordeaux: Ausonius Éditions.

Gleason, Maud W. 1995. *Making Men: Sophists and Self-Presentation in Ancient Rome*. Princeton: Princeton University Press.

1999. "Truth Contests and Talking Corpses," in James I. Porter, ed., *Constructions of the Classical Body*. 287–313. Ann Arbor: University of Michigan Press.

2001. "Mutilated Messengers: Body Language in Josephus," in Simon Goldhill, ed., *Being Greek under Rome: Cultural Identity, the Second Sophistic, and the Development of Empire*. 50–85. Cambridge: Cambridge University Press.

2012. "Shock and Awe: The Performance Dimension of Galen's Anatomy Demonstrations," in Christopher Gil, Tim Whitmarsh, and John Wilkins, eds., *Galen and the World of Knowledge*. 85–114. Cambridge: Cambridge University Press.

2020. "Aretaeus and the Ekphrasis of Agony." *Classical Antiquity* 39: 153–87.

Goldhill, Simon. ed. 2001a. *Being Greek under Rome: Cultural Identity, the Second Sophistic, and the Politics of Imitation*. Oxford: Oxford University Press.

2001b. "The Erotic Eye," in Simon Goldhill, ed., *Being Greek under Rome: Cultural Identity, the Second Sophistic, and the Development of Empire*. 154–94. Cambridge: Cambridge University Press.

2002. *Who Needs Greek? Contests in the Cultural History of Hellenism*. Cambridge: Cambridge University Press.

2007. "What is Ekphrasis For?" *Classical Philology* 102: 1–19.

ed. 2008. *The End of Dialogue in Antiquity*. Cambridge: Cambridge University Press.

González, Julián, and Crawford, Michael H. 1986. "The Lex Irnitana: A New Copy of the Flavian Municipal Law." *Journal of Roman Studies* 76: 147–243.

Goodenough, Erwin R. 1923. *The Theology of Justin Martyr*. Jena: Walter Biedermann.

1938. *The Politics of Philo Judaeus: Practice and Theory*. New Haven: Yale University Press.

Goodman, Martin. 1988. *The Ruling Class of Judaea: The Origins of the Jewish Revolt against Rome, A.D. 66–70*. London: Cambridge University Press.

1996. "Judaea," in Alan K. Bowman, Edward Champlin, and Andrew Lintott, eds., *The Cambridge Ancient History, Vol. X: The Augustan Empire, 43 B.C.–A.D. 69*. 737–81. Cambridge: Cambridge University Press.

Gordon, W. M., and Robinson, O. F. 1988. *The Institutes of Gaius*. London: Duckworth.

Graeber, David. 2011. *Debt: The First 5,000 Years*. Brooklyn: Melville House.

Gray, Benjamin. 2015. *Stasis and Stability: Exile, the Polis, and Political Thought, c.404–146 BC*. Oxford: Oxford University Press.

Grelle, Francesco. 1963. *Stipendium vel tributum: L'imposizione fondiaria nelle dottrine giuridiche del II e III secolo*. Naples: Jovene.

Gross, Simcha. 2018. "A Persian Anti-Martyr Act: The Death of Rabba bar Naḥmani in Light of the Syriac Persian Martyr Acts," in Geoffrey Herman and Jeffrey L. Rubenstein, eds., *The Aggada of the Bavli and its Cultural World*. 211–42. Providence: Brown Judaic Studies.

2024. *Babylonian Jews and Sasanian Imperialism in Late Antiquity*. Cambridge: Cambridge University Press.

Gruen, Erich S. 2002. *Diaspora: Jews amidst Greeks and Romans*. Cambridge, MA: Harvard University Press.

Gualandi, G. 2012. *Legislazione imperiale e giurisprudenza*. 2nd ed. 2 vols. Bologna: Bononia University Press.

Guarino, Antonio. 1994 [1969] "Gaio e l''edictum provinciale'," in *Pagine di Diritto Romano*. 279–95. Naples: Jovene.

Guerber, Éric. 2009. *Les cités grecques dans l'Empire romain: Les privilèges et les titres des citès de l'orient hellénophone d'Octave Auguste à Dioclétien*. Rennes: Presse Universitaire de Rennes.

Haas, Christopher. 1997. *Alexandria in Late Antiquity: Topography and Social Conflict*. Baltimore: Johns Hopkins University Press.

Haensch, Rudolf. 1992. "Das Statthalterarchiv." *Zeitschrift der Savigny-Stiftung fur Rechtsgeschichte (Romanistische Abteilung)* 109: 209–317.

1994. "Die Bearbeitungsweisen von Petitionen in der Provinz Aegyptus." *Zeitschrift für Papyrologie und Epigraphik* 100: 487–546.

1997. "Zur Konventsordnung in Aegyptus und den übrigen Provinzen des römischen Reiches," in B. Kramer, W. Luppe, H. Maehler, and G. Poethke, eds., *Akten des 21. Internationalen Papyrologenkongresses*. 320–91. Stuttgart: Teubner.

2015. "From Free to Fee?: Judicial Fees and Other Litigation Costs during the High Empire and Late Antiquity," in Dennis P. Kehoe, David M. Ratzan, and Uri Yiftach-Firanko, eds., *Law and Transaction Costs in the Ancient Economy*. 253–72. Ann Arbor: University of Michigan Press.

Hagedorn, Dieter, and Jördens, Andrea. 2006. "Ein unbekannter Proculus und das Verbot der paenula: Eine Neuedition von BGU XVI 2558." *Zeitschrift für Papyrologie und Epigraphik* 156: 169–78.

Halfmann, Helmut. 1979. *Die Senatoren aus dem östlichen Teil des Imperium Romanum bis zum Ende des 2. Jahrhunderts n. Chr.* Göttingen: Vandenhoeck & Rupprecht.

Hall, Linda Jones. 2004. *Roman Berytus: Beirut in Late Antiquity*. London: Routledge.

Hammer, Reuben. 1986. *Sifre: A Tannaitic Commentary on the Book of Deuteronomy*. New Haven: Yale University Press.

Hansen, William. 1998. *Anthology of Ancient Greek Popular Literature*. Bloomington: University of Indiana Press.

Harker, Andrew. 2008. *Loyalty and Dissidence in Roman Egypt: The Case of the Acta Alexandrinorum*. Cambridge: Cambridge University Press.

Harland, Philip A. 2003. *Associations, Synagogues, and Congregations: Claiming a Place in Ancient Mediterranean Society*. Minneapolis: Fortress Press.

Harper, Kyle. 2016. "The Environmental Fall of the Roman Empire." *Daedalus* 145: 101–11.

Harries, Jill. 1999. *Law and Empire in Late Antiquity*. Cambridge: Cambridge University Press.

2001. "Resolving Disputes: The Frontiers of Law in Late Antiquity," in Ralph W. Mathisen, ed., *Law, Society, and Authority in Late Antiquity*. 68–82. Oxford/New York: Oxford University Press.

2006. *Cicero and the Jurists: From Citizen's Law to Lawful State*. London: Duckworth.

2007. *Law and Crime in the Roman World*. Cambridge: Cambridge University Press.

2014. "Triple Vision: Ulpian of Tyre on the Duties of the Proconsul," in Jesper Majbom Madsen and Roger David Rees, eds., *Roman Rule in Greek and Latin Writing: Double Vision*. 193–209. Leiden: Brill.

Harris, W. V. 1985. *War and Imperialism in Republican Rome, 327–70 B.C.* Oxford: Clarendon Press.

2001. *Restraining Rage: The Ideology of Anger Control in Classical Antiquity*. Cambridge, MA: Harvard University Press.

Harris, W. V., and Holmes, Brooke. eds. 2008. *Aelius Aristides between Greece, Rome, and the Gods*. Leiden: Brill.

Hartog, Hendrik. 1985. "Pigs and Positivism." *Wisconsin Law Review* 1985: 899–935.

2012. *Someday All This Will Be Yours: A History of Inheritance and Old Age*. Cambridge, MA: Harvard University Press.

Hartog, Paul. 2013. *Polycarp's Epistle to the Philippians and the Martyrdom of Polycarp*. Oxford: Oxford University Press.

Haug, Brendan J. 2017. "Water and Power: Reintegrating the State into the Study of Egyptian Irrigation." *History Compass* 15. https://doi.org/10.1111/hic3.12394.

Hauken, Tor. 1998. *Petition and Response: An Epigraphic Study of Petitions to Roman Emperors, 181–249*. Bergen: Norwegian Institute at Athens.

Hayes, Christine. 2015. *What's Divine about Divine Law? Early Perspectives*. Princeton: Princeton University Press.

Heck, Paul L. 2002. *The Construction of Knowledge in Islamic Civilization: Qudāma B. Ja'far and His Kitāb al-Kharāj wa-Sinā'at al-Kitāba*. Leiden: Brill.

Heffernan, Thomas J. 2012. *The Passion of Perpetua and Felicity*. Oxford: Oxford University Press.

Hekster, Olivier. 2023. *Caesar Rules: The Emperor in the Changing Roman World (c. 50 BC – AD 565)*. Cambridge: Cambridge University Press.

Heller, Anna. 2006. *Les bêtises des Grecs: Conflits et rivalités entre cités d'Asie et de Bithynie à l'époque romaine (129 a.C. – 235 p.C.)*. Bordeaux: Ausonius Éditions.

Henderson, John. 2001. *Telling Tales on Caesar: Roman Stories from Phaedrus*. Oxford/New York: Oxford University Press.

Herbert, A. P. 1927. *Misleading Cases in the Common Law*. London: Methuen.

Herrmann, Peter. 1990. *Hilferufe aus römischen Provinzen*. Hamburg: Vandenhoeck & Rupprecht.

Herz, Zachary. 2018. "Playing the Judge: Law and Imperial Messaging in Severan Rome." PhD, Columbia University.

2025. *The God and the Bureaucrat: Roman Law, Imperial Sovereignty, and Other Stories*. Cambridge: Cambridge University Press.

Hin, Saskia. 2007. "Class and Society in the Cities of the Greek East: Education during the *Ephebeia*." *Ancient Society* 37: 141–66.

Holum, Kenneth G. ed. 1988. *King Herod's Dream: Caesarea on the Sea*. New York: Norton.

Hombert, Marcel, and Préaux, Claire. 1952. *Recherches sur le recensement dans l'Égypte romaine (P. Bruxelles inv. E. 7616)*. Leiden: Brill.

Honoré, A. M. 1962. *Gaius*. Oxford: Clarendon Press.

1994. *Emperors and Lawyers*. 2nd ed. Oxford: Clarendon Press.

2002. *Ulpian: Pioneer of Human Rights*. Oxford: Oxford University Press.

Hopkins, Keith. 1978. "Divine Emperors or the Symbolic Unity of the Roman Empire," in *Conquerors and Slaves: Sociological Studies in Roman History* 197–242. Cambridge: Cambridge University Press.

1993. "Novel Evidence for Roman Slavery." *Past & Present* 138: 3–27.
2018 [1980]. "Taxes and Trade in the Roman Empire (200 B.C. – A.D. 400)," in Keith Hopkins and Christopher Kelly, eds., *Sociological Studies in Roman History*. 213–59. Cambridge: Cambridge University Press.
Horden, Peregrine, and Purcell, Nicholas. 2000. *The Corrupting Sea: A Study of Mediterranean History*. Oxford: Blackwell.
Horstkotte, H. 1996. "Die 1804 Konventseingaben in P.Yale 61." *Zeitschrift für Papyrologie und Epigraphik* 114: 189–93.
Hübner, Sabine, and Ratzan, David M. eds. 2009. *Growing Up Fatherless in Antiquity*. Cambridge: Cambridge University Press.
Huebner, Sabine R. 2019. *Papyri and the Social World of the New Testament*. Cambridge: Cambridge University Press.
Hulsebosch, D. 2005. *Constituting Empire: New York and the Transformation of Constitutionalism in the Atlantic World, 1664–1830*. Chapel Hill: University of North Carolina Press.
Humfress, Caroline. 2007. *Orthodoxy and the Courts in Late Antiquity*. Oxford: Oxford University Press.
2011. "Law and Custom under Rome," in Alice Rio, ed., *Law, Custom, and Justice in Late Antiquity and the Early Middle Ages*. 23–47. London: Hellenic Studies Institute.
Humphries, Mark. 2019. *Cities and the Meanings of Late Antiquity*. Leiden: Brill.
Huschke, Ph. Eduard, Seckel, Emil, and Kübler, Bernhard. 1909. *Iurisprudentiae Anteiustinianae Reliquias in usum maxime academicum compositas*. 2 vols. Leipzig: Teubner.
Ibbetson, David. 2005. "Epiclassical Law," in Alan K. Bowman, Peter Garnsey, and Averil Cameron, eds., *The Cambridge Ancient History, Vol. XII: The Crisis of Empire, A.D. 197–337*. 200–7. Cambridge: Cambridge University Press.
Inowlocki, Sabrina. 2004. "The Reception of Philo's *Legatio ad Gaium* in Eusebius of Caesarea's Works." *Studia Philonica* 16: 30–49.
2006. *Eusebius and the Jewish Authors: His Citation Technique in an Apologetic Context*. Leiden: Brill.
Isaac, Benjamin H. 1990. *The Limits of Empire: The Roman Army in the East*. Oxford: Clarendon Press.
Ish-Shalom, Tal A. 2021. "Provincial Monarchs as an Eastern Arcanum Imperii: 'Client Kingship', the Augustan Revolution and the Flavians." *Journal of Roman Studies* 111: 153–77.
Israelowich, Ido. 2019. "Land Surveyors and the Roman Court." *Revue internationale des droits de l'Antiquité* 66: 135–53.
Jacoby, Susan, and Ochs, Elinor. 1995. "Co-construction: An Introduction." *Research on Language and Social Interaction* 28: 171–83.
Jakab, Éva. 2005. "Sale with Earnest Money in the Papyri," in Robert W. Wallace and Michael Gagarin, eds., *Symposion 2001: Vorträge zur griechischen und hellenistischen Rechtsgeschichte (Evanston, Illinois,*

5.–8. September 2001). 199–217. Vienna: Verlag der Österreichischen Akademie der Wissenschaften.

James, Sarah A. 2014. "The Last of the Corinthians? Society and Settlement from 146 to 44 BCE," in Steven J. Friesen, Sarah A. James, and Daniel N. Schowalter, eds., *Corinth in Contrast: Studies in Inequality.* 17–37. Leiden: Brill.

Janiszewski, Paweł, Stebnicka, Krystyna, and Szabat, Elżbieta. 2015. *Prosopography of Greek Rhetors and Sophists of the Roman Empire.* Trans. by Dorota Dzierzbicka. Oxford: Oxford University Press.

Johnson, A. C. 1936. *Roman Egypt to the Reign of Diocletian.* Edited by Tenney Frank. Baltimore: Johns Hopkins Press.

Jones, A. H. M. 1940. *The Greek City from Alexander to Justinian.* Oxford: Clarendon Press.

Jones, C. P. 1971. *Plutarch and Rome.* Oxford: Clarendon Press.

1978. *The Roman World of Dio Chrysostom.* Cambridge, MA: Harvard University Press.

1987. "Stigma: Tattooing and Branding in Greco-Roman Antiquity." *Journal of Roman Studies* 77: 139–55.

1990. "Heracles at Smyrna." *American Journal of Numismatics* 2: 65–76.

2007. "Juristes romains dans l'orient grec." *Comptes rendus des séances de l'Académie des Inscriptions et Belles-Lettres* 151:3: 1333–59.

2011. "Julius Nikanor Again." *Zeitschrift für Papyrologie und Epigraphik* 178: 79–83.

2012. "Joys and Sorrows of Multiple Citizenship: The Case of Dio Chrysostom," in Anna Heller and Anne-Valérie Pont, eds., *Patrie d'origine et patries électives: les citoyennetés multiples dans le monde grec d'époque romaine. Actes du colloque international de Tours, 6–7 novembre 2009.* 213–19. Paris: de Boccard.

2017. "Strabo and the 'Petty Dynasts'," in Laurence Cavalier, Marie-Claire Ferriès, and Fabrice Delrieux, eds., *Auguste et l'Asie Mineure.* 349–56. Bordeaux: Éditions Ausonius.

Jördens, Andrea. 2009. *Statthalterliche Verwaltung in der römischen Kaiserzeit: Studien zum Praefectus Aegypti.* Stuttgart: Franz Steiner Verlag.

2010. "Öffentliche Archive und römische Rechtspolitik," in Katja Lembke, Martina Minas-Nerpel, and Stefan Pfeiffer, eds., *Tradition and Transformation: Egypt Under Roman Rule (Proceedings of the International Conference, Hildesheim, Römer- and Pelizaeus-Museum, 3–6 July 2008).* 159–79. Leiden: Brill.

2020. "*Aequum et iustum*: On Dealing with Law in the Province of Egypt," in Kimberley Czajkowski and Benedikt Eckhardt, eds., *Law in the Roman Provinces.* 19–31. Oxford: Oxford University Press.

Judt, Tony. 2005. *Postwar: A History of Europe since 1945.* London: William Heinemann.

Kahana, Maoz, and Mayse, Ariel. 2017. "Hasidic halakhah: Reappraising the Interface of Spirit and Law." *AJS Review* 41: 375–408.

Kahana, Menahem I. 2006. "The Halakhic Midrashim," in Shmuel Safrai, Zeev Safrai, Joshua Schwartz, and Peter Tomson, eds., *Compendia rerum Iudaicarum ad Novum Testamentum. Section 2, The Literature of the Jewish People in the Period of the Second Temple and the Talmud. Volume 3: The Literature of the Sages.* Assen: Royal van Gorcum.

Kantor, Georgy. 2009. "Knowledge of Law in Roman Asia Minor," in Rudolf Haensch, ed., *Selbstdarstellung und Kommunikation: Die Veröffentlichung staatlicher Urkunden auf Stein und Bronze in der römischen Welt.* 249–65. Munich: C. H. Beck.

2013. "Law in Roman Phrygia: Rules and Jurisdictions," in Peter Thonemann, ed., *Roman Phrygia: Culture and Society.* 143–67. Cambridge: Cambridge University Press.

2015. "Greek Law under the Romans," in Edward M. Harris and Mirko Canevaro, eds., *The Oxford Handbook of Ancient Greek Law.* Oxford: Oxford Handbooks Online.

2016. "Local Law in Asia Minor after the Constitutio Antoniniana," in Clifford Ando, ed., *Citizenship and Empire in Europe, 200–1900: The Antonine Constitution after 1800 Years.* 45–62. Stuttgart: Franz Steiner.

2017a. "Property in Land in Roman Provinces," in Georgy Kantor, Tom Lambert, and Hannah Skoda, eds., *Legalism: Property and Ownership.* 55–74. Oxford: Oxford University Press.

2017b. "*Qui in consilio estis*: The Governor and His Advisers in the Early Empire." *Istoricheskij Vestnik* 19: 50–87.

Kantor, Georgy, Lambert, Tom, and Skoda, Hannah. 2017. "Introduction: Property and Ownership: An Overview," in Georgy Kantor, Tom Lambert, and Hannah Skoda, eds., *Legalism: Property and Ownership.* 1–27. Oxford: Oxford University Press.

Karambelas, Dimitris. 2020. "Herodes Atticus in Trial: Procedure and Verdict," in Athina Dimopoulou, Andreas Helmis, and Dimitris Karambelas, eds., *ΙΟΥΛΙΑΝ ΒΕΛΙΣΣΑΡΟΠΟΥΛΟΥ ΕΠΑΙΝΕΣΑΙ: Studies in Ancient Greek and Roman Law.* 375–90. Athens: Greek Epigraphic Society.

Karla, Grammatiki A. 2016. "The Literary Life of a Fictional Life: Aesop in Antiquity and Byzantium," in Carolina Cupane and Bettina Krönung, eds., *Fictional Storytelling in the Medieval Mediterranean and Beyond.* 313–37. Leiden: Brill.

Kaster, Robert A. 1995. *C. Suetonius Tranquillus, De Grammaticis et Rhetoribus.* Oxford: Clarendon Press.

2005. *Emotion, Restraint, and Community in Ancient Rome.* Oxford: Oxford University Press.

Katsari, Constantina, and Mitchell, Stephen. 2008. "The Roman Colonies of Greece and Asia Minor: Questions of State and Civic Identity." *Athenaeum* 95: 219–47.

Katzoff, Ranon. 1972. "Precedents in the Courts of Roman Egypt." *Zeitschrift der Savigny-Stiftung fur Rechtsgeschichte (Romanistische Abteilung)* 89: 256–92.

Keenan, James G. 1985. "Village Shepherds and Social Tension in Byzantine Egypt." *Yale Classical Studies* 28: 245–59.

Keenan, James G., Manning, Joseph G., and Yiftach-Firanko, Uri. eds. 2014. *Law and Legal Practice in Egypt from Alexander to the Arab Conquest.* Cambridge: Cambridge University Press.

Kehoe, Dennis P. 1992. *Management and Investment on Estates in Roman Egypt during the Early Roman Empire.* Bonn: Rudolf Habelt.

2007. *Law and the Rural Economy in the Roman Empire.* Ann Arbor: University of Michigan Press.

Kelly, Benjamin. 2010. *Petitions, Litigation, and Social Control in Roman Egypt.* Oxford: Oxford University Press.

Kelly, C. 2004. *Ruling the Later Roman Empire.* Cambridge, MA: Harvard University Press.

Kennell, Nigel M. 1995. *The Gymnasium of Virtue: Education and Culture in Ancient Sparta.* Chapel Hill: University of North Carolina Press.

1997. "Herodes Atticus and the Rhetoric of Tyranny." *Classical Philology* 92: 346–62.

2009. "The Greek Ephebate in the Roman Period." *International Journal of the History of Sport* 26: 323–42.

Kirbihler, François. 2016. *Des Grecs et Italiens à Éphèse: Histoire d'une intégration croisée (133 a.C – 48 p.C.).* Bordeaux: Ausonius Éditions.

Kloppenborg, John S. 2020. *Christ's Associations: Connecting and Belonging in the Ancient City.* New Haven: Yale University Press.

Kokkinia, Christina. 2004a. "The Philosopher and the Emperor's Words: Trajan, Flavius Archippus and Dio Chrysostom." *Historia* 53: 490–500.

2004b. "Ruling, Inducing, Arguing: How to Govern (and Survive) a Greek Province," in L. de Ligt, H. W. Singor, and Emily Ann Hemelrijk, eds., *Roman Rule and Civic Life: Local and Regional Perspectives.* 39–58. Amsterdam: J. C. Gieben.

2015–16. "The Design of the 'Archive Wall' at Aphrodisias." *Τεκμήρια* 13: 9–55.

König, Jason. 2005. *Athletics and Literature in the Roman Empire.* Cambridge: Cambridge University Press.

Kotrosits, Maia. 2015. *Re-thinking Early Christian Identity: Affect, Violence, and Belonging.* Minneapolis: Fortress Press.

Kovelman, Arkady B. 1991. "From Logos to Myth: Egyptian Petitions of the 5th–7th Centuries." *Bulletin of the American Society of Papyrologists* 28: 135–52.

Krause, Jens-Uwe. 2014. *Gewalt und Kriminalität in der Spätantike.* Munich: C. H. Beck.

Kruse, Thomas. 2013. "Bevölkerungskontrolle, Statuszugang und Archivpraxis im römischen Ägypten," in Michele Faraguna, ed., *Archives and Archival Documents in Ancient Societies (Trieste 30 September – 1 October 2011).* 307–32. Trieste: Edizioni Università di Trieste.

Kuhn, Annika B. 2013. "Herodes Atticus and the Quintilii of Alexandria Troas: Elite Competition and Status Relations in the Greco-Roman East." *Chiron* 42: 421–58.

Kunkel, W. 1966. *An Introduction to Roman Legal and Constitutional History*. Trans. by J. M. Kelly. Oxford: Clarendon Press.

1967. *Herkunft und soziale Stellung der römischen Juristen*. 2nd ed. Cologne: Böhlau Verlag.

2001. *Die römischen Juristen: Herkunft und soziale Stellung*. Cologne: Böhlau Verlag.

Kurke, Leslie. 2011. *Aesopic Conversations: Popular Tradition, Cultural Dialogue, and the Invention of Greek Prose*. Princeton: Princeton University Press.

Lapin, Hayim. 2012. *Rabbis as Romans: The Rabinnic Movement in Palestine, 100–400 C.E.* Oxford: Oxford University Press.

Lavan, Myles. 2013. *Slaves to Rome: Paradigms of Empire in Roman Culture*. Cambridge: Cambridge University Press.

2016. "The Spread of Roman Citizenship, 14–212 CE: Quantification in the Face of High Uncertainty." *Past & Present* 230: 3–46.

2020. "Devastation: The Destruction of Populations and Human Landscapes and the Roman Imperial Project," in Katell Berthelot, ed., *Reconsidering Roman Power: Roman, Greek, Jewish, and Christian Perceptions and Reactions*. 179–205. Rome: École Française de Rome.

2021. "Roman Citizenship, Marriage with Non-citizens, and Family Networks," in Myles Lavan and Clifford Ando, eds., *Roman and Local Citizenship in the Long Second Century CE*. 103–39. Oxford: Oxford University Press.

Lavan, Myles, and Ando, Clifford. eds. 2021. *Roman and Local Citizenship in the Long Second Century CE*. Oxford: Oxford University Press.

Lavan, Myles, Payne, Richard E., and Weisweiler, John. eds. 2016. *Cosmopolitanism and Empire: Universal Rulers, Local Elites, and Cultural Integration in the Ancient Near East and Mediterranean*. New York: Oxford University Press.

Le Teuff, Béatrice. 2012. "*Census*: les recensements dans les provinces de l'empire romain d'Auguste à Dioclétien." PhD, Université Michel de Montaigne Bordeaux 3.

Leesen, Tessa G. 2010. *Gaius Meets Cicero: Law and Rhetoric in the School Controversies*. Leiden: Martinus Nijhoff Publishers.

Lehne-Gstreinthaler, Christine. 2019. *Iurisperiti et oratores: Eine Studie zu den römischen Juristen der Republik*. Vienna: Böhlau Verlag.

Lendon, J. E. 1997. *Empire of Honour: The Art of Government in the Roman World*. Oxford: Clarendon Press.

2022. *That Tyrant, Persuasion*. Princeton: Princeton University Press.

Lenel, Otto. 1889. *Palingenesia Iuris Civilis*. 2 vols. Leipzig: Bernhard Tauchnitz.

Lenski, Noel. 2018. "Framing the Question: What Is a Slave Society?," in Noel Lenski and Catherine Cameron, eds., *What Is a Slave Society? The Practice of Slavery in Global Perspective*. 15–57. Cambridge: Cambridge University Press.

Lepelley, Claude. 1979–1981. *Les Cités de l'Afrique romaine au Bas-Empire*. 2 vols. Paris: Études Augustiniennes.

1983. "Quot curiales, tot tyranni: L'image de décurion oppresseur au Bas-Empire," in Edmond Frézould, ed., *Crise et redressement dans les provinces européennes de l'Empire (milieu du IIIe = milieu du IVe siècle ap. J.-C.)*. 143–56. Strasbourg: AECR.

Lerouxel, F. 2015. "The βιβλιοθήκη ἐγκτήσεων and Transaction Costs in the Credit Market in Roman Egypt," in Dennis P. Kehoe, David M. Ratzan, and Uri Yiftach, eds., *Law and Transaction Costs in the Ancient Economy*. 162–84. Ann Arbor: University of Michigan Press.

Letteney, Mark. 2023. *The Christianization of Knowledge in Late Antiquity: Intellectual and Material Transformations*. Cambridge: Cambridge University Press.

Levick, Barbara. 1967. *Roman Colonies in Southern Asia Minor*. Oxford: Clarendon Press.

Lewin, Ariel. 1995. *Assemblee popolare e lotta politica nelle città dell'impero romano*. Florence: La Giuntina.

Lewis, Naphtali. 1981. "The Prefect's Conventus: Proceedings and Procedures." *Bulletin of the American Society of Papyrologists* 18: 119–29.

1983. *Life in Egypt under Roman Rule*. Oxford/New York: Clarendon Press.

1997. *The Compulsory Public Services of Roman Egypt*. Florence: Edizioni Gonnelli.

Licandro, Orazio, and Palazzolo, Nicola. 2021. *Papirius Iustus: Libri XX de constitutionibus*. Rome: L'Erma di Bretschneider.

Liebeschuetz, J. H. W. G. 1972. *Antioch: City and Imperial Administration in the Later Roman Empire*. Oxford: Clarendon Press.

2001. *Decline and Fall of the Roman City*. Oxford: Oxford University Press.

Liebs, Detlef. 1993. *Die römische Jurisprudenz in Afrika: mit Studien zu den pseudopaulinischen Sentenzen*. Berlin: Akademie Verlag.

2002. "Umwidmung: Nutzung der Justiz zur Werbung für die Sache ihrer Opfer in den Märtyrerprozessen der frühen Christen," in Walter Ameling, ed., *Märtyrer und Märtyrerakten*. 19–46. Stuttgart: Franz Steiner Verlag.

Lim, Richard. 1995. *Public Disputation, Power, and Social Order in Late Antiquity*. Berkeley: University of California Press.

Lintott, A. W. 1993. *Imperium Romanum: Politics and Administration*. London: Routledge.

Litwa, M. David. 2022. *Carpocrates, Marcellina, and Epiphanes: Three Early Christian Teachers of Alexandria and Rome*. London: Routledge.

Lo Cascio, Elio. 2015. "The Imperial Property and Its Development," in Paul Erdkamp, Koenrad Verboven, and Arjan Zuiderhoek, eds., *Ownership and Exploitation of Natural Resources in the Roman World.* 62–70. Oxford: Oxford University Press.

Lupher, David A. 2003. *Romans in a New World: Classical Models in Sixteenth Century Spanish America.* Ann Arbor: University of Michigan Press.

Ma, John. 2013. *Statues and Cities: Honorific Portraits and Civic Identity in the Hellenistic World.* Oxford: Oxford University Press.

2024. *Polis: A New History of the Ancient Greek City-State from the Early Iron Age to the End of Antiquity.* Princeton: Princeton University Press.

MacCormack, Sabine. 1981. *Art and Ceremony in Late Antiquity.* Berkeley: University of California Press.

MacCoull, L. S. B. 1988. *Dioscorus of Aphrodito: His Work and His World.* Berkeley: University of California Press.

Mackil, Emily. 2023. "Assessing the Scale of Property Confiscation in the Classical Greek World," in Myles Lavan, Daniel Jew, and Bart Danon, eds., *The Uncertain Past: Probability in Ancient History.* 53–92. Cambridge: Cambridge University Press.

MacMullen, Ramsay. 1974. *Roman Social Relations, 50 B.C. to A.D. 284.* New Haven: Yale University Press.

1990 [1986]. "Judicial Savagery in the Roman Empire," in *Changes in the Roman Empire: Essays in the Ordinary.* 204–14. Princeton: Princeton University Press.

2000. *Romanization in the Time of Augustus.* New Haven: Yale University Press.

2008. *Voting about God in Early Church Councils.* New Haven: Yale University Press.

Madsen, Jesper Majbom. 2020. *From Trophy Towns to City-States: Urban Civilization and Cultural Identities in Roman Pontus.* Philadelphia: University of Pennsylvania Press.

Maffi, Alberto, Stolte, Bernard H., and Viarengo, Gloria. eds. 2021. *Herennius Modestinus: Excusationum Libri VI* Rome: L'Erma di Bretschneider.

Magalhães de Oliveira, Julio Cesar. 2020. "Late Antiquity: The Age of Crowds?" *Past & Present* 249: 3–52.

Magie, David. 1950. *Roman Rule in Asia Minor to the End of the Third Century After Christ.* 2 vols. Princeton: Princeton University Press.

Magnani, Adriano. 2009. *Il processo di Isidoro: Roma e Alessandria nel primo secolo.* Naples: Società Editrice Il Mulino.

Maiuro, Marco. 2012. *Res Caesaris: Ricerche sulla proprietà imperiale nel Principato.* Bari: Edipuglia.

Malka, Orit. 2019. "Disqualified Witnesses between Tannaitic Halakha and Roman Law: The Archeology of a Legal Institution." *Law and History Review* 37: 903–36.

Malka, Orit, and Paz, Yakir. 2019. "Ab hostibus captus et a latronibus captus: The Impact of the Roman Model of Citizenship on Rabbinic Law." *Jewish Quarterly Review* 109: 141–72.

Mantovani, Dario. 1993–1994. "Il 'bonus praeses' secondo Ulpiano: Studi su contenuto e forma del 'de officio proconsulis' di Ulpiano." *Bolletino dell'Istituto di Diritto Romano* 96: 203–67.

2011. "Rivelazioni sulla *salus principis* e tattici per sottrarsi al processo: il secondo editto di Augusto ai Cirenei alla luce del *Officio Proconsulis* di Ulpiano," in E. Stolfi, ed., *Giuristi e Officium: L'elaborazione giurisprudenziale di regole per l'esercizio del potere fre II e III secolo d.c.* 195–214. Naples: Edizioni Scienfiche Italiane.

2018. *Les juristes écrivains de la Rome antique: Les oeuvres des juristes comme littérature.* Paris: Les Belles Lettres.

Markovits, Inga. 2010. *Justice in Lüritz: Experiencing Socialist Law in East Germany.* Princeton: Princeton University Press.

Marotta, Valerio. 1991. *Mandata Principum.* Turin: G. Giappichelli.

2000–2004. *Ulpiano e l'impero.* 2 vols. Naples: Loffredo.

2024. "Between Tyre and Rome: A Biography," in Massimo Brutti, Valerio Marotta, Fara Nasti, Aldo Schiavone, and Emanuele Stolfi, eds., *Roman Jurists at Work: Four Portraits.* 135–59. Rome: L'Erma di Bretschneider.

Martin, Dale B. 1990. *Slavery as Salvation: The Metaphor of Slavery in Pauline Christianity.* New Haven: Yale University Press.

1995. *The Corinthian Body.* New Haven: Yale University Press.

Mascellari, Roberto. 2016. "La descrizione di atti criminosi e violazioni nei papiri: ΥΒΡΙΣ, ΑΙΚΙΑ, ΠΛΗΓΑΙ, ΒΙΑ," in Rudolf Haensch, ed., *Recht haben und Recht bekommen im Imperium Romanum: Das Gerichtswesen der Römischen Kaiserzeit und seine dokumentarische Evidenz.* 483–521. Warsaw: Journal of Juristic Papyrology.

Mason, Steve. 2016. *A History of the Jewish War, A.D. 66–74.* Cambridge: Cambridge University Press.

Mattern, Susan P. 2008. *Galen and the Rhetoric of Healing.* Baltimore: Johns Hopkins University Press.

Mayer, Emanuel. 2012. *The Ancient Middle Classes: Urban Life and Aesthetics in the Roman Empire, 100 BCE – 250 CE.* Cambridge, MA: Harvard University Press.

McClish, Mark. 2019. *The History of the Arthaśāstra: Sovereignty and Sacred Law in Ancient India.* Cambridge: Cambridge University Press.

McGing, B. C. 1998. "Bandits, Real and Imagined, in Greco-Roman Egypt." *Bulletin of the American Society of Papyrologists* 35: 159–84.

McGinn, Thomas A. J. 2013. "Roman Children and the Law," in Judith Evans-Grubbs and Tim Parkin, eds., *The Oxford Handbook of Childhood and Education in the Classical World.* 341–62. Oxford: Oxford University Press.

McLynn, Neil B. 1994. *Ambrose of Milan: Church and Court in a Christian Capital.* Berkeley: University of California Press.

McNamee, Kathleen. 1998. "Another Chapter in the History of Scholia." *Classical Quarterly* 48: 269–88.

2007. *Annotations in Greek and Latin Texts from Egypt.* New Haven: American Society of Papyrologists.

Mebane, Julia. 2024. *The Body Politic in Roman Political Thought.* Cambridge: Cambridge University Press.

Meeks, Wayne A. 2003. *The First Urban Christians: The Social World of the Apostle Paul.* 2nd ed. New Haven: Yale University Press.

Mélèze Modrzejewski, Josef. 1970. "La règle de droit dans l'Égypte romaine (État des questions et perspectives de recherches)," in Deborah Samuel, ed., *Proceedings of the Twelfth International Congress of Papyrology.* 317–77. Toronto: Hakkert.

1988. "'La Loi des Égyptiens': le droit grec dans l'Egypte romaine," in Basil Mandilaras, ed., *Proceedings of the XVIII Congress of Papyrology.* 383–99. Athens: Greek Papyrological Society.

1995. *The Jews of Egypt: From Rameses II to Emperor Hadrian.* Trans. by Robert Cornman. Philadelphia: Jewish Publication Society.

Merry, Sally Engle. 1990. *Getting Justice and Getting Even: Legal Consciousness Among Working-Class Americans.* Chicago: University of Chicago Press.

Metzger, Ernest. 2004. "Roman Judges, Case Law, and Principles of Procedure." *Law and History Review* 22: 243–75.

Meyer, Elizabeth A. 2004. *Legitimacy and Law in the Roman World: Tabulae in Roman Belief and Practice.* Cambridge: Cambridge University Press.

2006. "The Justice of the Roman Governor and the Performance of Prestige," in A. Kolb, ed., *Herrschaftsstrukturen und Herrschaftspraxis: Konzepte, Prinzipien, und Strategien der Administration im römischen Kaiserreich.* 167–80. Berlin: Akademie Verlag.

2016. "Evidence and Argument: The Truth of Prestige and its Performance," in Paul J. du Plessis, Clifford Ando, and Kaius Tuori, eds., *The Oxford Handbook of Roman Law and Society.* 270–82. Oxford: Oxford University Press.

Millar, Fergus. 1992. *The Emperor in the Roman World (31 B.C. – A.D. 337).* 2nd ed. London: Duckworth.

1993. *The Roman Near East, 31 BC–AD 337.* Cambridge, MA: Harvard University Press.

2002. *Rome, the Greek World, and the East.* 3 vols. Chapel Hill: University of North Carolina Press.

2004. *Rome, the Greek World, and the East, Vol. II: Government, Society, and Culture in the Roman Empire.* Raleigh: University of North Carolina Press.

2004 [1983]. "Empire and City, Augustus to Julian: Obligations, Excuses, and Status," in H. Cotton and G. M. Rogers, eds., *Government, Society, and Culture in the Roman Empire, Vol. II: Rome, The Greek World, and the East.* 336–71. Chapel Hill: University of North Carolina Press.

2004 [1986]. "A New Approach to the Roman Jurists," in H. Cotton and G. M. Rogers, eds., *Rome, the Greek World, and the East, Vol II: Government, Society, and Culture in the Roman Empire.* 417–34. Chapel Hill: University of North Carolina Press.

2004 [1999]. "The Greek East and Roman Law: The Dossier of M. Ch. Licinius Rufinus," in H. Cotton and G. M. Rogers, eds., *Rome, the Greek World, and the East, Vol II: Government, Society, and Culture in the Roman Empire.* 435–64. Chapel Hill: University of North Carolina Press.

2006 [1990]. "The Roman Coloniae of the Near East: A Study of Cultural Relations," in H. Cotton and G. M. Rogers, eds., *Rome, the Greek World, and the East, Vol. III: The Greek World, the Jews, and the East.* 164–222. Chapel Hill: University of North Carolina Press.

Minns, Denis, and Parvis, P. M. 2009. *Justin, Philosopher and Martyr: Apologies.* Oxford: Oxford University Press.

Mitchell, Margaret M. 2008. "Gentile Christianity," in Margaret M. Mitchell and Frances M. Young, eds., *The Cambridge History of Christianity.* 103–24. Cambridge: Cambridge University Press.

Mitchell, Stephen. 1976. "Requisitioned Transport in the Roman Empire: A New Inscription from Pisidia." *Journal of Roman Studies* 66: 106–31.

1979. "Iconium and Ninica: Two Double Communities in Roman Asia Minor." *Historia* 28: 409–38.

1993. *Anatolia: Land, Men, and Gods in Asia Minor.* 2 vols. Oxford: Clarendon Press.

1995. *Cremna in Pisidia: An Ancient City in Peace and in War* London: Duckworth/Classical Press of Wales.

Mnookin, Robert H., and Kornhauser, Lewis. 1979. "Bargaining in the Shadow of the Law: The Case of Divorce." *Yale Law Journal* 88: 950–97.

Moatti, Claudia. 1993. *Archives et partage de terre dans le monde romain (IIe siècle avant – Ier siècle après J.-C.).* Rome: École française de Rome.

2015. *The Birth of Critical Thinking in Republican Rome.* Trans. by Janet Lloyd. Cambridge: Cambridge University Press.

Mommsen, T. 1899. *Römisches Strafrecht.* 2 vols. Leipzig: Duncker and Humblot.

Monoson, S. Sarah. 2016. "*Aesop Said So*: Ancient Wisdom and Radical Politics in 1930s New York." *Classical Receptions Journal* 8: 90–113.

Monson, Andrew. 2012. *From the Ptolemies to the Romans: Political and Economic Change in Egypt.* Cambridge: Cambridge University Press.

Montiglio, Silvia. 2000. *Silence in the Land of Logos.* Princeton: Princeton University Press.

Morley, Neville. 2011. "Cities and Economic Development in the Roman Empire," in Alan K. Bowman and Andrew Wilson, eds., *Settlement, Urbanization, and Population*. 143–60. Oxford: Oxford University Press.

Moss, Candida. 2010. "On the Dating of Polycarp: Rethinking the Place of the Martyrdom of Polycarp in the History of Christianity." *Early Christianity* 1: 539–74.

2013. "Polycarphilia: The Martyrdom of Polycarp and the Origins and Spread of Martyrdom," in Clare K. Rothschild and Jens Schröter, eds., *The Rise and Expansion of Christianity in the First Three Centuries of the Common Era*. 401–17. Tübingen: Mohr Siebeck.

Muller, Hannah Weiss. 2017. Subjecthood in the Atlantic World. In Oxford Bibliographies Online.

Musurillo, H. A. 1954. *The Acts of the Pagan Martyrs: Acta Alexandrinorum*. Oxford: Clarendon Press.

1961. *Acta Alexandrinorum: de mortibus Alexandriae Nobilium fragmenta papyracea Graeca*. Leipzig: B. G. Teubner.

Nasrallah, Laura Salah. 2003. *An Ecstasy of Folly: Prophecy and Authority in Early Christianity*. Cambridge, MA: Harvard Theological Studies.

2019. *Archaeology and the Letters of Paul*. Oxford: Oxford University Press.

2024. *Ancient Christians and the Power of Curses: Magic, Aesthetics, and Justice*. Cambridge: Cambridge University Press.

Neer, Richard. 2005. "Connoisseurship and the Stakes of Style." *Critical Inquiry* 32: 1–26.

Nelson, Carroll A. 1979. *Status Declarations in Roman Egypt*. Amsterdam: A. M. Hakkert.

Nicolet, Claude. 1991. *Space, Geography, and Politics in the Early Roman Empire*. Ann Arbor: University of Michigan Press.

Niehoff, Maren R. 2003. "Circumcision as a Marker of Identity: Philo, Origen and the Rabbis on Gen. 17:1–14." *Jewish Studies Quarterly* 10: 89–123.

2018. *Philo of Alexandria: An Intellectual Biography*. New Haven: Yale University Press.

Nirenberg, David. 2013. *Anti-Judaism: The Western Tradition*. New York: W. W. Norton.

Noam, Vered. 2003. *Megillat Ta'anit: Versions, Interpretation, History, with a Critical Edition* [*Hebrew*]. Jerusalem: Yad Ben-Zvi.

2006. "Megillat Ta'anit – The Scroll of Fasting," in Shmuel Safrai, Zeev Safrai, Joshua Schwartz, and Peter Tomson, eds., *Compendia rerum Iudaicarum ad Novum Testamentum. Section 2, The Literature of the Jewish People in the Period of the Second Temple and the Talmud. Volume 3: The Literature of the Sages*. 339–62. Assen: Royal van Gorcum.

Nogrady, Alexander. 2006. *Römisches Strafrecht nach Ulpian: Buch 7 bis 9 De officio proconsulis*. Berlin: Duncker & Humblot.

Nonet, Philippe. 1978. "For Jurisprudential Sociology." *Law and Society Review* 10: 525–45.

Noreña, Carlos. 2011. *Imperial Ideals in the Roman West: Representation, Circulation, Power*. Cambridge: Cambridge University Press.

2012. "The Ethics of Autocracy in the Roman World," in Ryan K. Balot, ed., *A Companion to Greek and Roman Political Thought*. 266–79. Malden: Wiley-Blackwell.

Nörr, Dieter. 2003 [1973]. "Iurisperitus sacerdos," in Tiziana J. Chiusi, Wolfgang Kaiser, and Hans-Dieter Spengler, eds., *Historiae iuris antiqui: Gesammelte Schriften*. 851–68. Goldbach: Keip Verlag.

Nutton, Vivian. 1978. "The Beneficial Ideology," in Peter Garnsey and C. R. Whittaker, eds., *Imperialism in the Ancient World*. 209–21. Cambridge: Cambridge University Press.

O'Meara, Dominic. 2003. *Platonopolis: Platonic Political Philosophy in Late Antiquity*. Oxford: Clarendon Press.

Oakes, Peter. 2019. "The Christians and Their *politeuma* in Heaven: Philippians 3:20 and the Herakleopolis Papyri," in Katell Berthelot and Jonathan Price, eds., *In the Crucible of Empire: The Impact of Roman Citizenship on Greeks, Jews, and Christians*. 141–63. Leuven: Peeters.

Oertel, Friedrich. 1917. *Die Liturgie: Studien zur ptolemäischen und kaiserlichen Verwaltung Ägyptens*. Leipzig: B. G. Teubner.

Olivelle, Patrick. ed. 2013. *King, Governance, and Law in Ancient India: Kauṭilya's Arthaśāstra*. Oxford: Oxford University Press.

Oliver, James Henry. 1989. *Greek Constitutions of Early Roman Emperors from Inscriptions and Papyri*. Philadelphia: American Philosophical Society.

Ophir, Adi, and Rosen-Zvi, Ishay. 2018. *Goy: Israel's Others and the Birth of the Gentile*. Oxford: Oxford University Press.

Oudshoorn, Carolien. 2007. *The Relationship between Roman and Local Law in the Babatha and Salome Komaise Archives: General Analysis and Three Case Studies on Law of Succession, Guardianship and Marriage*. Leiden: Brill.

Pagels, Elaine. 1979. *The Gnostic Gospels*. New York: Random House.

Papathomapoulos, Manoles. 1990. *Ὁ Βίος τοῦ Αἰσώπου. Ἡ Παραλλαγή G: Κριτικὴ ἔκδοση μὲ Εἰσαγωγὴ καὶ Μετάφραση*. Ioannina: University of Ioannina.

Parássoglou, G. M. 1978. *Imperial Estates in Roman Egypt*. Amsterdam: A. M. Hakkert.

Patterson, Orlando. 1985. *Slavery and Social Death: A Comparative Study*. Cambridge, MA: Harvard University Press.

Payne, Richard E. 2015. *A State of Mixture: Christians, Zoroastrians, and Iranian Political Culture in Late Antiquity*. Oakland: University of California Press.

Peachin, Michael. 1994. "The Case of the Heiress Camilia Pia." *Harvard Studies in Classical Philology* 96: 304–41.

1996. *Iudex vice Caesaris: Deputy Emperors and the Administration of Justice during the Principate.* Stuttgart: Franz Steiner Verlag.

2004. *Frontinus and the curae of the curator aquarum.* Stuttgart: Franz Steiner Verlag.

2007. "Attacken und Erniedrigungen als alltägliche Elemente der kaiserzeitlichen Regierungspraxis," in Rudolf Haensch and Johannes Heinrichs, eds., *Herrschen und Verwalten: Der Alltag der römischen Administration in der Hohen Kaiserzeit.* 117–25. Cologne: Böhlau Verlag.

2011a. "Introduction," in Michael Peachin, ed., *The Oxford Handbook of Social Relations in the Roman World.* 2–36. Oxford: Oxford University Press.

ed. 2011b. *The Oxford Handbook of Social Relations in the Roman World.* Oxford: Oxford University Press.

2015. "Augustus' Emergent Judicial Powers, the 'Crimen Maiestatis', and the Second Cyrene Edict," in Jean-Louis Ferrary and John Scheid, eds., *Il princeps romano: autocrate o magistrato? Fattori giuridici e fattori sociali del potere imperiale da Augusto a Commodo.* 497–554. Pavia: IUSS Press.

Pernot, Laurent. 2008. "Aelius Aristides and Rome," in William V. Harris and Brooke Holmes, eds., *Aelius Aristides between Greece, Rome, and the Gods.* 175–201. Leiden: Brill.

Perry, Ben Edwin. 1936. *Studies in the Text History of the Life and Fables of Aesop.* Haverford: American Philological Association.

1952. *Aesopica.* Urbana: University of Illinois Press.

Peters, Julie Stone. 2008. "Legal Performance, Good and Bad." *Law, Culture, and the Humanities* 4: 179–200.

Petsalis-Diomidis, Alexia. 2010. *"Truly Beyond Wonders": Aelius Aristides and the Cult of Asklepios.* Oxford: Oxford University Press.

Pferdehirt, Babara, and Scholz, Markus. eds. 2012. *Bügerrecht und Krise: Die Constitutio Antoniniana 212 n. Chr. und ihre innenpolitischen Folgen.* Mainz: Verlag des Römisch-Germanischen Zentralmuseums.

Pharr, Clyde. ed. 1952. *The Theodosian Code and Novels (with the Sirmondian Constitutions).* Princeton: Princeton University Press.

Piotrkowski, Meron M. 2019. *Priests in Exile: The History of the Temple of Onias and Its Community in the Hellenistic Period.* Berlin: de Gruyter.

Pollard, Nigel. 2000. *Soldiers, Cities, and Civilians in Roman Syria.* Ann Arbor: University of Michigan Press.

Pölönen, Janne. 2004. "Plebeians and Repression of Crime in the Roman Empire: From Torture of Convicts to Torture of Suspects." *Revue internationale des droits de l'Antiquité* 51: 218–57.

Pomeroy, Sarah B. 2007. *The Murder of Regilla: A Case of Domestic Violence in Antiquity.* Cambridge, MA: Harvard University Press.

Pont, Anne-Valérie. 2020. *La fin de la cité grecque: métamorphoses et disparition d'un modèle politique et institutionnel local en Asie Mineure, de Dèce à Constantin.* Geneva: Droz.

2022. "Citoyenneté et participation civique des juifs et des chrétiens d'après les règlements grecs et romains, d'Auguste au IVe siècle," in Nicole Belayche and Anne-Valérie Pont, eds., *Participations civiques des juifs et des chrétiens dans l'Orient romain*. 33–83. Geneva: Droz.

Potter, David S. 1993. "Martyrdom as Spectacle," in Ruth Scodel, ed., *Theater and Society in the Classical World*. 53–88. Ann Arbor: University of Michigan Press.

Premo, Bianca. 2005. *Children of the Father King: Youth, Authority, and Legal Minority in Colonial Lima*. Chapel Hill: University of North Carolina Press.

2017. *The Enlightenment on Trial: Ordinary Litigants and Colonialism in the Spanish Empire*. New York: Oxford University Press.

Price, S. R. F. 1984. *Rituals and Power: The Roman Imperial Cult in Asia Minor*. Cambridge: Cambridge University Press.

Pucci ben Zeev, Miriam. 1998. *Jewish Rights in the Roman World: The Greek and Roman Documents Quoted by Josephus*. Tübingen: Mohr Siebeck.

Puech, Bernadette. 2002. *Orateurs et sophistes grecs dans les inscriptions d'époque impériale*. Paris: Librairie Philosophique J. Vrin.

Puliatti, Salvatore. ed. 2020. *Callistratus*. Rome: L'Erma di Bretschneider.

Purcell, Nicholas. 1990. "The Creation of Provincial Landscape: The Roman Impact on Cisalpine Gaul," in Thomas Blagg and Martin Millett, eds., *The Early Roman Empire in the West*. 7–29. Oxford: Oxbow Books.

2005. "Romans in the Roman World," in Karl Galinsky, ed., *The Cambridge Companion to the Age of Augustus*. 85–105. Cambridge: Cambridge University Press.

Purpura, Gianfranco. 1992. "Gli editti dei prefetti d'Egitto." *Annali del Seminario Giuridico dell'Università di Palermo* 42: 487–671.

2009. "I papiri e le costituzioni imperiali in Egitto." *Aegyptus* 89: 155–220.

ed. 2012. *Revisione ed integrazione dei Fontes Iuris Romani Anteiustiniani. Studi preparatori II: Auctores – Negotia*. Milan: Giappichelli Editore.

Quass, F. 1993. *Die Honoratiorenschicht in den Städten des griechischen Ostens: Untersuchungen zur politischen und sozialen Entwicklung in hellenistischer und römischer Zeit*. Stuttgart: Franz Steiner.

1996. "Zum Problem der Kultivierung brachliegenden Gemeindelandes kaiserzeitlicher Städte Griechenlands." *Tekmeria* 2: 82–119.

Quayson, Ato. 2007. *Aesthetic Nervousness: Disability and the Crisis of Representation*. New York: Columbia University Press.

Raggi, Andrea. 2004. "The Epigraphic Dossier of Seleucus of Rhosus: A Revised Edition." *Zeitschrift für Papyrologie und Epigraphik* 147: 123–38.

2006. *Seleuco di Rhosos: Cittadinanza e privilegi nell'oriente Greco in età tardo-repubblicana*. Pisa: Giardini Editori e Stampatori.

Ramgopal, Sailakshmi. 2016. "Romans Abroad: Associations of Roman Citizens from the second century BCE to the third century CE." PhD, University of Chicago.

Rebillard, Éric. ed. 2017. *Greek and Latin Narratives about the Ancient Martyrs*. Oxford: Oxford University Press.

Reger, Gary. 2020. "A Letter of Septimius Severus to the Lykian League on the Misbehavior of Soldiers. A New Inscription from Choma (Hacımusalar Höyük), Northern Lykia." *Chiron* 50: 253–85.

Reynolds, Joyce. 1982. *Aphrodisias and Rome*. London: Society for the Promotion of Roman Studies.

Rhodes, P. J., and Lewis, David M. 1997. *The Decrees of the Greek States*. Oxford: Clarendon Press.

Riccobono, Salvatore, Baviera, Giovanni, Ferrini, Contardo, Furlano, Giuseppe, and Arangio Ruiz, Vincenzo. eds. 1940. *Fontes Iuris Romani Anteiustiniani*. 3 vols. Florence: S. A. G. Barbèra.

Richardson, Seth. 2012. "Early Mesopotamia: The Presumptive State." *Past & Present* 215: 3–49.

2014. "Mesopotamian Political History: The Perversities." *Journal of Ancient Near Eastern History* 1: 61–93.

2017. "Before Things Worked: A 'Low Power' Model of Early Mesopotamia," in Clifford Ando and Seth Richardson, eds., *Ancient States and Infrastructural Power: Europe, Asia, and America*. 17–62. Philadelphia: University of Pennsylvania Press.

Richland, Justin B. 2008. *Arguing with Tradition: The Language of Law in Hopi Tribal Court*. Chicago: University of Chicago Press.

Richlin, Amy. 2007. *Marcus Aurelius in Love*. Chicago: University of Chicago Press.

Riedlberger, Peter. 2020. *Prolegomena zu den spätantiken Konstitutionen, Nebst einer Analyse der erbrechtlichen und verwandten Sanktionen gegen Heterodoxe*. Stuttgart: fromann-holzboog.

Riess, Werner. 2001. *Apuleius und die Räuber: Ein Beitrag zu historischen Kriminalitätsforschung*. Stuttgart: Franz-Steiner Verlag.

Rigsby, Kent J. 1985. "On the High Priest of Egypt." *Bulletin of the American Society of Papyrologists* 22: 279–89.

1996. *Asylia: Territorial Inviolability in the Hellenistic World*. Berkeley: University of California Press.

Rilinger, Rolf. 1988. *Humiliores-Honestiores: Zu einer sozialen Dichotomie im Strafrecht der römischen Kaiserzeit*. Munich: R. Oldenbourg.

Rives, James. 2005. "Flavian Religious Policy and the Destruction of the Jerusalem Temple," in Jonathan Edmondson, Steve Mason, and James Rives, eds., *Flavius Josephus and Flavian Rome*. 145–66. Oxford: Oxford University Press.

2009. "Diplomacy and Identity among Jews and Christians," in Claude Eilers, ed., *Diplomats and Diplomacy in the Roman World*. 99–126. Leiden: Brill.

Rivière, Yann. 2004. *La cachot et les fers: détention et coercition à Rome*. Paris: BELIN.

2016. "Introduction. *Confiscare, publicare, vindicare*: Esquisse lexicale et procédurale des confiscations romaines," in Clément Chillet, Marie-Claire Ferriès, and Yann Rivière, eds., *Les confiscations, le pouvoir, et Rome de la fin de la République à la mort de Néron*. Bordeaux: Ausonius Éditions.

Rizakis, Athanasios. 1998. "*Incolae-Paroikoi*: Populations et communautés dépendantes dans les cités et les colonies romaines de l'Orient." *Revue des Études Anciennes* 100: 599–617.

2004. "L'emphytéose sous l'Empire en pays Grec," in Simone Follet, ed., *L'Hellénisme d'epoque romaine: Nouveux documents, nouvelle approches (Ier s. a.C. – IIIe s. p.C.). Actes de Colloque international à la mémoire de Louis Robert, Paris, 7–8 juillet 2000*. 55–76. Paris: de Boccard.

2015. "Expropriations et confiscations des terres dans le cadre de la colonisation romaine en Achaïe et en Macédoine." *Mélanges de l'école française de Rome – Antiquité* 127: 2–23.

Rizakis, Athanasios, and Zoumbaki, Sophia. 2017. "Local Elites and Social Mobility in Greece under the Empire: The Cases of Athens and Sparta," in Athanasios Rizakis, Francesco Camia, and Sophia Zoumbaki, eds., *Social Dynamics under Roman Rule: Mobility and Status Change in the Provinces of Achaia and Macedonia*. Athens: National Hellenic Research Foundation.

Robert, Louis. 1994. *Le Martyre de Pionios, Prêtre de Smyrne (ed. C.P. Jones and G.W. Bowersock)*. Washington, DC: Dumbarton Oaks Research Library and Collection.

2007 [1977]. "La titulature de Nicée et de Nicomédie: La gloire et la haine," in Denis Rousset, ed., *Choix d'écrits*. 673–703. Paris: Les Belles Lettres.

Rodriguez, Chris. 2010a. "Le PSI inv. 123: Un nouveau fragment des Acta Isidori?" *Revue historique de droit français et étranger* 88: 449–53.

2010b. "Les *Acta Isidori*: Un procès pénal devant l'Empereur Claude." *Revue historique de droit français et étranger* 88: 1–41.

2012. "Caracalla et les Alexandrins: coup de folie ou sanction légale?" *Journal of Juristic Papyrology* 42: 229–72.

Roller, Matthew B. 2001. *Constructing Autocracy: Aristocrats and Emperors in Julio-Claudian Rome*. Princeton: Princeton University Press.

Romano, David Gilman. 2003. "City Planning, Centuriation, and Land Division in Roman Corinth: Colonia Laus Iulia Corinthiensis and Colonia Iulia Flavia Augusta Corinthiensis," in Charles K. Williams II and Nancy Bookidis, eds., *Corinth, Volume 20: The Centenary, 1896–1996*. 279–301. Athens: The American School of Classical Studies at Athens.

Ronconi, A. 1966. "Exitus illustrium virorum." *Reallexikon für Antike und Christentum* 6: 1258–68.

Rosen-Zvi, Ishay. 2011. *Demonic Desires: Yetzer Hara and the Problem of Evil in Late Antiquity*. Philadelphia: University of Pennsylvania Press.

2012. *The Mishnaic Sotah Ritual: Temple, Gender, and Midrash*. Leiden: Brill.
2014. "Rereading *herem*: Destruction of Idolatry in Tannaitic Literature," in Katell Berthelot, Joseph E. David, and Marc Hirshman, eds., *The Gift of the Land and the Fate of the Canaanites in Jewish Thought*. 50–65. New York: Oxford University Press.
2023. "Rabbis as *Nomikoi*? Questioning a New Paradigm: A Response to Yair Furstenberg." *Journal for the Study of Judaism* 55: 1–13.
Rostovtzeff, M. 1957. *The Social and Economic History of the Roman Empire*. 2nd ed. 2 vols. Oxford: Clarendon Press.
Roueché, Charlotte. 1984. "Acclamations in the Later Roman Empire: New Evidence from Aphrodisias." *Journal of Roman Studies* 74: 181–99.
Rowlandson, J. 1998. *Women and Society in Greek and Roman Egypt*. Cambridge: Cambridge University Press.
Rubenstein, Jeffrey L. 2003. *The Culture of the Babylonian Talmud*. Baltimore: Johns Hopkins University Press.
Ruiz-Montero, Consuelo. 2014. "The Life of Aesop (rec.G): The Composition of the Text," in Edmund P. Cueva and Shannon N. Byrne, eds., *A Companion to the Ancient Novel*. 257–71. Chichester: John Wiley & Sons.
Runia, David. 1993. *Philo in Early Christian Literature*. Minneapolis: Fortress Press.
Saba, Sara. 2013. *The Astynomoi Law from Pergamon: A New Commentary*. Mainz: Verlag Antike.
Saller, Richard P. 1980. "Promotion and Patronage in Equestrian Careers." *Journal of Roman Studies* 70: 44–63.
1994. *Patriarchy, Property and Death in the Roman Family*. Cambridge: Cambridge University Press.
2002. "Framing the Debate over Growth in the Ancient Economy," in Walter Scheidel and Sitta von Reden, eds., *The Ancient Economy*. 251–69. New York: Routledge.
Sallmann, Klaus. ed. 1997. *Die Literatur des Umbruchs: von der römischen zur christlichen Literatur, 117 bis 284 n. Chr*. Munich: C. H. Beck.
Sänger, Patrick. 2019. *Die ptolemäische Organisationsform Politeuma: Ein Herrschaftsinstrument zugunsten jüdischer und anderer hellenischer Gemeinschaften*. Tübingen: Mohr Siebeck.
Sarat, Austin. 1985. "Legal Effectiveness and Social Studies of Law: On the Unfortunate Persistence of a Research Tradition." *Legal Studies Forum* 9: 23–31.
Sartre, Maurice. 2005. *The Middle East under Rome*. Trans. by Catherine Porter and Elizabeth Rawlings. Cambridge, MA: Belknap Press.
Scarano-Ussani, Vincenzo. 1981. "I 'beneficia principalia' in un dibattito fra primo e secondo seculo." *Labeo* 27: 315–30.
Scheidel, Walter. 2015. "The Early Roman Monarchy," in Andrew Monson and Walter Scheidel, eds., *Fiscal Regimes and the Political Economy of Premodern States*. 229–57. Cambridge: Cambridge University Press.

Scheidel, Walter, Morris, Ian, and Saller, Richard P. eds. 2007. *The Cambridge Economic History of the Greco-Roman World.* Cambridge: Cambridge University Press.

Schiavone, Aldo. 2012. *The Invention of Law in the West.* Trans. by Jeremy Carden and Antony Shugaar. Cambridge, MA: Belknap Press.

Schmidt-Hofner, Sebastian. 2008. *Reagieren und Gestalten: Der Regierungsstil des stätrömischen Kaisers am Beispiel der Gesetzgebung Valentinians I.* Munich: Verlag C. H. Beck.

Schmitz, Thomas. 1997. *Bildung und Macht: zur sozialen und politischen Funktion der zweiten Sophistik in der griechischen Welt der Kaiserzeit* Munich: C. H. Beck.

Schulz, Fritz. 1946. *History of Roman Legal Science.* Oxford: Clarendon Press.

Schwartz, Saundra. 2017. *From Bedroom to Courtroom: Law and Justice in the Greek Novel.* Aarhus: Barkhuis.

Schwartz, Seth. 2001a. *Imperialism and Jewish Society, 200 BCE – 640 CE.* Princeton: Princeton University Press.

2001b. "The Rabbi in Aphrodite's Bath: Palestinian Society and Jewish Identity in the High Roman Empire," in Simon Goldhill, ed., *Being Greek under Rome: Cultural Identity, the Second Sophistic and the Development of Empire.* 335–61. Cambridge: Cambridge University Press.

Selden, Daniel L., and Vasunia, Phiroze. eds. forthcoming. *The Oxford Handbook of the Literatures of the Roman Empire.* Oxford: Oxford University Press.

Seston, William, and Euzennat, Maurice. 1961. "La citoyenneté romaine au temps de Marc Aurèle et de Commode, d'après la Tabula Banasitana." *CRAI* 105: 317–24.

Shackleton Bailey, D. R. ed. 1980. *Cicero: Epistulae ad Quintum Fratrem et M. Brutum.* Cambridge: Cambridge University Press.

Shaw, Brent D. 1984. "Bandits in the Roman Empire." *Past & Present* 105: 3–52.

1993. "The Passion of Perpetua." *Past & Present* 139: 3–45.

1996. "Body/Power/Identity: Passions of the Martyrs." *Journal of Early Christian Studies* 4: 269–312.

2003. "Judicial Nightmares and Christian Memory." *Journal of Early Christian Studies* 11: 533–63.

2009. "State Intervention and Holy Violence: Timgad/Paleostrovsk/Waco." *Journal of the American Academy of Religion* 77: 853–94.

2011. *Sacred Violence: African Christians and Sectarian Hatred in the Age of Augustine.* Cambridge: Cambridge University Press.

2013. *Bringing in the Sheaves: Economy and Metaphor in the Roman World.* Toronto: University of Toronto Press.

2015. "Augustine and Men of Imperial Power." *Journal of Late Antiquity* 8: 32–61.

2016. "Lambs of God: An End of Human Sacrifice." *Journal of Roman Archaeology* 29: 259–91.
Sherk, Robert K. 1969. *Roman Documents from the Greek East: Senatus Consulta and Epistulae to the Age of Augustus*. Baltimore: Johns Hopkins University Press.
1988. *The Roman Empire: Augustus to Hadrian*. Cambridge: Cambridge University Press.
Sherwin-White, A. N. 1963. *Roman Society and Roman Law in the New Testament*. Oxford: Clarendon Press.
1972. "The Roman Citizenship: Its Development into a World Franchise." *ANRW* 1.2: 23–58.
1973. *The Roman Citizenship*. 2nd ed. Oxford: Clarendon Press.
Sidebottom, Harry. 2006. "Dio Chrysostom and the Development of *On Kingship* Literature," in Diana Spencer and Elena Theodorakopoulos, eds., *Advice and Its Rhetoric in Greece and Rome*. 117–57. Bari: Levante.
2009. "Philostratus and the Symbolic Roles of the Sophist and Philosopher," in Ewen Bowie and Jaś Elsner, eds., *Philostratus*. 69–99. Cambridge: Cambridge University Press.
Sidwell, Keith. 2004. *Lucian: Chattering Courtesans and other Sardonic Sketches*. London: Penguin Books.
Siegert, Folker, Maier, Johann, and Lötzsch, Johann. eds. 2023. *Rechtsgeschichtlicher Kommentar zum Neuen Testament, Band 1: Einleitung, Arbeitsmittel und Voraussetzungen*. Berlin: de Gruyter.
Sievers, Joseph, and Levine, Amy-Jill. eds. 2021. *The Pharisees*. Grand Rapids: Wm. B. Eerdmans Publishing Co.
Sizgorich, Thomas. 2006. "Reasoned Violence and Shifty Frontiers: Shared Victory in the Late Roman East," in H. A. Drake, ed., *Violence in Late Antiquity: Perceptions and Practices*. 157–76. Aldershot: Ashgate.
2009. *Violence and Belief in Late Antiquity: Militant Devotion in Christianity and Islam*. Philadelphia: University of Pennsylvania Press.
Smail, Daniel Lord. 2016. *Legal Plunder: Households and Debt Collection in Late Medieval Europe*. Cambridge: Harvard University Press.
Smallwood, E. Mary. 1956. "Some Notes on the Jews under Tiberius." *Latomus* 15: 314–29.
1961. *Philonis Alexandrini Legatio ad Gaium*. Leiden: Brill.
Smith, Andrew M. 2013. *Roman Palmyra: Identity, Community, and State Formation*. Oxford: Oxford University Press.
Smith, Martin Ferguson. 1992. *Diogenes of Oinoanda: The Epicurean Inscription*. Naples: Bibliopolis.
Smith, R. R. R. 1998. "Cultural Choice and Political Identity in Honorific Portrait Statues in the Greek East in the Second Century A.D." *Journal of Roman Studies* 88: 56–93.
Smith, R. R. R., and Ward-Perkins, Bryan. eds. 2016. *The Last Statues of Antiquity*. Oxford: Oxford University Press.

Smolin, Nathan Israel. 2024. *Christ the Emperor: Christian Theology and the Roman Emperor in the Fourth Century AD*. Oxford: Oxford University Press.

Souris, George A., and Haensch, Rudolf. 2009. "RECAM III 112 (SEG 48, 1583): Abuse of Power by Members of the Roman Administration and the Imperial Reaction," in Rudolf Haensch, ed., *Selbstdarstellung und Kommunikation: Die Veröffentlichung staatlicher Urkunden auf Stein und Bronze in der römischen Welt*. 349–63. Munich: C. H. Beck.

Spawforth, Antony. 1989. "Roman Sparta," in Paul Cartledge and Antony Spawforth, eds., *Hellenistic and Roman Sparta: A Tale of Two Cities*. 93–211. London: Routledge.

1996. "Roman Corinth: The Formation of a Colonial Elite," in A. D. Rizakis, ed., *Roman Onomastics in the Greek East: Social and Political Aspects (Proceedings of the International Colloquium on Roman Onomastics, Athens, 7–9 September 1993)*. 167–82. Athens: Research Center for Greek and Roman Antiquity, National Hellenic Research Foundation.

Stadter, Philip A. 2006. "Pliny and the Ideology of Empire: The Correspondence with Trajan." *Prometheus* 32: 61–76.

Steel, Catherine. 2004. "Being Economical with the Truth: What Really Happened at Lampsacus?," in Jonathan Powell and Jeremy Paterson, eds., *Cicero the Advocate*. 234–51. Oxford: Oxford University Press.

Steinhauer, Georgos. 2010. "C. Iulius Eurycles and the Spartan Dynasty of the Euryclids," in Athanasios Rizakis and Cl. E. Lepenioti, eds., *Roman Peloponnese III: Society, Economy, and Culture under the Roman Empire: Continuity and Innovation*. 75–87. Athens: National Hellenic Research Foundation.

Stern, Menachem. 1974. *Greek and Latin Authors on Jews and Judaism*. 3 vols. Jerusalem: The Israel Academy of Sciences and Humanities.

Stradzins, Estelle. 2019. "The King of Athens: Philostratus' Portrait of Herodes Atticus." *Classical Philology* 114: 238–64.

Strassi Zaccaria, Silvia. 1988. *L'Editto di M. Sempronius Liberalis*. Trieste: Giulio Bernardi Editore.

Swain, Simon. 1989. "Favorinus and Hadrian." *Zeitschrift für Papyrologie und Epigraphik* 79: 150–58.

1996. *Hellenism and Empire: Language, Classicism, and Power in the Greek World, AD 50–250*. Oxford: Clarendon Press.

Syme, Ronald. 1958. *Tacitus*. 2 vols. Oxford: Clarendon Press.

Tacoma, Laurens E. 2015. "Imperial Wealth in Roman Egypt: The Julio-Claudian ousiai," in Paul Erdkamp, Koenrad Verboeven, and Arjan Zuiderhoek, eds., *Ownership and Exploitation of Land and Natural Resources in the Roman World*. 71–87. Oxford: Oxford University Press.

Talbert, Richard J. A. 1984. *The Senate of Imperial Rome*. Princeton: Princeton University Press.

Taubenschlag, Rafael. 1955. *The Law of Greco-Roman Egypt in the Light of the Papyri, 332 B.C. – 640 A.D.* 2nd ed. Warsaw: Państwowe Wydawnictwo Naukowe.

Tcherikover, Viktor A. 1964. "Was Jerusalem a 'Polis'?" *Israel Exploration Journal* 14: 61–78.

Tcherikover, Viktor A., and Fuks, Alexander. 1957–64. *Corpus Papyrorum Judaicarum*. 3 vols. Cambridge: Magnes Press/Harvard University Press.

Thomas, Yan. 2011. "L'institution juridique de la nature: Remarques sur la casuistique du droit naturel à Rome," in Marie-Angèle Hermitte and Paolo Napoli, eds., *Les opérations du droit*. 21–40. Paris: Seuil/ Gallimard.

Thonemann, Peter. 2004. "Polemo, Son of Polemo (Dio, 59.12.2)." *Epigraphica Anatolica* 37: 144–50.

2011. *The Maeander Valley: A Historical Geography from Antiquity to Byzantium*. Cambridge: Cambridge University Press.

2013a. "Phrygia: An Anarchist History, 950 BC–AD 100)," in Peter Thonemann, ed., *Roman Phrygia: Culture and Society*. 1–40. Cambridge: Cambridge University Press.

2013b. "Rev. of Sara Saba: The Astynomoi Law of Pergamon." *sehepunkte* 13.5.

Thornton, John. 2001. "Gli *aristoi, l'akriton plethos* e la provincializzazione della Licia." *Mediterraneo Antico* 4: 427–46.

Tilly, Charles. 2006. *Why? What Happens When People Give Reasons ... And Why*. Princeton: Princeton University Press.

Tobin, Jennifer. 1997. *Herodes Attikos and the City of Athens: Patronage and Conflict under the Antonines*. Amsterdam: J. C. Gieben.

Tomson, Peter. 1990. *Paul and the Jewish Law: Halakha in the Letters of the Apostle to the Gentiles*. Leiden: Brill.

Tropper, Adnan. 2022. *A Tragedy of Errors: Bar Qamtza and the Fall of Jerusalem*. Cincinatti: Hebrew Union College Press.

Tuori, Kaius. 2007. *Ancient Roman Lawyers and Modern Legal Ideals: Studies on the Impact of Contemporary Concerns in the Interpretation of Ancient Roman Legal History*. Frankfurt am Main: Vittorio Klostermann.

2016. *Emperor of Law: The Emergence of Roman Imperial Adjudication*. Oxford: Oxford University Press.

Valvo, Alfredo. 2010. "Le condizioni del buon governo: Temi 'municipali' nel *De Officiis* e nel *De Re Publica*," in Laurent Lamoine, Clara Berrendonner, and Mireille Cébeillac-Gervasoni, eds., *La praxis municipale dans l'Occident romain*. 21–29. Clermont-Ferrand: Presses universitaires Blaise-Pascal.

van den Horst, Pieter W. 2003. *Philo's Flaccus: The First Pogrom*. Leiden: Brill.

van Minnen, Peter. 2016. “Three Edicts of Caracalla? A New Reading of P.Giss. 40.” *Chiron* 46: 205–21.

van Nijf, Onno. 2004. “Athletics and *Paideia*: Festivals and Physical Education in the World of the Second Sophistic,” in Barbara Borg, ed., *Paideia: The World of the Second Sophistic*. 203–27. Berlin: de Gruyter.

2008. “The Social World of Tax Farmers and Their Personnel,” in Michel Cottier, Mireille Corbier, C. V. Crowther, Jean-Louis Ferrary, Barbara Levick, Olli Salomies, and Michael Wörrle, eds., *The Customs Law of Asia*. 279–311. Oxford: Oxford University Press.

2012. “Political Games,” in Kathleen M. Coleman, Jocelyn Nelis-Clément, and Pierre Ducrey, eds., *L'organisation des spectacles dans le monde romain*. 47–95. Geneva: Fondation Hardt.

Vega Navarette, Natalia. 2017. *Die Acta Alexandrinorum im Lichte neuerer und neuester Papyrusfunde*. Cologne: Ferdinand Schöningh.

Venticinque, Philip. 2016. *Honor among Thieves: Craftsmen, Merchants, and Associations in Roman and Late Roman Egypt*. Ann Arbor: University of Michigan Press.

Veyne, Paul. 1976. *Le pain et le cirque: Sociologie historique d'un pluralisme politique*. Paris: Le Seuil.

Vidas, Moulie. 2021. “What Is a *Tannay*?” *Oqimta* 7: 21–96.

Wacke, Andreas. 1980. “Die potentiores in den Rechtsquellen: Einfluß und Abwehr gesellschaftlicher Übermacht in der Rechtspflege der Römer.” *ANRW* 2.13.1: 562–607.

Wallace-Hadrill, Andrew. 1982. “Civilis Princeps: Between Citizen and King.” *Journal of Roman Studies* 72: 32–48.

Walzer, Michael. 1987. *Interpretation and Social Criticism*. Cambridge, MA: Harvard University Press.

Waterfield, Robin. 2010. *Polybius: The Histories*. Oxford: Oxford University Press.

Watson, Alan. ed. 2009 [rev., orig. 1988]. *The Digest of Justinian*. Philadelphia: University of Pennsylvania Press.

Watts, Edward Jay. 2010. *Riot in Alexandria: Tradition and Group Dynamics in Late Antique Pagan and Christian Communities*. Berkeley: University of California Press.

Weaver, Paul. 2002. “Consilium praesidis: Advising Governors,” in Paul McKechnie, ed., *Thinking Like a Lawyer: Essays on Legal History and General History for John Crook on His Eightieth Birthday*. 43–62. Leiden: Brill.

Weisweiler, John. 2015. “Making Masters, Making Subjects: Imperial Ideology and Memory Policy in the Early Roman Empire and in the Later Roman State,” in Karl Galinsky and Kenneth Lapatin, eds., *Cultural Memories in the Roman Empire*. 66–85. Los Angeles: J. Paul Getty Museum.

Weitzman, Steven. 1999. “Forced Circumcision and the Shifting Role of Gentiles in Hasmonean Ideology.” *Harvard Theological Review* 92: 37–59.

Welch, Kimberly M. 2019. "William Johnson's Hypothesis: A Free Black Man and the Problem of Legal Knowledge in the Antebellum United States South." *Law and History Review* 37: 89–124.

Welles, C. Bradford. 1974 [1934]. *Royal Correspondence in the Hellenistic Period.* Chicago: Ares Publishers (repr.).

Wenger, Ayelet. 2023. "The Aesopic Wisdom of Tevi: A Tale of Two Tongues." *Jewish Quarterly Review* 113: 591–614.

Whitman, James Q. 2008. *The Origins of Reasonable Doubt: Theological Roots of the Criminal Trial.* New Haven: Yale University Press.

2012. *The Verdict of Battle: The Law of Victory and the Making of Modern War.* Cambridge, MA: Harvard University Press.

2025. *From Masters of Slaves to Lords of Land: The Transformation of Ownership in the Western World.* Cambridge: Cambridge University Press.

Whitmarsh, Tim. 2001. *Greek Literature and the Roman Empire: The Politics of Imitation.* Oxford: Oxford University Press.

2013. *Beyond the Second Sophistic: Adventures in Greek Postclassicism.* Berkeley: University of California Press.

Wieacker, Franz. 1959. *Textstufen klassischer Juristen.* Göttingen: Vandenhoek & Ruprecht.

Williams, Bernard. 2005. *In the Beginning Was the Deed: Realism and Moralism in Political Argument.* Princeton: Princeton University Press.

Wilson, Andrew, and Bowman, Alan K. eds. 2017. *Trade, Commerce, and the State in the Roman World.* Oxford: Oxford University Press.

Wirszubski, Ch. 1950. *Libertas as a Political Idea at Rome during the Late Republic and Early Principate.* Cambridge: Cambridge University Press.

Woloson, Wendy A. 2009. *In Hock: Pawning in America from Independence through the Great Depression.* Chicago: University of Chicago Press.

Woolf, Greg. 1996. "Monumental Writing and the Expansion of Roman Society in the Early Empire." *Journal of Roman Studies* 86: 22–39.

1998. *Becoming Roman: The Origins of Provincial Civilization in Gaul.* Cambridge: Cambridge University Press.

2006. "Pliny's Province," in Tønnes Bekker-Nielsen, ed., *Rome and the Black Sea Region: Domination, Romanization, Resistance.* 93–108. Aarhus: Aarhus University Press.

Yannakakis, Yanna. 2008. *The Art of Being In-Between: Native Intermediaries, Indian Identity, and Local Rule in Colonial Oaxaca.* Durham: Duke University Press.

Yiftach-Firanko, Uri. 2003. *Marriage and Marital Arrangements: A History of the Greek Marriage Document in Egypt, 4th Century BCE–4th Century CE.* Munich: C. H. Beck.

2009. "Law in Greco-Roman Egypt: Hellenization, Fusion, Romanization," in Roger S. Bagnall, ed., *The Oxford Handbook of Papyrology.* 541–60. Oxford: Oxford University Press.

2020. "Order and Chaos in Roman Administrative Terminology," in Kimberley Czajkowski and Benedikt Eckhardt, eds., *Law in the Roman Provinces*. 32–43. Oxford: Oxford University Press.

Yngvesson, Barbara. 1993. *Virtuous Citizens, Disruptive Subjects: Order and Complaint in a New England Court*. New York: Routledge.

Zimmerman, M. 1996. "Probus, Carus, und die Räuber im Gebiet des Pisidischen Termessos." *Zeitschrift für Papyrologie und Epigraphik* 110: 265–77.

Zuiderhoek, Arjan. 2009. *The Politics of Munificence in the Roman Empire: Citizens, Elites, and Benefactors in Asia Minor*. Cambridge: Cambridge University Press.

Index

Studies in Legal History
(continued from page ii)

Alastair McClure, *Trials of Sovereignty: Mercy, Violence, and the Making of Criminal Law in British India, 1857–1922*
Marie-Amélie George, *Family Matters: Queer Households and the Half-Century Struggle for Legal Recognition*
Simon Devereaux, *Execution, State and Society in England, 1660–1900*
Giuliana Perrone, *Nothing More than Freedom: The Failure of Abolition in American Law*
Christian G. Fritz, *Monitoring American Federalism: The History of State Legislative Resistance*
Ada Maria Kuskowski, *Vernacular Law: Writing and the Reinvention of Customary Law in Medieval France*
E. Claire Cage, *The Science of Proof: Forensic Medicine in Modern France*
Kristin A. Olbertson, *The Dreadful Word: Speech Crime and Polite Gentlemen in Massachusetts, 1690–1776*
Edgardo Pérez Morales, *Unraveling Abolition: Legal Culture and Slave Emancipation in Colombia*
Lyndsay Campbell, *Truth and Privilege: Libel Law in Massachusetts and Nova Scotia, 1820–1840*
Sara M. Butler, *Pain, Penance, and Protest: Peine Forte et Dure in Medieval England*
Michael Lobban, *Imperial Incarceration: Detention without Trial in the Making of British Colonial Africa*
Stefan Jurasinski and Lisi Oliver, *The Laws of Alfred: The Domboc and the Making of Anglo-Saxon Law*
Sascha Auerbach, *Armed with Sword and Scales: Law, Culture, and Local Courtrooms in London, 1860–1913*
Alejandro de La Fuente and Ariela J. Gross, *Becoming Free, Becoming Black: Race, Freedom, and the Law in Cuba, Virginia, and Louisiana*
Elizabeth Papp Kamali, *Felony and the Guilty Mind in Medieval England*
Jessica K. Lowe, *Murder in the Shenandoah: Making Law Sovereign in Revolutionary Virginia*
Michael A. Schoeppner, *Moral Contagion: Black Atlantic Sailors, Citizenship, and Diplomacy in Antebellum America*
Sam Erman, *Almost Citizens: Puerto Rico, the U.S. Constitution, and Empire*
Martha S. Jones, *Birthright Citizens: A History of Race and Rights in Antebellum America*

Julia Moses, *The First Modern Risk: Workplace Accidents and the Origins of European Social States*
Cynthia Nicoletti, *Secession on Trial: The Treason Prosecution of Jefferson Davis*
Edward James Kolla, *Sovereignty, International Law, and the French Revolution*
Assaf Likhovski, *Tax Law and Social Norms in Mandatory Palestine and Israel*
Robert W. Gordon, *Taming the Past: Essays on Law and History and History in Law*
Paul Garfinkel, *Criminal Law in Liberal and Fascist Italy*
Michelle A. McKinley, *Fractional Freedoms: Slavery, Intimacy, and Legal Mobilization in Colonial Lima, 1600–1700*
Karen M. Tani, *States of Dependency: Welfare, Rights, and American Governance, 1935–1972*
Stefan Jurasinski, *The Old English Penitentials and Anglo-Saxon Law*
Felice Batlan, *Women and Justice for the Poor: A History of Legal Aid, 1863–1945*
Sophia Z. Lee, *The Workplace Constitution from the New Deal to the New Right*
Mitra Sharafi, *Law and Identity in Colonial South Asia: Parsi Legal Culture, 1772–1947*
Michael A. Livingston, *The Fascists and the Jews of Italy: Mussolini's Race Laws, 1938–1943*

Printed by Integrated Books International,
United States of America

The Judgment of the Provinces

Roman law is justly famous, but what was its relationship to governing an empire? In this book, Ari Z. Bryen argues that law, as the learned practice that we know today, emerged from the challenge of governing a diverse and fractious set of imperial subjects. Through analysis of these subjects' political and legal ideologies, Bryen reveals how law became the central topic of political contest in the Roman Empire. Law offered a means of testing legitimacy and evaluating government, as well as a language for asking fundamental political questions. But these political claims did not go unchallenged. Elites resisted them, and jurists, in collaboration with emperors, reimagined law as a system that excluded the voices of the governed. The result was to separate, for the first time, "law" from "society" more broadly, and to define law as a primarily literate and learned practice, rather than the stuff of everyday life.

Ari Z. Bryen is Associate Professor in the Department of History and the Department of Classical and Mediterranean Studies at Vanderbilt University. He is the author of *Violence in Roman Egypt: A Study in Legal Interpretation* (2013).

ANKERWYCKE YEW

STUDIES IN LEGAL HISTORY

See the Studies in Legal History series website at
http://studiesinlegalhistory.org/

Studies in Legal History

Other books in the series:

James M. Campbell, *Reluctant Abolitionists: Britain and the End of the Colonial Death Penalty*
Sonia Tycko, *Captured Consent: Contract Labor in English Charity, Colonization, and War, 1600–1700*
Jenny Huangfu Day, *Transborder Fugitives, Extradition, and Political Crimes in Modern China*
Maurits den Hollander, *Court, Credit, and Capital: Amsterdam's Insolvency Legislation in the Dutch Golden Age*
Zachary Herz, *The God and the Bureaucrat: Roman Law, Imperial Sovereignty, and Other Stories*
Kevin Arlyck, *The Nation at Sea: The Federal Courts and American Sovereignty, 1789–1825*
Ivan Lee, *Extradition and Empire: Sovereignty and Subjecthood in Hong Kong*
James Q. Whitman, *From Masters of Slaves to Lords of Lands: The Transformation of Ownership in the Western World*

(Continued after the Index)

The Judgment of the Provinces

The Roman Empire and the Origins of Law and Society

ARI Z. BRYEN
Vanderbilt University

CAMBRIDGE
UNIVERSITY PRESS

CAMBRIDGE
UNIVERSITY PRESS

Shaftesbury Road, Cambridge CB2 8EA, United Kingdom

One Liberty Plaza, 20th Floor, New York, NY 10006, USA

477 Williamstown Road, Port Melbourne, VIC 3207, Australia

314–321, 3rd Floor, Plot 3, Splendor Forum, Jasola District Centre, New Delhi – 110025, India

103 Penang Road, #05–06/07, Visioncrest Commercial, Singapore 238467

Cambridge University Press is part of Cambridge University Press & Assessment, a department of the University of Cambridge.

We share the University's mission to contribute to society through the pursuit of education, learning and research at the highest international levels of excellence.

www.cambridge.org
Information on this title: www.cambridge.org/9781009730372

DOI: 10.1017/9781009730341

When citing this work, please include a reference to the DOI 10.1017/9781009730341

First published 2026

Cover image: MET/BOT / Alamy Stock Photo.

A catalogue record for this publication is available from the British Library

A Cataloging-in-Publication data record for this book is available from the Library of Congress

ISBN 978-1-009-73037-2 Hardback

To Kim

Contents

Figures

Acknowledgments

This book has taken a long time, and bears the marks of many friends, colleagues, and institutions. It began as a very different project, during a postdoctoral fellowship at New York University's Institute for the Study of the Ancient World, in 2008–2009. The time that I spent in New York allowed me to read broadly in law and social science. A conversation with Rob Tempio encouraged me to move from my stated project to paint on a broader canvas. The immediate result of this was an article, eventually published in 2012, that served as the framework for my broader thinking about how to tell the story of the changes of law in the Roman world over the course of the Roman period, broadly conceived. A subsequent fellowship from the American Council of Learned Societies (the heroic "New Faculty Fellows" program, designed to protect vulnerable PhDs in the wake of the 2008 economic crisis) allowed me to spend two years in the Departments of Rhetoric and Classics at the University of California, Berkeley. My time at Berkeley was formative for exposing me to new modes of thinking about rhetoric and language, about how speech might act in the world, and about how law and legality inflected and emerged from such speech acts. The Rhetoric department is also, in some key respects, a department devoted to investigating the meaning and consequences of a commitment to *logos*; my time there thus casts a long shadow over the manuscript as a whole. My special thanks at Berkeley are due to Marianne Constable, who saw the potential of the earlier versions of this book, and who encouraged me to read